Musical Boxes and Other Musical Marvels — A Decade of Enjoyment

ANGELO RULLI
Editor

The Musical Box Society International

Musical Boxes and Other Musical Marvels — A Decade of Enjoyment

Rulli, Angelo, 1943—

ISBN 0-9150000-02-4
Library of Congress Cataloging-in Publication Data.

Includes indexed table of contents.

To Those Who Care For And About Mechanical Music

PREFACE

This book is the second anthology published by the MBSI. The first such book is titled *The Silver Anniversary Collection*. Edited by William Edgerton, it was published in 1974 and is a 1,000-page book comprising many relevant articles published in the MBSI *Technical Bulletin* from 1949-1974. This second book brings together many of the important articles published in the *Technical Bulletin* from 1975-1985. The information uncovered during this decade has clarified and enhanced much of what was previously known. Because of the great number of important articles which appeared in the *Bulletin* from 1975-85, the Trustees have chosen to publish two volumes, this being the first. The second volume is expected to be published in 1988. Tune listings and copies of catalogs are not included.

In 1986 the *Technical Bulletin* was renamed the *Technical Journal* and was first published in the larger 8½″ by 11″ format. This book marks the closing of the 17-year era of the smaller-sized magazine.

Topics featured in this anthology cover a vast range of mechanical musical instruments from automata to zithers. The articles reflect the knowledge of experts and collectors around the world who write, without benefit of financial reward, because they want to share what they have learned.

FOREWORD

The Musical Box Society is devoted to all forms of mechanical music. Therefore, the Society has the responsibility of sharing information which is related to and promotes the value of mechanical music as an art form and as an important aspect of the musical history of this and other cultures.

It is difficult to imagine life without music. Yet, until the advent of mechanical music, only those learned in a musical skill and who could afford an instrument for their home had the opportunity to hear secular music other than in the concert hall or on the street corner. In regard to the latter, the organ grinder played a major role in providing music to the masses.

With the advent of mechanical music, people of all means were able to enjoy music in the privacy of their own home or to hear a nickelodeon at a local saloon or restaurant. And the era of music for people of all classes was born.

The importance of mechanical music is easily lost in the myriad of electronic musical wonders in today's society. It is only in the context of a society without music for all people that mechanical music can be truly understood and appreciated for the significant role it played in the transition of America from a rural, farm-oriented society to that which emerged after the industrial revolution.

This book celebrates the wealth of knowledge that was published in the MBSI *Technical Bulletin* from 1975-1985. That decade saw the most prolific amount of information since the turn of the century. This information is due, in part, to the renaissance of interest in mechanical music today as attested to by the retail sales of musical boxes, the increasing number of makers of mechanical music—from musical boxes to street organs—throughout the world and the increase in membership in the MBSI.

As is noted in the dedication, without the members/authors who devoted their time and talent in caring for mechanical musical instruments and to writing articles, this book could not have been possible. The Society Trustees provided the financial support and leadership necessary to fulfill the goals of the Society by affirming the publication of this book.

Selecting nearly 500 pages of articles from the 2,400 pages which were published in the decade in review was not easy. In so many ways, each of the articles which was originally printed deserved to be recognized in this book. Realistically, that wasn't possible. And, it is important to note those articles which stand out and deserve to be recognized as important references.

The following are some of the criteria which we used in selecting the articles knowing that the book would be less than 500 pages in length: general appeal, article appeal, authenticity, new information, author recognition, technical or historical merit and reference value.

One of the disappointments in the selection process was that some aspects of mechanical music did not receive their deserved recognition. That's because very little was written, for example, in the areas of nickelodeons and orchestrions.

This book involved the talent and cooperation of many members of the MBSI, each of whom, like the editor, volunteered their time and energy including MBSI members Frank Metzger, Coulson Conn, James Spriggs, Joseph Schumacher, Ralph Schack, and Gary Stevenson who each assisted in the selection of articles; Al Choffnes, Q. David Bowers, Bud and "B" Bronson, Fred Dahlinger, Nancy Fratti, Alan Lightcap, Art Reblitz, Harvey Roehl, Shirley Kopp, Elton Norwood and Tim Trager each of whom contributed to the Glossary.

I wish to especially acknowledge the diligent and unselfish assistance of Ralph Heintz and Steve Ryder who assisted me in making the final decisions.

The articles herein celebrate a form of music which will not be re-created in this lifetime. We are indebted to those who have taken the time to record information which will be read and appreciated by those who know the value and enjoyment of mechanical music.

The Glossary is the first ever compiled under the auspices of the MBSI. It is not meant to be a definitive glossary, but rather the beginning of a process which may last several years. Defining one glossary which can be endorsed by a majority of those interested in this field is a challenging task. The first important step has now been taken. It is now up to readers to provide input to the leadership of the Society regarding suggestions for the Glossary so the final product will reflect the scholarly and practical attention which it deserves.

Angelo Rulli
St. Paul, Minnesota
July, 1987

TABLE OF CONTENTS

ORCHESTRIONS

LARGE ORGANS

SMALL ORGANS

PIANOS

STRINGS

TOYS, SELF-PLAYING

OTHER RELATED SUBJECTS
ART, HISTORY, REFERENCE

PHONOGRAPHS

THE CAROUSEL OF LIFE

Kevin Sheehan

A wisp of steam and steady chuffing
Reed horns just out of tune undaunted blare
A child's expression blurred with colored lights
And peals of laughter echo through the night
Little clasping hands reflect in silvered glass
A ship's bell sounds, oddly out of place
The smell of salt and wood and grease
Of popping corn and candy fleece

The need to lean inside grows stronger
As the carousel of life still faster turns
Though leaning inward we look out and try to focus
On something still for just a fleeting moment
But the centrifuge keeps turning
And we must ride it out

Now the din of pounding wheels and rumbling gears
Blends with the organ's plaintive cheers
All too soon the ride of life is done
So like the roundabout's brief whirls
But for the children the carousel keeps turning
Again for just a quarter

Automata

ARCHIMEDES AND HERO — AN HISTORICAL NOTE

Ralph Heintz

here has been a long-standing argument on whether Archimedes or Hero of Alexandria can be considered to be the "Father of Mechanical Music." Translations from the works of both men have indicated each was responsible for the design of at least *automata,* if not actual mechanical music. There are also indications that the automata of Archimedes could produce sounds, qualifying them, by only a slight stretch of the imagination, as mechanical music (See "On the Construction of Water Clocks," *MBSI Bulletin,* Volume XXVI, No. 1 pp 26-32). The main question seems to be the dates on which these designs were set down on paper. Unfortunately, the patent office was not much better then than it is now. There is nothing in the documents to indicate seniority or prior art, and we are forced to use other information to determine which came first.

Archimedes' lifetime has been fairly well established. He was born around B.C. 287 and died in B.C. 212. Hero, on the other hand, is usually specified "2nd century B.C. to 2nd century A.D." Allowing for inaccurate dating, he *could* have known Archimedes, and if the dating were really inaccurate, he might even have been inventing at the same time Archimedes was running about with his clothes off shouting, "Eureka." One thing of which we can be relatively sure; Hero did not live for four hundred years, or even for two hundred years.

A brief comment by A. G. Drachman in a review of a translation of Hero's *Automata* provides a clue that may finally set the question to rest. He states: "Hero has been dated from the 2nd century B.C. to the 2nd A.D., but his position has now been clarified by O. Neugebauer from a reference to a solar eclipse which must have been that of A.D. 62."

A gap of this size is too great to be absorbed by inaccurate dating, regardless of whose government came up with the figures. So, on the basis of this information, we must give the nod to Archimedes. The problem for future investigation will be, "Where does Philon fit into the picture, and why has he not received the same degree of publicity as the other two?"

5

VICHY'S CLOWN

Stephen H. Ryder

$\mathcal{P}$ICTURED opposite is a life-size automaton built in the Parisian workshop of Vichy some time near the turn of the century. The clown cranks the barrel organ as would a normal man, the drive power emanating from within the clown--not the organ. Meanwhile, the clown turns his head, blinks his eyes, and keeps time with the baton in his left hand. Atop the organ are seated three articulated monkeys, all activated by the same mechanism.

The large monkey in a striped costume, seated on the front corner, is given to drink; his left arm brings the bottle to his mouth several times before he nods off. At this point, the clown interrupts his time-keeping to strike the monkey on the head.

The monkey in the center simulates playing the banjo, and the smallest is an acrobat on a ladder. The former was built more than once by Vichy, because an identical banjo-player with a self-contained movement has been found in a private collection.

This entire automaton-piece was presumably spring-driven, and the barrel organ actually played. It is no mean feat for a normal man to crank an organ of this size, so one can imagine what it took to wind up the clown. Vichy might have built this for an exhibit, which could explain the conglomeration of sizes and genres of automata.

This photograph is reprinted with the kind permission of member Michel Bertrand of Bullet/Ste.-Croix, Switzerland. Mr. Bertrand is the successor to the Vichy firm, and he says that this piece has not been seen since it left the workshop..

THE MAGIC CUPBOARD

Murtogh Guiness

𝒯HE MAGIC CUPBOARD is a special musical automaton which I have just recently acquired. The cupboard measures two feet nine inches high, by two feet wide, by nine inches deep. When the mechanism is started, the boy, holding a cookie in his left hand, moves his hand toward the door. At that moment a fly runs up the side of the door.

Inside of the cupboard there is a cookie jar which, in an instant, turns into the face of an old lady — presumably the boy's grandmother. Her mouth moves, as if scolding the boy for trying to take food, and her eyebrows move up and down. In response he puts his tongue out at her, and she in turn grimaces at him. Finally, a mouse appears behind the piece of cheese on the shelf.

The piece was made by Vichy of Paris, circa 1880. It is mostly composed of mica — a gelatin/silicate made in several layers — and the starting knob is in the shape of an acorn, a Vichy trademark. ■■

THE PRIEST AUTOMATA

Frank Metzger

$\mathcal{T}$HE handsome young priest pictured in this article has just surfaced among the drifting mass of art and antiquity that passes through the London salesrooms of Christie's. It is sure to add an important chapter to the history of automata. The style of the wooden body and the steel clockwork mechanism which gave him life suggest that he was made in the 16th century by German-trained craftsmen in Spain. Although there is a mass of legend about automata made during the period for Charles V, King of Spain and Holy Roman Emperor, (they were said to include a fly which soared through the air and returned to its master's hand), very little tangible evidence of free-standing automata as early as this has survived.

Stories of marvelous animated statues of oracles and deities go back to antiquity, but the oldest surviving mechanical figures are invariably associated with clocks. Those rather gross giants who hammer the bell on the clock tower in St. Mark's Square in Venice are the most famous of the clock automata which became popular with richer and more ambitious civic authorities in Western Europe from the 13th century.

The Arabs seem to have started a fashion for entertaining their guests at banquets with table decorations which, at the touch of a lever, would assume a life of their own. By the 17th century European nobility were commissioning similar devices from the ingenious clockmakers and silversmiths of Augsburg and Nuremburg. A silver galleon might sail down the center of the table, bearing miniature casks of wine; or Diana the Huntress might trundle down the table on a wheeled stag, whose removable head would provide a loving cup.

We may reasonably guess that the little priest in Christie's, in times much earlier than these, was intended for the banquet table of a devout Catholic king or nobleman of Spain. His wooden body and working parts must originally have been concealed beneath a splendid cassock. When in full working order, with his clockwork wound, he would move smoothly along on two wheels, directed by a third smaller wheel from behind which probably shifted so as to give him a zig-zag movement from side to side of the table. Two little articulated feet would have moved under the front of the cassock to give a life-like impression of walking. As he progressed, his head moved from side to side, his eyes, eerily lifelike in their sockets, glanced to right and left, and his lips moved slightly as if in silent prayer. His left hand was repeatedly pressed to his chest in a gesture of obeisance, while his right hand was raised and lowered as if in benediction. Perhaps

9

the noble host astounded his guests by entrusting this miniature cleric with pronouncing grace after meat.

It is merely speculation, and at this distance of time the idea sounds somewhat irreligious. Yet the marvel of the object, the sense that the skills which could devise it must be God-given, most likely were stronger than fears of irreverence. Certainly we know that in some seventeenth and eighteenth century monasteries and convents clerically-garbed automata were set to guard the gates, and silently admitted guests before retreating into the picturesque grottoes in which they were installed.

Until the little priest finds his way into a museum, is restored to vitality (all the works are still there, though needing adjustment) and properly researched, we can only guess at his origins and purpose.

The figure anticipates the greatest days of automata by a whole century and a half. Still dependent on clockwork mechanisms and elaborate arrangements of levers and wires, the achievements of the eighteenth century makers of automata are even today astounding.

Automata were only a very small part of the creative life of the inventor Jacques Vaucanson, whose other accomplishments included the perfection of rubber hose-pipe and (before Jacquard) a loom that could weave patterned material. Yet it was the three animated figures that he showed to the Royal Academy of Sciences in 1738 which ensured his popular and lasting fame. The audiences that flocked to see them wherever they were shown during the next thirty years or more were astounded by the flautist who could play twenty airs on any flute put into his hand, or the ambidextrous shepherd who played a drum and whistle at the same time. The biggest thrill though was a small, gilded duck who obligingly demonstrated all the processes of ingestion and digestion.

The eventual fate of Vaucanson's automata remains a mystery. They were in Germany, where Goethe saw and described them, in the 1780's. In the 1790's Napoleon talked of bringing them back to France, but then had his attention distracted. After that they vanished. Perhaps one day, like the little Spanish priest, they will arrive on Christie's doorstep.

Happily the masterworks of the other great automata-makers of the eighteenth century, the brothers Jacquet-Droz, have survived, and may be seen, restored to brilliant order in the museum of Neuchatel, Switzerland, the makers' home town. There a tiny, solemn, bare-foot boy sits at a table and draws a variety of pencil sketches, yet another writes amiably "Soyez les bienvenus a Neuchatel" ("Be the welcomed ones to Neuchatel"). Their elder sister performs on a miniature piano-forte. The bouquet on her coursage rises and falls as she breathes, and between each faultlessly executed piece she bows graciously to the public.

With their slight mechanical jerkiness and momentary hesitations, these lively double-centarians seem infinitely more marvelous than all the perfect electronic robots of Disneyland's ghoulish Hall of Presidents. And of course, the little Spanish priest is (pardon his celibacy) the daddy of them all. ⚜

Cylinder Musical Boxes

The 'Fabrique' and the Musical Box Industry in Geneva in 1867

Pierre Germain

$\mathcal{I}$N the 18th century Geneva was well known for its production of richly decorated watches and snuffboxes. Around 1785, one of its best periods, 100,000 watches were sold annually. The activities connected with the production and the decoration of watches, clocks, snuffboxes, small boxes, etc., were part of what was known in Geneva as the *Fabrique* (the Factory). It had a peculiar organization, worth describing, since tuned steel teeth were first used by the watchmakers and because, later on, the makers of musical boxes became influential members of the system.

The Fabrique consisted of craftsmen and merchants, the latter acting as intermediaries between the makers and the outside world. Around 1785 one Genevese out of five was a member of the Fabrique, showing how important this industry was for the economy of a town with 25,000 inhabitants. The workshops were small, often consisting of very few people, and in this French-speaking city, such a shop was called a *cabinet* hence the name *cabinotier* given to the workers of the Fabrique.

There existed, therefore, a multitude of small independent workshops and very few large ones. There was no factory as such, and even the blanks of the watches were not made in Geneva but imported from nearby France or Switzerland (Geneva joined the Swiss Confederation only in September of 1814). The craftsmen were highly specialized and the work so divided that an old document lists as many as 50 different crafts. It is not surprising to learn that teenagers were needed to transport pieces from one workshop to another, and the district of Saint-Gervais, where most of the 'cabinets' were installed, was a lively and typical part of Geneva.

Since nearly all of the production had to be exported, the merchants were an essential part of the structure. They placed the orders with the different shops and independent craftsmen in and outside Geneva, often delivering the gold, the pearls, and other precious materials, advancing money when needed, etc. Take as an example the pair of singing-bird boxes, piece number 175, from Jean-Frédéric Leschot, the partner and later on the successor of the two Jaquet-Droz. He ordered the blanks of the two mechanisms in December 1802, but it was not until April 1804 that the pair of boxes was ready. During this period I traced at least five independent workshops or craftsmen who participated in the making, Leschot distributing the tasks. Three were in Geneva, but two were in the Vallée de Joux, a Swiss valley in the Jura mountains some 30 miles north of Geneva, in the canton of Vaud.

Obliged to export, the Genevese merchants were superbly organized, and this was subsequently true for the musical box industry. Traveling with their collection, they regularly visited the dealers abroad, participating in the major fairs throughout Europe. The most important traders had branches in key cities like Paris and London, and even in places such as Constantinople in Turkey. It is well established also that many Piguet et Meylan watches with automata and musical mechanisms were sold in China, often via London.

For Geneva, as for most of the Western countries in Europe, the turn of the century was indeed a difficult period, politically and economically. Social unrest similar to the French Revolution took place in Geneva, which even had a short-lived Terror in 1794. After many vicissitudes, in 1798 the Republic of Geneva, independent since 1536, was annexed by France, its powerful neighbor. The French ruled Geneva for 15 years, until the very end of December 1813. Obviously, this period was a difficult one for the Fabrique, so highly dependent on foreign commercial relations.

Particularly acute from 1806 onwards was the Continental blockade enforced by Napoleon, the French Emperor. All merchandise of English origin or merely suspected to be of English origin was seized, and often burnt in a public square. It was nevertheless during these critical times that watchmakers in Geneva began to use hard steel teeth to produce music, in an attempt to replace the delicate bell-playing carillon in a musical watch. These teeth were plucked by pins inserted in a rotating support, and, in Geneva, the idea was first proposed by Antoine Favre in 1796.* For several years it was not seriously marketed, not only because the economic situation was difficult but also because by 1796 Favre was already 62 years old. In April 1802 Jean-Frédéric Leschot presented, as a novelty, a jeweled ring with an automaton and a musical mechanism. He sold a pair of such rings, one bearing the number 169, to Duval and Michely in London. It was almost certainly Isaac-Daniel Piguet who made the mechanism, and in a letter from Leschot to Duval, one learns that this kind of ring was no longer fashionable by 1805. On the other hand I found evidence that the system initially proposed by Favre was widely used in Geneva by 1808. The steel teeth were often, if not always, associated with an automaton in a watch, in a snuffbox, or in some other, jeweled piece, and clearly in those times the musical instrument of vibrating teeth played only a modest and secondary role.

The true musical boxes, i.e. boxes where the music part played a major role, did not appear, I shall guess, much before 1815. They really came into existence when the first cylinder musical boxes with lateral key-winding, i.e. the cartel type, were marketed. A series of circumstances made this type

* We are well aware of the interesting and challenging article of Arthur Ord-Hume *(The Music Box* 1975, volume 7, p. 50) questioning the date, place, and author(s) of the invention of the tuned steel tooth in Europe. In the present article we are sticking to what happened in Geneva.

attractive; for instance, the loading of the bass teeth with small blocks of lead, together with the possibility of muting teeth efficiently by steel dampers, a damper being a curled spring made of a flat wire, beneath the fine end of the tooth, reportedly invented by François Nicole in 1814. Also an important incentive was the restoration, with the departure of the French in 1813, of commercial relations with foreign countries, such as England.

The combination of these technical inventions and a better economic climate gave a boost to the musical box industry, and, around 1815, a new branch appeared in the Fabrique: the making of musical boxes. Some of the makers were still watchmakers, but one finds an increasing number of clockmakers and mechanics, better qualified for the cartel techniques. By 1817 the Fabrique counted 300 workers on musical boxes.

The Genevese musical box industry progressed steadily during the first half of the 19th century. The French occupation was followed by what historians of Geneva have called the "27 years of happiness" *(27 ans de bonheur)*, and in 1820 the Fabrique was again booming, although an increasing part of the Geneva watch was done outside, in the Jura mountains. The town nevertheless remained, as today, a trade center for watchmaking and jewelry. During these years, there was great prosperity. Although still confined in its impressive fortifications, the part of Geneva along the Rhône river was remodeled in the 1830's according to a well-thought-out urbanistic plan. This rebuilding affected Saint-Gervais, the main district of the Fabrique, and gave, for instance, to the Nicole Frères (nothing to do with François Nicole) the opportunity to move into a new house at 17, rue Kléberg, where the brothers lived for some 50 years. Last year, at the end of 1975, the house of the Nicole Frères, a beautiful old house with a wooden 'cabinet' on top, was unfortunately being demolished.

This period of happiness deteriorated during the 1840's, and the political crisis in Geneva culminated in 1847 with the adoption of a democratic constitution, the basis of the one in existence today. A sizable fraction of the Fabrique's craftsmen were unemployed, and in 1849 many watchmakers were engaged in the demolition of the fortifications.

In the 1850's new buildings were erected on the former fortifications, and soon after a public square named the *Place des Alpes* appeared. In the musical box industry, the Place des Alpes is a well-known location. There and nearby, the most important makers of musical boxes and singing birds had their workshops and/or salesrooms: Brémond, Lecoultre, Rivenc, Conchon, Allard, Langdorff, Baker-Troll, Bruguier, Greiner, etc. It was also in the 1850's that Sainte-Croix, in the Swiss Jura mountains, began slowly but steadily to supplant Geneva in the making of musical boxes. An indication is the list of the Swiss exhibitors of musical boxes at the 1851 Exhibition in London, the first great international exhibition, to be followed by many others. There were three firms from Geneva (Ducommun-Girod, Gay and Luquin, Métert and Langdorff), three from Sainte-Croix, two from the Vallée de Joux. We do not take into account two Genevese merchants more specialized in watchmaking and jewelry than in musical boxes.

Let's now skip 15 years and come to the year 1867. It was the year of the Great Exhibition in Paris, which attracted 10 million visitors. The waltz of Johann Strauss, 'The Blue Danube,' a tune frequently found on our musical boxes, met with a great success, after a dead start in Vienna the year before. In America, the Civil War had come to an end two years before, and it was the time of a gigantic industrial expansion in oil, steel, and railroads.

In the 1867 Paris exhibition - - as in the other exhibitions - - the musical boxes were part of the 'Musical Instruments' section. Fourteen Swiss exhibitors displayed musical boxes and singing birds. Five were from Geneva, the others from Sainte-Croix or nearby. It shows the progress made by Sainte-Croix, which today remains the Swiss, and even the European, production center of musical movements.

In February 1868 the Chamber of Commerce of Geneva presented in a public session the results of an inquiry on the watchmaking, jewelry, and musical box industries. The title of the report, precisely, reads:

"Enquête sur la situation de la fabrique d'horlogerie, de bijouterie et de boîtes à musique à Genève"

Rapport présenté au nom de la Chambre de Commerce en séance publique à l'Association commerciale et industrielle genevoise le 21 février 1868 par M.E. BROCHER VERET.

The introduction for this 37-page booklet explains how the inquiry had been conducted. Four hundred circulars and questionnaires were printed and sent, in October 1867, to "all the addresses where it was assumed it would provoke useful returns." It is also said that these three branches of the Fabrique were the most representative ones of Geneva industry.

To compare the relative importance of the musical box industry we shall first extract from the report some information concerning the two other sectors.

The jewelry sector was represented by 40 firms employing altogether 750 people. The production amounted to five million Swiss francs per year, 90 percent of it being exported.

In the watchmaking industry one found 146 firms, 83 producing and trading watches and 63 making accessories such as cases, dials, etc. The total of the yearly sales was 11 million Swiss francs, again nearly 90 percent for exportation. Unfortunately the report does not give the number of people employed. About 60,000 watches were sold annually, but the author of the report confesses that it is sometimes difficult to define a 'Geneva watch' since one-half to three-fourths of the watch was not made in Geneva; only two firms were producing all the parts of the watch. As from the beginning of the century, small watches for women remained a Genevese specialty, although "they are often copied elsewhere; the jeweled part uses too much gold, and the models do not change often enough." I give those details because they illustrate the conservatism of the Genevese and their tendency to concentrate on articles of luxury. The same trend will be found later on in the musical box industry.

In 1867, according to the report, the situation in the musical box industry was better than in the two other sectors. The report said that it was "in full prosperity," and it even claimed that "our musical boxes are everywhere the first ones and on many markets the only ones." This last remark is chauvinistic, to say the least, and we shall come back to the competition endured by the Genevese later on.

The 1868 report contains interesting remarks on the improvements introduced in musical boxes during the former decade. Drums, bells, castanets, and finally an organ have been incorporated in the boxes. All these additions had led to the 'orchestra box.' It also mentions as a recent addition: a reed organ with a keyboard "at the disposal of the artist." Talking about the musical box with a reed organ *(Voix célestes)*, I have strong reasons to believe that Joseph Ravel, the father of the French composer Maurice Ravel, first proposed it in 1859. Joseph, an engineer by education, was a maker of musical boxes in Geneva for a couple of years. (Alfred Chapuis in his *Histoire de la boîte à musique* noted a Joseph Ravel, maker of musical boxes in a directory of addresses in 1860, but he was not sure that he was Maurice's father.)

In 1867 the musical box industry in Geneva consisted of:

6 firms assembling the parts of the boxes, selling the final product,
    and employing 200 people,
7 firms making the parts, and employing 300 people,
2 firms making singing birds.

The yearly production was estimated at 0.8 million Swiss francs. In the number of people employed, the musical box industry was therefore not much behind the jewelry sector, with its 750 people. To the watchmaking industry it was still a poor relation, and this is probably the reason why most of the historians, when writing about the industry in Geneva during the 19th century, have not, or only superficially, mentioned the musical box industry.

This 'benign neglect' is somewhat unjustified, since Sainte-Croix has been better treated by Chapuis although in 1867 its production was not so much larger. It is the *Société industrielle et commerciale de Sainte-Croix* itself that estimates at 700 the number of workers in the musical box industry. They belonged to some 30 workshops or firms, two-thirds working on small pieces (tabatières) and one-third on large pieces (cartels). The total of the yearly Sainte-Croix production was estimated at 1.3 million Swiss francs, only 50 percent more than the Geneva sales.

We have no figures for the French production, mainly concentrated at Sainte-Suzanne, near Switzerland, in the hands of Auguste L'Epée, who founded the firm in 1839. According to the well-documented article of Roger J. Vreeland (*Silver Anniversary Collection*, pp. 96-104), in 1867 the firm of L'Epée was just recovering from a series of trials concerning the infringement of music editions by the makers of musical boxes. From 1863 until 1866 Auguste L'Epée had been obliged to use only airs in the public domain. These limitations and the expensive trials had severely affected production. In 1866 the French maker won the trial, and in 1867, the production was on the increase, although he did not exhibit in Paris.

Let's come back to the production in Geneva. The 1868 report gives the figure of 6,000 musical boxes per year, the prices ranging from 40 to 1,000 Swiss francs, exceptionally to 5,000 francs. A small box (tabatière type, I guess) cost 40 francs, and the price of an average-sized cartel box was around 250 francs. Most of the boxes were exported, "although the sales in Geneva were increasing." Concerning the singing birds, a hundred pieces were made annually, their value ranging from 500 to 1,500 francs. Though it is not mentioned in the report, I suppose that it concerned singing-bird boxes rather than birds in cages.

Since we have been quoting prices, let us give an indication of the salaries in Geneva around 1867. It will give, by comparison, some idea of the relative value of an average box. The workers were sometimes paid daily or monthly, but more often they did piecework. A watchmaker, for ordinary work, could earn five Swiss francs a day, and for more qualified work up to eight francs. A woman's daily pay was closer to three francs. Assuming that 250 francs was the price of an average cartel box, one might conclude that a standard musical box of a cartel type represented, in 1867, about two months' salary of a skilled worker. Another point of comparison is the salary of a town counselor in 1864: 5,000 Swiss francs per year. It is amusing to note that we can buy today an antique musical box proportionally cheaper than a new one could have been bought a hundred years ago. Of course, such a comparison is arbitrary and must not be taken too seriously.

Concerning the salaries in 1867, the report points out that they were lower in Geneva than in Britain and Paris but higher than in Germany. They were surely higher in Geneva than in the Swiss Jura by a factor of two, at least. Furthermore, the cost of living in the Jura mountains was less, and there was plenty of woman-power available. The cost of living in Geneva must have been relatively high, since the report, which in general reflects the employer's point of view, recognizes that life for an ordinary watchmaker with a family was not easy.

I cannot resist quoting the report on social aspects, for some of the problems evoked are still with us. The future watchmaker began his apprenticeship when 12 to 16 years old, and it lasted four to six years. The report adds: "but in general one learns until 30, and one improves oneself until 40." Apprenticeship was a sour point for the Fabrique. The number of apprentices was declining, partly due to the hostility of the workmen themselves, keen to keep this number low. Concerning the problem of daily pay versus piecework, the report's author is of the opinion that, although the workmen wanted to be paid on a daily basis, piecework was better "for improvement of the products and the development of the workmen's abilities."

Let's come back to the situation of the musical box industry in Geneva at the end of 1867. The report unfortunately gives no details on the six firms assembling the boxes, the seven making parts, and the two producing singing birds. I have therefore tried to establish the list of these firms, using the information available. The list is less easy to draw than one would expect. Just to give an example, the directories around 1867 enumerate many firms under the heading "makers of musical boxes," but some of these firms were obviously merely selling the boxes, taking no part whatsoever in their manufacture. It is even more difficult to trace the makers of parts (combs, blanks, etc.) for they were often mechanics, at best the heads of small workshops, and not necessarily restricting themselves to the production of components for musical boxes

Nevertheless we are almost certain that the six firms, employing altogether 200 people, assembling and trading musical boxes were:

> Nicole Frères
> Ducommun-Girod
> C. Lecoultre
> D. Langdorff
> B.-A. Brémond
> Th. Greiner

Hereafter, we have summarized the information concerning these firms in 1867 and their place in the musical box industry during the 19th century.

NICOLE Frères

In 1867 the head of the firm was David-Elie Nicole (1792-1871) in partnership, most probably, with his son Pierre-François-Emile (1835-1910). The address was 17, rue Kléberg, in the Saint-Gervais district. The firm had been founded around 1815 by the two brothers David-Elie and Pierre-Moïse. The latter died in 1857 and David-Elie in 1871, after which his son, Pierre-François-Emile, continued to run the firm until 1881 or thereabouts. Around that time Charles-Eugène Brun took it over. The firm was registered in London in 1881, keeping a branch in Geneva.

For more details, see the article of Cyril de Vere Green in *The Music Box*, volume 4, pp. 234-240, or *Silver Anniversary Collection* pp. 148-160.

C. LECOULTRE

In 1867 the head was Charles-François Lecoultre (1834-1914) and the address 12, rue des Alpes, not far from the Place des Alpes (the house still exists today but became No. 18 around 1880). Charles was the son of François-Charles, also a maker of musical boxes. François founded the LECOULTRE firm about 1828. Charles succeeded François circa 1865, and around 1871 Charles handed over the firm to Auguste Perrelet. Until 1874, Perrelet was associated with Louis-Auguste Grosclaude, and the trade name of the firm was A. PERRELET et Cie. After 1874 Grosclaude left the firm to run his own business, L.-A. GROSCLAUDE, from about 1875 to 1879. The firm A. PERRELET disappeared when its owner died in 1900.

For more information on the Lecoultre family, see the article of Olin L. Tillotson in the *Bulletin*, volume XIII, pp. 70-74.

Th. GREINER

In 1867, the address of Théodore-Jean Greiner (1820-1868) was probably 3, rue Sismondi, a street close to the Place des Alpes. We do not know the exact date of foundation, but the firm was in existence in 1857. From 1858 to circa 1863 Greiner was associated with Baptiste-Antoine Brémond under the trade name T. GREINER et B. BREMOND. In 1867 Greiner was again on his own and won a bronze medal in the Paris exhibition. He died a year later, his wife continuing for a while to own the firm. Ami Rivenc took over the Greiner firm about 1870 under the trade name of A. RIVENC et Cie. The Rivenc firm ceased to exist in 1898 when Ami died.

B.-A. BREMOND

Baptiste-Antoine Brémond (1834-1925) was the head of this firm for about 40 years. In 1867 his address was still 7, rue Pradier, for he moved to the Place des Alpes only in 1873. In the second half of the century this firm was probably the most important one and its boxes the best ones in Geneva. Baptiste-Antoine, a jeweler by education, was at first the partner of Théodore-Jean Greiner (T. GREINER et B. BREMOND). The association lasted about five years (1858 to circa 1863). Brémond ran his own firm until 1902, when he went bankrupt. Let us remember, in passing, that in 1859 he married Anaïs, the daughter of David Langdorff, also one of the six Genevese makers of musical boxes in 1867.

Details on Brémond can be found in an article published in the *Bulletin*, volume XXI, pp. 81-84.

D. LANGDORFF

In 1867 the firm was owned by David Langdorff (1804-1873) and located in Saint-Gervais, at 13, rue de Coutance. He claimed that the firm had been founded in 1838. What is sure is that he was in 1844 the partner of Isaac-Henri Métert, the grandfather of Henri Métert, who at the end of the century worked for the NICOLE Frères and died in London in 1933. The association was known as METERT et LANGDORFF and was dissolved in 1852. After David's death in 1873, the firm was owned by his son John-Baptiste in association with David's wife, under the trade name John LANGDORFF et Cie. In 1898 the trade name became John LANGDORFF and the firm ceased to exist in 1902 when John became a partner of Jean Billon (Billon-Haller) in the Société anonyme des Fabriques réunies des Boîtes à Musique, anciennes Maisons RIVENC, LANGDORFF et BILLON.

DUCOMMUN-GIROD

In 1867 the firm was owned by Louis Ducommun (1821-circa 1885) in partnership with his young brother Jean (1830-1899). They won a bronze medal at the 1867 Paris exhibition. The address was 15, quai des Etuves, on the right bank of the Rhône river in the Saint-Gervais district. Louis and Jean were the sons of Frédéric-Guillaume Ducommun, who married Jeanne-Catherine Girod and founded the famous firm F.-W.

DUCOMMUN-GIROD ('W' stands for William, i.e. *Guillaume* in French). Frédéric was first associated with a certain Custot from about 1820 to about 1828, the name of the firm being CUSTOT et DUCOMMUN. After Frédéric's death in 1862, his two sons continued to run the firm, apparently keeping the name of the father: DUCOMMUN-GIROD. In 1868 the firm was dissolved. The younger brother, Jean, became a maker of blanks for musical boxes. Louis, in 1869, associated himself with Louis Mittendorff, creating the firm Louis DUCOMMUN et Cie., which subsisted until circa 1872.

For more details, see *The Music Box,* volume 7, pp. 59-60.

As for the two firms of singing-bird boxes, one of the two was surely headed by Charles-Abraham Bruguier the son (1818-1891). His address was the "5, rue des Pâquis" often found scratched on existing mechanisms. (For more details on the Bruguiers, see the *Bulletin*, volume XXII, pp. 1-16.) I am not sure about the other firm. It could be the workshop of Jacques Bruguier (1801-1873), the brother-in-law of Charles-Abraham, but it could also be that of Ami-François-Napoléon Rochat (1807-1875).

The seven firms making parts for musical boxes pose more problems. I have assumed that the report's author had in mind only the makers of blanks and/or combs (the makers of blanks of musical boxes did not always provide the combs). I do not believe that the report counted the spring makers or the makers of accessories such as drums, and so forth. With these assumptions, the seven firms in 1867 were probably:

Société anonyme libre de l'ancienne Maison BILLON et ISAAC
J. Kuntz
A. Kimmerling (the father)
L. Kimmerling (the son)
A. Mouchet
M. Simond
A. Jacquillard,

although I cannot exclude as possible candidates:

F. Dadier (comb maker)
J. Ducommun (who made blanks, but somewhat later than 1867, I guess)
F. Alder (mostly a tool maker).

The most important firm was surely the first one, and it made blanks, combs, and springs. The detailed story of the successive BILLON firms has been written by my daughter, Suzanne Maurer, (see the *Bulletin,* volume XXI, pp. 182-188). The trademark of the Billons was composed of the letters SBI, and they are often found underneath the cast comb-base. The three letters stand for SOCIETE BILLON et ISAAC, which became the Société anonyme libre de l'ancienne Maison BILLON et ISAAC on January 1, 1867. The firm B.-A. BREMOND, for instance, often used SBI blanks, and it is also known that the Billons sold blanks to makers in Sainte-Croix.

It would obviously be quite instructive to find more about these makers of combs and blanks: who were they, to whom did they sell, what were their marks? Answering these questions would certainly explain the similarities between musical mechanisms from different firms. Unfortunately, reliable information is difficult to find.

The conclusions of the February 1868 report are interesting. Its author's opinion is that, basically, nothing was wrong with the structure of the Fabrique. The difficulties, according to him, had to be imputed essentially to the circumstances prevailing at the time in European industry. We wonder if he was not too optimistic.

The report recommends a few actions to be taken concerning the type of watches produced, as well as a more extensive use of machine-tools. It proposes to maintain and even enhance "high-class watchmaking and jewelry," but suggests also producing "good standard watches" in order to compete with the watchmakers of the Swiss Jura. To the mechanization of the Fabrique, the report devotes a few paragraphs. It is noted that Geneva firms, except a few, do not use many of the mechanical facilities available. The author's opinion is that:

> ... the use of machine-tools has drawbacks ... it pays a premium for mediocrity ... it slows down the professional development of the worker, but modern industry is nevertheless forced to use more and more of these machines.

and he concludes:

> ... let us nevertheless try to see that the machine-tools will be the slaves and that man will remain the master."

Does this last sentence not sound familiar to those worried by the invasion of computers into our private lives?

The issue of mechanization throughout the Fabrique was indeed a crucial one. For the musical box industry, the resistance by the Genevese firms to fully mechanized manufacturing led Sainte-Croix to supersede Geneva. This transfer was a slow one, beginning around 1850. By 1900 Sainte-Croix had won the battle, the production of Geneva being negligible.

Amazingly, this process was correctly forecast and analyzed in 1878 by Etienne Dufour, a workman in the Genevese musical box industry. Dufour, together with another worker, had been selected by the makers to visit the international exhibition held in Paris in 1878. Back in Geneva, he wrote up a report, making, in substance, the following remarks:

> For its musical box industry, Geneva seems to have a definite tendency to abandon the manufacturing of standard items. I ask myself if it is appropriate to abandon this type of production and if a consequence of this trend would not be for Geneva to lose just what it should like to keep: namely, the making of large boxes.
>
> Comparing the large and small types, one must not forget that, in spite of its apparent inferiority, the small musical box will remain the most in demand and the best adapted to transport, due to: 1) its lesser volume, 2) its remarkable suitability to introducing music in many items, adding value to them.

I address my remarks to the Makers (Dufour uses the polite French expression: *Messieurs les Fabricants.*) *It is my personal impression that the Genevese industry of musical boxes would lose enormously in this projected change from the standard type of production that permits keeping the workman busy on a regular basis.*

Etienne Dufour, probably working in one of the six Genevese firms listed earlier, precisely analyzed in 1878 what would happen to Geneva, and why it would happen, if the production of the tabatière movements were to be abandoned. He was proved to be right. ■■

B. A. BREMOND

Pierre Germain and Suzanne Maurer

$\mathcal{L}$ITTLE is known about the history of the Geneva makers, and even Alfred Chapuis in *Histoire de la boîte à musique* does not tell much about them. This led us to dig, a few months ago, into the written material available in Geneva and, as a result, to collect a sizable amount of firsthand and, often, original information. The firm B.A. BREMOND was one of the first investigated, and it is a pleasure to summarize hereafter part of our results.

Baptiste Antoine Brémond was born in August, 1834, and the family was living at rue du Rhône 137, the present 82 (the house no longer exists). His father Philippe and his grandfather Charles Abraham were jewellers, and so were Baptiste Antoine and his eldest brother Charles Abraham. According to the *Dictionnaire historique et biographique de la Suisse* the Brémonds settled in Geneva in 1698, having come from Uzès (France).

We have a photocopy of a contract indicating that the firm GREINER & BREMOND was founded in February of 1858, and the signatures of the two partners are reproduced here. The association was to last five years, and

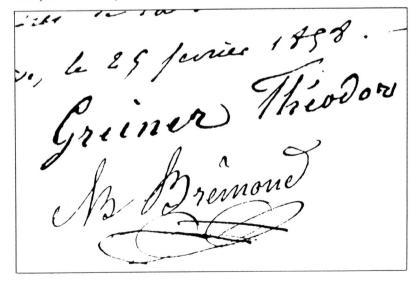

in the agreement Théodore Greiner is indicated as a musical-box manufacturer *(fabricant de pieces à musique)* while Brémond is mentioned as a merchant only. The claim, made later on by Brémond, that his firm was founded in 1858 is therefore only partially correct, this date corresponding to the beginning of its association with Greiner.

A year later, Baptiste Antoine married Anaïs Langdorff, the daughter of David and the sister of John (David and John Langdorff being the well-known makers of musical boxes).

Around 1861 we find the firm GREINER & BREMOND established in rue Sismondi. The street was located in a new ward built on the site of the old fortifications that had been demolished some time before. This ward was to be a manufacturing and trade center for musical boxes, with firms like CONCHON, ALLARD & CIE., etc.

In a directory of 1866 we find, still in the same district, the firm B.A. BREMOND installed at rue Pradier 7. It is therefore probable that the association with Greiner was not renewed at the end of the contract in 1863. Théodore Greiner was to die a few years later, in 1868.

At the Great Exhibition of Paris in 1867 the firm B.A. BREMOND received a bronze medal, and in 1873 we found the following quotation:

> *Mr. B.A. Brémond, you are hereby appointed Manufacturer of Musical Boxes to His Royal Highness the Prince of Wales. Given under my hand and seal at Marlborough House this first day of March 1873.*
> *(signed) W. Knollys, Comptroller.*

This Prince of Wales was the future King Edward VII.

MUSICAL BOX MANUFACTORY

B.-A. BRÉMOND

Fabrique de PIÈCES A MUSIQUE en tous genres.

PIÈCES A MUSIQUE — ARTICLES FANTAISIE A MUSIQUE
OISEAUX CHANTEURS — AUTOMATES, ETC., ETC.

Grands salons de vente au rez-de-chaussée.

GENÈVE   PLACE DES ALPES   GENÈVE

FABRIK VON SPIELWERKEN JEDER ART

ADVERTISEMENT FOUND IN A DIRECTORY OF 1879.

Brémond wrote in 1876 a report on the proposal by the French government to raise the customs duties on imported musical boxes. It is quite interesting to read, for this new tariff was seriously to affect the ability of the Swiss to compete in the French market, by favoring the French manufacturer Auguste L'Epée.

In 1878 Baptiste Antoine was appointed by the Swiss government to one of the Commissions of the Paris Exhibition, where the firm once again won a bronze medal. It was this year also that Brémond began his public life, being from 1878 to 1886 town-councilor of Geneva, and for two years (1880-1882) a deputy of the legislative body of the Canton of Geneva. He made several interventions in the councils, but we found nothing worth reporting on. Let us just mention that even now a *Député au Grand Conseil* is a personage in the public life of the Canton.

Brémond always advertised a great deal. For instance, reproduced here, is an advertisement published in 1879, showing that the firm was trading not only in musical boxes but also in singing birds, automata, etc., though probably not manufacturing them. Ten years later, in 1889, another advertisement, also shown here, mentions for the first time the trade name *A la Lyre D'Or* (At the Golden Lyre). In December 1891, in the *Journal de Genève*, a significant Genevan newspaper, we have found an amusing ad:

> ... *large choice of presents for Christmas and New Year, 20% discount ... Goods shipped to all countries.*,

its last sentence being in English.

By 1880 the official address was rue des Alpes 2. The building still exists at the corner, rue and place des Alpes, and the business card in the possession of the Frattis (see Vol. XX, No. 6, p. 352) shows the Lake as viewed from the premises of the factory. There was -- and still is -- a square between the house and the Lake.

Brémond did not participate at the National Exhibition of Geneva in 1896, a very important Swiss event. This came as a surprise to us, for Allard, Conchon, Langdorff & fils, Baker & Cie., not to mention numerous Sainte-Croix makers, did participate. Why was Brémond absent?

We finally arrive at 1902, a year of sorrow for Brémond: he went bankrupt. We found a note written and signed by him, dated 4th September 1902 and addressed to the Tribunal. In this note, he, Baptiste Antoine Brémond, 'fabricant de pièces à musique, rue des Alpes 2,' being insolvent asks to be declared bankrupt. For this 68-year-old man, once a political figure in town, this bankruptcy must have been a tragedy; from a domestic point of view, he had to move to a smaller flat and get rid of his servant.

By then, the firm B. A. BREMOND had existed for about 40 years (ca. 1863 to 1902) following the five-year association of GREINER & BREMOND (1858 -- ca. 1863).

After the bankruptcy, there still remains a mystery, for, under the heading of musical boxes, the directories continue to list Brémond: as B.A. BREMOND until 1908, as Ph. BREMOND until 1913, and as Firm

A LA LYRE D'OR

PLACE DES ALPES

En face le monument du duc de Brunswick

GENÈVE

FABRIQUE DE BOITES A MUSIQUE

B.-A. Brémond

BOITES A MUSIQUE	MUSIKWERKE U. SPIELDOSEN
EN TOUS GENRES	ALLER ART
en QUALITÉ SOIGNÉE	in SORGFÆLTIGER AUSFUHRUNG
Derniers perfectionnements	Letztere Verbesserungen
ARTICLES POUR L'EXPORTATION	ARTIKEL FÜR DEN EXPORT
AIRS DE TOUS LES PAYS	MELODIEN ALLER LÆNDER
PRIX MODÉRÉS	MÆSSIGE PREISE
ADRESSE TÉLÉGRAPHIQUE :	TELEGRAMM-ADRESSE :
BREMONDUS-GENEVE	BREMONDUS-GENEVE
TÉLÉPHONE N° 493	TÉLÉPHONE N° 493

FROM L'ANNUAIRE DU COMMERCE SUISSE (1889).

BREMOND until 1916. Ph. Brémond almost certainly stands for Philippe Albert Brémond (1863-1930), son of Baptiste Antoine – his only son, we believe. Philippe was an accountant and probably spent some time in New York in the 1880's. We have not, as yet, cleared up this mystery, although we have a clue.

Baptiste Antoine Brémond died in October of 1925 in Geneva at the respectable age of 91. A journalist wrote a short necrology, pointing out (we translate):

> ... *his firm remained flourishing until the phonograph was invented* ...

He was certainly right. ▪ ▪

MARTIN FRERES

Howard M. Fitch

$\mathcal{A}$LTHOUGH some makers of cylinder musical boxes placed their names on their products in one way or another, many did not, to the great frustration of collectors who would like to have some idea of where, when, and by whom their cherished boxes were made. In a few instances, such as the L'Epée boxes sold by the firm of Thibouville-Lamy, certain uniform details of construction or secondary evidence of various kinds enable attribution to be made with a fair degree of certainty, but a great many quality boxes are and will probably remain unidentifiable. Two boxes of excellent quality that are unmarked as to maker but can be traced to the Martin family in l'Auberson, Switzerland, have come to our attention during the past year, and we will describe them in some detail in the hope that further information about this family will be forthcoming from our members.

We have been able to find very little in the literature regarding the Martins as makers of musical boxes, although Martin is an old name in the Ste.-Croix area, with members represented in various trades and industries of the region. In his book *Histoire de la Boîte à Musique et de la Musique Mécanique* (Scriptar S. A., Lausanne, 1955), Prof. Alfred Chapuis chronicles the origin and development of mechanical musical instruments, including the beginnings of the cylinder musical-box industry in the early nineteenth century through its growth in that century and ultimate decline in the first two decades of the twentieth century. He lists (page 201) among the nine makers in the Ste.-Croix area exhibiting at the first National Swiss Exposition in 1883 at Zurich "Henri Martin, founded in 1874, l'Auberson"; lists (page 211) Henri Martin as a member of a committee of comb tuners in the Ste.-Croix region that was formed in 1911 to study ways to reverse the alarming decline in numbers and ability among tuners and to attract more apprentices to the trade; and states (page 212) that the year 1914 marked the end of the production of large cylinder boxes. In a list by Chapuis (page 287) of makers active in the Ste.-Croix area in 1914, the name Martin does not appear.

One of the Martin boxes was shown to us when we visited the Florida home of members Helen and Frank Kenyon in the Spring of 1978, and we are indebted to Frank for permission to examine and photograph the box and the documentation that came with it. The interchangeable movement is of the rather rare type known as *Flûte-basse*, i.e. it has a reed-organ section using low-pitched reeds to accompany the conventional comb. The organ does not overpower the music from the comb, as is frequently the case with the more usual *Flutina* or *Voix-céleste* reed-organ accompaniment, and the effect is very pleasing. The well-arranged tunes are all operatic, and as may be seen from the photos the mechanism, case and matching table are of

MARTIN FLUTE-BASSE INTERCHANGEABLE BOX.

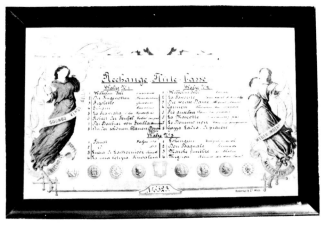

ONE OF THE FRAMED TUNE CARDS.

32

INTERIOR VIEW OF THE FLUTE-BASSE BOX.

FIVE CYLINDERS STORED IN THE TABLE'S DRAWER.

excellent quality throughout. The two multi-colored tune cards, one of which is illustrated here, for the six cylinders bear a striking resemblance to the tune sheet lent to us by Vicki Glasgow from a Heller Overture box (see page 170 of the Spring-Summer 1977 *Bulletin*, Vol. XXIII, No. 2) and were lithographed by the same lithographer, Habernal & Co. of Vienna. It was Vicki's conclusion that her box was not typical of Heller construction, and it is interesting to speculate that hers was a Martin box sold under the Heller name.

Two letters that were with the *Flûte-basse* box give information regarding its sale and are of particular interest in that they link the box with the Martins and carry a surprisingly late date for the sale new of an item of this sort. If the price of $1,500.00 seems low, it should be borne in mind that in 1928 our currency was freely convertible into gold at about $30.00 an ounce, so the amount was equivalent to about 50 ounces of gold. Gold was recently selling as high as $245.00 an ounce, and even at $200.00 an ounce the price would be about $10,000.00. We reproduce here the letterhead and a free translation into English of the contents of the two letters. (Note: The first initial of Mr. French's name differs in the headings.)

Manufacture de Pièces à Musique en tous genres

FONDÉE EN 1870

FRANCIS MARTIN

CHÈQUES ET VIREMENTS POSTAUX II-1194

TÉLÉPHONE N° 4

BANQUES
SOCIÉTÉ DE BANQUE SUISSE, LAUSANNE
BANQUE CANTONALE VAUDOISE, LAUSANNE

AUBERSON (VAUD) SUISSE
GARE SAINTE-CROIX

192

LETTERHEAD OF THE DEALER WHO SOLD THE BOX.

19 July, 1928

Mr. L. M. French
111 North Street
Seymour, Conn., U.S.A.
(Present address: Hotel Victoria, Interlaken)

My dear Sir:

We hereby confirm our conversation today concerning your purchase from us of a musical box No. 6523, Interchangeable *Flûte Basse*, in a box 100 by 50 by 40 cm. with a table 125 by 75 by 75 cm. conforming to the box and table in the last figure in our catalogue, for the price of $1,500 (fifteen hundred dollars) delivered to your home set up and in operable condition.

This *Flûte* musical box has six cylinders with eight airs each, for a total of 48 tunes. These cylinders are kept in the drawer of the table. Shipment will be made in September-October of 1928. Payment will be on delivery, the musical box being at your home in operating condition.

We ask you as a matter of formality to be kind enough to confirm this agreement, giving us also at the same time the name of the bank where we may obtain information.

With our very best wishes,

for   F. Martin
S. Martin, Ing.

P.S. You may give us your confirmation in English.

Among the friends made by Jere Ryder when he spent the Summer of 1977 in Switzerland is Mr. Claude Martin of Ste.-Croix, who has been kind enough to supply us through Jere with some information on the Martin family. The two brothers who founded the firm of Martin Frères in 1870 were Paul (who had four children) and Louis (who had three children). One of Paul's children was named John, and his son Claude is thus a grandson of one of the founding brothers. Paul and Louis had a third brother, Emile, not one of the founders, who had five children, one of whom was Francis Martin, whose letterhead we reproduce and who was thus a nephew of the founding brothers. According to Mr. Claude Martin, Francis was in fact a dealer, not a maker, and handled pieces made by Cuendet Frères (of Auberson) as well as those of Martin Frères.

Mr. Claude Martin owns a musical box made by his grandfather, Paul, that has never been out of the family. It is a handsome interchangeable box with three cylinders, two of which are stored in a separate box. The lithographed tune card, although equally attractive, does not resemble those of the *Flûte-Basse* box previously described. It is headed 18 airs, 12 pouces / *Rechange* 18 airs, *Musique Harpe Harmonique Piccolo* Zither; this appears to be of the type listed as item 82 on page 7 of the Martin Frères catalogue, but in interchangeable format. The six tunes listed for each of the three cylinders are nearly all operatic. Unfortunately, the photos of this box presently available to us would not reproduce well, and we hope at some future date to be able to publish detailed photos of this box and its tune sheet.

This article leaves many questions unanswered, including when the Martin Frères firm went out of business, information about its successors, if any, information about its relations with other makers in the area, and a more detailed genealogy of the family, with dates. We also wonder where the Henri Martin firm and Henri Martin, comb tuner, listed by Chapuis fit into the picture, as well as the engineer S. Martin connected with the Francis Martin firm. We sincerely hope that our members and their friends in the Ste.-Croix area can supply us with this information while it is still available. It seems likely that there are people still alive who have some remembrance of the firm and may even have family accounts and records (all of which could be scattered or lost forever in a relatively few years) that would shed much light on its activities.■ ■

⌐ SHOP ⌐OTES ⌐

Joseph E. Roesch *

A Peugeot Frères Trademark

*J*N the Winter 1976 *Bulletin*, I discussed the signature 'P.F' that has shown up on the mainsprings of several of the music boxes I have repaired over the last few years. British member Mike Gilbert rounded out our knowledge of the identity of 'P.F' by submitting a sketch of a Peugeot Frères trademark consisting of the profile of a man-in-the-moon accompanied by an imprint of the manufacturer's name. More recently,

George Worswick has sent me an excellent photo of the same trademark shown in Mike's sketch. The photo, which certainly resembles nothing so much as a man-in-the-moon automaton, is reproduced here.

*7 Gregor Court, Liverpool, N. Y. 13088.

On the basis of present evidence, it seems that Peugeot Frères used two trademarks: 'P' and 'F' separated by a lozenge, with the letters 'B.S.G.D.G.' beneath, and the more interesting version shown here. Mr. Worswick asks which of these might be the earlier version, a question that seems difficult to determine. The patent marking 'B.S.G.D.G.' would have been used only during the 15-year period of the patent, suggesting that the man-in-the-moon version was used after the expiration of the patent. It is not uncommon to rely on a trademark for protection when patent protection has expired. Perhaps one of our French members could locate this particular patent, the dates of which would provide positive evidence of the period during which the 'B.S.G.D.G.' was used. ■ ■

PAILLARD'S
'GLORIA'

Mark and Nancy Fratti

𝒥N the Autumn 1975 *Bulletin*, in an article called "Groovy Box," by Murtogh Guinness, we saw one of Paillard's many ingenious variations of interchangeable-cylinder boxes. Here is another, this one called the 'Gloria,' which was patented on January 19, 1892. As a matter of fact, there were two patents issued to Eugène Tuller of Ste. Croix, Switzerland, on the same day. U. S. Patent No. 467,388 was assigned to M. J. Paillard & Co., of New York, N. Y.; the application was filed on November 10, 1891. (Mr. Tuller already had Swiss patent No. 3,742 covering these "certain new and useful Improvements in Music-Boxes.") An examination of the patent drawings will show that many of the features were very closely followed in the finished product. U. S. Patent No. 467,485, also issued to Eugène Tuller, a citizen of the Republic of Switzerland, residing at Ste. Croix, was not assigned; application for this one was filed April 20, 1889. Its object was to provide a much longer running time with one winding, using a shaft and gearing on the under side of the bedplate. Earlier, U. S. Patent No. 364,554 was issued on June 17, 1887, to Tüller (with an umlaut this time) and also assigned to Paillard. This patent was listed on the bottom of a Gem Sublime Harmonie Interchangeable box, and the drawing for it was reproduced in the Christmas 1971 *Bulletin*, Vol. XVIII, No. 2, page 102.

The unusual, and most obvious, feature of the Gloria model is the 'under-slung' drive mechanism. As Figure 1 illustrates, the spring power is transferred from the barrel to a brass gear (connected to the supporting bridge) and then to a steel gear connected by a polished shaft to the main drive wheel (on left). This large wheel drives both the cylinder and governor simultaneously. Even the safety check is underneath the bedplate.

Figure 2 shows the governor assembly with drive wheel and cylinder in place. As opposed to the upward motion of the typical endless screw, the drive pressure here is downward, with the jewel at the bottom bushing. Attached to the detent is a double-bent arm that extends through the bridge and thus acts as a clamp to hold the cylinder while playing. It is this locking device (shown as *J* in *Figures 5* and 6 of the patent drawings), which is activated by the start-stop lever and which prevents lifting the right end of the cylinder shaft from its bearings other than at the end of a tune, together with another locking device at the other end of the shaft, that form the

FIGURE 1. UNDERSIDE OF THE BEDPLATE, CYLINDER REMOVED.

essence of the previously mentioned U.S. Patent No. 467,388. A pin L' (shown in *Figure 1* of the patent drawings) entering through slot Q' into groove Q (shown in *Figures 2* and *3* of the patent drawings) prevents lifting the left end of the cylinder shaft from its bearing except at the end of a tune, and the two devices in combination effectively and automatically lock the cylinder in place throughout the playing of a tune.

The spring is indirectly wound from the left side by an outside crank turning a small reduction gear that is connected to a larger winding gear (Figure 3).

All in all, a very ingenious mechanism, and one well thought of by Paillard, if we may quote once more from a previous *Bulletin* (Winter 1975, Vol. XXI, No. 1, page 29), where an 1895 advertisement states, in part:

FIGURE 2. VIEW FROM RIGHT FRONT OF MOVEMENT.

39

E. TULLER.
MUSIC BOX.

No. 467,388.   Patented Jan. 19, 1892.

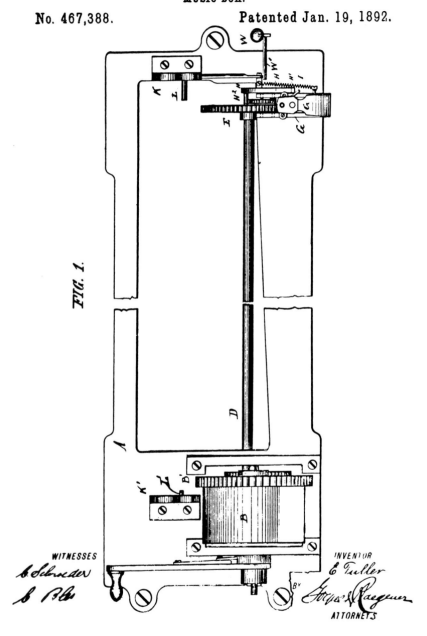

FIG. 1.

WITNESSES

INVENTOR
E Tuller

BY

ATTORNEYS

E. TULLER.
MUSIC BOX.

No. 467,388.　　　　　　　　　　　　Patented Jan. 19, 1892.

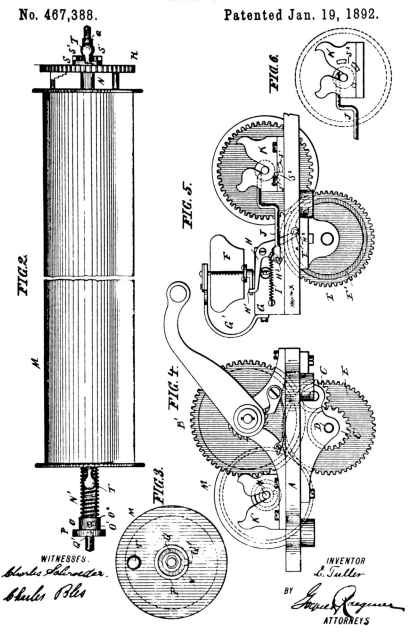

WITNESSES.
Charles Schroeder.
Charles Bles

INVENTOR
E. Tuller

BY

ATTORNEYS

41

FIGURE 3. VIEW OF LEFT END OF THE GLORIA MOVEMENT.

PAILLARD'S latest inventions, the "GLORIA" and "COLUMBIA," are considered the very acme of perfection -- the highest development of the art. ■ ■

FORTE PIANO

H. A. V. Bulleid

$\mathcal{F}$rom the earliest days of the larger type of cylinder musical boxes — around 1820—makers sought to avoid the monotony of uniform volume, and they did so mainly by reinforcing the louder passages of the music with chords. The base of the box, which is the sounding-board, correspondingly increased in size with the larger cylinders and this markedly improved the sound-radiation efficiency, particularly of the lower frequencies. Larger and stiffer comb teeth also gave improved volume in the middle and bass range.

These developments naturally caused the makers to think about achieving *contrasts* in volume by increasing or reducing the lift of the comb teeth and thereby the volume to suit the louder and softer passages of the music.

Single-comb Forte Piano

This early method of achieving volume contrast is now always referred to as "single-comb Forte Piano" and used longer cylinder pins for the loud passages and shorter pins for the softer passages. It was also sometimes achieved by altering the rake of the pins. In both methods intermediate lift, and therefore intermediate volume, was possible for crescendos. Examples were described on page 261 of the Winter 1980 *Bulletin* of the MBSI in an article by David Wells.

As workshop accuracy improved in the 1830 to 1850 period, and with it less time needed for fitting adjustments, the excessive time devoted to adjusting cylinder pins was gradually eliminated; and so I think it is unlikely that many Forte Piano boxes were made depending on the rake of the pins. But undoubtedly, many were made with long and short pins, which was not a difficult manufacturing problem; the short pins would be first fitted, ground and raked and the cylinder then pricked and normally finished for the long pins.

No indication of which were long and short pins was needed and so none was made. This meant that after damage these cylinders are virtually impossible to restore perfectly; and also when the tune sheet was lost, they would probably not even be recognized as Forte Piano movements.

Twin-comb Forte Piano

Apart from the extra work in cylinder manufacture, the main disadvantage of the single-comb arrangement was that the different amount of lift to give loud or soft volume was very small. Therefore, extra accuracy was needed in pin lengths, comb-tooth lengths, comb placing and particularly in damper setting, which all added further manufacturing problems. So it is not surprising that the musical box makers, probably but not certainly spearheaded by Nicole Freres, standardized about 1845 on the twin-comb arrangement for Forte Piano.

At that time all musical boxes were, naturally enough, fitted with combs which gave the maximum practicable volume—simply because lack of volume was always a basic disadvantage. So the twin-comb Forte Piano box came to have a normal comb referred to as the Forte comb occupying about two thirds of the cylinder length with a weaker, Piano comb occupying the remaining third. Of course this meant that extra cylinder length was now needed for the Forte Piano effect which was accordingly established at the luxury end of the makers' range.

Presumably this "standard" evolved after a comparatively short time, helped by the fact that the musical box makers were mostly a close-knit community in the small area from Geneva to Ste. Croix, with many components and sub-assemblies made by local specialists and supplied to several makers. But while it was evolving, there must have been many boxes made with different ratios of Forte and Piano teeth, and certainly there must also have been made a number with normal standard comb teeth in both combs, and relying on different lift for different volume as was done in the single-comb arrangement.

Luckily just such a Forte Piano box has come to light. It is by the much-respected, Geneva-maker Ducommun Girod, serial number 22386, about 1850, in a plain case. It plays twelve airs at two per turn. The Forte comb has 89 teeth and the Piano comb 33, but both combs have teeth of practically equal stiffness and the *piano* effect is achieved by setting the Piano comb to give reduced lift. However, it was obviously better to make the Piano-comb teeth weaker and keep to full lift of all teeth, and this must have been quickly accepted by all concerned.

Tooth Dimensions

There was considerable variation in the stiffness decided upon by different makers. Nicole Freres consistently used very weak Piano teeth and examples from other makers are also given in the .accompanying table.

In this table tooth positions are counted from the bass end of the comb. Tooth length is measured from tip to root under comb; width is measured at about midpoint of a tooth; and thickness is measured at the thinnest part. Stiffness calculated from these tooth measurements involves several assumptions but is the best practical guide. The figures are relative, not absolute, and are multiplied by 1000 for clarity.

Other notes on the table:

1. Nicole Forte combs are of exactly the same stiffness as the combs on their contemporary single-comb boxes.

2. Nicole Freres differs from other makers by having the treble ends of the two combs adjacent. This looks more elegant because adjacent teeth have the same amount of lift.

3. The Ducommun Girod movement quoted is early and is not typical.

4. The comparatively large number of teeth in the Ami Rivenc Piano comb is an unusual feature.

Loudness

The stiffness of a tooth is proportional to its width multiplied by the cube of its thickness and divided by its length. The volume of sound from a tooth is proportional to its stiffness and the amount of lift.

It is generally accepted that for a perceptible increase in loudness the sound energy has to be increased by 25 per cent. This is explained on page 221 of *Science & Music* by James Jeans, Dover Publications, New York (Library of Congress catalog card no. 68-24652).

About four times this "threshold" difference is needed to give good contrast between loud and soft musical passages, and therefore the theoretical difference between the stiffness of Forte and Piano comb teeth should be about two to one. The Langdorff and Ami Rivenc examples in the table come close to this and they give good contrast. Nicole and L'Epee have used decidedly weaker Piano teeth giving more contrast but at the risk of the *piano* passages being too soft. However,

COMPARISON OF FORTE AND PIANO COMB TEETH

Maker serial no. & approx. date	Cylinder length, inches	No. of tunes	Comb type and no. of teeth	Position of a teeth (440Hz)	Tooth dimensions in mm.			Relative stiffness	Stiffness rate Forte to Piano
					length	width	thickness		
Nicole Freres 40767 1865	17½	8	Forte 87 Piano 42	29 & 30 11 & 12	29.2 26.5	1.98 1.90	0.66 0.43	195 57	3.4 to 1
Langdorff 6622 1865	13	6	Forte 86 Piano 40	28 & 29 9	24.7 21.4	1.83 1.45	0.61 0.53	168 101	1.7 to 1
Ducommun Girod 22386 1850	12¾	12 at 2/turn	Forte 89 Piano 33	32, 33, 34 8 & 9	24.6 22.2	1.65 1.78	0.56 0.51	118 106	1.1 to 1
Ami Rivenc 29290 1875	13	4	Forte 115 Piano 70	32 & 33 11 & 12	25.0 20.2	1.24 1.35	0.64 0.48	130 74	1.8 to 1
L'Epee 11543 1860	13¾	4	Forte 137 Piano 62	45 & 46 13 & 14	25.7 23.0	1.30 1.26	0.66 0.42	145 41	3.5 to 1

the human ear is extremely accommodating and all these boxes give very satisfactory performances assuming, of course, that they are listened to in an appropriate setting and without extraneous noises.

The Forte Piano effect is essentially subtle and cannot be emphasized, as some restorers attempt, by setting the Forte comb closer for increased volume. This introduces undesirable harmonics which are poison to a musical ear.

Tune Arrangers

The main problem facing the tune arrangers was that the aftersound of a *forte* passage tended to drown the opening notes of a following *piano* passage. This problem grew more pronounced as later cylinder boxes become even larger and with correspondingly better sound radiation. Therefore, the arrangers curtailed heavy chords immediately before *piano* passages and tended to avoid *piano* passages in the later and generally noisier stages of a tune. They must have envied the curtailment of aftersound by the felt dampers in a piano which permit a clean break from a loud to a soft passage unless the dampers are lifted by the loud pedal.

The arrangers often gave *Piano* comb passages some bass support from the Forte comb, and often in the finale of a tune both combs were played; but, particularly with the weaker Piano combs, the additional volume was scarcely significant.

The Forte Piano Era

Forte Piano musical boxes first appeared in about 1845. Their heyday was in the 1860's. Nicole Freres referred to them as "Pianoforte," but they, and other makers, often omitted the description from their tune sheets.

Probably the main reason, apart from cost, why the Forte Piano effect disappeared after about 1880 and never appeared on disc machines was that the last quarter of the nineteenth century was a period when noisier rather than quieter effects were wanted—so why should anyone pay extra money for parts of each tune to be at half strength?

Luckily an appreciation of Forte Piano subtleties has now returned.

♪

Nostalgia, Restoration and Love

Ruth C. Bornand

℃HE original Bornand family pin-making lathe is back in business again. Used by music-box workers in Switzerland since 1840, this lathe, as others then in use, was foot-powered. It has now been electrified and is turning out the sticks of cylinder pins *(goupilles)* by the millions.

The last member of the family to use this lathe in Switzerland was Camille Bornand of Neuchâtel, uncle of my husband, the late Adrian V. Bornand (1900-1949). Camille had been sending pins to the Bornands in Pelham, N.Y., from the time his brother, Adrian's father, the late Joseph Bornand (1873-1940) had come to the United States in 1887 with a Mr. Jaccard and a Mr. Cuendet, to restore music boxes here. He continued making and sending pins up to the time of his death in 1965. The lathe was subsequently shipped to the author, who was – and is -- still carrying on the family music-box tradition.

PIN-CUTTING LATHE SEEN FROM THE FRONT.

In the early years of music-box manufacture in Switzerland, the pinning of the cylinders was done extensively in the homes of the makers by the women in their families as 'piece work,' and even today, the making of the pins and the re-pinning of the cylinders is done by women.

The lathe is simple to operate. The wire is threaded through the tailstock; a lever is pushed to advance it into position; a pin is notched and filed -- then another, until approximately 50 pins have been made. The wire is then cut off, as pins in sticks of this size are most easily handled in the re-pinning process. Different sizes of wire must be used in order to match the various sizes originally used in the cylinders. The proper hardness is also important, because if the wire is too hard (such as piano wire) it can wear the points of the comb.

REAR VIEW OF THE LATHE.

When the owner of a music box is told a cylinder needs re-pinning, it usually raises the question, "How is this done?" Briefly, the cement is first removed from the inside of the spoiled cylinder, which is then put into a bath of acid that eats the old pins out without harming the cylinder itself.

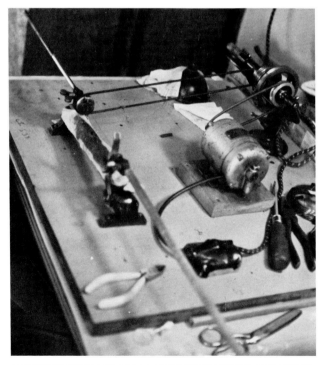

READY TO OPERATE, THE LATHE WITH MOTOR ATTACHED.

Following this, the cylinder is thoroughly cleaned, and all new pins are inserted; the cylinder is re-cemented, and the pins are ground to the height of the original pins. The cylinder is re-cleaned, then polished and lacquered, ready to be installed in the cleaned and repaired mechanism. All this is not as simple as it sounds – many hours of hard, tedious handwork are involved, but today's scarcity of fine music boxes makes this an important feature of the restoration process when it is called for. The largest cylinder we have re-pinned was 19 inches long and five inches in diameter and belonged to a fine three-overture box. It required about 48,500 pins and took over 50 hours for the re-pinning work alone.

This pin lathe is a nostalgic part of the Bornand family history and an indispensable item in our music-box restoration work of today – the salvaging of fine instruments, which if not re-pinned would never sing again. This is by no means meant as a technical article, only one of nostalgia, restoration, and love, as indicated by the title. ■■

Recording Pin Patterns
for Musical Analysis

David R. Young

𝒲HEN a music box has been torn down for re-pinning, the pins etched out, and the cylinder cleaned up, there exists an ideal opportunity to record the hole pattern of the cylinder. This pattern could be used by those members of our group interested in the music and its arrangement, those interested in developing numerical control for new pinning techniques (page 26, Autumn 1967 *Bulletin*) and those who just like to collect raw data for future analysis.

As a photographer and novice restorer, I don't do any re-pinning myself and so have not had an opportunity to record any pin patterns yet, but an idea has occurred to me which should make it quite easy to do. As the adjacent diagram shows, the technique involves wrapping the cleaned cylinder with photographic paper that is then exposed to light through the holes. The paper is processed and dried and then shows the pattern for analysis. The entire process should take less than 30 minutes and should cost less than one dollar per cylinder. Here are some suggestions for those who'd like to try it.

Any kind of photographic paper for making black-and-white prints will do, though the new resin-coated papers (such as Kodak's Polycontrast RC) are easier to wash and dry. Since we are only trying to record black dots on white paper the type of paper used is not at all critical. Photographic papers for black-and-white prints are sensitive to blue or blue and green light and must be handled under a suitable safelamp. The type to use is described on the paper's box. Almost all black-and-white papers can be handled in red light, so if you have a ruby bulb about it may just do the trick.

Wrap the paper snugly about the cylinder, taking care to start the edge of the paper at the end-of-tune space. Trim the paper so that it does not overlap, and secure it with rubber bands. If the paper overlaps there will be poor contact between the paper and the cylinder at the lap, and this will make the dot pattern 'fuzzy' at that area.

Expose the paper by passing a lamp down through the cylinder. It is easy to make up such a lamp using a small battery and flashlight bulb. Solder leads to the base of the flashlight bulb (or a grain-of-wheat lamp for you snuffbox re-pinners), and pass them through a plastic drinking straw to form a handle. For larger cylinders you may choose to glue the lamp to a length of wood or plastic dowel as shown in the drawing. A suitable size

51

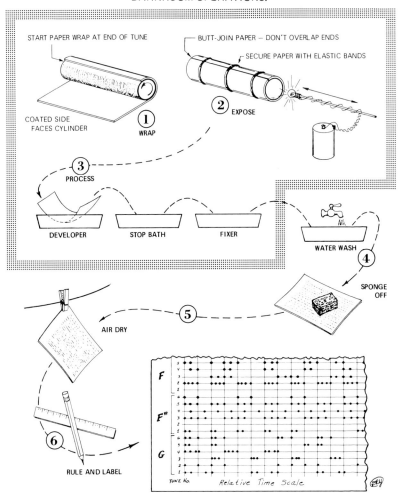

dowel may be screwed into the lamp socket of a standard flashlight. Extending the connections from the socket to the lamp at the far end of the dowel would make the battery and lamp 'wand' a completely self-contained instrument. The exposure time will have to be determined by trial and error, though the timing will not be very critical. Too long a time will cause the dots to become larger and may cause adjacent dots to merge. Too little exposure will cause gray dots (or no dots!) to form. The optimum would be a sharp black dot.

Chemicals for processing are described in the literature that accompanies the paper package. Rather than mixing up large quantities, you can use Kodak's Tri-Chem pack, which makes eight ounces each of the developer, stop bath, and fixer, and which costs about 65c. This is sufficient for an evening's work. Times for the chemical steps are described in the aforementioned paper data-sheet but are, typically: developer, one to one and one-half minutes; stop bath, 20 seconds; fixer, five minutes. A water wash is necessary to remove the chemicals, which would cause staining of the image if left in the paper. The wash time is dependent upon the paper type. The resin-coated papers require only four to five minutes' washing. The non-coated papers require a one-hour wash for single-weight (thin) papers and a two-hour wash for double-weight (thick) papers. These times may be reduced dramatically if a Hypo Clearing Agent solution is used prior to the wash bath.

Drying goes faster if the paper is first squeegeed or sponged off. If there are water droplets on the paper it will dry unevenly, causing wrinkles to form. Resin-coated papers dry in about 10 minutes, with no special equipment required. Non-resin-coated papers absorb more water and take longer to dry. They should dry overnight between two sheets of photographic blotting paper (Photographic blotting paper, unlike regular blotting papers, is made without sulphur compounds that might stain the pictures), or between clean sheets of linen and under a light weight to hold the paper flat while drying.

If the photographic paper has a fine matte surface, such as Kodak's 'N' surface, it is very easy to add final lines and notations, using a finely sharpened pencil. A piece of fine sandpaper will help you to keep that pencil sharply pointed.

The finished chart of the tune will now resemble the chart for setting chime barrels drawn back in 1696 and illustrated on page 19 of the Autumn 1973 *Bulletin.* The difference is that ours was made *after* pinning.

Since some of my readers will be pattern makers, and others will be pattern users, and others will have questions to ask about specific chemicals, papers, and so on, I hereby offer to act as a clearing house for any questions on this project. I'll be glad to help you with photographic problems or to put you in touch with the makers or users of the patterns. If you send me enough data perhaps we can generate a follow-up article for the *Bulletin* as well.

■■

Which Damper Wire Should I Use?

Olin L. Tillotson

$\mathcal{F}$OR YEARS, I've been collecting and restoring musical boxes and have enjoyed those feelings of real satisfaction that attend the insertion of the last case-screw and washer, or the last wipe of the polishing cloth, or whatever it is for you. I'm sure you recognize the feeling that I'm talking about -- to sit back and relax and listen to the fruits of your labors can be a real treat.

Too often, unfortunately, I've been less than satisfied with the sound produced by my boxes after spending seemingly endless hours at re-pinning or dampering or fussing about. It's not that I'm so much of a perfectionist, although I prefer my musical boxes to sound *musical* -- that occasional squawk, whistle, or squeak really does detract from an otherwise musical performance. Most such imperfections can be traced to faulty or absent dampers. My own indifferent dampering ability has given me cause for concern, and latterly I've conjured all kinds of means by which I might improve upon my technique. We're told that with combs requiring only the replacement of the odd damper, the thickness of dampers on adjacent teeth could be gauged and a new one fitted accordingly. Sometimes when I seem to have meticulously followed all such accepted rules, I'm still left with a damper or two that won't behave. In analyzing the circumstances of such an instance as described, I've been led to the conclusion that damper wire, coming from a variety of sources, varies not only in thickness but also, to a degree, in tensile strength as well. Thus, many a repairman can attest to the fact that a tooth fitted with a given thickness of damper wire may not perform properly when replaced by damper wire of exactly the same thickness, length, width, and contour. This being the case, if one is to expect a perfect job, it becomes necessary to develop a functional test to predetermine a damper that will work.

At first I thought of a star-wheel type of device that would strike a tooth a number of times successively, and if the damper didn't work properly, it could then be replaced. While this would obviously help, it would still involve a certain trial-and-error insertion of dampers, and this can be both tedious and frustrating. What's needed is a sure means of selection of the appropriate damper wire *prior* to its insertion into the comb and formation into a damper.

Having reached this conclusion, I began to experiment with bits of damper wire and a comb and arrived at a very satisfying technique. First, I removed all existing dampers, being sure to retain the damper pins. These I stored, in order, by affixing them to a large piece of masking tape that had been numbered, being careful to account for dampers that could not be removed intact and would require drilling out. (I do this with a pivot drill bit mounted in a flexible-shaft Foredom drill at slow speed with plenty of oil. Incidentally, have a supply of clock pins of assorted sizes on hand for making new damper pins.) I have not tried this technique on combs for cylinders less than eight inches in length. Given these circumstances, it has not been necessary to test for damper size with damper pins in place. For smaller movements, it might be necessary to perform the following tests with damper pins in place.

After the dampers are all removed, I clean the comb with naphtha. If the comb teeth require repointing by stoning, this should be done now. When all is in readiness for the installation of new dampers, I mount the comb, with tuning weights uppermost, onto a heavy wooden board, being careful to have all teeth free to vibrate their entire length.

Having damper wire in thickness multiples of .0005-inch, from .002-inch to .007-inch, I then fashion a test damper in each thickness of a length and contour appropriate to the comb being tested. These test dampers are inserted into any convenient handle. I use Q-Tips, cutting off the end with the cotton swab. For ease of identification, I band the handles according to size, i.e.: .002-inch - two bands; .0035 inch - three and one-half bands, etc.

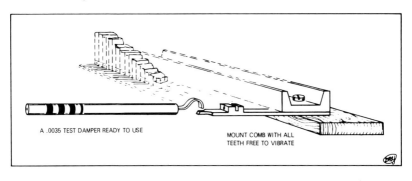

A .0035 TEST DAMPER READY TO USE

MOUNT COMB WITH ALL
TEETH FREE TO VIBRATE

Starting at the extreme treble end of the comb and using the blunt end of a toothpick to pick the teeth indeed, I make my way down the comb, testing to see if a damper is required. A small mark is placed on the comb base between the teeth to mark the start of each new size, and the size is scribed between the marks for my own reference. With a little practice, even with combs no longer having a trace of shellac to indicate where quill or feather dampers are required, it is possible to detect the need for dampers. Starting with the lightest test damper available, i.e., .002-inch or .0025-inch, I apply its tip to the tooth-point immediately on its being plucked, listening for its effect, plucking and damping alternately and rapidly in imitation of the actual circumstances wherein a damper would be required. An appropriate damper will cause the sound to cease immediately, with no accompanying side effects. As one heads down the comb, it is found that if a damper is too light a whistling sound will accompany its contact with the tooth-point. If, on the other hand, the damper is too stout for the job, a low-squeaking, or even grating, sound will be heard. Don't depend on the accuracy of my adjectives, though -- make a set of test dampers and have a go yourself. With patient listening, you'll soon discern the differences in sound created by what I shall, for lack of better terms, call over-dampering or under-dampering effects, with sometimes only one size of damper wire performing properly for a given tooth.

Some real advantages become quite apparent with the use of this technique. First of all, there is the pure pleasure of very often hearing a perfect comb on first re-mounting it to the movement -- which is certainly more than can be said for all previous techniques I've used. Second, we seldom can know if the dampers are original or not, and if not, we certainly can't have any guarantee of their effectiveness – only careful and patient listening will tell. If you've spent many hours, as I have done, trying to locate a faulty damper, you know what a frustrating job that can be. Replacing even a few obviously faulty dampers often doesn't do the trick. A *really* foolproof method, even though involving the complete replacement of all the dampers, is worth the time and effort. More often than not, it takes less time than the tedious task of searching out the offending dampers, with attendant frustrations at dismounting and remounting the comb from the movement half a dozen times or more. Even if all you care to do is replace one damper, the use of test dampers appears to me to be a surer, quicker means of determining the correct size to use than to gauge its thickness by those on adjoining teeth.

One word of caution: the test dampers you make will be good for only that damper wire from which the test damper was taken. If you buy wire of the same size from another vendor (even from the same vendor, perhaps), it becomes necessary to make a new test damper and label it appropriately. To do so will ensure that your technique will continue to succeed.

I'd be pleased to hear how you deal with *your* dampering problems. Good luck! ■ ■

༄ TOOTH TIP WEAR, II ༄

George Worswick

ℐN my article in the last issue (pages 72-73), I suggested that good sound quality depends to some extent on lack of wear of pins and tooth tips. Still, it is a fact that *wear must take place, however slowly.* Wear can occur for the following reasons, in chronological order:

Pin-damper contact; of no significance.

Pin-stationary tooth contact; very hard pin could start to gouge into tooth tip.

Pin-vibrating tooth contact; similar to last effect, but greater in intensity, as multiple-contact takes place.

Sliding of pin along underside of tooth tip; wears groove, of little consequence *except at drop-off point.*

Drop of tooth from pin. In fact, this includes two events: tooth drops to produce sound, and pin rises (it *is* microscopically flexible).

So far, so good, but if pin or tooth tip are worn (whatever the reason), the drop is not 'clean' or 'crisp'; if the tooth slides off the pin sideways, on its return stroke it will almost certainly strike the underside of the pin, producing a sound similar to damper trouble, at the same time probably 'killing' the natural sound of the tooth. If it fails to kill this sound and continues to vibrate, it will vibrate sideways as well as up and down; as the

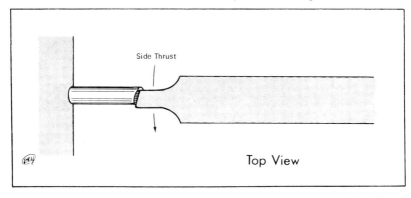

WORN PIN AND TOOTH TIP; CONTACT ALONG THE SLOPING FACES MUST RESULT IN SIDEWAYS MOTION.   *(Drawings by David R. Young.)*

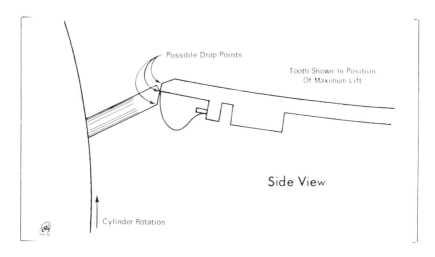

Possible Drop Points

Tooth Shown In Position
Of Maximum Lift

Side View

Cylinder Rotation

A WORN PIN LIFTING A WORN TOOTH TIP; SEPARATION COULD
OCCUR AT ANY TIME AFTER THE STAGE SHOWN, VARIABLE FROM
TUNE TO TUNE, AND FROM TURN TO TURN ON THE SAME TUNE.

tooth is not tuned for sideways vibration, this higher-pitched sound will make one suspect the tuning of a tooth farther up the scale. Even 'normal' wear results in the tooth dropping at some indeterminate instant, perhaps striking the underside of the pin with rather less violence than previously described, but with similar consequences, i.e. a 'bad' sound.

Wear may take place because the pin is very hard, because the comb teeth are stiff, or because the presence of a grinding paste consisting of old oil and dust contributes to tooth-tip damage. Without re-pinning, the first cannot be rectified; the second may be reduced by setting the comb to play slightly quieter; and the last is a matter of ensuring that a regularly played box be kept in a clean atmosphere and that tooth tips be cleaned occasionally with a dry artist's brush. *If*, however, the pins are radial, as on most re-pinned cylinders, they may be re-ground, and the improvement in sound can be quite surprising. Tooth tips would require 'cutting back' so that the pin operates on a flat underside of tip, and drops off a very thin full-width tip; viewed end-on, the thickness of the end should be *just* visible, *not* sharp.

Earlier, I mentioned the fact that the tooth plucks the pin; if the pins are not secure in the cylinder, or if the filler has come away from the inside of the cylinder (a condition easily determined by lightly tapping the empty spaces between pins with a hard plastic object and listening for the different sound from certain areas), a hot spin should rectify this fault. One risk involved is that if the pin is not secure in the brass it *may* move during this process and leave you with further corrections to be made. It is not possible to correct this problem by local heating. Musically, the result of the fault is a 'dullness' of sound quality.

Finally, ONLY as a last resort should tuning be considered, and then only by a competent restorer, as an incorrectly re-tuned comb will sound far worse than it did previously. ■ ■ **58**

CYLINDER CIRCLES III

George Worswick

ℛEADERS may consider me obsessed with cylinders, as the title suggests; not quite true, but I do find of particular interest an aspect of musical boxes that is literally 'inside information,' normally seen only by those who dismantle cylinders.

The photographs illustrate endcaps of three cylinders and show a sort of 'progression.' Endcaps are a reasonably tight fit in the ends of the brass tube, and are sometimes secured by two or three brass pins. The length of the portion within the tube is made use of by three methods; the earlier two prevent the removal of the cap after pinning, so any filler would need to be inserted through the bearing holes in the endcaps.

In Figure 1, the pin holes are drilled through the endcap, and are not opened to a larger diameter; this presumes a sequence of fitting endcaps, drilling, and then pinning.

FIGURE 1.

In Figure 2, the same process is followed, but the pin holes are enlarged to provide access of filler to the pins, though a few notches are sometimes cut into the edge.

In Figure 3, we see the most usual type of endcap; the drill presumably leaves a mark on the cap, and this mark is then filed away to allow for the length of the pin to enter without bending.

Returning to Figure 1, the remainder of the old pin has gouged a groove in the endcap; the larger hole for the brass pin is quite obvious; what is left of the pin in the cap is quite secure and can be removed with acid or careful

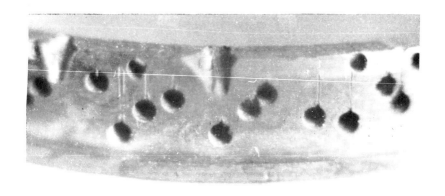

FIGURE 2.

tapping out. Figure 2 also shows the groove that is created by removing the cap; the hole for the brass pin is not readily identifiable.

Frequently, the points of the pins used with the first two types are obviously filed by hand, whereas the later type may have machine-made pins.

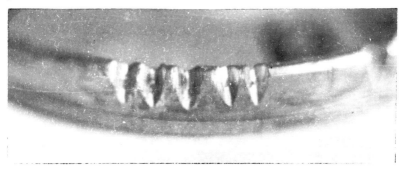

FIGURE 3.

ADDITION to my two-part article on "Tooth Tip Wear" that appeared in the last two issues (see pages 72 and 171). The reader might infer that *all* piano wire is too hard for repinning cylinders. Regretfully, the term 'piano wire' can mean genuine music wire, or harder spring-steel wire that will sometimes be almost brittle, incapable of being bent into line with tooth tips without danger of fracture. I would suggest that a rule-of-thumb test would be to bend it *sharply* to an angle of 30 to 45 degrees, and observe, by bending it further by hand, whether any strength has been lost. If it snaps at the bend, discard it. ■ ■

TUNING, TEMPERING AND MUSICAL BOXES

Elton M. Norwood

$\mathcal{O}$ne of the most difficult areas of musical box restoration involves tuning the boxes to the intended original tuning. Major tuning is required when many teeth have been replaced, when someone has changed all the damper pins, when the steel in the comb has rusted or when metal fatigue has occurred. Lesser tunings are required in instances of isolated broken teeth or tips or when a tooth is obviously out-of-tune; however, great care should be taken to keep the original tuning intact for future generations to appreciate.

This article is not intended to show you how to tune, but to make you aware of the complexity of the problems without getting extremely technical. Problems usually involve choosing the correct tuning or type of temper that might be needed. To address these problems, we need to look at some historical tunings, their beginnings and how they relate to musical boxes.

For those who are not musically inclined, a few explanations of musical terms are appropriate. Since most of you know what "C" is on a piano, that "C" can be equated to the octave or "1" (See Diagram No. 1). For those of you who have seen the numbers (or symbols, dots, and lines) inscribed underneath the comb, they indicate a given note in a musical scale. Some are written in "do re mi" scale.

Makers of musical boxes indicated the "do" in every key, depending upon the music. For the sake of simplicity, we will stick with "C" as being "do". Now the fifth tone above "do" is "sol" or "G", and the third is "mi" or "E", and one octave is "C" to the next "C." Also, there is a circle of twelve fifths in any given octave, including the accidentals (black keys on a piano). This should be enough to get us started and new words will be explained as we proceed.

With any given note, its fifth and third tones are part of the sound which is considered the natural harmonic or overtone of that particular note. All octaves are tuned perfectly with themselves; hence, "C" and the octave "C" above are perfectly in tune. If we listen carefully when we hear the "C" sound, we will also hear its fifth "G" resound an octave above. Now the problem: if we tune all 12 fifths in any given octave perfectly to the natural harmonics which are considered pure (or "just") tones, by the time we get to the last fifth, we will discover that it is too large and will not fit into the octave. When played, that fifth will howl unpleasantly, thereby earning its name — "the wolf." There is no way of tuning all the intervals pure or perfect, so we must temper or *compromise the tuning*. (In Latin, *temperamentum* means "the proper balance in a mixture.")

We are interested in this because harmonics and acoustics play a major role in producing those qualities in a musical box that we all enjoy. We must find the correct tempering system that will work best for the music and enrich the natural harmonic structure. Many times in the tuning of a musical box, we can save the original tuning by correcting the few notes that are out of tune. This is done by making a scale of what the notes are and playing various intervals to find the sour notes. Likewise, we can sometimes determine the types of tempered systems used. Please be aware that there is no quick, easy solution for tuning a 19th-century instrument as there were many tuning systems. Today we use an equal temperament system for tuning instruments. It does not work for antique musical boxes as will be explained later. At this point, a thumbnail sketch of the history of tuning might be helpful in the understanding of where the musical box fits in terms of tuning and what was and is still available.

The Greek scholar Pythagoras (about 500 B.C.) determined the conditions under which two musical tones sounded together would produce a pleasing combination. This gave rise to the Pentatonic (or five-note) scale, Diatonic, Greek Chromatic, and Greek Enharmonic scales. Pythagorean tuning was used from the beginning of keyboard instruments through the Renaissance. Just intonation tuning had only limited use during the sixteenth and seventeenth centuries. Meantone temperament was used extensively from the beginning of the sixteenth century into the early eighteenth century and continued into the nineteenth century. Well-temperaments were used from the late seventeenth century into the early nineteenth century. Quasi-equal temperaments were practiced throughout the nineteenth century and equal temperaments from the late nineteenth century to the present. Now that we have been exposed to all these tuning systems, we should find out what they mean. Remember a tuner of the early nineteenth century had to be aware of all these earlier tuning systems. Very likely, when he or she tuned Mrs. Van Tutti's harpsichord, the owner wanted to meantone temper as she played basic or simple music and it sounded quite lovely. When he or she tuned the organ at church, well-temper was used as the organist had to be able to play in all keys.

In the Middle Ages, the fifths were kept pure but the thirds suffered (Pythagorean tuning) and only the fifths and fourths were used in the tuning procedure which produced the so-called "wolf interval." This rendered half of the keyboard unusable. At the end of the fifteenth century, musicians wanted to use more than half the major (C-E-G) triads dictated by the restrictive Pythagorean system.

In 1496, Franchinus Gafusius was fist mentioned in tempering or compromising the best and worst of sounds from just tuning of keyboard instruments. Just intonation did contain some pure major and minor thirds, but many were musically unusable. Maybe we should explain more of the tempering problems. There is no way of tuning all intervals pure. All temperaments are compromises which can be reached in a infinite number of ways. Musically, octaves must remain pure; however, we find that the pure fifths are too large to produce a pure octave and pure major third is much too small, which makes opposing demands on temperament. Pure fifths give wide thirds and pure thirds results in narrow fifths.

Harmonically, the intervals are either in tune or out of tune. Completely in-tune intervals are know as pure (or "just") intervals. Intervals that are purposely out of tune to a very small and tolerable degree are known as "tempered" intervals. Scale systems that require the use of one or more intervals are know as temperaments.

In 1523, Pietro Aron came up with meantone temperament. His was a divergence from the Pythagorean intonation, but related to just intonation. His temperament is notable because it preserves the pure major third and all of its major thirds are pure. Also, "D" is exactly in between "C" and "E." Since Aron's system of temperament was used into the nineteenth century, quite likely it was used in some musical box tunings -- probably those boxes that had very basic music.

A great deal of experimentation occured in the seventeenth century. Some attempts were made with keyboard instruments having compound keys that were slightly sharper or flatter which were used to accomodate music when modulating (that is, going from one key to another by a succession of chords). This was cumbersome at best and never caught on, but the idea was adopted by some makers of musical boxes. When programming their music onto a cylinder, makers simply added an extra note or two of the same value, the extras being slightly sharper or flatter for use in modulating. This method easily kept the music pure for harmonic and acoustic considerations.

The onset of well-tempered tunings gave rise to a large class of unrestricted, circulating, twelve-tone temperaments which do not include present-day equal temperament. In these temperaments, all the possible chord combinations can be used in vertical harmony with acceptable musical results, leaving modulation unrestricted. In well-temper, the key tonalities are variable in their color without being offensive to the ear and are as close to just intonation as possible; at the same time accommodating transposition into all keys. One such tuning system that we have found in musical boxes is the Marpurg Temperament which compromised only three fifth tones and left nine pure tones. We are sure there are dozens of other systems used along with the tuner's discretion.

By the time musical boxes were invented, tuners of the day were well versed in the art of tuning as their work involved the tuning of harpsichords, pianofortes and organs. In dealing with a musical comb, there existed the same types of problems that keyboard instruments had. Very likely, there was a good deal of discussion between tuners and musical-box makers concerning inherent tuning problems. The tuner probably suggested the master-comb idea which could eliminate many problems and allow a non-musician to tune musical boxes. A master-comb consists of a chromatic scale with a sliding "do" which allowed tuning in any key. Later, as the industry grew, tuners were employed on a full-time basis and when a maker produced a very special piece, it was the master tuner who did the work.

The purpose of making you aware of all of these early tunings is to widen your awareness of what the possibilities were for tuning musical boxes. Today's tuning devices can be helpful but are not to be used as an end in themselves. To completely rely on them to do the work of tuning will surely destroy the personality and character of the box. These tuning devices are made for today's tunings known as 1/12 diatonic comma equal temperment, which is a complete compromise of the music, the fifths being all flattened by 1/12. Using equal-temper tuning, you can play in all keys without hearing the "wolf." However, we dearly pay for these freedoms: there are no single pure intervals and the thirds are poor, giving the triad an insecure sound which is restless in nature. There is no differentiation between keys, the melodic tensions are reduced and temperament is difficult to set.

If you insist on using this method of setting temper in your musical box, you will destroy its tonal color and kill the personality created for that particular instrument. For those who still wish to tune your musical boxes, remember there is one chance to do it correctly. The restorer spends a great deal of time in deliberation and in listening to what is best for a musical box after it has fallen into the hands of the well-intended. If the tuning is not correct, more effort goes into reconstruction of a new musical reality, and the old one is lost forever. Setting temper is a technique of listening to individual intervals and tuning them exactly to the necessary requirements of the musical box. This can be done only by sure and careful practice.

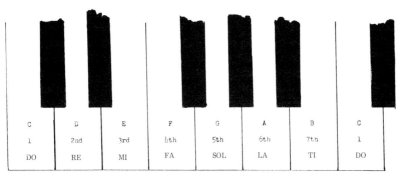

C	D	E	F	G	A	B	C
1	2nd	3rd	4th	5th	6th	7th	1
DO	RE	MI	FA	SOL	LA	TI	DO

"C" to "C" is one Octave which is tune pure.

Footnote: Theory and tuning information is highly technical and, for the most part, extremely difficult to wade through. This article attempts to present information in easily-understandable terms with as few musically-complex terms as possible, such as mathematics, ratios, cents differences, etc. For those of you who wish further detailed information, the following books are recommended:
Theory and Tuning: *Aron's Meantone Temperament and Marpurg's Temperament "I"*, John W. Link, Jr., Tuners Supply Company, Winter Hill, Boston 45, Mass.
The Equal-beating Temperaments, A Handbook for Tuning Harpsichords and Forte-pianos, with tuning techniques and tables of fifteen historical temperaments, by Owen Jorgensen, Sunbury Press, P.O. Box 1778, Raleigh, North Carolina 27602.
Harpsichord Tuning, course outline, G.C. Klop, Sunbury Press.

PIN ACCURACY
IN CYLINDER MUSIC BOXES

David Wells

𝒯HE LABORS of the music arranger in the shop of a music-box maker must surely have been the most consequential of all tasks undertaken to produce the beauty and magic of a musical box. In conjunction with the timbre of the comb, it was the nuance and clever editing of the musical score that gave birth to the heart of the instrument. This phase was by far the most creative and placed particular demands on the arranger to conform to the rigid mechanical limits of the mechanism while bringing forth a tune which was able to inspire and endure repeated listening while still retaining its charm.

More complex orchestration made the accuracy of the pins more critical so that the tolerance of acceptable accuracy was very small indeed. The transposition of the melodies onto the cylinder was crucial, and mistakes were often made and later corrected once the music was heard. Also of utmost importance was the accurate angling forward or "justification" of the pins. (In many shops, women did the pin work because of their expertise with such things as embroidery and crochet, which required similar attention to detail and a lot of patience.) After justification, it was necessary to align all the pins with the tips of the teeth once the correct comb placement was found. Second and third placement attempts were usual. The last refinement process was called "terminage". This final level of pin accuracy was what placed the music box in a wholly musical realm without the distractions of any mechanical concern.

The development of metal dampers in the 1820's by François Nicole[1] was important in eliminating unpleasant secondary noises from the music. But his accidental discovery of putting a thick layer of cement inside the cylinder[2] and the advent of justification added a great deal to the quality of the sound, giving it a sense of depth, clarity and delicacy. Toward the latter part of the 19th century, in response to commercial demand, some makers began to find ways of short-cutting the very time-consuming phases of cylinder-box production. One such practice was to leave the pins straight out on the cylinder and dispense with justification altogether. To accomodate the correct angle of contact for actuating the dampers sufficiently, these makers increased the angle of the comb and flattened the curl of the dampers, providing the correct stilling action on the moving tooth (Figure 1).

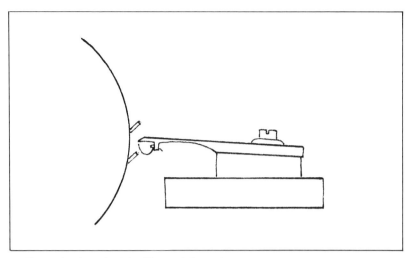

Figure 1a. A comb with a "flat angle", justified pins, and a rounded damper curl.

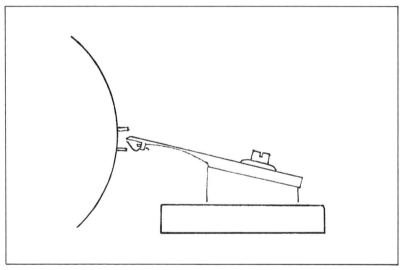

Figure 1b. Later development using a steeper comb angle, unjustified pins, and flatter damper curl.

Sometimes, in the restoration of this type of machine, there arises a problem of pins "skidding" along the damper in a longer contact than needed, causing a slight croaking noise just before the note sounds. One remedy is to check the comb placement (too close), or alter the curl of the damper slightly. Unfortunately, on a music box where the justification was eliminated, the richness of the arrangements was often sacrificed in favor of quick production.[3]

67

If a justified cylinder is repinned but not justified again, there is a risk of wearing slight indentations in the under surface of the tips by the scooping action of the freshly ground sharp edges of the pin heads. This is especially true if the comb is set too close, as is frequently done, or for notes that are played with the dampers missing. If hard wire was used for the new pins, the result can be drastic.

During the period around 1845, some makers of piano-forté movements (loud and soft expression) utilized long and short pins — angling the long pins at two or three different positions, which lessened their plucking strength — while pins playing soft notes were set in shorter and left straight out.[4] The result was a sound that modulated in a very flowing fashion. This also called for an indentation or hook in the underside of the tooth tip to accomodate increased damper functioning with the variety of pin positions. This kind of music box is the most difficult to restore, requiring musicianship of the magnitude used in the original procedure.

Whether a cylinder is repinned or not, the importance of pin straightening should not be overlooked. The absolute placement of the comb against the pins demands that *every pin* be aligned perfectly. Every note must be heard clearly. This requirement of complete restoration involves many contributing factors. If there is any comb work done, it is necessary that the tip of each tooth register with the corresponding dot or line on the cylinder, located in the space between the tunes. The width of the tip must also exactly match the original to prevent buzzing against closely packed pins. If the tooth tilts to one side, and straightening it is not possible, all the pins plucking that note will have to be tilted to correspond, causing possible interference with adjacent notes. Because the drilling of the pin holes was susceptible to human error and the fallibility of quite basic machinery, instances occur when, even with correct comb placement, some pins will have to be tilted slightly left or right to come up squarely underneath each tip. Even if the pin is tilted considerably so as to present the corner rather than its face, it must strike the damper and tip in the center (Figure 2). It is not possible to derive real clarity in the music unless this principle of "coming up square" is practiced. This is true of *all* cylinder boxes. To arrive at a level of strict accuracy, several separate go-throughs of pin straightening are necessary. The more exact the straightening, the fewer times are needed, though try as one might, there are some pins which were overlooked or tilted too far in the previous straightening. The first go-through can be done by viewing the cylinder in an overall fashion, catching the obvious cases. However, it is necessary to use the comb as your standard for subsequent straightenings. Therefore, finding the acceptable comb placement should be done before too much pin adjustment is started. This helps eliminate the problem of "muddying" the music with incorrect adjustment, adding greater trouble to the restoration and increasing the possibility of weakening the pins, causing them to break out. In double checking the angle of justification, it helps to switch perspectives and view the pins down the length of the cylinder.

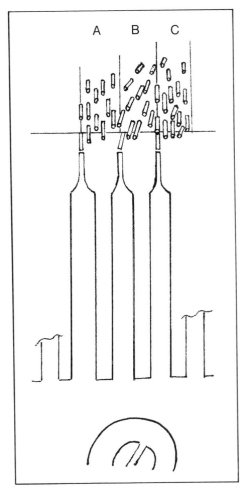

Figure 2.

A. Pins accurately drilled and straightened to align with the tooth tips.

B. All pins drilled out of register with tip but angled to come up squarely under the tip. Some cases occur where the tooth itself is out of register with its dot on the cylinder; this requires the same pin treatment.

C. Occasional misdrilled pins are angled to come into line with the other pins in that tune.

The overlap of the tips into the arc of moving pins is slightly lighter for the treble notes than for the bass. For example, the bass teeth might overlap .004″ and lift the thickness of the tooth, flexing halfway down the length. The treble teeth may overlap just .001″ and lift just enough to be seen, yet emanate a clear delicate tone in balance with the bass. Some makers' combs are more responsive to this kind of careful placement (Nicole, Ducommun-Girod, Lecoultre, etc.), however, every box has its own best placement.

Because these procedures put a great deal of strain on the eyes and neck, it is understandable to note the importance of a good, movable light source such as a drafter's desk lamp (cross lighting from two sources is best), an elevated table to avoid prolonged hunching over, and a high-quality magnifier visor or watchmaker's loupe. These are indispensible for good results and freedom from headaches.

The pin straightening tool (called a 'courbette')[5] can be easily made from a hypodermic needle (size 22 or 23 for most pins) fitted on a brass rod which is screwed into a wooden handle for comfort. When straightening or justifying short pins (.002″ long) the inside of the needle tends to get scraped out of shape by the edge of the pin face as it resists bending because of its shortness. Continuous honing of the tool with a fine Arkansas stone is needed to keep the hole round and tight so that there is no slippage of the pin, giving an inaccurate bend. Rotating the tool as you go helps wear the inside of the needle more evenly.

When a cylinder has what would be considered long pins (.035″ or longer) there is a need for greater accuracy in the pin's angle because a small amount of visible difference in the justification angle will produce a large disparity in the music; a cloudy or jumbled tune is the result (Figure 3). This is especially true of very fat or very thin cylinders (over 2½″ or under 1″ in diameter). The more extreme large- or small-radius cylinders exaggerate the effect of the pin position at the contact point between pin and tooth.

Some cylinders have specific types of orchestration such as mandoline or tremolo arrangements, involving many trills and extensive use of runs, counter-melodies or broad chording. Accuracy with this kind of pin straightening must ultimately be done by ear. Visual adjustment can take you most of the way, but the uniformity of sound makes the music the final judge. Minute variations in pin position can best be found when all other steps are finished. The cylinder can be played slowly and the few remaining rough spots can be unraveled more easily, leaving the last vestige of the mechanical element hidden by beautiful music.

With machines that have multiple combs, especially long-cylinder movements, synchronizing the combs can sometimes be quite a problem. In

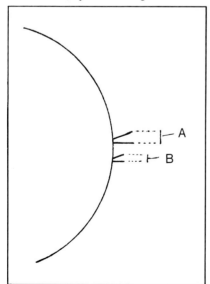

Figure 3.
Longer pins (A) require greater accuracy of justification than shorter pins (B). Apparent visual accuracy does not guarantee musical accuracy.

some cases where a bad synchronization problem exists, every possibility must be investigated to correct the problem. One solution can sometimes be found in the very small leeway available in the justification angle. One comb can be brought into synchronization by advancing or backing off the angle to compensate for the discrepancy without detriment to the accuracy of the music. This of course takes great care, musical experience, and patience.

Briefly, these are some of the aspects of pin accuracy and the relationship of the pins to the other elements of the instrument. One has to marvel at the absolutely refined and distinct skills the makers of these machines had. Such a simple idea, and such an involved path of execution! It is, however, a labor of love, because the joy these musical boxes bring to the world spans many generations. ■■

Notes

1. Chapuis, A., *The History of the Musical Box,* MBSI Publication, 1980, p. 152.

2. Ibid, p. 154.

3. An exception to this occurs on some early fat-cylinder machines which used very short pins left unjustified. Usually the overlap of the pins and tips was very slight and the slender, supple teeth provided very little resistance.

4. Wells, D., *Malignon Pianoforte,* MBSI *Bulletin* Vol. XXVI, Winter, 1980.

5. Chapuis, A., *The History of the Musical Box,* MBSI Publication, 1980, p. 211.

HONING COMB TIPS

Joseph E. Roesch

𝒯HE PROPER REMOVAL of the wear on the tips of a musical box comb is an important procedure which has not, I think, been adequately described in the current literature. The procedure which is apparently favored by British authorities is most fully described in Graham Webb's *The Cylinder Musical Box Handbook* (Faber & Faber, 1968), pp. 92–93. The interested reader should consult Webb's fine book (now unfortunately out of print) for a full description of that procedure. The method of honing which I describe in the following pages seems to be the preferred procedure of American restorers, and it is a procedure for which I freely confess a personal bias.

Most combs probably do require some degree of honing, and I always check for indications of that need as part of a standard overhaul. The indications are both auditory and visual. An audible clicking sound in the music is one indication of worn tooth tips. It is true that the clicking can be caused by other factors, such as rounded cylinder pins or fallen-away cement inside the cylinder. In such cases the pins can be lightly touched up in the lathe (provided they are not raked forward), and the cylinder can be properly "recemented". The visual indication of worn teeth is apparent because the tips fall off the cylinder pins. A worn tooth will drop off the pin sideways, which causes a visible "wobble" in the vibration of the tooth. This, of course, produces an impure tone. Finally, an examination of the tips with a loupe will confirm the need for honing.

The amount of wear will depend on how much the box has been played and on the relative hardness of the pins and the tips. Wear is likely to be particularly prominent on the tips of combs which have played for years just slightly out of register with the cylinder pins; in this case, you may well find that fully half of each tip has been worn away! Mechanisms from musical clocks — if they have, indeed, played every hour on the hour for the last eighty years or so — will show very deep wear. I recently had dramatic confirmation of this fact while restoring an Olbrich movement which is in the base of a well-known clock from the former Alec Templeton collection. This clock was one of Templeton's favorites, and he dubbed it "Robert the Devil" because one of its two tunes is an aria from Meyerbeer's 1831 opera of the same name. Templeton would not tolerate in his collection any piece that did not "zack" (Templetonian for "work" or "run"), and poor Robert obviously "zacked" a lot! Wear was extensive on the whole movement but nowhere so severe as on the comb tips. Over the years, the pins had cut a slot in the tips that was nearly a sixteenth of an inch deep. With proper honing, however, and a bit of retuning, Robert now "zacks" again to the satisfaction of his present owner, Howard Fitch.

What about tuning? Will it be affected by the removal of metal from the tips? The answer has to be "yes". By the physical laws governing the tone of a vibrating tooth, any removal of weight from the tips (especially from the treble teeth) will necessarily raise the pitch. Where the tip wear is not severe, however, the honing produces minor alterations only, and the relative pitch of the comb with reference to itself is not likely to be adversely affected. To be on the safe side, however, it is a good idea to record the value of each individual tooth before honing. For this purpose, I use a Peterson 400 strobe tuner with a contact pick-up. I rule off a piece of paper with seven lines for the octaves and then proceed to read the notes from the comb, going from bass to treble. Numbering each tooth on its proper octave line, I record the note and the cents correction. I read the comb in the key of "C" on the tuner, without regard to the actual key of the comb, since my only purpose here is to provide a reference base to return to after honing if necessary.

If, after honing, the comb does not "sound right", I re-check the tuning for significant variations — they are most likely to occur in the unleaded teeth. A small amount of scraping at the back of the tooth (at the point of flexure) will restore the original values. I stress the word "small" because if overdone, metal must be removed from near the tip to bring the pitch back up again. Instead of scraping near the point of flexure, a bit of weight (solder) can be added near the tip to lower the pitch, but I find this practice objectionable on aesthetic grounds; furthermore, adding weight to the tip of the very treble teeth sometimes produces an impure tone.

Unfortunately, all dampers must be removed before honing can be carried out. More than once, I have had to remove perfectly good dampers (perhaps ones just recently installed in an earlier repair), but the extra work is worth it in terms of results. The "wobble" produced by worn tips often causes contact between a damper wire and an *adjacent* pin, and the resulting squeak will wrongly be blamed on poor dampering when the worn tips are really the problem. Properly honed tips, good dampering, and straight cylinder pins — this is the "triple formula" for clear, harmonious sound.

When removing the dampers, do not pull out the pins. Rather, snap or cut the wires about half way back. This will leave adequate clearance for honing, and enough wire will be left to grab with pliers as an aid to removing the pins when you re-damper. That little bit of protruding wire can very often save the trouble of drilling out a stubborn pin. It is a particularly convenient "handle" for pulling pins which allow no access from the rear of the damper anvil (pins which are said to "go into the lead").

The dampers have been cut; all other comb work (tip and tooth repair) has been done — now we are ready to hone the tips. A perfectly flat plate of either steel or glass is needed. Ideally, the plate should be a piece of machinist's precision ground flat stock; but a piece of ground and polished plate glass is cheaper and easier to obtain. Glass will serve well enough, but it should be checked periodically against a good, metal straight edge and discarded if it becomes warped or worn. Whether of steel or glass, the plate should be ¼-inch thick about 4-inches wide and of a convenient length to work with (about 10 inches).

Wrap a sheet of wet-or-dry abrasive paper *tightly* around the plate; the paper will adhere more closely to the glass if it is thoroughly wetted first. In that event, rinse the comb in alcohol after honing to remove any water. The grit of paper used should not, I feel, be coarser than 400; 220 or 320 will, of course, cut more quickly, but speed is not the objective here. The 400 grit will hone away the wear fast enough, and it will leave the tips reasonably smooth. The final pass across the comb tips may be made with 600 or even 800 grit for the smoothest finish possible.

Hold the comb upside down (tuning weights up) and parallel to the ground in one hand; hold the plate *exactly* perpendicular to the tips in the other hand. Now, pass the plate straight across the tips with moderate and even pressure; be very careful not to exert more pressure on the treble tips than on the other tips. After a few passes with the plate, brush the tips with a small paint brush to remove the abrasive and steel dust. With a loupe, examine the tips to see if all the wear has been removed — you want to stop as soon as you are satisfied that the wear is gone. If it can be seen that one or two tips still show wear while the others have been sufficiently touched, it may be that those tips are a bit shorter than the others. If those tips are still untouched after another pass or two, it would be wiser to replace them than to hone down all the other tips to that length.

To test the evenness of the tips, hold them perpendicular against the plate (with the abrasive paper removed), and move comb and glass around under the light until you can see the tips mirrored in the plate. You will be able to see the tips meeting and "touching" their mirror images; those tips which are too short will show a gap between the image and the real tooth.

After the honing is completed, you will see under the loupe that the tips now have blunted ends. If the tips are left in this condition, the pins will scrape as they move across the tips, and the drop of the tooth from the pins will be sluggish, which affects both the tone of the tooth and the timing of the music.

In original manufacture, the tips were bevelled to reduce thickness at the very end. This bevel must now be restored to each tip, one at a time. To do this, secure the comb in a smooth-jawed vise with the tips pointing up and the upper surface of the comb against the moveable jaw of the vise. Support each tip from behind with a piece of pegwood as you stone or file the bevel. An India or Arkansas stone slip is satisfactory for the job, but you can also use a fine-cut (#4 or #6 Swiss) narrow file. If the tips are close together, slightly elevate the one you are working on with the pegwood. Enough of the original bevel will be left to serve as a guide — file or stone away (in the forward direction only) at that bevel angle until the very end of the tip has been reduced to the proper thickness. Go slowly and carefully, removing the swarf with a brush and checking constantly with a loupe. Do not produce an actual knife edge, as this would soon wear away, rather, the goal is a slightly blunted end. I would estimate that the thickness at the very extremity of the tip should be about .010″. Note that the bevel angle on the treble tips is very slight — these tips are thin to begin with; if too much of a bevel is filed, the chances of appreciably altering the pitch of these teeth is increased.

As a final check on the work, once again "mirror" the tips in the glass to see if perhaps the mark was overshot on a few tips. This is not likely to have happened if care was taken to preserve at least some edge at the tips in restoring the bevel; however, if it did happen, there is little choice but to replace the offending tips and very carefully (this time) bring them to the proper length and bevel, constantly checking the progress against the glass or steel plate.

After a comb has been honed, it may require some re-setting to bring it into proper depth with the cylinder pins. This is not always the case; sometimes a comb is originally set up a little too close, in which case honing often results in precisely the desired setting. Before proceeding with the dampering, it is wise to check the depthing — the less the comb is moved after dampers are in place, the less likely they are to be damaged. Unless a comb has required rather vigorous honing, not much depthing should be required. A single piece of medium-weight typing paper under the back edge of the comb may well do the trick. My own preference is not to use paper shimming — rather, I bend the dowel pins ever so slightly *backward*, thus moving the comb forward. A pair of Channel-Lock pliers works well for this purpose (one jaw against the dowel, the other against the back edge of the comb). Having secured a satisfactory depthing and having verified the registration of the cylinder, the comb can now be dampered. That, however, is the subject of another article which has already appeared in *The Silver Anniversary Collection* of the M.B.S.I. ■■

Manivelles

SCHOENHUT'S MERRY-GO-ROUND WITH MUSICAL WORKS

Joseph H. Schumacher

A. SCHOENHUT'S ANIMATED MUSICAL MERRY-GO-ROUND.

𝕿OY FORMS of the carousel, especially those with musical movements, were favorites of children for many years. A fine example from the mid-1920's is Schoenhut's animated merry-go-round, which uses a hand-cranked musical box (manivelle) located in the base to supply both its motion and its musical accompaniment.

Attractively painted and decorated with stenciling, the toy's base is made of fiberboard and wood and is twelve and one-fourth inches square. Its revolving platform, ten inches in diameter, holds eight stationary cast-metal animals (pairs of horses, lions, tigers, and camels, standing two abreast, with detachable boy and girl riders) and two wooden chariots (sea horse and swan). The animals, figures, and chariots are painted by hand in attractive colors. A cloth canopy in alternating colors, topped with the American flag on a staff, completes the toy.

The heart of the merrry-go-round is a single-air musical movement with a 36-tooth comb stamped with the 'Anchor' trademark of Thorens. In addition, "Swiss-Made" is marked on the baseplate. The Hermann Thorens Company of Sainte-Croix, Switzerland, was a maker of small musical movements for assembly in such diverse articles as photograph albums, musical chairs, hand-carved bowls, musical steins and jugs, fancy wood cases, and the like. At the present time Thorens is still actively in business,

DETAIL OF MUSICAL MOVEMENT, SHOWING 'ANCHOR' TRADEMARK, ENDLESS SCREW, AND WOODEN WHEEL WITH RUBBER RING.

BASE SEEN FROM ABOVE.

in Auberson, Switzerland; Jean Paul Thorens, a direct descendant of the earlier makers, is director of the Swiss operations.

The toy's operation is quite simple. The platform rests on wooden rollers fixed to the inside of the base and is supported in the center by a dowel extending upward from the base. This dowel fits into an abutting hole in the platform's center post. The musical-box cylinder is driven by an endless screw that engages in the great wheel. A long shaft on this screw extends through the front of the base and is threaded to the crank handle. If the crank is turned backwards (counterclockwise), the handle will loosen, thus preventing damage to the comb. A grooved wooden wheel fitted with a rubber ring is attached to the shaft near the crank end, and the outer edge of the underside of the platform rides on this wheel. When the crank is turned, the platform rotates counterclockwise and the musical box plays. For each full play of the musical movement the platform revolves 10 times.

The producer of the merry-go-round was the well-known toymaker, the A. Schoenhut Company of Philadelphia, Pennsylvania. This firm was

81

established in 1872, and by 1933 occupied the impressive group of buildings shown in the accompanying illustration; the location was the southwest corners of East Hagert and Sepviva Streets. They also had a New York sales office at 215 Fourth Avenue. They made toys of superior quality -- pianos, wooden dolls, doll-houses, circus figures, and so forth. One of their most popular was the 'Humpty-Dumpty Circus,' consisting of an extensive variety of unbreakable jointed wooden animals and figures. Although the A. Schoenhut Company is no longer in business, O. Schoenhut, Inc. -- operated by relatives of members of the original firm -- continues to make toy pianos in Philadelphia. Mr. William Zimmer, President of this corporation, was of considerable assistance in my investigations and supplied a Xerox of an original sheet from A. Schoenhut's 500-page 1925 *Toy and Doll Catalogue* that lists the merry-go-round. This item was first catalogued in 1924 and appeared in subsequent catalogues through 1927. Two sizes were available -- the one under study was number 920/10, and a smaller version with fewer animals and figures was number 920/5. They were priced at $120 and $48 a dozen, respectively ($120 is equivalent to about $480 at today's prices, based on the Consumers' Price Index). All goods were shipped F.O.B. Philadelphia. Mr. Zimmer commented that this was an expensive toy for the 1920's, and consequently they probably did not sell many of them. Also, in

LION WITH DETACHABLE BOY RIDER.

SCHOENHUT'S EXTENSIVE MANUFACTURING FACILITIES IN 1933.

CLOSE-UP OF A BOY AND A GIRL RIDER.

SCHOENHUT'S TOY MERRY-GO-ROUND
With Music

MADE STRONG AND SUBSTANTIAL—FINISHED IN BRIGHT COLORS

A Swiss Music Works produces the music.

By turning a small crank handle on one side of the case the platform revolves and at the same time the music works plays.

A small pulley is attached to the crank so that it can be driven by a small electric motor.

A long-felt want in every toy department.

A very amusing and attractive toy.

A toy that every child has been longing for!

Illustrating
No. 920/10 Size: Base, 12¼ x 12¼ Inches; Height, 17 Inches

The base is made of wood, the animals and figures of metal artistically painted, the canopy is finished in bright colors.

The whole Toy has a rich and realistic appearance.

Each packed in a strong pasteboard box

920/10   (Mac)   Weight, 7 lbs. each, packed...Per dozen, **$120.00**
Size: Base, 12¼ x 12¼ Inches; Height, 17 Inches

SMALLER SIZE
920/5   (Mor)   Weight, 3½ lbs. each, packed...Per dozen, **$48.00**
Size: Base, 9½ x 9½ Inches; Height, 14½ Inches

In ordering goods, always give number. When ordering by telegraph, use code words

17

PAGE FROM A. SCHOENHUT'S 1925 TOY AND DOLL CATALOGUE.

their 1925 catalogue, a full page was devoted entirely to the merry-go-round to promote the sale of this 'expensive' item.

The book *Toys and Banks with Their Prices at Auction*, published by Ledbetter's Antique Auction Gallery in Phoenix, Arizona, describes and pictures in color an identical toy that was sold at a public auction in May of 1973 for $350. Schoenhut toys of all varieties are extremely popular with collectors today, and good specimens bring astonishing prices. ■ ■

Miniatures

C. MARGUERAT

Pierre Germain

*C*HARLES ARMAND MARGUERAT was born in October 1887 near Lausanne, at Lutry (Canton of Vaud, Switzerland), and married Lucie Alexandrine Marie Fralon (or Fialon). He must have settled in Geneva around 1914 since his daughter Simone-Emilie was born in August of 1914 in Geneva, although Charles himself did not appear in a Geneva directory until 1915.

From 1915 to 1919 he is listed as a watchmaker, his address being rue de Savoie, 9. From 1920 to his death in 1931 he lived at avenue de la Gare des Eaux-Vives, 18, only two blocks away from his first house. From 1920 to 1925 he is still listed as a watchmaker, but in 1926 he suddenly appears as a manufacturer of automata (*fabricant d'automates*). In 1927 and onwards he is mentioned simply as a manufacturer (*industriel*).

MARGUERAT OVAL SILVER-GILT BIRD BOX HAS A BASKET-WEAVE DESIGN ON THE SIDE AND BOTTOM, AND DEEP BLUE ENAMEL OVER ENGINE-TURNING ON THE TOP AROUND THE PAINTING ON THE CENTER POP-UP LID. THERE IS A WATCH SET INTO THE FRONT, AND ALL EDGES HAVE BANDS OF INCISED FORMAL DESIGNS.

He died on August 1, 1931, in Geneva. There is still a house at 18, avenue de la Gare des Eaux-Vives, and it could be the place where Marguerat worked, but it would need a check to be sure. Incidentally, the gare des Eaux-Vives, in a suburb of Geneva, is a railway station, terminal of some trains coming from nearby France. The 'buffet' of the station is a simple but well-known restaurant . . . but this is another story.

In March of 1929 C. Marguerat took a Swiss patent (No. 134992) for a case suitable for the watchmaking industry. He was not in the *Trade Register*, and we are pretty sure about this fact. This implies that his firm was rather small, otherwise an inscription in the *Register* would have been compulsory. This lack of registering is unfortunate because it would have given us the exact foundation date of the *Manufacture d'Oiseaux Chanteurs, C. Marguerat.*

RUBBER STAMP ON HEAVY CARDBOARD SPACER IN BOTTOM OF BOX.

Nevertheless, the information gathered by my wife and my daughter permit fixing the date of C. Marguerat singing-bird boxes between 1920 and 1931, most probably in the second half of this period. As far as cases are concerned, I suspect that, as usual, they came from another manufacturer. ■■

THREE TABATIERES

David A. R. Tallis

A SIDE from the items* shown in Pierre Germain's article about two early Lecoultres, I have a few other items in my collection worthy of note.

One is a small two-air movement with undampered comb screwed up from below the bedplate. It plays 'Ranz des Vaches' and 'Finale from *Cenerentola*' by Rossini very well and is contained in a snuffbox of sycamore made in Scotland near Mauchlaine. The lid has a penwork drawing of Waterloo -- Wellington and N.B. (see Figure 1). All is original, but the movement is unsigned.

FIGURE 1.   THE BATTLE OF WATERLOO IS SHOWN ON THE LID.

Another unsigned movement is in a composition snuffbox decorated with a central oval miniature and with corner scrollwork of pewter wire (Figures 2-A and 2-B). It plays the 'Prayer from *William Tell*' and 'Ranz des Vaches.' Now, the punch line -- the comb has 56 teeth and is one and seven-eighths inches wide; the bedplate is two and three-fourths inches wide. I know of only three others of this size.

M.B.S.I. Bulletin, Vol. XXII, No. 1, pages 34, 35, and 38.

89

FIGURE 2-A.   UNCOMMON TREATMENT
OF A COMPOSITION SNUFFBOX LID.

FIGURE 2-B.   VERY SMALL TWO-AIR MOVEMENT, UNSIGNED.

FIGURE 3-A. A RUINED CASTLE IS ON THE LID OF THIS TIN BOX.

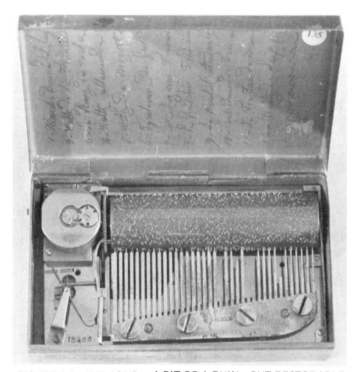

FIGURE 3-B. THE COMB -- A BIT OF A RUIN -- BUT RESTORABLE.

Figures 3-A and 3-B show a small 12-air two-per-turn movement that is four inches wide and is contained in a transfer-decorated tin box. The comb is stamped 'F. NICOLE' and the bedplate 'FRERES NICOLE' and '13266.' There has been a run, and the comb needs five teeth and ten tips. This box is rare, but up to now I have chickened out of the needed restoration. ■■

LISTENING
TO MUSICAL-BOX
MOVEMENTS

James O. Spriggs

𝕿HERE are quite a few important musical-box movements that are mute, for all practical purposes, due to having become separated from their cases through unfortunate circumstances, or perhaps because they were never fitted in a case in the first place. Some complete boxes, such as musical seals, and some snuffboxes and manivelles, are so quiet that the possibilities for enjoyment of their sound are quite limited, especially for groups of people or when there is any noise present. Also, there are occasions while making repairs or adjustments when it is expedient to listen to movements separate from their cases. The usual solution for making these movements audible is the makeshift conscription of a handy table top. I believe these frequently unique and irreplaceable mechanisms deserve a voice more in keeping with their capabilities.

A musical movement, by itself, is very quiet for two reasons. The teeth are small, so they displace very little air when vibrating. Also, because they are very small in terms of a wavelength of sound at their frequency of vibration, the sound pressure they do generate on one side of the tooth can rush around to the other side before it can be propagated outward. At the highest frequency likely to be encountered, say 4400 Hz, a wavelength is still three inches long -- large when compared to the width of the tooth, or even of the movement itself. Some means must be found for vibrating a surface that is large compared to a wavelength, or, alternatively or additionally, another way found for preventing the positive pressure being cancelled by the negative.

One solution consists of a box, dedicated to the purpose, that has a soundboard as its upper surface, similar to the soundboard of a piano and of some of the larger disc boxes. A few hours of work to make such a box will be quite rewarding in enhancing the appreciation of the music so laboriously and artfully incorporated in these instruments. The sudden burst of sound when a movement is placed on the soundboard is quite impressive.

The considerable problems of making a box from scratch are avoided by starting with a shadow box, obtainable from art stores. A suitable size for small and medium sized movements is eight by ten by two and one-half inches. In the shadow box* I purchased, the back was one-eighth-inch plywood, which seemed to be a good thickness for the sounding-board top. On its inner surface, for a margin of about an inch adjacent to the four

SOUND BOX WITH SPRUCE RIBBING FITTED AND GLUED IN PLACE. NOTE THINNED AREA BEYOND RIBBING.

sides, this plywood was thinned to about one third of its thickness by means of a straight routing bit in a drill press. Next, ribs were made of about one-fourth by three-fourths-inch spruce and feathered at the ends where they approach the edge of the un-routed center portion of the plywood top. They were then fitted on edge, in a pattern similar to that of the British flag to cover this center portion, and glued in place. A rectangle of ribs connecting the radial ribs is desirable. If a rectangle of thin plywood, also obtainable at art stores, is glued on to cover this rectangle, a very stiff box structure is achieved. The objective is to make most of the area of the top of

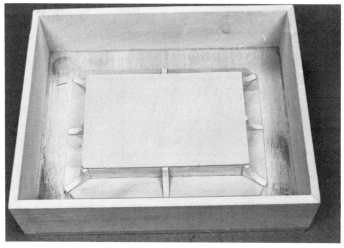

COVER GLUED TO RIBBING, COMPLETING INNER STRUCTURE.

93

the box move as a unit similar to a piston, with the bending occurring at the periphery, which should be as flexible as durability will allow. If a piece of half-inch plywood, preferably cabinet grade (no voids), is glued on the bottom and rubber feet mounted at the corners, the box is functionally complete. The appearance is considerably improved if veneer is glued first to the ends and then to the sides of the box and a finish applied to the entire outer surface.

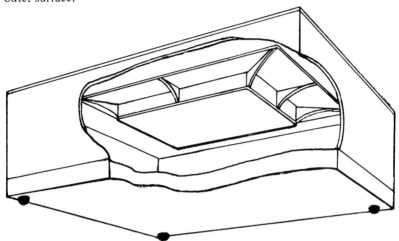

CUT-AWAY DIAGRAM AS SEEN FROM BELOW.

The particular box described resonates at about middle 'C' with a 2.5 oz. movement. The importance of making the box this large (8 x 10 x2½ inches) or larger is seen from the following: a tooth on a 2.5 oz. cylinder movement may be as small as 0.027-inch wide by 0.017-inch thick and about 0.500-inch long, but since only one end vibrates, the effective mass is only about one-half the total, and involves a weight of about 0.0005 oz. Since the movement weights 2.5 oz., the ratio of weights is 5,000:1, so the ratio of motion of the movement to tooth is 1:5,000. A tooth might have been displaced 0.010-inch by the pin on the cylinder as it starts to vibrate, so the movement and consequently the surface of the box vibrates only ± 2 millionths of an inch at most. Fortunately, the human ear is remarkably sensitive and can hear a displacement of the air of only a ten-thousand-millionth part of an inch, so a box with a vibrating area several inches square can be quite audible.

An obvious question is whether the sound could be enhanced by adding an opening to the box as in a violin, guitar, or other stringed instrument. The effect of such a hole is to make the box into a Helmholtz resonator, the volume of the box and the area of the hole determining the resonant frequency. Although this can be done (and the right size might be about two inches in diameter to make it resonant just below the lowest note of the movement I was using), my limited experimentation showed no advantage over a completely closed box. Incidentally, the resonant frequency can easily be determined by fitting a tube on the end of a stethoscope and inserting it in the hole, at the same time striking notes on a piano until the sound is augmented. Sensitivity is increased by moving the tube in and out of the hole as each note is struck.

An interesting and thoughtful book for background reading is *Fundamentals of Musical Acoustics* by Arthur H. Benade (Oxford University Press, 1976). Chapter 9, entitled "The Vibrations of Drumheads and Soundboards," particularly relates to this article.

A REPAIRER'S PLEASURES
or
"Why Do Repairers Repair?"

Frank Metzger

𝒟ESPITE the expense associated with quality mechanical-music repair services these days, most repairers will tell you that their income from repairs is not huge when figured on dollars earned per hour spent. In fact, very often it is quite small. Lest you stop reading at this point let me hasten to add that this is *not* a plea for higher repair fees, nor a complaint about repair fees as such. Rather, I would like to use this introduction as a means of pointing out to you, dear reader, why many repairers repair, or rather why this repairer in particular finds repairing rewarding, not so much financially, but, what is much more important, psychologically.

In order to be able to 'show and tell' you without too much delay, I will not dwell long on two of repairing's great pleasures: *Problem-Solving* and *People-Pleasing*. Obviously, if problem-solving is your thing, repairing antique mechanical music gives you plenty of opportunity to exercise your mind and hands. In fact, almost never does one get an article for repair that does not have an associated problem to be solved before the repair is right. The approach to solving the problem, with its associated pleasurable tension, and the breakthrough to the heart of the problem, with a resultant release from that tension and thus a great sensation of pleasure, provide an exhilerating experience of which I never tire.

Then, too, the second pleasure—people-pleasing—has its rewards; not as intense as problem-solving, but longer lasting. What occurs, in me at least, is a transfer of pleasure—from the recipient of the repair to me. It's not so much the verbal thanks one gets (though every repairer will tell you that those can go a long way) as the sensation created internally by viewing the pleasure of the recipient as he or she examines your accomplishment.

The greatest pleasure of all, however, comes from the communication that takes place between the repairer and the long-gone craftsman who created the piece. No—I'm not talking about voices from the past nor any other psychic phenomenon. The communication I'm thinking about takes place through the medium of craftsmanship—the evidence of artistry and love to be found in the details and hidden places of our hobby's artifacts.

In this article I propose to take you on a photographic tour of my private pleasures. Photographs that I have taken over a period of time show, sometimes in unexpected ways, a repairer's pleasures. A simple but good example of what I am discussing can be seen in Figure 1, which shows an F. Lecoultre snuffbox

Figure 1.

movement. Look at Arrow A. The bracket for the escape wheel clearly shows the craftsman's eye for beauty. The scrollwork is purely decorative, and, I'll bet, done primarily for the craftsman's own pleasure. Note, too, at Arrow B the graceful way the stop lever has been cut. Later movements by lesser makers, though they may play well, never show the attention to detail that early ones, such as this example, do.

In Figure 2, Arrow A shows an early version of the Geneva lock. Though the Geneva lock with which we are all familiar maintains its own position between revolutions, this one, as you can see, has a little retaining spring to hold it in

Figure 2.

Figure 3.

position. The Geneva in this photo is probably not original, but the spring is. Just look at its graceful design. If you have ever tried to make one of these, you'll know it took real effort to add the pleasing shape to what is already a complex problem of metal cutting, hardening, and tempering.

There are more details of the same movement to be seen in Figure 3. Arrow A

Figure 4.

shows the chamfered edges on the spring housing, Arrow B the gentle curve cut in the comb for clearance of the adjustment screws, and Arrow C the proud stamp of the maker. Note, too, by the way, that in this early movement the comb is still completely hand cut.

Sometimes something truly unusual comes along for repair. Figure 4 shows a so-called 'Mauchline' box, many of which were made with great skill and care by Scottish watchmakers in the last years of the 18th century and the beginning of the 19th century. (These were also sometimes known as 'Lawrencekirk' boxes, although the latter tended to be even finer than this example.) With typical Scottish thrift, they made them of the wood of the sycamore tree, which grew in profusion in

Figure 5.

Ayrshire where these hand-painted wooden boxes were produced. Among outstanding characteristics of these boxes were the fine painting, usually done with India ink and either pen or brush, and their *concealed hinges*. These appear to have been invented by James Sandy, a bed-ridden cripple who devoted his time to working on a variety of optical, scientific, and musical instruments, including the boxes in which they were contained. Boxes such as the one shown in Figure 4 are rare indeed when they contain a musical movement. Note in the photo, at Arrow A, the presentation plaque ("From A. Brodie to John Stirling Esq. of Gray Bank"). Very often these boxes were made on commission as gifts. Note also the ivory start/stop button at Arrow B. Figure 5 shows the top of the same box, with its carefully executed hunting scene drawn in India ink on a yellow background.

Finally, in Figure 6 you can see that not only the top of the box is hinged, but also the bottom of the box so that the musical movement may be seen. Note at

Figure 6.

Arrow A the concealed hinges (which show magnificent craftsmanship), and note also that this is a very early three-tooth-per-section comb. At the moment, I have not yet repaired this, but the movement plays very nicely and the wooden box gives it beautiful resonance.

On occasion, when a repair comes in something really startling may be seen. Figure 7 shows the underside of a musical seal that belongs to one of our most discriminating, but also anonymous, collectors. The inscription—"Horatio Nelson to Lady Hamilton"—refers, of course, to Lord Nelson's famous liaison with Lady Hamilton (the wife of the English Ambassador to the Kingdom of the Two Sicilies), which began about 1798 and continued until he was killed in the Battle of Trafalgar (against the Spanish and French fleets) in 1805. The seal dates from around 1800, and there is no reason to doubt the authenticity of the inscription. It is exciting to hold a piece of history in your hand!

Clearly, the old craftsmen took their time when they wanted to make something beautiful. Here in Figure 8 is a fine musical *nécessaire* made of mother-of-pearl with a framework of ormolu (gilded brass). The arrows point to one of the hand-engraved mother-of-pearl plaques (A) and to the different gilded-brass castings (B,C,D) used in the case-work. Such boxes were made in the *'Palais Royale'* (a street in Paris, France), which in the early 19th century was the home of craftsmen who specialized in mother-of-pearl (or nacre) work. (See my article in *The Music Box,* Vol. 5, No. 3, page 146). Inside the box (Figure 9) are elegant fittings of mother-of-pearl, steel, and gold. When I opened this box, I noted with wry amusement that an early craftsman had made a graceful thread-winder of mother-of-pearl (Arrow A), and a later 'not-so-craftsman' had made a rather amateurish

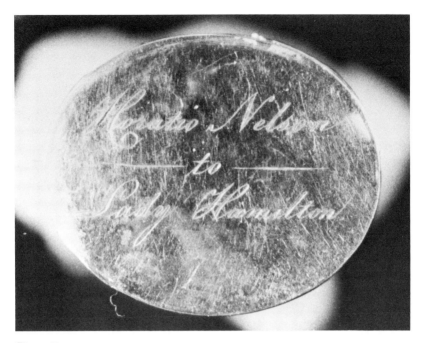

Figure 7.

Figure 8.

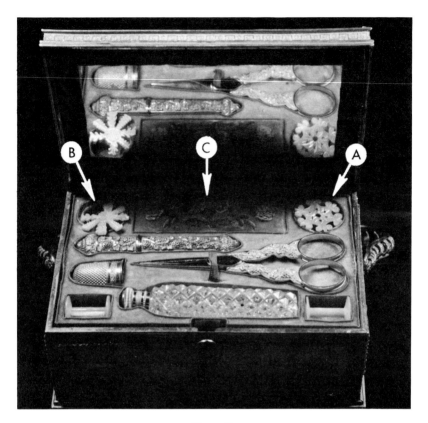

Figure 9.

replacement (Arrow B). Note, also, at Arrow C, the beautiful embroidery in colored silk and silver and gold threads.

An added bonus was apparent in the music compartment in the form of a rare musical movement, shown in Figure 10. Almost every detail here is different, as those of you who are familiar with these movements will quickly note. The square-tipped offset teeth (A), the comb cut out for the change lever (B), the blued screws (C) (characteristic of French makers—in clocks, too), and the slit in which the escape wheel runs (D). The Geneva female (E) is neatly made, but is a replacement; the curve of the lobes does not exactly match the curve of the male Geneva.

Figure 11 is an enlargement of the name—"ARNAUD.F!"—which is quite rare and, as far as I know, not previously listed as a musical-box maker. It must have been an apprentice who struck the name stamps—once illegibly (Arrow B), once upside down (also B), and finally properly (Arrow A). The craftsman who made this movement was really sure of himself—Arrow C points to the *non-adjustable* stops for the change-lever.

Figure 10.

Repairing, of course, often is prosaic—similar pieces to be done again and again—but occasionally one comes along that is truly singular. Here, in Figure 12, is a bird-box of exquisite design and execution by Blaise Bontems, circa 1880. The heavy silver case is beautifully engraved and the enamel lid very well painted in fine detail. My job was to repair the interior—it was (and is) a two-bird box, a very rare and short-lived specialty. Rochat made one about 1820, which is illustrated in Chapuis, and Blaise Bontems made the only others I know of, circa 1870-1890. These, of which this is a fine specimen, are much simpler than the Rochat and are cleverly adapted from a single-bird movement. (The cams are the same, and there is only one whistle. A special lever transfers the movement first to one bird, then to the other, and then to both at once.) Since this one, I've repaired two more—both

Figure 11.

103

Figure 12.

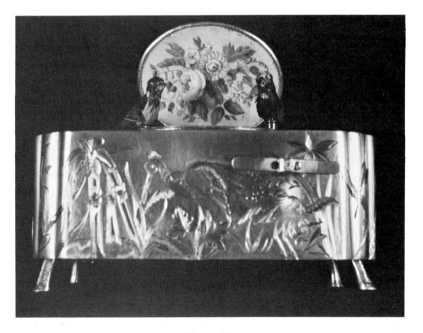

Figure 13.

Figure 14.

by Blaise Bontems—one in a tortoise-shell case and one in a silver-gilt engraved case. Figure 13 shows the two colorful little birds and the well-enamelled underside of the lid.

Not long ago, I repaired the silver musical snuffbox with disc movement shown in Figure 14. There was not much wrong—the on/off lever was broken and a long-ago repairer had used poor case screws to fasten the case. Figure 15 shows the beautiful radial-disc movement, with 16 of its 32 teeth visible. Note the true craftsmen at work again, with curves, fillets, and pretty scrolls (denoted by arrows) to take the mechanism a little out of the ordinary, to express the maker's sense of beauty. In Figure 16, at Arrow A are the hallmarks that reveal almost the whole story—DH (Daniel Hockley), TB (Thomas Bosworth), London, 1814/15 (T). Also, in Figure 16, if you will look closely, is an interesting example of the desire of a repairer to insure his immortality by leaving his mark in the work. Mr. C. Cohen

105

Figure 15.

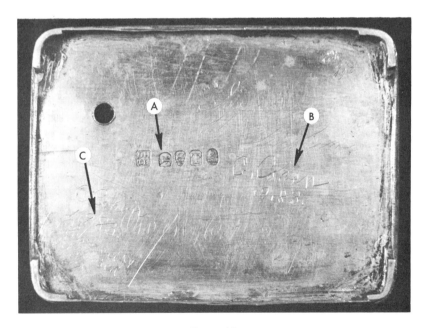

Figure 16.

Figure 17.

signed his name and the date 1/9/83 once (Arrow B) and then, just to make sure, signed it again (Arrow C) and wrote "cleaned and repaired" under the date. There is presently a repairer in our Society who writes his full name, address, zip code, and telephone number, usually twice, in every piece he repairs. Although future historians may be grateful for this, I'm not sure it is a good practice to follow.

The last series of photos shows a most unusual piece—probably one of a kind—that I had the pleasure of repairing a few months ago. It is a musical automaton in

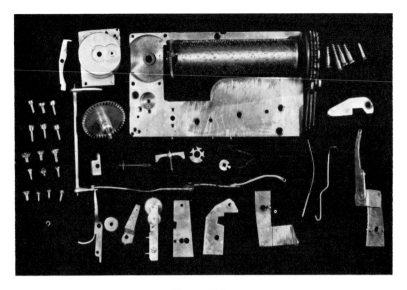

Figure 18A.

Figure 18B.

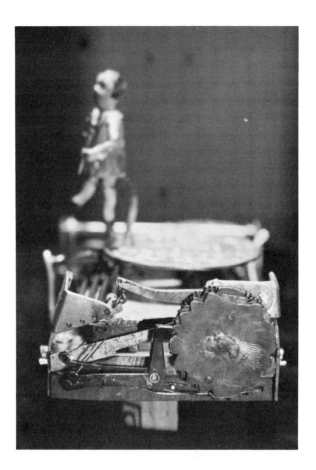

Figure 19.

bird-box format. Many of you will have seen the illustration of it on page 90 of David Bowers's *Encyclopedia of Automatic Musical Instruments*. The photo was supplied by Rita Ford, who owned the box at the time. Janet Fead, who is the proud owner now, showed it to many of us at the Annual Meeting in Cleveland in 1977. Here are some photos of the inside that have never before been published. This is a truly ingenious 'Rube Goldberg' device, which to me speaks of the old craftman's rule— "The more complicated it is (or appears), the more fun it is to make"—just the opposite of today's "Do it easy" philosophy. Figure 17 shows a side view of the movement. The little violin player is really a mini-marionette whose head, arm, and leg move by strings and who is supported by a hidden lever. Figures 18-A and 18-B show many (but not all) of the parts that make up this cleverly executed automaton. It was clearly built *ad hoc,* unlike the beautifully designed and executed earlier pieces (this one dates to the 1890's or so), but it nevertheless shows the inventiveness of the artisan. You can tell it was built piece by piece, trial and error, by the shape of the components, by the extra holes, and by the crudeness

109

Figure 20.

of certain parts. Figure 19 shows the four cams that provide the action and the levers that pull the strings and raise the figure. Finally, Figure 20 shows the little manikin at rest—fiddle at ready—waiting to amuse us all again.

I hope you agree that it's sometimes "the little things that count" and that there is beauty to be found in the details of our hobby, not only in its music, but also in its history and its craftsmanship. *That's* why repairers repair! ■■

NECESSAIRES

Marguerite Fabel

*M*echanical music takes on many forms and styles. I have found one of the most facinating of all to be the necessaire. (The name necessaire is derived from necessaire de reparations — necessary repair kit.) Collecting music boxes is my husband Clarence's hobby, but since I usually am with him to look for them, and since we occasionally find a necessaire, I decided they would be a good item for me to collect.

Some necessaires are very simple, as depicted in Photo 1. This one has an inlaid case with bone-handled sewing implements, as seen in Photo 1a. The musical unit is 3″ long with a five-tooth-per-section comb and plays two tunes. There is no identification mark, which is typical of the necessaires in our collection. Most necessaires have a thimble, scissors, bodkin, needle case and embroidery punch. There can be other items such as bobbins, a small bottle containing a white powder (I wonder if this was originally smelling salts in case you pricked a finger while sewing?), button hook, crochet hook, knife and needle threader.

Photo 1. A "simple" necessaire.

Photo 1a. The inlaid case with bone-handled implements.

Photo 2. A domed case.

Photo 2a. Showing the glass cover.

Photo 2b. Mother-of-pearl trimmed with gold.

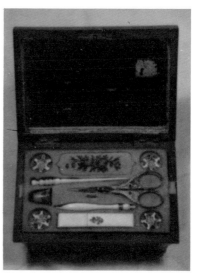

Photo 3. An inlaid domed case.

Photo 3a. A gold thimble inscribed "Laura."

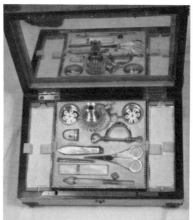

Photo 4. A large version - 9½" x 6¼".

Photo 4a. The round, cut-glass bottle with a telescope in the center.

Photo 4b. Open view.

Photo 5. The largest, 8¼" x 12".

Photo 5b. The silver toiletry implements.

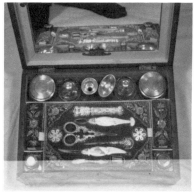

Photo 5a. The silver sewing implements.

Photo 5c. An open view of the movement.

Photo 6. A rather common type in the form of a piano.

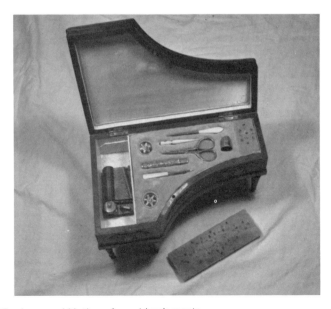

Photo 6a. Ivory and Mother-of-pearl implements.

There are also necessaires with ivory, mother-of-pearl trimmed with gold, silver steel and silver implements. All early necessaires seem to have the same type five-tooth-per-section musical unit with two tunes. Some cases had a domed top as in Photo 2, or a nice glass cover over the musical unit as shown in Photo 2a. Others had a paper-covered tin for the top cover. The one in Photo 2b is made of mahogany with mother-of-pearl implements trimmed with gold. The start and stop levers for this box are on the bottom.

The necessaire in Photo 3 is a light-colored, rectangular, wooden box, trimmed with brown wood and marquisites. It contains ivory implements decorated with painted flowers and a gold thimble on which is inscribed "Laura" (See Photo 3a). The levers for this box are at the back.

The large necessaire in Photo 4 is 9½″ x 6¼″ and has a little plaque with "Souvenir" inscribed on it. An unusual feature of this box is a round, cut-glass bottle (Photo 4a) with a small telescope in the center. This has mother-of-pearl, gold-trimmed implements. It also has a paper-covered tin cover, and the start and stop levers are in the back (Photo 4b). On the bottom of the case is a paper label with the inscription: "LE. Kesul, Faiseur de Toutes, Socles de Marchandises, en Maroquin, Cassettes de Voyage -- A', St. Petersbourg." (L.E. Kesul, Maker of all, Merchandise Stands, in Morocco leather, Traveling Cases -- At St. Petersburg.") This has marquisite trim on the corners and edges.

The largest and most elaborate box is 8¼″ x 12″ with marquisite trim (Photo 5). This is probably a personal traveling case. It has the sewing implements in the top tray, and they are lavishly decorated in silver (Photo 5a). There are two round bottles with silver tops, a silver eye cup and a silver funnel in the back of the box (Photo 5b). The lower tray has a comb, scissors, toothbrush, bodkin, bobbins and a needle punch (Photo 5c). The mirror in the lid can be lifted out and there is a pocket behind this for storing paper and such stationery.

Another rather common type of necessaire is the baby grand piano style, as seen in Photo 6. I have seen these with ivory and with mother-of-pearl implements (Photo 6a). I have also seen a necessaire with automata (little figures that moved as the music played).

Necessaires are nice items and add a quality dimension to a collection of mechanical music. Even if some of the implements are missing, do not hesitate to purchase one if the musical unit is there. You can find sewing implements at antique shows and in antique shops. ♩

116

Disc Musical Boxes

THE
KALLIOPE MAKERS

Hendrik H. Strengers

$\mathcal{U}$P TO NOW not a single author has mentioned the names of the Kalliope-makers. *The Disc Musical Box Handbook* (Graham Webb, 1971), on page 191, in a list of disc muscial boxes gives: "Kalliope. Made in Leipzig, Germany. There is very little known about the manufacturers of these boxes . . . " (See also on page 211). Only Roy Mosoriak has given their names -- as patentees, but not as the manufacturers of the famous Kalliope disc boxes. For years I tried to discover their identities. Some time ago I had some correspondence with the Industrie- und Handelskammer Leipzig (the Chamber of Industry and Commerce) and with Dr. Helmut Zeraschi, the director of the Musikinstumenten-Museum der Karl Marx Universität at Leipzig, but they convinced me that "nowadays probably nowhere in Leipzig can any trace be found concerning the Kalliope history. You have to consider the fact that during World War II Leipzig was bombed out so intensively that even the underground archives were lost forever."

Were all my efforts in vain? Certainly not, but how to start again? The solution seems very simple. As you know, Kalliope is one of the nine Muses in Greek mythology. (Orpheus was considered to be her son.) Her name means 'with beautiful eyes,' and she was the patroness of epic poetry. And how was she depicted? With CERA and STILUS (in English: wax tablets and stylus), so you can guess where I might find the solution of the Kalliope riddle -- in the written sources of musical history in Leipzig, or downstream in the rich-flowing reports of industrial and commercial activities from the last quarter of the nineteenth century and the first decade of the present one. To these papers points Kalliope's stylus!

1. Registration of trademarks.
2. *Zeitschrift für Instrumentenbau* (Journal for the construction of instruments), published from 1880 by Paul de Wit.
3. Announcement and registration of German and United States patents.
4. Registration of (trade-)samples.
5. Reports of the Leipzig Fair *(Leipziger Messe)*.
6. Advertisements.
7. Data from the trade-register of the Imperial district court at Leipzig.
8. History of the Association of the German wholesale dealers in musical products.

The Makers and the Trademark.

My first discovery was a magnificent reproduction of the Kalliope trademark, published by Paul de Wit in his *Zeitschrift für Instrumentenbau* (1 February 1896, page 351). *(See Figure 1.)* Trademark No. 11006, K. 1364. Registered on 11 November 1895 for the firm of KALLIOPE, FABRIK MECHANISCHER MUSIKWERKE ESPENHAIN, WACKER UND BOCK, Leipzig-Gohlis, Dorotheenstrasse 20, in compliance with the request of 6 September 1895. Description of the business: Production of mechanical musical instruments. List of products: mechanical musical instruments and accessories.

FIGURE 1.

Two questions then arose: 1) How to find more data about these persons, and 2) Is 6 September 1895 the first date of importance in the Kalliope history? To start with the second question: There is a German patent, No. 84740, which concerns the installation of dampers for steel combs in mechanical musical instruments, standing in the names of E. WACKER and BOCK, Leipzig-Gohlis, Louisenstrasse 3, and valid from 12 January 1895. *(See Figures 2A and 2B.)* The following points are clear:

* * *

Auf die hierunter angegebenen Gegenstände ist den Nachgenannten ein Patent von dem bezeichneten Tage ab unter nachstehender Nummer der Patentrolle ertheilt.

No. 84740. Dämpfervorrichtung für Stahlstimmen in mechanischen Musikwerken. — E. Wacker & Bock, Leipzig-Gohlis, Louisenstr. 3. Vom 12. 1. 95 ab.

FIGURE 2-A.

* * *

Klaſſe 51. Muſikaliſche Inſtrumente.

Nr. 84740 vom 12. Januar 1895.

E. Wacker & Bock in Leipzig-Gohlis. — Dämpfervorrichtung für Stahlſtimmen in mechaniſchen Muſikwerken.

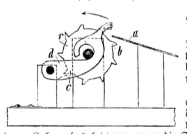

Der neben dem Anreißrädchen *r* angeordnete Dämpferhebel *d* wird unmittelbar vor dem Anreißen der Stimmen *a* durch einen Zahn *b* des Rädchens *r* von einem anderen Zahn *c* des letzteren gegen die Stimme gedrückt.

Das Neue an der Vorrichtung besteht nun darin, daß von dem Anreißzahn *b* die Stimme *a* und zusammen mit dieser der entgegen der Bewegungsrichtung des Anreißzahnes gegen die Stimme gedrückte Dämpferhebel *d* so weit gehoben werden, daß letzterer von der angeriſſenen Stimme nicht mehr berührt wird und durch Reibung in der gehobenen Lage verbleibt.

FIGURE 2-B.

Espenhain is not mentioned (why not?); the address is not the same; and the first name of Wacker begins with 'E.' In the jigsaw puzzle we now have the corner pieces. 12 January 1895 is the earliest date I have discovered, but it is of course possible that there were earlier activities, although I cannot trace them.

The first question, about the persons involved, is far more interesting. The final solution is given by the registration of a trade-sample

121

(Gebrauchsmuster), shown in Figure 3. No. 242258, W 17586, 24 December 1904. Record for a phonograph, registered in behalf of: EMIL WACKER, Leipzig-Gohlis, Wilhelmstrasse 9, and RICHARD BOCK, Leipzig-Eutritzsch,

* * *

Nr. 242 258. Schallplatte für Sprechmaschinen, mit auf in die Rückseite derselben eingepreßtem Papier aufgedrucktem, der Tonzeichnneg zu Grunde liegendem Texte. Emil W a c k e r , Leipzig - Gohlis, Wilhelmstr. 9, u. Richard B o c k, Leipzig-Eutritzsch, Geibelstr. 20. 24. 12. 04. W. 17 586.

FIGURE 3.

Geibelstrasse 20. The unsurpassed author Roy Mosoriak gives their complete names in his book *The Curious History of Music Boxes* (1943) on page 69: CHRISTIAN HEINRICH RICHARD BOCK (co-patentee No. 543,286, July 23, 1895) and EMIL MORITZ ANTON WACKER (idem). This United States patent concerns the same subject as the above-mentioned German patent No. 84740 -- a damping device for music boxes. *(See the drawings and technical explanation for the U. S. patent at the end of this article.)*

The only person whose Christian names we still have to find is Espenhain. Look for another registration of a trade-sample -- and here it is! *(Figure 4.)* No. 47764, E 1312, 26 September 1895. Music box, registered

* *
*

Gebrauchs-Muster.

Eintragungen.

No. 47764. Spieldosenwerk mit einer Friktionszwinge zum Ausschalten des Sperrkegels für geräuschloses Aufziehen desselben. Max Espenhain, Leipzig-Gohlis, Dorotheenstrafse 20. 26. 9. 95. — E. 1312.

FIGURE 4.

in behalf of MAX ESPENHAIN, Leipzig-Gohlis, Dorotheenstrasse 20. I suppose the puzzle has been solved now. The address mentioned in Figure 1 is the address of Max Espenhain. The date of the request was 6 September 1895, and nearly the same date is given for the registration of the trade-sample in behalf of Max Espenhain, whose complete name was GUSTAV MAX ESPENHAIN, as I will show further on.

Establishment of the Limited-liability Company 'Kalliope-Musikwerke A.G.,' 18 May 1898.

So far as I know, all other interesting papers concerning the Kalliope Musikwerke A.G. (Kalliope Music-Works, Ltd.) are lost forever, but this contract was published by Paul de Wit on 31 July 1898. Because we know very little about the company, the translation of this contract gives us a clear insight into German law and trade customs at the end of the nineteenth century, and supplies financial and personnel data of the company. Translation: 14 July 1898. Registration on folio 10059 of the trade-register of the Imperial district court at Leipzig: The limited-liability company Kalliope Music-Works (Kalliope-Musikwerke Aktien-Gesellschaft) is registered in continuation of the Kalliope-Firm (Kalliope Firma Espenhain, Wacker & Bock) and is established at Leipzig. At the same time it is announced that the owners of the shares of the company are the original owners of the Firm and that their capital amounts to 600,000 Marks, divided into 600 nominal shares of 1,000 Marks each. Fellow members of the committee are: GUSTAV MAX ESPENHAIN -- merchant, EMIL MORITZ ANTON WACKER -- director of the factory, CHRISTIAN HEINRICH RICHARD BOCK -- director of the factory; all three residents of Leipzig.

The following statement is published: The partnership contract has been drawn up on 18 May 1898. (Note: See Ord-Hume, *Clockwork Music,* 1973, page 320. The author does not mention the earlier Firm.) The aim of the company is the taking over and continuation of the existing factory at Leipzig-Gohlis, hitherto under the charge of the Kalliope Firm Espenhain, Wacker & Bock, to produce mechanical musical instruments and related articles and to deal in these products. It is allowed that the company participate in other similar companies, or take over and continue such companies. The committee consists of one or more (fellow) members, appointed by the Supervisory Board. The company can be committed legally: 1) when the committee consists of one person only, by the signature of this person or of two deputy managers; 2) when the committee consists of more (fellow) members, by the signature of two members of the committee, or of one member and of one deputy manager, or of two deputy managers. The shareholders' meetings are convened by the committee or the Supervisory Board, insofar as no other people have the power to do so in accordance with the law. The notice takes place by a single public announcement with the understanding that there must be a period of at least 18 days between the day of the announcement and the day of the shareholders' meeting. All announcements issued by the company are published in the *Deutschen Reichsanzeiger* (German Government Newspaper) in such a way that -- if issued by the committee -- the fellow members of this committee give their names, and -- if issued by the Supervisory Board -- the chairman of this Board or his deputy member give their names.

The open trade-partnership of the Kalliope Firm Espenhain, Wacker & Bock (factory of mechanical musical instruments at Leipzig-Gohlis) brings in its interest in the real property as registered on folio 916 of the land-registry office at Leipzig-Gohlis (Note: this folio was lost, alas!), as well as all assets and liabilities -- with the exception of private accounts -- in agreement with the approved balance-sheets of 31 December 1897, while

13,200 Marks must be added as estimated value for the above-mentioned lands, in behalf of the company.

The Firm and its three partners, the gentlemen GUSTAV MAX ESPENHAIN, EMIL MORITZ ANTON WACKER, and CHRISTIAN HEINRICH RICHARD BOCK, surrender all their protective duties, such as patents, protected trade-samples, trademarks, and so on, in behalf of the company at the surrender value of 1 (one) Mark. The assets transferred to the company amount to 296,585.22 Marks and the liabilities to 122,999.36 Marks, so that the total price to take over the Firm amounts to 173,585.86 Marks. This price will be paid to the Kalliope Firm Espenhain, Wacker & Bock by ready money with 585.86 Marks and by delivering 173 shares (of 1,000 Marks each) in the newly established company. As a special compensation for the surrender of patents, protected trade-samples, trademarks, and other protective duties, the partners of the transferred open trade-partnership acquire 600 shares in the profit of the company. (Note: 600 shares each, or 200 shares a head for the three partners? That is not clear. The following paragraphs deal with the participation in the net profits of the company and with the liquidation of the company; because they are not pertinent to this article, I have omitted them. Hereafter follows an important enumeration of all persons concerned in this contract.)

Founders of the limited-liability company 'Kalliope-Musikwerke A.G.' are:

1) the open trade-partnership of the Kalliope Firm, Espenhain, Wacker & Bock (factory of mechanical musical instruments at Leipzig-Gohlis),
2) the owner of the factory, Mr. Gustav Max Espenhain, for himself,
3) the owner of the factory, Mr. Emil Moritz Anton Wacker, for himself,
4) the owner of the factory, Mr. Christian Heinrich Richard Bock, for himself,
5) the merchant, Mr. Ernst Simon (of the Firm Ernst Holzweissig Nachfolger) at Leipzig,
6) and the merchant, Mr. Carl Otto Dietrich (of the Firm Wilhelm Dietrich), for himself;

these have taken over the shares. The Supervisory Board consists of:

7) the *Commerzienrath* (commercial advisor), Mr. Henri Palmié, Dresden.
8) the lawyer, Dr. Hans List, Leipzig,
9) the private individual, Mr. Arthur Pekrun, Dresden,
10) the consul, Mr. Charles de Liagre, Leipzig, and
11) the banker, Dr. Paul Harrwitz, Leipzig.

As chartered accountants, in accordance with article 209 h of the commercial code in the edition of the National law, dated 18 July 1884, there have been appointed Mr. Carl Eduard Jacobi, legally sworn chartered accountant at Leipzig, and Mr. Richard Lambert, teacher at the public Commercial School at Leipzig; their written account may be looked over by anyone at this place (Trade-register of the Imperial district court), while a duplicate may be obtained on payment of the usual fee.

Worth mentioning are the following points: In the year 1897 the Association of the German manufacturers of musical instruments *(Verein Deutscher Musikwerke-Fabrikanten)* was founded on November 15th. For the committee seven persons were chosen; two of them came from music-box factories: H. Preussner (from the former Paul Ehrlich factory) and Espenhain (from the Kalliope factory). Preussner was the director of his factory, but Espenhain is mentioned in the Kalliope contract as merchant and owner, but not as director as Wacker and Bock were.

Another very interesting matter is that the Association of the German wholesale dealers in musical products had acquired the rights of sole sale of Kalliope products almost from the very beginning, and that two of the six founders of the Kalliope-Musikwerke A.G. were members of the Association, namely, Ernst Simon and Carl Otto Dietrich. *(See Figure 5.*

Verein Deutscher Musikwaaren-Grossisten
in Leipzig.

Den Herren Interessenten bringen wir hierdurch zur gefl. Keuntnifs, dafs der

Verein Deutscher Musikwaaren-Grossisten

dessen Mitglieder untenstehend verzeichnet sind, den

═══════ Allein-Vertrieb ═══════
der

Symphonion-,Orphenion-
und
Kalliope-Musikwerke,

sowie deren Noten übernommen hat, und dafs diese 3 Fabrikate in der Folge **nur** von den untenstehenden Firmen zu **einheitlichen** Preisen und Conditionen bezogen werden können. Da die **Symphonion-Musikwerke-Fabrik** unter der vorzüglichen Leitung ihres Herrn Directors Paul Lochmann (der Erfinder der Musikwerke mit auswechselbaren Noten) in den nächsten Wochen mit **so hervorragenden Neuheiten** in Musikwerken und Automaten auf dem Markte erscheinen wird, dafs die Polyphon-Musikwerke dadurch vollständig ersetzt werden, haben wir uns entschlossen, in der Folge unsere Aufmerksamkeit ausschliefslich den Musikwerken

Symphonions, Orphenions und Kalliope,

sowie sonstigen etwa noch erscheinenden, wirklich guten Instrumenten zuzuwenden. Wir rathen den Herren Interessenten, in der nächsten Zeit nur den nothwendigsten Bedarf in Polyphon-Musikwerken **bei** uns zu decken, damit sie später freie Hand haben zum Ankauf **unserer** Neuheiten.

Da der **Verein Deutscher Musikwaaren-Grossisten** nur aus Firmen besteht, denen ebenso wie den Herren Händlern an der gesunden Entwickelung des Musikwaaren-Geschäftes auf streng rechtlicher Basis gelegen ist, so geben wir uns der Hoffnung hin, auch ferner das Vertrauen unserer werthen Abuehmer wie bisher zu geniefsen.

Unsere Preisliste kommt in den nächsten Tagen zum Versandt und bitten wir, uns auch ferner mit ihren werthen Aufträgen zu beehren.

Ernst Holzweifsig Nachf., Leipzig.	J. M. Bon, Leipzig.	Adalbert Hawsky, Leipzig.
E. Dienst, Leipzig-Gohlis.	H. L. Ernst, „	Ludwig&Fries,Frankfurt/M.
Wilhelm Dietrich, Leipzig.	Kraft Behrens, „	P. H. Hahn & Co., Dresden.
Berger & Würker, „	C. H. Weigel, „	Plato & Co., Berlin.
Ludwig Hupfeld, Leipzig-Eutritzsch.	Zuleger & Mayenburg, „	K. Hellbrunn Söhne, „
Jul. Heinr. Zimmermann, Leipzig.	Wilhelm Benzing, „	Deurer & Kaufmann, Hamburg.

FIGURE 5.

Advertisement of the Association of the German wholesale dealers in musical products, dated 1 April 1896, concerning the sole sale of Kalliope products.) The date of the advertisement, 1 April 1896, is important for two reasons: 1) the Association's first official year started on 28 February 1896; the sole sale of the (practically brand-new) Kalliope products was one of the main objects, and 2) It gives clear evidence that Kalliope was one of the best makes, right from the start.

Short History: Facts and Figures.

The Kalliope Firm came into operation in 1895, or perhaps a little earlier. As far as I know, the first catagloue was printed in 1895 (See some illustrations of models in the *Encyclopedia* by David Bowers, page 109). The trademark was registered on 11 November 1895 for the Firm *(See Figure 1)*. The Muse Kalliope is not depicted with her usual attributes of tablet and stylus, but with a wind-instrument, while three cherubs surround her, one with a Pandean pipe and the other two dancing. This trademark was used very rarely, even in advertisements, but you may see it as a decoration of the under side of the lid of model No. 42 on page 108 of Bowers' *Encyclopedia*. The period of validity was 10 years; after that the copyright expired. *(See Figure 6.)* The Government Newspaper

* * *

Nr. 11006 (K. 1364) R.-A. v. 26. 11. 95.
(Inhaber „Kalliope" Fabrik mechanischer Musikwerke Espenhain, Wacker & Bock, Leipzig-Gohlis.) Gelöscht am 20. 11. 1905.

FIGURE 6.

(Reichsanzeiger, abbreviated *R.-A.*), dated 26 November 1895, had published the original trademark, but it was struck off the list on 20 November 1905. The Kalliope makers had designed a new one, shown in Figure 7. Translation: Announcement, 14 August 1905. Kalliope Music-Works Ltd., Leipzig, Bitterfelderstrasse 1 (the address of the factory).

* * *

Nr. 84018. K. 10559.

KALLIOPE

14. 8. 1905. Kalliope-Musikwerke, Akt.-Ges., Leipzig, Bitterfelder Straße 1. 23. 12. 1905. G.: Herstellung und Vertrieb von Musikwerken, Spieldosen, Musikautomaten, Drehdosen, band- und scheibenförmigen Notenblättern, Harmoniums, Sprechmaschinen, Schalldosen, Schallplatten für Sprechmaschinen. W.: Musikwerke, Spieldosen, Musikautomaten, Drehdosen, band- und scheibenförmige Notenblätter, Harmoniums, Sprechmaschinen, Schalldosen, Schallplatten für Sprechmaschinen. — Beschr.

FIGURE 7.

Registration 23 December 1905. Description of the business: Production and sale of musical products, musical boxes, coin-operated musical automata, manivelle boxes, music sheets in the form of perforated rolls and discs, harmoniums, speaking-machines, phonographs, sound discs (or records, if you prefer) for speaking-machines. List of products: idem.

The letter-type of the new trademark is different from the type used for the discs (disc types D, E, F. See my previous article in the **MBS** Winter *Bulletin* 1976, pages 64-66). This description of the products brings us to some remarks concerning the financial results, and the following very instructive table:

Year	Net Profits	Dividend
1898	77,034 Marks	8% (48,000 Marks)
1899	86,178 Marks	8%
1900	80,099 Marks	8%
1901	57,691 Marks	8%
1902	61,591 Marks	8%
1903	64,961 Marks	8%

In 1904 and 1905 only a six percent dividend was paid, but in the years 1902 and 1903 a debenture-loan was placed, to a total amount of 500,000 Marks. That was an enormous sum in those days. In 1901 the total sales were 100 percent higher than the year before. On the occasion of the first lustrum 3,000 Marks was granted to the joint employees, and it was paid in 1904.

Now, back to the products. Reports of the Leipzig Fair, catalogues, and advertisements tell something about the new models and products. The most important items are mentioned here, year by year:

1896:   Models No. 61 (61 teeth), No. 82 (82-teeth), with respective 34- and 45-centimeter discs; a 120-tooth model; a coin-operated wall-mounted automaton, No. 109; and a giant model No. 150. (Easter Fair; Hupfeld advertisement.)

1897:   A coin-operated wall-machine with 156 teeth, 64½-cm discs, and a playing time of one and three-fourths minutes.

1898:   There was no show of models at the Easter Fair because the Association of the German wholesale dealers in musical products had guaranteed the sale of a quantity of products. At that time there were 10 models available. A poster (80 cm high and 51 cm wide) was made, with a lithograph showing three little girls listening to a Kalliope musical box in a shop. At the end of the year, a 27-page illustrated price list (in quarto form) was issued, with the models depicted in red-brown woodcuts and the text printed in black. The cover is of light green moiré paper, with the word 'Kalliope' printed in gold. (Note: Has anyone seen the poster lithograph or the 1898 price list?)

1899:   Many new models at the Easter Fair, 38-tooth manivelle, No. 10; 38-tooth table model, No. 38; idem 49-tooth, No. 49; wall-machines with 120, 164, 216, and 268 teeth and the same

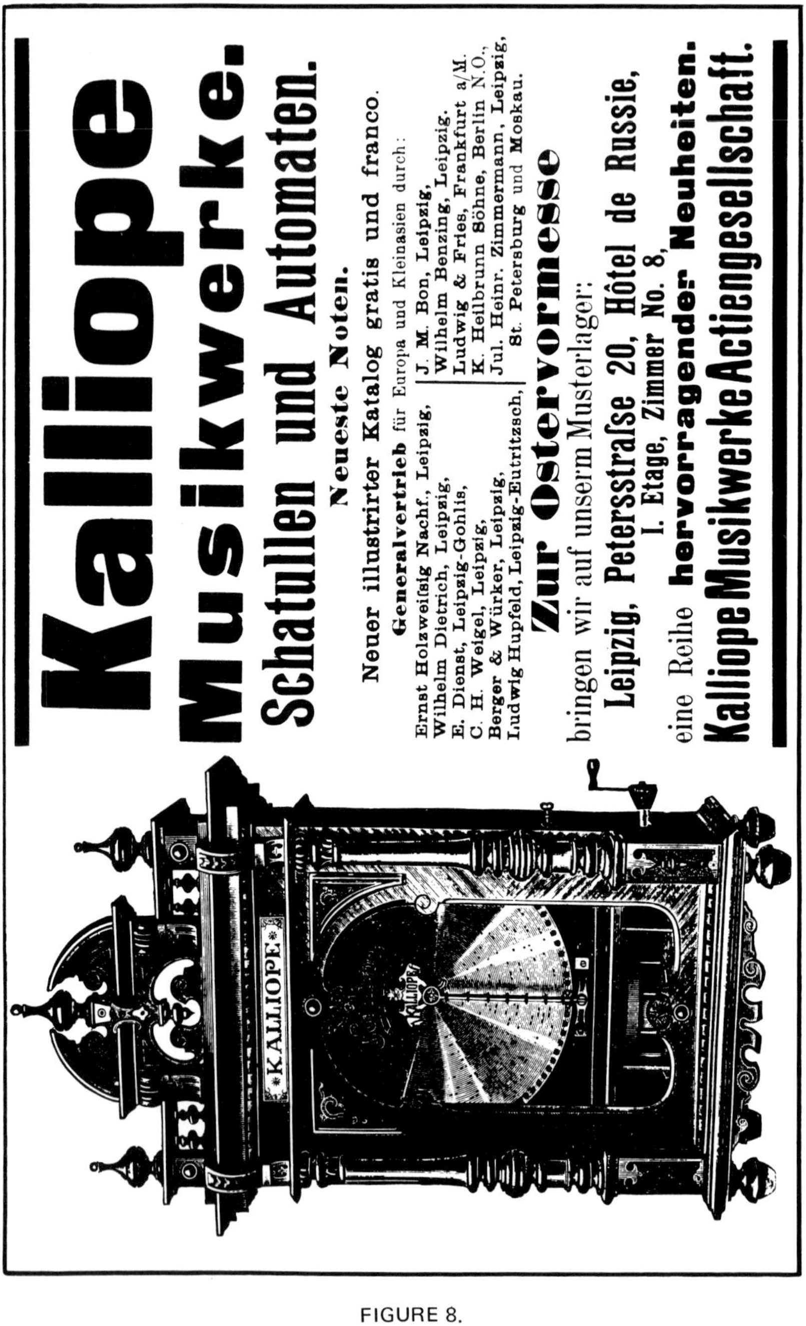
Kalliope
Musikwerke.
Schatullen und Automaten.
Neueste Noten.
Neuer illustrirter Katalog gratis und franco.
Generalvertrieb für Europa und Kleinasien durch:
Ernst Holzweifsig Nachf., Leipzig,
Wilhelm Dietrich, Leipzig,
E. Dienst, Leipzig-Gohlis,
C. H. Weigel, Leipzig,
Berger & Würker, Leipzig,
Ludwig Hupfeld, Leipzig-Eutritzsch,
J. M. Bon, Leipzig,
Wilhelm Benzing, Leipzig,
Ludwig & Fries, Frankfurt a/M.
K. Heilbrunn Söhne, Berlin N.O.,
Jul. Heinr. Zimmermann, Leipzig,
St. Petersburg und Moskau.
Zur Ostervormesse
bringen wir auf unserm Musterlager:
Leipzig, Petersstrafse 20, Hôtel de Russie,
I. Etage, Zimmer No. 8,
eine Reihe hervorragender Neuheiten.
Kalliope Musikwerke Actiengesellschaft.
KALLIOPE

FIGURE 8.

model numbers; and a No. 104 with a very beautiful case. A fine example of such a case may be seen in the advertisement dated 11 February 1899 *(shown in Figure 8)*. (Note: The 1898 catalogue is mentioned, and the address of the showroom at the Easter Fair -- Petersstrasse 20, Hotel de Rûssie, first floor, room number 8.)

1900: Wall-machine No. 200, with 12 bells and 158 teeth (64½-cm discs); idem No. 300, with 12 bells and 75-cm discs and a matching base cabinet; a 'Gnome' Automat, No. 1 'Burghaus' that vends chocolates or cigarettes; at the Autumn Fair: a wall-machine with eight saucer bells and four tremolo bells that replace the drum; and finally, a 'Billard-Musik-Automat' named 'Veritas.' (Note: In an advertisement dated 1 June 1900, this remarkable instrument, produced by Ed. Pfeffercorn & Co. in Mersburg, was described. In return for depositing a coin, you get the billiard balls and the music starts -- in this case by means of a Kalliope disc. After a certain interval, the balls disappear, the available time being checked by a built-in clock.)

1901: A tall wall-machine, No. 201, with 158 teeth and 10 (Note: This is a misprint, there are 12) sound-bars. On 1 September 1901 Paul de Wit, in his *Zeitschrift für Instrumentenbau* (Page 889), mentions for the first time the center spindle as a winding post; earlier models with this system of winding do not exist (Note: I do not know whether this is right or wrong); and the costs of production can be reduced 30 percent with this system.

1902: The famous Panorama Automat with the racing horses, which run as the music plays (shown in Bowers's *Encyclopedia,* page 110); small table models with six and ten bells; and a very small 26-tooth model.

1904: Paul de Wit reports *(Zeitschrift für Instrumentenbau,* 11 March 1904, page 477) the start of the production by the Kalliope Music-Works of speaking-machines named 'Odeon'; the great advantage, he writes, is that the discs can be used on both sides. (Note: Mr. de Wit compares the double-sided record with the normal disc of the music box.) This report is very interesting, because the machines were shown at the Easter Fair. The trademark 'Odeon' was announced on 17 October 1903 and registered 4 February 1904 in behalf of the International Talking Machine Company, Ltd., Berlin Weissensee, Lehderstrasse 22-24. The Kalliope manufacturers (and other producers, such as the Zonophone Company) could use this trademark, hardly a month after the registration, because German law did not offer protection at once, but only after a certain period. The same rule was in force for a Gebrauchsmuster (Trade-sample), so it is understandable that an advertisement in the *Phonographische Zeitschrift* (Vol. 6, No. 18, page 402) warns the customers against abuse of the trade-sample standing in the name of A. N. Petit (German Gebrauchsmuster No. 148105, United States Patent No. 749,092).

Anyway, the whole question is very intriguing. Still another type of product was made for the first time by the Kalliope Music-Works in 1904: harmoniums, fitted with the American system of stops.

Several noteworthy points are mentioned now. There are many Kalliope catalogues, published in 1895, 1898, 1900, 1903, and 1911 -- and probably other catalogues exist. In the 1911 catalogue, it is stated that the disc-numbers are constant for any one tune (Note: Sometimes the model number is placed before the tune number), although many of the tunes were not available in all sizes. After that year, many new tunes were issued (Note: I suppose about 100). Particularly worth noting is the fact that this catalogue ends with a picture of the factory, and above, at the right, in very small letters, is: *Eigene Arbeiterhäuser Kolonie* (a number of houses for the employees of the factory). In those days such progressiveness was an exception. During World War I (1914-1918) business ran down, so in 1919 the Kalliope Music-Works was merged into Menzenhauer & Schmidt. The director of this firm was Henry Langfelder, Rungestrasse 17, Berlin. (See Bowers's *Encyclopedia*, pages 108, 136, and 359.)

Patents.

In the section 'The Makers and the Trademark,' some patents are mentioned; there are more than 10 German patents concerning Kalliope manufacture. They bear the names of C. H. R. Bock, alone or with E. M. A. Wacker, or the name of the Firm, and afterwards the Company, but never that of G. M. Espenhain. Why? The solution is given in a later section on Gustav Max Espenhain.

The possibility of the infringement by Ferdinand Schaub of Kalliope's patent concerning the center-wound spring-barrel is very unlikely (See MBS *Silver Anniversary Collection,* pages 282-283; Bowers's *Encyclopedia,* page 136; Roy Mosoriak, *The Curious History of Music Boxes,* pages 58 and 127). The patent of Schaub, No. 538,468, is dated 30 April 1895, and Paul de Wit on 1 September 1901 reported for the first time the same system used by the Kalliope makers. Besides, the registration of a trade-sample, No. 154813, concerning this matter is dated 13 May 1901. How to reconcile these two data? *(See Figure 9.)* Translation in short: Spring-barrel for

* * *

No. 154813. Federtriebwerk für mechanische Musikwerke u. dgl. bei welchem die bewegende Kraft durch eine mit dem Federgehäuse verbundene Hülse vermittels eines auf letzterer befestigten Treiborganes direkt übertragen wird. Kalliope-Musikwerke, Aktiengesellschaft, Leipzig. 13. 5. 1901. K. 14234.

FIGURE 9.

mechanical musical instruments, in which the upper spring-barrel arbor is the drive shaft for the disc to be played. Kalliope Music-Works, Ltd., Leipzig. 13 May 1901. K. 14234. (Note: Who can prove that center-wound Kalliope models existed before the year 1901?)

As mentioned above, at least two United States patents exist: No. 543,286, 23 July 1895 (a damping device) and No. 555,757, issued to Bock alone on 3 March 1896 (a cylinder for a music box, consisting of a plurality of metal discs, a very complicated and never-used invention).

The Addresses.

I have found the following addresses, with the dates on which they are mentioned:

Gustav Max Espenhain, Dorotheenstrasse 20 (26-9-1895). *(Figure 4.)*

Emil Moritz Anton Wacker, Wilhelmstrasse 9, Leipzig-Gohlis (24-12-1904). *(Figure 3.)*

Christian Heinrich Richard Bock, Geibelstrasse 20, Leipzig-Eutritzsch (24-12-1904). *(Figure 3.)*

Probably these addresses are the private homes of the three Kalliope makers at these dates.

Another address is not clear: E. Wacker & Bock, Louisenstrasse, Leipzig-Gohlis (12-1-1895). *(Figure 2.)* I do not know the meaning of this address. Is it an address of the factory? The address of the Firm at the time of the registration of the trademark (11-11-1895) -- ten months later -- is Dorotheenstrasse 20, the same as that given for Espenhain. It is of course possible that Wacker & Bock both lived in the Louisenstrasse in 1895 and afterwards in different homes. The original building of the (then small) factory was in the Dorotheenstrasse at No. 20, and Gustav Max Espenhain moved to Dorotheenstrasse 27 (his address in 1901).

A new building for the factory was inaugurated on 17 March 1899 on the occasion of the shareholders' meeting in the Apelstrasse. The following year (1900), the address of the factory was Bitterfelderstrasse 1, and after that the address was always the same. So we can conclude that the factory's address was: Dorotheenstrasse 20 from 1895 to February 1899; and Bitterfelderstrasse 1 (at the corner of the Apelstrasse?), from March 1899 until the end *(Figure 10.)*

Kalliope Musikwerke, Bitterfelderstrasse 1, Leipzig. (Advertisement, dated 11 March 1900).

Gustav Max Espenhain and the Real Kalliope Makers.

Although Espenhain was involved in the original Kalliope Firm, Bock and Wacker were the real makers. A short partial biography gives evidence of this fact. The Firm's address (on 5 September 1895) was Dorotheenstrasse 20, where Espenhain lived on 26 September 1895. *(See Figures 1 and 4.)* On 15 November 1897 he was chosen as one (out of seven) of the fellow-members of the committee of the Association of the German manufacturers of musical instruments, but he is not mentioned as a director of the Kalliope factory. In the contract in behalf of the establishment of the Kalliope Musikwerke A.G. (Date: 18 May 1898) Espenhain is mentioned as a merchant and an owner of the factory, but Bock and Wacker are called owners *and* directors of the factory. Espenhain was only a fellow-member of the committee. On 22 November 1898 in the trade-register of the Imperial district court at Leipzig, it is recorded that Mr. Gustav Max Espenhain has resigned from this committee. (Note: A mention without comment; we can only guess why.) On 27 June 1899 Espenhain

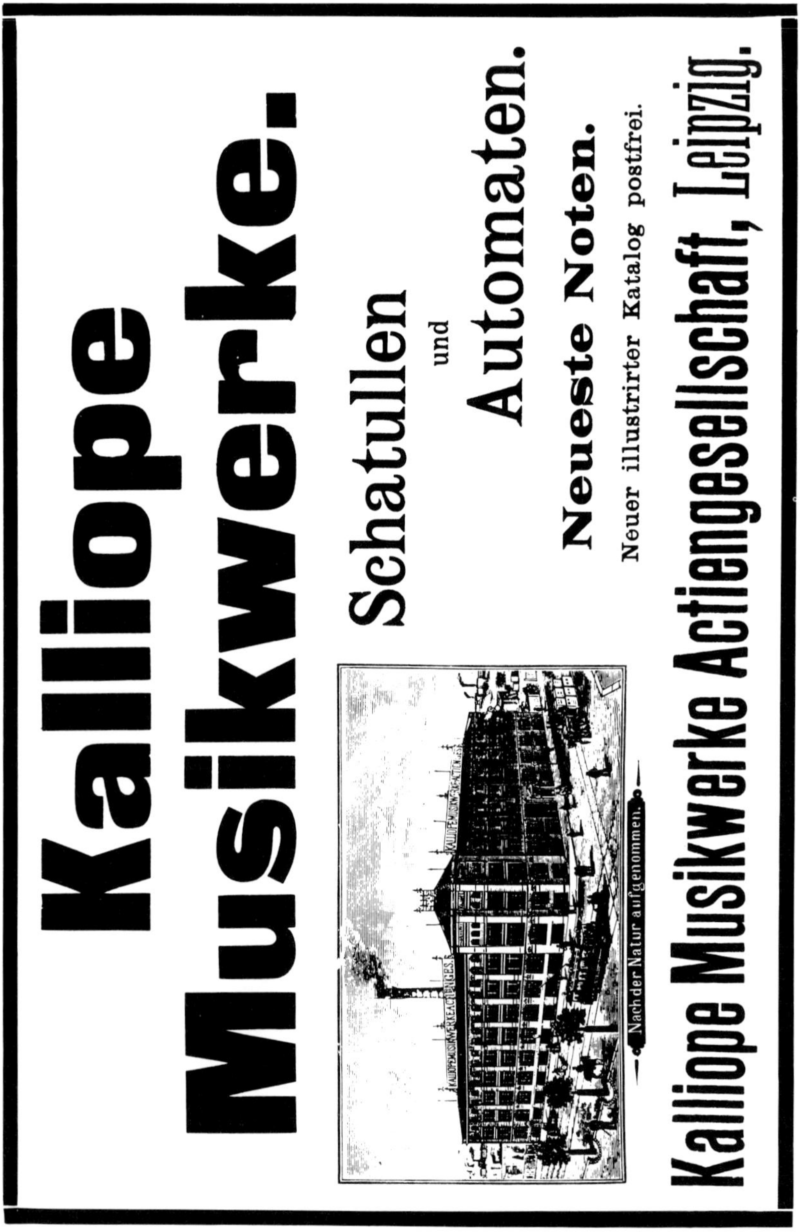

FIGURE 10.

voluntarily resigned from the committee of the Association of the German manufacturers of musical instruments. (Note: A logical step after his withdrawal from the Kalliope committee.) But now follows an unexpected development: Registration on folio 11134 of the trade-register at Leipzig; the Firma Apollo Musikwerke, Max Espenhain & Co. is registered. Address: Leipzig-Gohlis, Dorotheenstrasse 27. (Note: Not far from his original home). Founders are Gustav Max Espenhain -- merchant, Carl Heinrich Kretschmar and Paul Louis Gustav Lösche -- manufacturers of musical instruments. (Note: It's the same old story again.) Production of orchestrions, and so on. (See Bowers's *Encyclopedia,* page 706.) The Firm was founded 15 November 1900, and showed Piano-Orchestrions and Flute-Automata for the first time at the Easter Fair at Leipzig in 1901. The name 'Apollo' was announced on 27 December 1900 and registered on 31 May 1902. There is an unusually. long period between these two dates. *(See Figure 11.)* Espenhain seems to have been a difficult person to work with,

* * *

No. 54255. E. 2544.

27. 12. 1900. Gustav Max Espenhain, Leipzig-Gohlis. 31. 5. 1902. G : Fabrikation und Vertrieb von mechanischen Musikwerken und Theilen derselben. W.: Drehorgeln, Spieldosen, Orchestrions. — Beschreibung.

FIGURE 11.

because in the trade-register notice was given on 11 October 1902 that Mr. Lösche had resigned as a partner and that Mr. Kretschmar was shut out as a representative of the Firm. In 1903 Paul de Wit, the honest and impartial publisher of the *Zeitschrift für Instrumentenbau,* quarreled with the hot-headed Espenhain and declared that he was not an expert, but only a merchant, and with this statement my short biography of Espenhain ends. The conclusion can only be that he was neither a musical nor a technical man in the field of musical instruments -- his merits were in the main financial. As I have demonstrated in the section 'Patents,' the real makers were Christian Heinrich Richard Bock and Emil Moritz Anton Wacker. They built up the technical and musical qualities of the Kalliope products, and they produced one of the best makes in the field. In my opinion Kalliope boxes are equal to or perhaps better than most other German makes. The numerous patents point to this, and every collector knows that Kalliope boxes seldom fail, because of the genius of two now almost forgotten men, Bock and Wacker.

FIGURE 12. THE AUTHOR WITH A 45-CM DISC (NO. 56) FOR HIS KALLIOPE.

Epilogue.

My brother Theo is a professional photographer who works in the darkroom of the municipal museum of the Hague (Note: 's-Gravenhage, as we say in Dutch; it means 'The garden of the counts') a few steps away from our parental home. This museum has a famous musical library and a corner with mechanical musical instruments. When I visited him in the late fifties and early sixties and he needed some help for an artistic photograph in the quiet hours of the evening, I was always fascinated by a big Kalliope, a musical murmuring monster with crispy, croaking circles of solid steel. I never guessed that such things were for sale. As a boy I had collected some old Roman and Greek coins, and along the way I had made some friends among antique dealers. On a happy day in 1962 while I was visiting one of them, a merchant came in, and the conversation turned to musical boxes. The merchant was acquainted with a shopkeeper who offered a disc box for sale. After some cross-talk, we both walked through the city, and two miles away we went in the shop -- he for the tip, and I for the box. There on the floor was a rectangular wooden box with a bone shield on the lid and a pile of 52 rust-eaten discs, but -- how could it be -- the only thing I could read was 'Kalliope.' After a night of doubt, I came back with money (Oh, dear Mother!), and the box was mine. (Note: Style No. 40, with 36 teeth and 18-cm discs. Motor number 7278; serial number 87282.) That is the beginning of this story with a happy end. When my daughter Carolina was born in 1965 and my wife came home from the hospital, she was welcomed by my mother, who had just put a cent in a big Kalliope that was a twin of the museum monster. (Note: A coin-operated wall automaton, style No. 109, with 106 teeth and 45-cm discs. Serial number 161026. The words on

FIGURE 13. MR. STRENGERS PUTS ANOTHER PENNY IN HIS KALLIOPE.

the glass door are: *Ph. Hakkert Jr., Kon. Fabriek en Magazign van Musiekinstrumenten, Weste Wagenstraat 96, Rotterdam. Telefoon Interc. 407*, which translates: Ph. Hakkert, Jr., Royal factory and storehouse of musical instruments. Interlocal telephone number 407. The business is still in existence as a company with limited liability. Its former address was bombed in World War II, and the address is now Westblaak 13, Rotterdam.)

MUSICAL BOX LID PICTURES

Coulson Conn

𝒯HE COLLECTOR of musical boxes will find the beauty of disc machines is often enhanced by the variety of lid pictures used to decorate the cases. Manufacturers used many different scenes, personages, allegories, and designs. Many of the larger firms such as Polyphon and Kalliope used a wide array of pictures in an effort to appeal to a variety of tastes. Other firms, especially the small ones, used a characteristic picture which usually included the maker's name as a means of advertisement.

The Regina Co., although one of the three largest firms, usually used its trademark of the Queen Regina with surrounding cherubs. However, they

Figure 1. A most interesting photo. What appears to be a chapeau is in fact a disc, presumably a Kalliope since this is the maker of the box.

Figure 2. The characteristic lid picture of many small Symphonions, with a blue-green background and flesh-colored cherubs.

also used a listing of all tunes available, an inlaid "Regina" in the lid, and other pictures. Symphonion, another large manufacturer, also used several photos. The one depicted in this article is the one that most commonly identifies their pieces.

In this article I will share with you some of the characteristic motifs found in lid pictures. In some cases, such as the Perfection, the motif is also

Figure 3. The Troubador 11¾" box with sepia wash and black and brown printing.

Figure 4. This Komet 13" multi-colored picture is the most beautiful in my collection. The same emblem appears on the discs.

Figure 5. The 8¼" Celesta, an uncommon piece, is multicolored with a blue background.

Figure 6. A very rare Euterpephon with brown and gold hues over a light blue background.

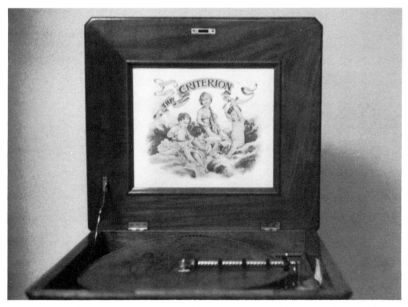

Figure 7. The characteristically pleasing Criterion 15" motif. A box made by F.G. Otto and Sons, Jersey City, New Jersey.

Figure 8. Another American-made machine, the 15" Triumph (identical to the Monarch) made by the American Musical Box Co. in New Jersey. This is apparently the only design they used.

Figure 9. The 10½" Perfection, an uncommon box made in Newark, New Jersey. This identical scene also appears on all Perfection discs.

Figure 10. A 18⅝" Polyphon with artwork made by Brian Clegg, Norfolk, England.

Figure 11. The 24½" Phoenix Twin, made by Brian Clegg. The scene is Mr. Clegg's creation.

found on the discs.

As an addendum, I call your attention to motifs taken from upright boxes. As these boxes do not have lids, the manufacturers often embellished their glass fronts with beautiful artwork.

I hope this brief jaunt through some of my lid pictures may stimulate you to be aware of this aspect of collecting. Although pictures are often a small and seemingly unimportant part of the box, they deepen our respect for the original craftsmanship and add a unique aesthetic beauty to these already beautiful machines. ♪

141

SYMPHONION EROICA IN SWEDEN

Bill Lindwall

ℐT was with great interest that I read Mr. Reblitz's article about music arrangements on Symphonion Eroica discs in the Autumn 1979 issue of the *Bulletin* (Vol. XXV, No. 2, p. 143). I have an Eroica in my collection and have, of course, observed that there are certain differences among the three-disc sets, but it never occurred to me to record the exact nature of the ways in which they differ. It was therefore with a lively curiosity that I spread out my 16 sets of discs on the floor and started to examine them. This is what I found, but first we must agree on the names of the four different types of sets that Mr. Reblitz mentioned in his article. What he called the first type, second type, and so forth, I decided to designate with Roman numerals, as Type I, Type II, and so on. In the following list you will consequently find I, II, III, or IV directly after the serial numbers that are stamped on the discs— except for Type II, of which there are none in my collection. Here we go!

Type I   All three discs are identical.

Type II   All three discs have identical musical arrangements, with discs A and B punched identically and disc C punched slightly in advance.

Type III   Discs A and B punched identically, with disc C having a different musical arrangement.

Type IV   All three discs are punched differently.

Set No.	Serial No.	Type	Title and Composer
1	6035	I	"Die Klosterglocken"
2	6105	I	"Letzte Rose" (Last Rose of Summer) from *Martha*, Flotow
3	8006	IV	"Finnländischer Reitermarsch"
4	8016	IV	"Spinn! Spinn!" Estländischer Volkslied
5	8032	IV	"Donau-Walzer," J. Strauss, Jr.
6	8033	IV	"Waldandacht," F. Abt
7	8040	IV	"Still ruht der See," H. Pfeil
8	8043	IV	"Wiener Blut," J. Strauss, Jr.

The Eroica's handsome case.

9	8053	IV	"Sei nicht bös," C. Zeller
10	8068	IV	"Meditation über das erste Präludium," J. S. Bach
11	8071	I	"Waltzer aus der Operette: Die Glocken von Corneville," O. Planquette
12	8079	IV	"Im kühlen Keller sitz ich hier," L. Fischer
13	8092	IV	"Unter dem Doppeladler," J. F. Wagner
14	8102	III	"La Paloma"
15	8132	IV	"Home, Sweet Home," H. R. Bishop
16	8156	III	"Glory to Thee, My God!" T. Tallis

May I also take this opportunity to relate the rather amazing story of my Eroica?

The instrument is coin-operated for five Swedish öre (about one cent) and was brought to Sweden around 1900 by a man who had a musical-

Eroica's machinery seen from the back.

144

All six combs in impressive array.

instrument shop in the Old Town of Stockholm. He could not sell it (perhaps because of the price), so it just stood there until he had to close the shop, for lack of business, about 1920. All of the instruments that did not find buyers (most of which I am told were mechanical ones) were stored in a garret room. Around 1940 the garret was cleared, and the workmen found the forgotten instruments. Most of the instruments were discarded, but the workers located a man who purchased some of them, including this Eroica. That man also had it stored, in a basement this time, until he passed away

Mr. Lindwall and disc set No. 8016 (Spinn! Spinn!).

some time ago. Since I happened to know him and his wife, I was privileged to take over the instrument.

The Eroica was seldom played, looks like new, and is in 100 per cent fine condition. In the back of the case there is a penciled notation "B 30/7 97" that I suppose means the instrument left the factory in the year 1897. The number 309723 is stamped on the upper left comb.

In the Bowers *Encyclopedia,* the diameter of the discs is given as 355 mm. — mine are 346 mm. in diameter. There are six combs, each with 50 teeth, giving a total of 300 notes; each comb is in two parts, one with 16 and the other with 34 teeth. The melody is played twice for each coin and the instrument has a magnificent sound.

As everyone knows, the Eroica was made by the Symphonion Musikwerke in Gohlis, a suburb of Leipzig, Germany. This company was the leading firm in the world during the time when mechanical musical instruments were made on a large scale, from the late 1880's to about 1900. In 1903 the company reported producing between 5,000 and 6,000 mechanical instruments of various kinds, a considerable production for that time. The firm barely survived the first years of the 1920's.

In conclusion, I wish Mr. Reblitz good luck in his further investigation of this matter of the three-disc sets for the Eroica.

THE NEW CENTURY
SOME QUESTIONS ANSWERED

Al Choffnes

A few years ago I was fortunate enough to meet a gentleman who had in his possession much of the business correspondence of a musical instrument dealer from Van Wert, Ohio. Dr. H. S. Ainsworth was a dentist in Van Wert and had a side-business of selling musical instruments (the ones you play yourself), and automatic musical instruments (the kind we collect). Much of the correspondence covered the years from 1880 through 1910, a period of great activity by the cylinder and disc music-box manufacturers.

One make of music box which fascinates me is the New Century because so little is known of its manufacturer. My introduction to the New Century music box was at a fellow collector's house who owned a four-comb table model in a cherry wood case. When the music box was played, the room was literally filled with a nicely-arranged melodious tune. The four-comb New Century was also one of the loudest playing music boxes I had heard at that point in my early days of collecting (and probably still is!).

After being properly impressed with the New Century's performance, I asked the owner if he knew any details about who manufactured the music box, where it was made, and when. From the name, we concluded that it was made some time after the turn of the century, rather well into the disc music box era. The case appeared to be of American design and manufacture, but there were no markings, patent plates, or identification of any kind on the case or movement. The only place a trade name appeared was on the discs. The owner and I speculated that its existence may have come about as the result of a U.S. importer's effort to avoid the duties which were levied on completed music boxes by importing the parts and assembling them into an American-made case. This seemed plausible, as the Mermod Freres disc music boxes were imported by Jacot in New York and assembled into cases here in the United States. If this were true, and the movements were imported, who was the European manufacturer? If the movements were not imported in the U.S., who was the domestic manufacturer? The following correspondence and trade literature appears to prove that the Symphonion Manufacturing Company of Asbury Park, New Jersey, was the distributor and possibly the manufacturer of the New Century line of disc music boxes. The initial distribution of the New Century began in early 1902.

No. 300 U.
SYMPHONION MECHANOPHONE.
Open View of the Instrument.

Cabinet Grand.   Long Running Movement.
Case Piano Finish, Mahogany or Oak.   120 Steel Tongues, 2 Combs.
Tuned in Chromatic Scale, 5½ Octaves.
Very Loud Orchestrion Tone.   Disc Drawer on Base.

No. 300 U.   Height, 77½ in., Width, 30 in., Depth, 24¼ in.
No. 300 U.   With 5 Cents Money Drop Attachment.
No. 300 U.   Polished Steel Music Discs, 20 in. Diameter.

Catalogue of Music for IMPERIAL SYMPHONIONS sent on application.

Two views of the overstocked model 300 U,
which allegedly was used for the New Century 18½ inch movement.

No. 300 U.

SYMPHONION MECHANOPHONE.

Closed View of the Instrument.

Description on page 18.

Catalogue of Music for IMPERIAL SYMPHONIONS sent on application.

The size range of New Century music boxes included 11½ inch, 15½ inch, and 18½ inch models. The 11½ inch model and 15½ inch models were available in either single or duplex-comb format, and were probably offered in table model case style only. The 18½ inch model was available as a single, duplex, four comb, four-comb tremolo zither, or duplex comb disc-shifting in table model or upright glass front, coin-operated styles.

It is interesting to note the passage in the letter to Dr. Ainsworth where Mr. Varrelman, President of Symphonion, mentions that the company had given up production of the 300 U automatic disc-changing Imperial Symphonion. Apparently Symphonion had produced a number of large cases to house the automatic disc-changing Imperial Symphonion and then had the problem of what to do with the cases. That problem was solved with the introduction of the New Century. The use of the leftover, large Symphonion automatic changer case explains why the small 18½ inch New Century movement was housed in the oversize upright case in which the surviving examples appear. The line drawing from a 1901 Imperial Symphonion catalog illustrates the discontinued automatic disc changer,

Symphonion Manufacturing Co.
Asbury Park, New Jersey
April 28, 1902

Mr. H. S. Ainsworth, D.D.S.102 East Main StreetVan Wert, Ohio

Dear Sir:

Your favor of April 25th to hand. We herewith enclose illustrated price sheet of our music boxes, and would say that we have given up making the 300 upright which was an automatically changing instrument, but which did not prove satisfactory. The chimes music box is one of our very best sellers, and is the only disc instrument made with chimes. It is therefore a great attraction as it can be heard at a long distance. We also enclose you our trade price list. We will send you the spring desired but will not make any charge for same as it is not worthwhile. The new boxes which we are making are called New Century and one style of this instrument is made so that an 18½ inch disc in making two revolutions, plays one long tune of three minutes duration whereas the largest sheets now made, 27½ inch in diameter, only play two minutes. This is the greatest improvement which has been made in music boxes since their advent in this country. We have not as yet issued a new catalogue for same. We enclose the net cash price list which will show you that the #478 is $100. And the tunes $1. each. Awaiting your favor, we remain,

Yours very truly,

Symphonion Mfg. Co.

The letter from the Symphonion Co. to Dr. Ainsworth is retyped here for easier readability. It implies that the cases left over from the production of the model 300 U were used for the New Century.[Ed.]

GEO VARRELMAN. PRES.   LIEBERS & A B C CODE 4TH ED. USED.   Telephone 150 Asbury Park

ASBURY PARK,
NEW JERSEY.

April 28, _____ 190 2.

Mr H. S. Ainsworth, D. D. S.,

102 East Main Street,

Van Wert, Ohio.

Dear Sir:-

Your favor of April 25th to hand. We herewith enclose
illustrated price sheet of our music boxes, and would say that we have
given up making the #300U upright which was an automatically changing
instrument, but which did not prove satisfactory. The chimes
music box is one of our very best sellers, and is the only disc instrument made with chimes. It is therefore a great attraction as it
can be heard at a long distance. We also enclose you our trade price
list. We will send you the spring desired but will not make any
charge for same as it is not worth while. The new boxes which we
are making are called New Century and one style of this instrument is
made so that an 18" disc in making two revolutions, plays one long
tune of three minutes duration whereas the largest sheets now made,
27-1/2" in diameter, only play two minutes. This is the greatest
improvement which has been made in music boxes since their advent in
this country. We have not as yet issued a new catalogue for same.
We enclose the net cash price list which will show you that the #478
is $100. and the tunes $1. each. Awaiting your favor, we remain,

Yours very truly,

SYMPHONION MFG. CO.

Photocopy of the original letter from the Symphion Co. to Dr. Ainsworth.

150

with the photo of a surviving example of the disc-shifting upright New Century housed in the same case.

Another interesting point worth noting involves the discs. The dealer promotional brochure devotes an entire paragraph to describing the merits of zinc used in the production of their discs. The zinc discs, however, proved unsatisfactory in operation due to the softness of the metal and the sharpness of the New Century's star wheel points. After a moderate number of disc revolutions the scoop-shaped projections would be cut by the star wheel with the resultant loss of notes and jamming of the disc due to partially - turned star wheels. This problem was intensified in the four - comb and disc-shifting models which use projections which were half the size of the other models to allow for passage of the disc over the second set of combs and between the star wheels of the first.

Apparently Symphonion music box manufacturers realized they had a problem with the zinc discs as they also manufactured steel discs which this writer has seen for the 15½ inch model.

The following photos will illustrate the various models and case styles that this author has found. The 11½ inch model has proven to be elusive. If one of our members has seen one, or owns one, the forwarding of such details would be appreciated.

Special thanks is given to fellow members Walt Bellm and Wayne Wolf for their help in providing the subjects for the following photographs.

Model no. 478. Upright Disc Shifting 18½ inch New Century no. 3214. Wayne Wolf Collection.

Model no. 260. Duplex 15½ inch New Century. Serial no. 1827. Walt Bellm Collection.

Model no. 278. Duplex 18½ inch New Century. Serial no. 2545. Walt Bellm Collection.

Model no. 478. Duplex (Double Revolution) 18½ inch New Century Disc Shifter. Serial No. 3246. Walt Bellm Collection.

Model no. 478. Duplex (Double Revolution) 18½ inch New Century Disc Shifter. Serial no. 3246. Walt Bellm Collection.

Model no. 412. New Century Double Duplex 18½ inch 4 Combs Tremolo Zither. Walt Bellm Collection. Serial no. 3093.

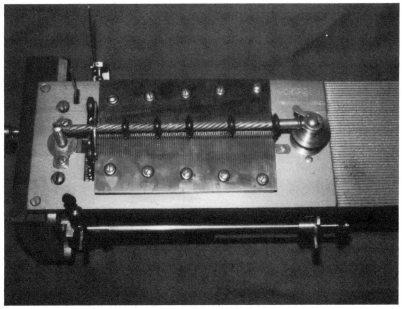

Model no. 478. Close-up of mechanism of 18½ Disc Shifting Duplex 18½ inch New Century Serial no. 2231. Wayne Wolf Collection.

Model no. 478. Close-up of motor assembly of New Century Disc Shifter Serial No. 2231 — 18½ inch. Wayne Wolf Collection.

Price list for the New Century — Circa 1902.

154

DESCRIPTION OF
The New Century Music Boxes.

NO. OF BOX	STYLE OF COMBS	DIAMETER OF DISC	LENGTH OF TUNE	NUMBER OF TUNE LIST
45	Single	11½ inch	50 seconds	1
245	Duplex	11½ "	50 "	1
60	Single	15 "	65 "	2
260	Duplex	15 "	65 "	2
78	Single	18½ "	1½ Minutes	4
278	Duplex	18½ "	1½ "	4
*478	Duplex (double revolution)	18½ "	3 "	6
†312	Double duplex 4 combs	18½ "	1½ "	7
‡412	Double duplex 4 combs Tremolo Zither	18½ "	1½ "	8

* In this box, the sheet makes two complete revolutions, playing one long tune of three minutes duration, or two tunes, each 1½ minutes in length, can be played one directly following the other, we having arranged many of the popular airs two on a sheet for this purpose.

† This style is especially loud in tone having four combs, each containing the same scale of 78 notes, so that the volume of sound from a single comb is quadrupled.

‡ Of the 312 teeth in these combs, 156 are actual notes, they being duplex, produce a clear and sweet tone never attained heretofore.

For further particulars we would refer you to the body of this circular and in addition, we would kindly call the attention of the trade to the playing duration of each size of our discs as compared with those of equal size used by our competitors, the playing length of one revolution or tune being greatly increased in all our numbers.

SYMPHONION MANUFACTURING CO.,

GEORGE VARRELMAN, PRESIDENT,

ASBURY PARK, N. J.

THE NEW CENTURY AND SYMPHONION MUSIC BOXES

What the Twentieth Century has
done for the Music Box Industry

ERE we to say that the perfect Music Box had been invented and was at hand, we can just picture the broad smile of derision that would cross your countenance at the thought and yet we DO say that we have come nearer to that than has yet been approached. This is a broad statement, and feeling sure that the subject is one of enough importance to you, we ask your kind indulgence *In which we introduce to you THE NEW CENTURY* with us for just a few minutes that we may endeavor to prove to you that what we say is true, and beg to call your attention to the description of our NEW CENTURY Music Boxes given on separate sheet.

You have probably noted from time to time the mention made in the trade papers or have heard through our traveling representatives that we have for the past year been working on something entirely new and novel in the Music Box line with the object in view of not only correcting the oft proven faults in disc instruments but to acquire the hitherto unrivaled sweet tone of the old Swiss cylinder boxes and use same in an instrument which will accomplish the results of the largest disc styles now on the market, but in a more condensed form. Much time and money have been spent in attaining these results *The reasons which lead up to THE NEW CENTURY* and we rejoice with you that we have succeeded far beyond our most sanguine hopes and expectations. As you well know, there have been but few decided improvements made in disc playing music boxes since their advent in this country and the prices as well as the value, therefore, have always been at about the same ratio. Feeling sure that the growing dissatisfaction so apparent among the majority of dealers handling such goods has been to some extent justified, and an indication that we as manufacturers catering to their wants must correct this feeling, we now present to your notice what we deem to be the most complete and novel line of instruments ever offered for sale. A more explicit explanation of them is surely apropos and to further substantiate the fact as set forth above, we invite your especial attention to a few of our more important styles.

Probably the most striking example of our new enterprise is style No. 478. The advantages of this instrument can readily be seen when you study closely the description given elsewhere and note that by arranging our 18½" sheet so that it will make two revolutions, to complete only one tune, it is possible to play much longer selections than are produced from the largest sheets now on the market. When you consider that our 18½" double revolution sheet plays 208 bars or measures of music, making the playing time of the disc nearly three minutes, while other instruments employing the same number of teeth in the comb, play less than one minute, and that the 27½" sheet of to-day plays only 132 bars or measures of music, you will comprehend more clearly that the longest of overtures and operatic selections can be played even more correctly on this style of "NEW CENTURY" than has been attempted here tofore. It is essential to note, too, that even in a single revolu. tion of this 18½" sheet, 104 bars or measures of music are played, while in the boxes of other makes containing the same number of teeth in the comb only 64 can be used. One revolution, therefore, of our disc is sufficient to play any of the popular melodies more completely than a disc having but 64 bars of music arranged on it; and that two tunes, each having 104 bars of music, can be arranged on our disc and can be played one following the other without removing same. A point in favor of the smaller sheet in the proportion of our 18½" as to the 27½" of heretofore is that it is much more easily handled than the larger, cumbersome style and, at the same time, the price per disc is less than half.

An instrument which will revolutionize the Music Box trade

Another style which will prove a big seller is our No. 312, which, while it has no more notes than our ordinary duplex comb box No. 278, using an 18½" disc, yet doubles the volume of same, for we have placed in this instrument a pair of double combs, exact duplicates, on each side of the bed-plate, and have arranged the discs so that 312 teeth are struck and played during the revolution of the tune, instead of 156, as are used when a single pair of combs only are in play, as in the ordinary duplex instrument. The volume of tone produced is truly wonderful, being loud enough for any purpose for which it might be needed, while the whole mechanism necessary requires no more space than the ordinary box. We wish to add that this is the first time that a four comb instrument has been made using the same size disc as the ordinary duplex or two comb instrument. Formerly in order to obtain the same volume of tone it was necessary to employ two instruments and two separate sheets, which not only caused a great inconvenience in the handling of the same, but increased the price nearly one hundred per cent.

'T'will remind you of a brass band

While the object of the last named box has been to provide an especially powerful toned instrument, we have continued in our experiments and have made another style, No. 412, which also has two sets of combs, one either end of the comb plate, but the nature of the combs being different, the quality of music obtained therefrom is much finer from the fact that those on the right of the plate are tuned differently in character from those on the left side, thereby making double the number of actual notes found in No. 312. That is to say, in No. 312 the same scale of 78 different notes is employed in each of the four combs, while in No. 412 there are 156 different notes or 312 duplex. The difference between actual teeth and actual notes must be noticed particularly in comparing these two last mentioned styles, and we do not hesitate to say that the music produced from

That singing quality of tone so desirable to lovers of artistic music

No. 412, both in quality and strength of tone, is the finest ever attained, not excepting any size of box or disc now on the market, for it is made "Sublime Harmony Mandolin Tremolo." This style, No. 412, is provided with a zither attachment which adds a very pleasing effect to the tone, and we might further say that ours is one that works properly and its use is optional.

Having described the three styles of unusual interest to you, we would say the balance of our numbers given in the list are operated on principles with which you are undoubtedly familiar in the regular instruments. A few words as to the strength *Worthy* and reliability of the movement will be appreciated *of special men-* upon investigation when we tell you that *tion* each and every NEW CENTURY in strument is fitted with a speed regulator which is abso lutely infallible, the adjusting of which produces a change in tempo which will not vary during the playing of the tune. Among the noticeable features in the motor used is the fact that it will not vary in speed from the time the spring is fully wound up until the last coil has done its work. This eliminates the disagreeable feature so often *At last* evident in the ordinary box, that as a spring is run *a perfect regulation* ning down, the tempo of the tune gradually *of speed* diminishes, and that, while being wound up, the tempo quickens gradually, making a very in harmonious change. Again, broken springs may be taken from the spring-barrels and new ones inserted without taking the movements from the cases which fact in itself is indeed a blessing. It is important to add that all the running gears used in the construction are made of solid bronze or nickel, as brass and cast iron, so generally used *Solid* heretofore, have been proven utterly worthless in wear *bronze and nickel* ing qualities. We point out these advan *parts* tages to you that you may more fully com prehend the fact that we have spared nothing to make this line of instruments as durable and strong as possible and in so doing we are confident that no other made instrument will stand comparison with THE NEW CENTURY.

After all, one of the strongest points is our tune sheet. Much has been said for and against tune sheets with and without projections, but we have struck a happy medium. The patent indentation used by us is not an actual perforation, which when engaging the star wheel produces a disagreeable clicking noise, but is an arrow shaped point which is so small and accurate that many more of such can be placed on our disc than on the same size of other makes. *Tune sheets--* There has been considerable prejudice against all zinc *no projections, no perforations,* discs used heretofore. The reason for this *what then?* has been, that the projections on same have broken off on account of their formation. This is en tirely obviated in our discs by the indentations used, and we furthermore guarantee to replace any disc on which these have become damaged in ordinary use. Zinc being a non-conductor of vibration is far preferable to steel, and dealers handling instruments using steel discs will also recall many instances of same rusting in stock often before being sold, let alone the fact that the buckling or crackling sound so evident while playing them is very obnoxious. These are objections unknown in THE NEW CENTURY discs.

Having described the line somewhat in general, we beg to state that next in importance to the instruments themselves, the method for selling and distributing same presents itself, and we wish to say that as has been the policy of our house during the past year, we will *Selling methods* continue to establish an agency in each town that but one dealer may reap the benefit not only of what local advertising he may do, but also the general publicity that we are giving and will give THE NEW CENTURY Music Boxes. We have found this to be the best plan, as the benefits arising from the conscientious efforts of an attentive and in *Publicity everywhere Policy of protection* terested dealer will add much to the popu larity of THE NEW CENTURY in struments and at the same time be a benefit to both him and ourselves. We guarantee the upholding of retail prices, and will do all in our power to have the dealers assist us in this policy.

We would ask you to bear in mind that we will continue the sale of Symphonion Music Boxes as heretofore and will use them as an adjunct to THE NEW CENTURY line. We will, of course, add new tunes at intervals *As to new tunes for Symphonions* to our Symphonion lists, and think that with the combination of the Symphonion and NEW CENTURY interests as we make them, you will find that we have the best and most profitable line of boxes, price, quality and appearance considered, that you have yet seen. We say little of the cases of the new instruments, reserving that as a surprise for you, but will add that the same up-to-date comparison speaks for them as that in the movement we have explained.

You should surely avail yourself of the opportunity of examining THE NEW CENTURY Boxes by ordering a sample line sent you, for we do not hesitate to say that after once having *It's up to you* seen and heard them, you will find them superior to any disc instruments of this kind. We invite at least your further inquiry, and stand ready to do all in our power to make the handling of our instruments agreeable and profitable to you.

SYMPHONION MANUFACTURING CO.,

GEORGE VARRELMAN, President,

ASBURY PARK, N. J.

THE NEW CENTURY AND SYMPHONION MUSIC BOXES.

We hope you have read this all carefully, profiting thereby, and wish to thank you again for the time and attention you have given us.

NEW CENTURY UPDATE

Al Choffnes

*S*ince publication of my last article on the New Century (*Bulletin*, Volume XXIX, No. 1), a good deal of information has come to light to make the New Century less mysterious. First of all, through the generosity of fellow MBSI member Mel Werner, an original catalog has been loaned for reproduction to accompany this article. You will note the catalog lists only table-model instruments. Conspicuously absent is the glass-front, vertical model in the over-sized case. This omission would lend further evidence to the fact that the vertical model was an afterthought to use the cases produced to house the Imperial Symphonion automatic disc changer which was never placed in production (see previous article).

In going through the catalog it is interesting to note the logic of the model numbering system. The smallest model of the New Century is one which plays an 11½″ peripheral-driven disc. The single-comb model contains one comb of 45 notes, hence is known as Model No. 45. The duplex-comb model has two combs of 45 notes each, and is called Model No. 245. All tunes for the 11½″ are listed in the 1000 series, or List of Tunes No. 1. This information was provided to the owner via a paper label tacked to the filler panel behind the bedplate, in much the same manner as disc information was provided to owners of the Imperial Symphonion instruments. To date, none of the 11½″ models have been observed.

The next model is the No. 60, which is a single-comb, 15″ instrument with 60 notes in the comb. The duplex model is designated No. 260, with 2 combs of 60 notes each. It is interesting to note the 15″ New Century , while using a disc only ½″ smaller in diameter than Regina (the industry leader), contained 16 fewer notes in the music comb. Perhaps this was New Century's method of beating Regina (and similar instruments) on a price basis while appearing to deliver the same sized instrument. In 1902 the 15″ duplex New Century was retail priced at $60.00, while the Style 11 (or equivalent) Regina was priced in the area of $75.00 to $85.00. (I have a June, 1900 Regina price list which shows a Style 11 priced at $75.00, retail.) All discs for the 15″ model are numbered in the 2000 series, or List of Tunes No. 2.

The largest and most popular model of New Century was the 18½″ disc player. This model was available in five different formats, using four different disc series:

    1. Single comb, single play, 78 notes, Model No. 78.

2. Duplex combs, single play, two 78-note combs, Model No. 278.
3. Duplex combs, disc shifter, two 78-note combs, Model No.478.
4. Double duplex combs, single play, four 78-note combs, tuned to 78 notes, Model 312.
5. Double duplex combs, single play, four 78-note combs, tuned to 156 notes, Model No. 412.

Model Nos. 78 and 278 are pretty similar to the common disc music boxes to which we have become familiar (with the exception of the duplex-comb tuning which I will discuss in a future article). Both play 4000 series discs, or Tune List No. 4. The models become quite unusual with No. 478, which is a disc-shi ing, duplex-comb instrument. The tune discs for Model No. 478 are arranged in such a way as to play two distinct melodies in two revolutions of a single disc. To accomplish this, the center post is moved about $\frac{1}{16}''$ to the left after the first tune is played. This movement will bring an entirely new set of disc projections into play on the star wheels to produce a second tune. It is also important to mention that the production width of the disc-shifting and four-comb discs is half of that found on the single or duplex-comb (non-shifting) instrument's 4000 series discs. On the disc shifter, the projections for the second tune pass between the star wheels which are playing the first tune, and vice-versa. All disc-shifter tunes (Model No. 478) are in the 6000 series, or Tune List No. 6.

A further variation of the engineering used on the disc shifter is employed on the four-comb models. Model No. 312 uses two duplex sets of combs which are tuned alike, for a total of 312 music teeth. The discs for No. 312 and No. 412 look similar to the disc-shifter's disc, with the exception of there being no "blank" (projectionless) spot at the beginning of the disc. This "blank" spot is used to accomplish disc shifting on Model No. 478. However, since Model Nos. 312 and 412 are non-shifting, single-play instruments, the area which normally would be blank is used for projections to play the left-hand comb pair in harmony with the right-hand comb pair. All tunes for Model No. 312 are in the 7000 series, or List of Tunes No. 7.

The top-of-the-line New Century Model was No. 412 which used two duplex-comb pairs tuned to 156 different notes, with a total of 312 comb teeth. The only easily observable difference between No. 312 and No. 412 is the addition of a zither on one of the left-hand combs of Model No. 412. The discs used on the four -comb No. 412 look identical to those used on No. 312, but the programming is different, as the comb tuning on the two four-comb models is different. Model No. 412 uses discs in the 8000 series, or List of Tunes No. 8.

Up to now I have described the model identification and mechanics of the New Century instruments and not said much about who actually made the New Century. Thanks to the correspondence I have had with Mr. Etienne Blyelle-Horngacher, who is the administrator of the Conservatoire Autonome Des Boites a Musique, in Geneva, Switzerland, I was informed that Paillard & Co. of Ste. Croix, Switzerland was the manufacturer of New Century movements and discs. Mr. Blyelle-Horngacher also mentioned that Paillard won a medal for the New Century at the 1906 Milano, Italy Exhibition. The Conservatoire in Geneva owns four-comb and disc-shifting instruments in upright cases which are quite different from those found in the United States.

One final note on the New Century discs. In my last article I mentioned that New Century, late in the period of production, made a change from zinc to steel discs. That information was in error as I mistook a bright and shiny, silvery-looking zinc disc as a steel disc. This shiny disc was in sharp contrast to most of the zinc New Century discs which are a dull grey in color. There are still no original steel New Century discs, to my knowledge, in existence.

There is quite a bit more to tell of the New Century story, and I will continue the tale in future articles.

The original New Century catalog is reproduced on the following pages. Portions of the text and photographs of Model Nos. 312 and 412 were missing from the original catalog.

THE

NEW CENTURY

MUSIC BOXES

C.H.LICHTY,
Pianos Talking Machines,
and everything Musical,
641 PENN STREET
READING, PA.

IN the following pages we have attempted to picture and describe somewhat briefly the NEW CENTURY MUSIC BOXES. This line of goods is the result of many years of study and experiment in the music-box line, years in which disappointment and sometimes failure have crept in, but feeling sure that there must be, hidden somewhere, a principle on which to build a music-box that would be more pleasing to the ear, and one which would prove to be of much less trouble to own and operate, we have persevered and we are now glad to present the NEW CENTURY INSTRUMENTS. When you study closely the points of merit as set forth in our description of the new methods introduced in these instruments, you will realize more fully their SUPERIORITY. In tone, we have approached nearer the clear, full, sweet volume of the old Swiss cylinder style than has ever been attained heretofore in any disc instrument. Again, we have increased materially the length of tune obtainable from each size of our discs over that possible from other makes of the same size, reaching a climax in our 18 ½ inch disc for No. 478, which retails for $1, and from which we obtain 208 measures of music as compared with the 27 ½ inch discs now on the market, which sell for $2, and on which are arranged only 132 measures. In other words, this 18 ½ inch disc plays a tune three minutes in length, while the old style 27 ½ inch disc plays but two minutes.

The factor most interesting to the purchaser of a music-box is as to its reliability and durability, the question, " WILL IT BE CONSTANTLY GETTING OUT OF ORDER?" is always among the first asked, and to meet this has been the principle object of our efforts.

The cause of trouble has been clearly shown in all previous disc music-boxes, to have been in the CONSTRUCTION OF THE MOTOR used for propelling the discs, and has been difficult to overcome, through the necessity of tremendous speed and its attendant friction and wear on the different parts. The man of a mechanical turn of mind will realize instantly how much more reliable our perfectly cut gears of BRONZE and NICKEL are over those of CAST IRON and   RASS used in all other makes. But the most marvelous impr   is in

163

the construction of our TWO-BALL EXPANDING GOVERNOR, which obtains for us an absolutely uniform speed, and a tempo regulator so sensitive that the most critical musical ear may be satisfied.

The tune discs used on the NEW CENTURY boxes are a most novel and practical invention. Much has been said for and against tune sheets with and without projections, but we have struck a happy medium. The patent INDENTATION used by us is not an actual perforation, which when engaging the star wheel produces a disagreeable, clicking noise, but is an arrow shaped point which is so small and accurate that many more of such can be placed on our disc than on the same size of other makes. There has been considerable prejudice against all zinc discs used heretofore. The reason for this has been,that the projections on same have BROKEN OFF on account of their formation, and because they were used to turn the star wheels; our indentations DO NOT turn the star wheels, but act simply as a guide for them, while the SOLID METAL of the disc actually does the lifting. We guarantee to replace any disc on which these become damaged in ordinary use. Zinc being a NON-CONDUCTOR OF VIBRATION is far preferable to steel, as it will not rust or give out that buckling or crackling sound so evident in steel discs while playing, which is very obnoxious. These are objections UNKNOWN in the NEW CENTURY discs.

We invite comparison and close inspection of any of our instruments or parts thereof, knowing as we do, that in PRINCIPLE, QUALITY and FINISH, they are far superior to any manufactured heretofore. In conclusion, we beg to state that we guarantee to replace, free of charge any instrument, part of same or disc of same, which becomes damaged or broken through a flaw in the metal or construction. Dealers handling our goods are instructed to uphold this principle at all times.

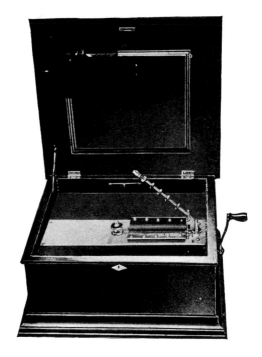

Nos. 78 and 278.

No. 78 New Century, Single Comb.

Tune Discs, 18 ½ inches in diameter. Playing duration of each tune one and one-half minutes.

Highly Polished Cases in either Mahogany or Oak. Dimensions 25 ½ x 23 ½ x 13 ¼ inches.

List of Tunes No. 4.

No. 278 New Century, Duplex Combs, Long Running Movement.

Tune Discs, 18 ½ inches in diameter. Playing duration of each tune one and one-half minutes.

Highly Polished Cases in either Mahogany or Oak. Dimensions 25 ½ x 23 ½ x 13 ¼ inches.

List of Tunes No. 4.

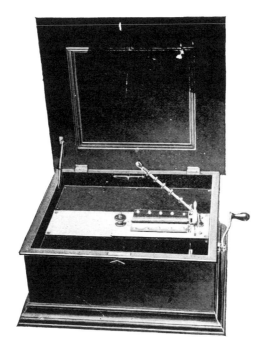

No. 478.

No. 478 New Century Soprano, Double Revolution, Duplex Combs, Long Running Movement.

Tune Discs, 18 ½ inches in diameter.

Highly Polished Cases in either Oak or Mahogany. Dimensions 25 ½ x 23 ½ x 13 ¼ inches.

List of Tunes No. 6.

In this instrument, the tune disc makes TWO COMPLETE REVOLUTIONS to play only ONE LONG TUNE THREE MINUTES IN DURATION OR TWO TUNES, EACH PLAYING ONE AND ONE-HALF MINUTES a single revolution being used for each tune. We have arranged many of the popular airs two on a sheet for this purpose. By adjustment of the change lever the tunes can be repeated or alternated at will.

DISC COLLECTING

Coulson Conn

The popularity of the disc musical box was based in part on the large amount of music which was available during the period of manufacture of the boxes, and even today updating with new tunes is possible to a slight extent. The large variety of discs has led to two groups of disc collectors. The first group is primarily interested in obtaining samples of as many possible makes and sizes of discs as can be found, collecting them for their own sake of uniqueness, originality, and, in some cases, beauty. The actual piece of music on the disc is usually not of importance to this collector, nor is it necessary for a box to play the disc. The criterion for collection is the physical condition of the disc, with graphic detail of paramount importance. The late John Bishop was a prominent collector of this type, and his collection of discs was kindly donated to The M.B.S.I. after his untimely death. Today's outstanding collector of this persuasion must surely be Bud Bronson, whose listing of collected discs borders on the unbelievable.

The second group of disc collector is primarily interested in the music contained in the discs; therefore, they tend to seek discs for those boxes which are owned, and they desire many tunes for each box. In many cases, certain tunes or types of music are of special interest. Obviously, the condition of the disc projections is of great importance, but the ornamentation and labeling may be less so. The tune is the thing. Perhaps the outstanding collector of this persuasion is Robin Timms of Great Britain, who is so conversant with the 11½" Polyphon that he apparently knows all the music produced for this instrument by name, tune, and number and is able to "read" the music from the discs by observing the projections as he turns a disc. In addition, he has expanded into the Regina discs which are compatible with this machine. Not content with acquiring almost all the discs produced for his 11½" Polyphon, Robin has expanded into personally orchestrating and making a large number of additional discs for these boxes. Of those with less specialized but more widespread interest in the music of disc machines, I would mention Michael Miles of East Sussex, Brian Clegg of East Anglia, Great Britain, (who has gone so far as to reproduce large varieties of discs) and myself.

My own efforts at disc collecting started out as an attempt to obtain as much pleasant music as possible for my boxes, later to include different varieties of discs which would, nevertheless, play on my boxes; and finally, in a few cases, to include a few discs which will not play on my machines. My collecting was originally limited to buying discs for my boxes as they became available but expanded dramatically with the purchase of my 15" New Century box. A few weeks before I acquired this instrument, the owner gave one of its 16 discs to John Bishop to include in his collection. Believing this was probably the only source of additional music for this rare box (actually I have since been lucky enough to find 20 others), I was delighted to hear from Al Choffness that copies could be made in England. I borrowed the disc from the Society and sent it to Norman Vince and Brian Clegg in Great Britain where a copy was made.

The knowledge that copies of many disc types could be made opened up new horizons. In general, if an original could be found, Brian could copy it. In the past several years he has copied at least 12 assorted makes and sizes of discs for me, plus types for other collectors. Now if discs can be copied, isn't it worthwhile to compile catalogs of the tunes made so that each collector can know what pieces are ultimately possible to obtain, perhaps through the help of fellow collectors?

And so I began compiling lists of various makes and sizes of discs; the most recent project involving the different series of 18" New Century discs where, along with Al Choffnes, I will list and publish the different tunes, then compile a bulk order from all interested parties and thus make it worthwhile for Brian to make dies to manufacture these most difficult discs.

One other unusual way of obtaining new tunes was to interest a musically learned and talented friend to orchestrate two pieces from "Pirates of Penzance" for Dwight Porter to produce. (I tried to interest Robin in doing Gilbert & Sullivan works, but he is presently doing a Leslie Monkton show, "The Arcadians," and will be occupied with this for some time.)

One need not get so involved as to try to obtain new music or reproductions to get further discs for musical boxes, however. It is surprising how many discs of various types are available unattached from the appropriate boxes. Some were apparently stored apart from their box and inadvertantly separated at time of sale, others were purposely "skimmed" at time of sale, and still others belonged to owners who wish to play only one or two particular pieces on a given box and are willing to sell some of the extra discs. With industrious looking, asking, and even advertising, most boxes can be enhanced with additional tunes. This has become a game of sorts with me, and I can say that all my boxes have at least one more disc to play than they did when I acquired them, and I specialized in rare boxes. (In one case the acquired discs didn't play, but that story is part of a different article.)

The first place to seek additional discs would be in local antique shops. It is surprising what may turn up, even stores that have no boxes may still have a supply of discs left over from a previously sold box or discs purchased separately. In looking for one type of disc you may frequently encounter others; I would urge you to jot down their make and size and the store address; someone else may be seeking just those discs or in the future, you may want or need them.

One of my greatest pleasures was buying a 17″ Britannia box already knowing where a supply of additional discs lay. Then when you hear of fellow collectors looking for something, pass on the word; not only will you make a friend, but often the effort bears rewards — the collector you are helping may come across what you need — this happened to me.

Another option would be to contact dealers who may also stock discs. Many of those listed in the ads in the *News Bulletin* stock moderate to large supplies of discs and are unfailingly helpful. If they don't have an item, they will try to suggest someone who does. Also, of course, our various meetings include marts where assorted goodies turn up. Next would be ads placed in the *News Bulletin* or the journals of sister organizations. If these fail, contact foreign dealers, try to borrow copies of your desired discs to get them copied or, if all else fails, drop me a note. I still have a list of people's wants and lists of discs scattered about and I've been able to help several seekers.

As two addenda, the following is a list of present-day producers of discs, and those discs which are interconvertible, as known to me. For disc producers we have:

DWIGHT PORTER - Randolph, VT

Reproduces Regina discs of practically all sizes; at one time he copied 19 5/8" Polyphon discs but has temporarily stopped. Plans to expand the types of discs in the future.

HARRY CARMEL - Worth, IL

Has Lloyd Kelly's machinery for reproducing Regina discs but to my knowledge, has not made any.

BARRY JOHNSON - Menlo Park, CA

Is in the process of building a machine for reproducing Stella discs. Expects to be operational in 1985.

PATCH PIERCE - England

Has copied and made new 11½" Polyphon and 12¼" Regina discs.

BRIAN CLEGG - Norfolk, England

Has reproduced a large assortment of makes and sizes. Keeps a master each time a disc is copied and so has an extensive reference library of discs. As he works on many different discs, he only makes one type at a time and may require some time to furnish discs.

Several years ago someone in England advertised Stella reproductions by an acid-etched process. I don't know whether these are still being done.

Discs which are interconvertible are as follows:

REGINA

Regina 8" - same as Polyphon 8" if you stretch the drive hole.

Regina 11½" = Polyphone 11½".

Regina 12¼" same comb set up as Polyphon/Regina 11½" and so can be used for copying; same for Universal 12¼".

Regina 15½" = Polyphon 15½" = Euphonia 15½" = Princess 15½" = Universal 15½".

F.G. OTTO

15½" Criterion, Olympia, Euphonion, Crown, and Sterling discs have the same comb set up but the center holes have different sizes. By changing the center hole, enlarging it or attaching metal with a smaller center hole, they can be interchanged.

20" Criterion and Olympia - as above.

TRIUMPH/MONARCH

These two boxes are the same with only different names. Also, the combs will play Regina 15½″ discs if they are hand turned, so these could serve as sources of tunes for reproducing.

BRITANNIA

Imperial is the same box with a different name.

Britannia 8⅛″ = Britannia 9″ with the combs the same and the drive mechanism (central versus rim) different (as Regina 11½″ and 12¼″).

Britannia 11¾″ and Orpheus 11¾″ are interchangeable.

Britannia 19⅝″ and Polyphon 19⅝″ are interchangeable.

MONOPOL 13⅝″ and SYMPHONION 13⅝″ are interchangeable.

SYMPHONION discs - actually Kalliope.

EDELWEISS 4½″ - new Thorens discs will play on this box.

A LIBELLION IN NORWAY

Trygve Kile

When musical boxes could be bought new, few people in Norway could afford to buy one. So today even Polyphons and Symphonions are uncommon here. Thus the collector's dream — to find one of those rare musical boxes — is not likely to be fulfilled in my country.

Nevertheless, some years ago the following advertisement could be read in a Norwegian newspaper:

SAMLERE
Libellyon spilledase nr. 2 m/14 band selges h. bydende.

Translation:

COLLECTORS
Libellion musical box no. 2 with 14 bands (books) for sale on the best offer.

I had never seen a Libellion before and had hardly read about it. But the phrase "with 14 bands" indicated a very interesting musical box. A check in my book indicated it was an extremely rare and interesting item.

So I immediately called the owner, who turned out to be a very talkative and business-minded lady. She told me that she had received a lot of calls, even from abroad, and she was offered enormous sums over the telephone. I was surprised to hear that, since I felt sure that nearly nobody here in Norway would be able to find out what a Libellion was.

According to the owner, the Libellion was a small one, but a play-through on the telephone seemed to come from a musical box in very good condition. The following weekend the Libellion would be demonstrated for every one interested, and the owner invited me to come.

Photo 1. The Libellion, No. 2.

Photo 2. Playing mechanism with comb.

Photo 3. A book for a Libellion, No. 2.

Photo 4. Inside of lid with some of the melodies available.

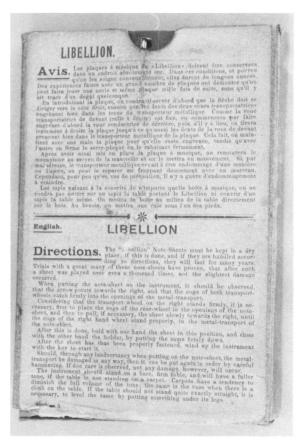

Photo 5. A book cover the the Libellion, No. 2.

I had to choose my strategy so I told her that I was unable to be there on that weekend because of the long distance between our cities. But, without giving an offer, I told her that I was very interested in the Libellion. So, if for any reason, it should not be sold during the weekend, I would very much appreciate a telephone call from her on Sunday evening. She promised to do that. I was anxiously awaiting her call, but Sunday passed without the telephone call I had hoped for. On Monday I called her again. She reported that dramatic things had happened. On Saturday her mother-in-law suddenly died. Consequently, she had not been able to demonstrate the Libellion for anyone, and she had not even taken care to write the addresses or phone numbers of any of the interested parties, except mine. So now she would be glad to sell the Libellion to me.

Shortly thereafter, my wife and I left to view the Libellion. It was indeed interesting to see it, as well as to meet the lady and her modest husband, who turned out to be the actual owner. The Libellion was a small one, and in beautiful, original condition. After several negotiations with the lady, the price became favorable, and we left as the happy owners of an extremely rare musical box.

In my literature on the Libellion, the size of ours was not described. I notified Q. David Bowers and Arthur W. G. Ord-Hume of my find; neither had ever heard of a Libellion model no. 2. The foldable, perforated cardboard books are 10 cm (3 5/16") wide. They vary in length from 2,70 m to 7,00 m and contain two, three or four melodies each. The comb has 34 teeth, but a bridge in the middle covers four teeth. Thus, 15 on each side are in use.

As will be known from Ord-Hume's book, *Musical Box. A Collector's Guide,* Allen & Unwin, 1982, the Libellion was devised by Friedrich Adolf Richter of Rudolstadt in Germany, and the action was performed by a complex system of sliding levers which comprised the mechanisms of the lever-plucker. The motor winds by a crank from the front of the case. Starting and stopping is performed by a vertical lever on the right front corner inside the box. Inside the lid there is a listing of a selection of musical books available containing book numbers, melody titles and length of each book. A picture of the factory and of medals awarded at the exhibitions of Chicago, Illinois, in 1893 and Paris, France, in 1900 can also be seen.

Two sizes of Libellion are known to exist today: one with 20 cm (7 7/8") books, and one with 29, 1 cm (11 9/16"). The number 2, with 10 cm (3 15/16") thus represents a third type.

Until now I have been unable to spot another Libellion of this size, and it should be very interesting to know if others exist, or if a fourth size (e.g., number 1?) might appear. This author and MBSI member Henk Strengers are, at present, researching the history of Fredrich Adolf Richter and would very much appreciate any information from other members about the Libellion and its inventor.

THE EUTERPEPHON AND A FRIEND

Coulson Conn

This article is dedicated to Howard and Helen Fitch, who had the good taste to buy picturesque discs and the kindness to sell them to someone who needed them.

$\mathscr{I}$N searching for rare disc musical boxes, you sometimes discover that the rare is even rarer than you thought! In the Frieberg auction of 1981 I was able to purchase a Euterpephon, a practically unknown make. This particular specimen had been photographed and published in *The Music Box, Volume 7, No. 4, page 149* (Photo 1). Later, in *Volume 9, No.8, page 379,* Arthur Ord-Hume described a second box which he saw in Walt Bellm's collection. In fine detail in five paragraphs he outlines a description of the box, the discs and unusual features, which he then uses in Sherlock Holmes style to trace the origins of the box.

As many of you probably do not have access to the *The Music Box* of 1980, let me quote extensively from Arthur's fine work: "The box (in Walt Bellm's collection) has one comb, an inside lid picture of a robed female playing two trumpets, one to each side of her face, (Photo 2), and a simple lid outer design with the name "Euterpephon" in script, (see Photo 3). On the lid picture there is a small rubber stamp which reads "Otto Pohland/Chemnitz/Uhren/ & Goldwaaren." An examination of the directories of the early years of this century provides the information that Otto Pohland was indeed in business at Kronenstrasse 26, Chemnitz, Germany. Managed by Alfred Pohland (in 1906), the business was established in 1887 as an agent for clocks and gold jewelry and was a dealer in mechanical instruments, talking machines and accessories.

The discs are printed in gold and black with an elaborate and typically ornate design of the period. A typical number is 2064 and there is

Photo 1. The Euterpephon disc musical box.

Photo 2. The inside lid picture.

the usual legend "Schutz Marke" (Trade Mark) under the figure of the large-mouthed muse, Euterpe.

But the real clue comes in the form of the disc projections. They are highly individualistic and readily identifiable. To begin with, they are not rectangular in form, but rather the punched-out end is pointed, and this pointed end is then folded back in the usual way until it is made to enter a small opening punched behind the projection. This second, smaller punching produces a sort of tiny scoop-shaped opening so that the point of the main projection engages in it. Naturally, this makes for a very strong projection which is supported by its rear or trailing edge.

The patent for this type of projection was taken out by Otto Helbig & Polikeit of Gohlis, Leipzig. The British patent, numbered 3941, is dated February 21st, 1896, and was secured in the name of the company's British agent, J. B. Howard.

Each of the square-tipped comb teeth in the bass to mid-range area (treble teeth are excluded) is drilled to accept a downwards-projecting damper wire. Helbig & Polikeit were granted a patent for a disc machine damper system, the United Kingdom number of which is 18,507, taken out on October 3rd 1895 in the name of agent C.A. Jensen.''

A good piece of research very nicely reported, and accompanied on page 381 with a nice photo of the box! However, it turns out that this is not the end of the story, but rather the beginning. After acquiring the box from the Freiberg auction, with the help of my good friend Norman Vince,

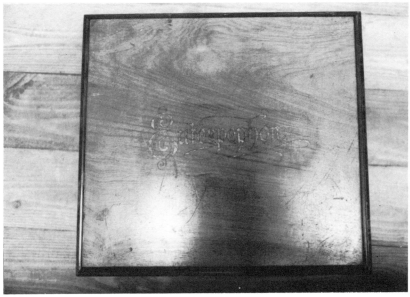

Photo 3. The outer lid design.

179

I had the broken tooth replaced, a working winding crank was acquired, and the box was cleaned. I then set out on that very crucial task which is also my own particular love and specialty: acquiring discs. And did I have a bonanza!

First, let me start by saying that the box does *not* play well with an 11 inch Polyphon disc as reported elsewhere. It is true that some of the Euterpephon discs are near in size to the 11½ inch Polyphon discs, but the Polyphon has 54 teeth in the comb and the Euterpephon has 56 teeth in its comb, a blatant difference! Second, a Polyphon disc on the machine gives random notes, but nothing suggesting a tune! So that option was out.

Arthur Ord-Hume described the discs on the Bellm machine and, had I recalled his article, I could have asked Mr. Bellm for the use of these discs to have them copied by Brian Clegg in England. Unfortunately, the articles on the Euterpephon had been glossed over by me earlier (I had read only paragraphs in a large article) and I had long forgotten them, so this was not available to me when I acquired the box. Therefore, I had to find old discs de novo! And then I learned that it really pays to communicate with fellow members of the musical box societies, because I discovered a hoard of discs, not in Europe, where these boxes were manufactured and sold, (I believe the Bellm Museum acquired its box through the Mekanisk Music Museum/American International Galleries Inc.), but here in the U.S.A.

Years ago members Howard and Helen Fitch had found a cache of unusual discs, and because they were so beautiful, they purchased them. These were Euterpephons, and when Helen heard I had a Euterpephon with no discs, she generously offered to let me have them. There were fourteen discs in all, many were well preserved and quite beautiful, and to my surprise, in two types and sizes!

Let me go back to Arthur Ord-Humes's article and quote some further sentences which I deleted above: "discs which measure 12¹⁄₁₆ inch in diameter are made of zinc." And "the discs are finely printed in gold and black with an elaborate and typically ornate design of the period." None of my discs fits this description; however, I do have several that are 12¹⁄₁₆ inch in diameter (and all are made of zinc), but these have two patterns. Either they have a lyre pattern with the word "Euterpephon" superimposed in a banner and use gold coloring for the design of the lyre, banner and surrounding sun rays, with black trimming and black printing of "Schutz Marke," "Euterpephon" and "Trade Marke" (Photo 4); or else they have a gold lyre but with no black edging, with "Schutz Marke" and "Trade Marke" in gold printing, and with the name "Euterpephon" on the banner in a negative fashion and lacking in color, ie., the zinc shows through the gold banner (Photo 5). All discs have gold rays and have the number above and the tune title below in German, English and French printed in black ink.

Photo 4. One version of disc design.

Photo 5. Another version of disc design.

In addition, five of the discs are not of the $12\frac{1}{16}$ inch size but are $11\frac{3}{8}$ inch in diameter. They are all black-trimmed and have black printing design, and fortunately played the same comb, so the only difference mechanically in the discs is that the larger ones have approximately $\frac{3}{8}$ inch of extra zinc about the rim. This arrangement is reminiscent of the $11\frac{1}{2}$ inch and $12\frac{1}{4}$ inch Reginas, which play the same combs but have a different (central versus peripheral) drive mechanism. But both sizes here are center driven, so one can only conclude that the one set of discs was made for a box which was slightly larger in size and needed more metal to reach the rollers of the disc supports. This is probably true since my box fits the $11\frac{3}{8}$ inch discs well, whereas the $12\frac{1}{16}$ inch discs play but overlap the edge of the box rather than rest on the rollers. I would assume, however, that the $12\frac{1}{16}$ inch discs fit well on the box in the Bellm collection.

Concerning the disc projections, there is again variance from those described. The $12\frac{1}{16}$ inch discs do indeed have the second punched hole, with a pointed primary projection bent backwards into it, identical to the described discs, but the smaller discs do not have the second punching, and the primary punching has a flat end so that it is the same as the Polyphon/ Regina projections.

Even this is far from the end of this tale, for while searching for a rare Sun disc for fellow member Bud Bronson, I returned to a store which frequently has unusual discs and which had had a Sun disc years ago. Alas, the Sun disc was gone but there was an unusual zinc disc with a sun ray type of design on it. I bought it for Bud and only after having it at home for some time, (I had planned to give it to him at the 1983 annual meeting in Philadelphia) did I realize that the pattern was like the periphery of the Euterpephon pattern, without the central lyre motif. Sure enough, it played on the box! Unfortunately there was only the one, but when I returned six months later, just after the 1983 meeting, lo and behold, there were 24 more discs that had been back in the stockroom for years! For reasons unknown they were never sold. And now the fun *really* increased.

Twenty-two of the discs were zinc with no printing except for the tune title and number which were done in black just like the Euterpephon described above. But the sizes were hardly uniform: $11\frac{7}{8}$ inch, 12 inch, $12\frac{1}{16}$ inch, $12\frac{1}{8}$ inch and $12\frac{3}{16}$ inch sizes were all there. Either they were made for boxes of very slightly different sizes, or the disc cutting was not too precise at the Euterpephon factory. But the real find involved the last two discs. Made of zinc and measuring $12\frac{1}{8}$ inch and $12\frac{1}{16}$ inch respectively, these two discs not only have different patterns but also have a different name: "Serenada." The large one has the common sun ray design with the name printed in a wavy pattern in gold across the open central area, on which no other mark appears (Photo 6). The other disc has an entirely different pattern — the name is of gold script across the top of the disc with gold lines and filigree enclosing it (Photo 7). Both discs have the numbers and titles printed in black in the usual pattern.

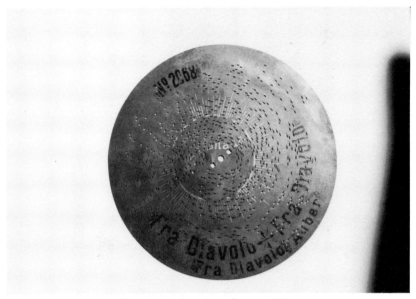

Photo 6. The mysterious "Seranada" disc.

So somewhere out there, there is, hopefully, one or more Serenada boxes. Why the makers of a rare type box whose production must have been very small should have felt compelled to produce some under a second name is unknown, but perhaps each distributor wanted his own brand name. Local names such as "Empress" for Mira boxes, "Princess or Universal" for Regina boxes, "Thorward" for Stella boxes, "Euphonion" for Polyphon or "The Imperial" for Britannia are all to be found. Mechanial differences in similar boxes are far from unknown. To quote Graham Webb in *The Musical Box Handbook,* Faber & Faber, 1971: "there are at least six different types of dampers used in the 15½ inch Polyphon alone." I am currently researching other examples of different mechanical mechanisms which were used in the same brand and size of box, including the Orpheus and Triumph/Monarch boxes — in spite of the small number of machines made — so the varying characteristics of the discs has precedence.

To continue with the differences in Euterpephon discs, let me record that the two Serenada discs have the projections made of two punchings as originally described; however, of the other twenty-three discs which I acquired in the fall of 1983, only four have these projections. The other nineteen have pointed primary projections as noted above, but they have no secondary holes punched, into which these pointed ends are pressed. Therefore, they are like Polyphon projections but the end, which is bent back and touches the disc surface, is pointed. None of them are like the 11⅞ inch discs earlier described, ie., with flat-ended projections.

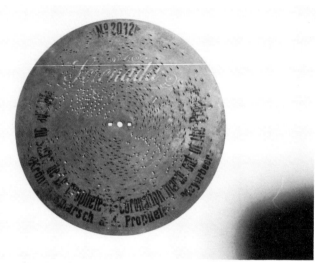

Photo 7. Another "Seranada" disc with a different design.

In closing, let me emphasize a few things. First, there is a tremendous advantage in exchanging information and helping each other out. Though these boxes are rare, disc copies can and have been made. My original fourteen Euterpephons are all copied in steel onto the 11⅜ inch size to play on my box. Also, it was through trying to help a fellow collector that I stumbled onto my hoard of 25 discs; and through the Fitches' kindness that I originally had discs for my machine. Second, if you have something unusual write it up and let us know. Your work may come back to help you. Lastly, does anyone know anything about the Serenada? Learning about it is a new goal for me, and playing Sherlock Holmes is fun for American musical box enthusiasts too! 𝄞

Orchestrions

BERNHARD DUFNER
THE UNKNOWN AMERICAN ORCHESTRION BUILDER

William H. Edgerton

⊘N Wednesday, January 19, 1898, a small funeral procession made its way down Genesee Street to the Pine Hill Cemetery in Buffalo, New York. Perhaps not one of the many people who witnessed it realized that it was bearing the remains of a man who enjoyed the unique distinction of being the only manufacturer of orchestrions in the United States. In fact, this uniqueness was preserved for several decades, until the early 1920's when Seeburg, Link, the Operators Piano Co., and others offered a type of orchestrion built with the piano as a base instrument. Who was this interesting man, Bernhard Dufner, and why have we not heard of him before now?

Bernhard Dufner's paternal grandfather, Anton*, was born about 1750 near Furtwangen, Germany, and was a clockmaker by trade. When called upon to repair a modest nine-pipe hand-played organ, Anton Duffner developed and perfected a clockwork attachment so that the organ would play by itself. After building several barrel-operated organs, and being concerned that he was musically inadequate, he pursued the acquaintance of a German musician to learn sufficient musical notation to be able to pin his barrels correctly. His first important instrument was a musical clock with 21 pipes. At that time in the then Kingdom of Baden, by tradition the front pew in the church was reserved for the Mayor and Councilmen, but Duffner's musical clock was regarded as so significant an invention by the townsfolk that he was seated for a time in front of the Mayor.

* *Die Uhrenmacher des hohen Schwarzwaldes und ihre Werke*, by Gerd Bender (Verlag Müller, Villingen/Schwarzwald, 1975), is an excellent source of information about Black Forest clocks and clockmakers and also has a large section on musical clocks and orchestrions made in that region. There were many Dufners who lived in the Black Forest, some of them spelling their names 'Duffner' and some 'Dufner' (and the same person may sometimes be referred to by either spelling). On page 444, Anton Duffner is introduced as a pioneer of the Black Forest flute clocks, a saddle-maker from Gütenbach (about five miles west and a little south of Furtwangen), who settled in the side-valley "Wanne" and practiced his craft there. He is listed as having been born in 1752 and dying in Furtwangen in 1834, although some sources give his death date as 1832. On page 447 there is a full-page portrait of him (20.5 by 24 cm), painted by Joh. Bapt. Laule, now in the Historische Uhrensammlung Furtwangen. Duffner is holding with both hands a small open *tabatière*, which seems to have a tune card on the inside of the lid. On the table there is a sheet of music with hand-notation, titled "Ländler." Perhaps this portrait was painted about the time he was studying music. – Ed.

Anton Duffner was unable to patent his musical clock, for there were no patent rights at that time, but he formed a partnership with some relatives to make barrel orchestrions. Their first instruments played dance and popular tunes, but the family partnership later developed larger and more elaborate mechanisms that could play operatic overtures and other classical music.

Anton Duffner died in 1834, and his son (Bernhard's father) succeeded him in business. Soon thereafter the second Duffner completed an elaborate instrument that he exhibited throughout the Kingdoms of Baden and Württemberg. When the King of the latter heard the orchestrion, he offered Duffner free citizenship, freedom from taxes, and a 10,000-florin annual pension to remain in Stuttgart and establish an orchestrion factory, but Duffner could not be tempted from his native Baden.

Bernhard Dufner served an apprenticeship with his father, and when the latter died in 1842, Bernhard, a third-generation member of the family to do so, carried on the business. Thinking there was a better opportunity for his craft in America, Dufner came to this country in 1867, settling in New York City, and then moving in 1868 to Buffalo, N. Y., where he spent the balance of his life. The Buffalo *City Directory* first listed Bernhard Dufner in 1869 as a laborer, then from 1871 to 1897 he was listed as an orchestrion

---

BERNHARD DUFNER,

MANUFACTURER OF

ORCHESTRIONS

HAND ORGANS,

AND ALL SORTS OF

AUTOMATIC OR SELF-PLAYING INSTRUMENTS.

Cylinders made on short notice. 795 Washington Street

ADVERTISEMENT FROM THE 1873 BUFFALO CITY DIRECTORY.

builder.* Toward the end of this period an Edward Dufner was listed at the same address. Edward later became a prominent Buffalo artist and joined the teaching staff of the Buffalo Art Students' League in 1934. In 1898, Anna Dufner, Bernhard's widow, was listed as a confectioner, offering baked goods at the same address. Obviously the loss of the man of the house forced his widow to assume family responsibilities, though it is difficult to picture a bakery kitchen displacing the workshop, lumber racks, and

---

* In Bender, *op. cit.*, on page 497 we learn that Adelbert Blessing (son of Makar Blessing of Weissenbach, in the Black Forest) migrated to America, and around 1876 was a musicwork maker in Buffalo. It is intriguing to speculate that he may have worked for Dufner, who was active as an orchestrion builder at that time and in that city. – Ed.

188

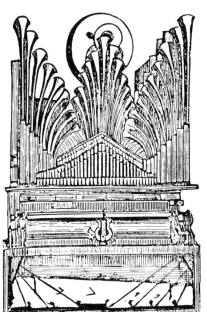

BERNHARD DUFNER,

MANUFACTURER OF

ORCHESTRIONS

AND ALL SORTS OF

Automatic or Self-Playing

INSTRUMENTS

795 Washington Street.

Cylinders made on Short Notice.

barrel-pinning gauges of a master orchestrion builder. Anna M. Dufner's name remained in the Buffalo directories until she died; her death occurred on March 4, 1938, at the age of 87.

On October 11, 1875, Dufner received U.S. Patent No. 168,561 covering improvements in organs. This patent was granted for improving the method of turning a rank of pipes on and off as a barrel-operated

BERNHARD DUFNER,

MANUFACTURER OF

ORCHESTRIONS

AND ALL SORTS OF AUTOMATIC OR SELF-PLAYING INSTRUMENTS.

No. 224 GOODELL STREET.

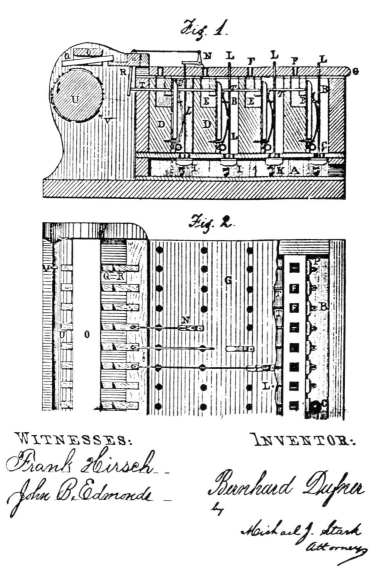

SKETCH OF BERNHARD DUFNER FROM THE COURIER
FOR JANUARY 30, 1898.
(Courtesy of the Buffalo and Erie County Historical Society.)

instrument is playing. Before Dufner's time a wooden slide, operated manually at the side of an instrument, was perforated with holes corresponding to interior windways controlling one or more ranks of pipes; thus, for a rank of 16 pipes there would be 16 holes in the slide. When the slide was in the open position, the wind could flow through the holes in the slide; when slid shut, the solid part of the slide effectively closed the wind-passage. Dufner's invention did away with the slide entirely and substituted pallet valves right in the wind chest, with the pallets activated automatically by keys riding on bridge pins on the barrel. When a bridge came along the pallet valve would be either open or closed. This was a much more scientific and accurate method of controlling the wind, and one not subject to problems caused by changes in humidity.

An interesting refinement of this barrel-activated pallet appears on the Dufner orchestrion described in this article: the first barrel pin activates the key, which self-latches in the open position. The next time a pin comes along the key unlatches. Very ingenious!

Dufner's pallet valve, though better, was more trouble to make and must have cost more than the slide, for slides continued to be used on 'monkey' organs, almost to the present time.

Dufner orchestrions were large, impressive instruments, extremely carefully crafted, and very likely of superior musical quality. Although Dufner's *City Directory* advertisements offered custom-made barrels on short notice, it is doubtful that more than three or four dozen complete instruments were made. When Dufner was asked to move to Rochester, N. Y., by a Mr. Powers, who had an Art Gallery there, so that he could make instruments on a 'large' scale, Dufner apparently preferred his adopted Buffalo. Powers did purchase, about 1878, a Dufner orchestrion that cost $12,000, and came with 60 pinned barrels. What an instrument that must have been!

Dufner seems to have had no desire for fame or publicity, which, together with his presumed small output, probably accounts for the fact that he was little known in Buffalo and only now has been 'discovered.' During the illness that ended with his death, he invented and copyrighted a musical chart to simplify the study of harmony in chords, but his name is not important in musical history. According to the Buffalo Bureau of Vital Statistics, he died at his home (Goodell and Oak Street) on January 15, 1898, at the age of 62 years, 6 months, and 15 days. It is not known if any of Dufner's five surviving children inherited any of his abilities or interests, or succeeded their father in business.

DUFNER'S GRAVESTONE, PINE HILL CEMETERY.

FULL VIEW OF INSTRUMENT.

The writer's interest in Bernhard Dufner was aroused after locating an orchestrion unquestionably made by a builder with the name of Dufner. While attending an auction outside Albany, N. Y., a bystander asked if I wanted to purchase a 'melodeon,' When I didn't show much enthusiasm, he then said it played a pinned barrel. Having well learned the rule of never telling a prospective seller that he doesn't know what he has and that there was no such thing as an instrument specifically called a barrel-operated melodeon (in this case), I cautiously expressed interest and agreed to meet the seller after the auction.

Located in the corner of a low-ceilinged basement, the orchestrion was in hundreds of pieces, and my concealed enthusiasm increased by the minute as we pulled out sections of the case for inspection. Then out came a

CLOSE-UP OF CARVED TOP.

photograph (probably 30 or 40 years old) that was much like the front view accompanying this article, and I knew we'd 'hit it big.' Not as 'big' as when Harvey Roehl discovered dozens of nickelodeons in a Rhode Island barn over two decades ago, but big nevertheless.

The instrument is impressive. When assembled, it stands ten feet, six inches high; five feet, six inches wide; and three feet, eight inches deep. Several ingeniously installed wooden rollers enable it to be easily moved in and out from the wall to allow access from the rear. The most important characteristic, however, is a near-mint state of preservation. Aside from some minor case damage at the mitered corners of the base that was caused by hurried disassembly, and a few distorted metal pipes, the instrument is about as mint, unrestored, as it is possible to find. The stencilling on the case is under some grime, but cleaning and polish is all the case has required. The chest will have to be releathered and the main wind-supply bellows recovered, but the level of craftsmanship was so high that not much else will be required. Even the chrome-plated parts were so heavily and well plated they will not have to be redone.

GOVERNOR, WITH BARREL REMOVED.

CLOSE-UP OF GOVERNOR.

The barrels are eight inches in diameter and 34 inches long. They have survived in an extraordinary state of preservation. Nine of the original ten barrels remain, and not one is cracked. Aside from a film of dust and an

END VIEW OF TYPICAL BARREL.

old-world appearance, they could have been made yesterday. The barrels are housed in a separate glass-fronted softwood cabinet. The programs are:

1. Telephone Waltz, Heilman
   Silver Wedding Waltz, Strauss
2. Overture to *Le Calife de Bagdad*, Boieldieu
3. Arias -- *Martha; Sonnambula; Trovatore*
4. *Orpheus* Selections, Offenbach
5. Glory Hallelujah; Home Sweet Home; Columbia the Pride of the Ocean; Old Folks at Home; Star Spangled Banner
6. Sacred Music
7. *Chimes of Corneville; Mignon; Fatinitza*
8. Wedding March; Inman March
9. Overture to *La Prison d'Edimbourg (Edinburgh)*, Carafa

B. DUFNER NAMEPLATE.

196

PIPEWORK; BELLS IN FOREGROUND, GOVERNOR TO THE RIGHT.

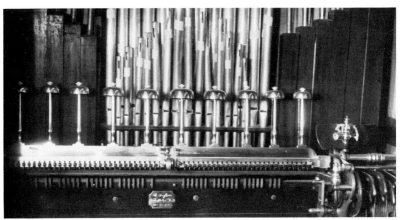

MECHANISM, BARREL REMOVED, SHOWING LOCATION OF NAMEPLATE.

There are 120 pipes in four ranks, including 12 brass trumpets, plus 10 bells. Three of the keys are latching keys as described above, so one rank must play continuously, and the barrel controls whether or not the other three ranks are playing. There are 58 keys, and allowing 10 for the bells, there must be 48 speaking notes. It is certainly an impressive instrument in specification, and time will tell whether it is impressive musically.

If luck is with us and some other projects get finished on schedule, the orchestrion may be playing in time for the 1980 M.B.S.I. Annual Meeting, which is to be held in Stamford, Connecticut. For the next year, it will be on display, unrestored, at the Mechanical Music Center in nearby Darien.■■

SO HERE'S TO POPPER FELIX —
AN AMERICAN SAGA

Rick Crandall

$\mathscr{I}$t all started with a nugget of gold.

Eureka, Comstock, Virginia City and Nevada City — all are towns whose roots go back to the post-Civil War days when men commonly pulled a pound of gold a day from the creeks of the "mother lode country."

In 1850 the inhabitants of one California settlement gathered to name their rapidly growing ville "Nevada," after the nearby, snow-covered mountains. Fourteen years later they met again to deal with the conflict in names with the adjacent state of Nevada, newly admitted into the Union. They solved the problem by affixing the word "City" after Nevada to distinguish their town.

Nevada City grew during the most boisterous of times to become one of California's boom cities because of the ore in the area. Extravagant sums were spent building homes and business establishments in grand Victorian style, many of which can still be seen today.

After the turn of the century, mining of silver and other ores was combined with lumbering to maintain prosperity. The town attracted all sorts of residents, many of whom were the rugged men typical of a western mining town. In the evenings you would find them in the Council Chamber Bar in the middle of town or on the corner of Pine and Broad Streets, looking for a drink. Tavern and saloon owners made a good living for themselves, but they had to make their occupation their lives, day and night. Saloons and cafes were focal points in busy towns, but they still experienced turnovers in ownership for a variety of reasons including owner fatigue, retirement and lack of financing.

In the year 1911 in Nevada City just such a turnover took place, making way for Ernest Schreiber to fulfill his ambition to become a proprietor by purchasing the Council Chamber Bar. He dubbed the establishment the Bismark, but later it became known as Schreiber's Restaurant and Cafe.

Ernest Schreiber was born in 1881 in Wuppertal (called Elberfeld then), Germany, 25 miles from Cologne. He struck out for America and landed a job at a restaurant in San Francisco. Every day he served some of the interesting people who came from a mining town in the Sierra foothills, where the streets were reputedly "paved with gold." So to Nevada City he went to further his fortunes.

Popper Felix, fully restored in the author's collection, July, 1983.

The Schreiber's Cafe building as the author saw it in 1981. The building was closed recently.

Schreiber's Cafe

Immediately on purchasing the Council Chamber Bar, he went about the task of setting up the bar, poolroom and restaurant in the style he wanted. In 1912 he started serving meals. His slogan, "Everything of the Finest Kind," was soon known to all. Schreiber's Cafe preserved the "gold rush saloon" motif with its long bar (along which he would slide brimming beer mugs) and fancy pool tables that today are prized pieces in collector's homes.

Nevada City townsman Bob Paine recalls in an article he wrote for the *Nevada City Nugget:*

"Everything in the place sold for 10 cents: Lee Stanley and Woodpecker Cigars, 10 cents; stein of beer, 10 cents. He (Ernest Schreiber) imported Arthur Allerman from Switzerland to be his chef — one of the best in this country of gourmets. Grass Valleyans by the dozen came on the electric street car on Sundays for a 6-course dinner — all you could eat for 24 cents per person."

Ernie Schreiber presided over the evening activities, tending bar, keeping order and ensuring that everyone had a good time. He always wore a white, floor-length apron, as though barkeeping was a scientific activity. If there was a science involved, then part of the formula for success was music, and so he journeyed back to his homeland to find one of the finest coin-operated music machines in the world for his cafe.

The Popper Felix in Germany

It happened on a vacation back to his home town of Elberfeld in 1921. As Bob Paine recollected:

"He came home to Broad Street with a German musical novelty that was to delight the patrons of Schreiber's corner for many years, a music box playing perforated musical rolls, that became famous as Felix."

Ernie Schreiber may have been purposefully looking for a coin-operated orchestra, or perhaps he just stumbled on one that met his criteria of "The Finest Kind." He did, in fact, end up buying a large classic machine built by one of the leading automatic orchestra manufacturers, Popper & Co. of Leipzig, Germany.

How he heard of the German Biergarten near Cologne, we don't know. There he found an establishment financially devastated by the effects of World War I, but still in possession of a most striking music machine — the Popper Felix, originally built from 1906 to 1908. The machine appeared awesome at first, at 10' high, 7½' wide and 4' deep, it was noticeable.

A large bay window adorned the upper-central part of the machine with a seemingly plain window in front and two beautiful art-glass side panels, each with a colorful picture of a famous castle on the Rhine. Below the bay window was the little door to the roll frame, made of crinkled, deep blue glass with a gold script "Felix" in keeping with Popper's practice of individually naming its machines.

Near the top center of the oak case was a rotating brass and jeweled wonderlight that showered the room in colored light beams when turned on. Adding another 12" in height on top of the case was a hand-wrought, gold-leafed metal sculpture of a floral bouquet inlaid with sparkling lights. Initially, with the machine turned off, Schreiber may not have noticed the 90 colored lightbulbs that lined the entire upper perimeter of the case, but they were ready to surprise and entertain him. At some point, he would have noticed the small brass plate framing a coin slot with the instruction, "10 pfennig."

With the drop of a coin, Felix literally came alive. Ernie Schrieber may not have known what to look at first. Undoubtedly, his eyes would have been transfixed on the bay window in which, almost magically, a beautiful woman appeared with a basket of flowers in one hand. The brilliantly-colored, painted picture would then have seemingly started to move. He would have seen her move her hand to the basket, take out some flowers, and throw them to the audience! At some point he would have been distracted by the perimeter lights flashing alternately in a sequence, all controlled by the mysteries within.

The wonderlight rotated and threw off jeweled rays of colored light. Two layered, round brass fixtures also rotated with oblong light bulbs creating a pinwheel effect. The overall feeling created was one of Felix sparkling in a dimly-lit room with a beautiful woman throwing flowers while inviting all to come and listen.

The author backlighting the moveable art glass scene for this photograph.

Listening was the best part. Once the music started, Ernie Schreiber would have found Felix had muscle. An orchestra of violins, flutes, viol da gambas, cellos, piccolos, clarinets, mandolins, piano and percussion including bass and snare drums, tympani, triangle, Chinese cymbal, xylophone and orchestra bells began to play a wide repertoire of music. Whether it was a waltz, march or a 20-minute opera piece that he first heard, it must have been enough for him to make the decision to buy Felix for his cafe in Nevada City, California.

Before long, Felix was on its way by boat to California. In pioneering tradition, it traveled through the Panama Canal, which at that time had been open for business for only five years. The boat trip for Felix ended on the northern California coast, and from there it proceeded by narrow gauge railroad to the "mother lode country." Little did anyone know then, but that trip was undoubtedly responsible for the survival of Felix, since most large machines did not make it through wars and reconstruction in Europe.

The Popper Felix in Nevada City

Felix arrived in Nevada City during the summer of 1921 with its art glass and instrumentation amazingly intact. Once installed and working, it became an integral part of nighttime Broad Street.

Bob Paine recalls:

"I am sure the mysterious insides had hundreds of working gremlin musicians. The mechanical orchestra . . . could play *The Parade of the Wooden Soldiers, The Blue Danube,* and all the Strauss waltzes. It took 20 minutes to play the opera *Carmen,* the roll was 200 feet long. Suddenly, little lights would come on in back of the colored glass front and a girl would appear to throw roses at the listener."

Felix must have been installed and working by the fall of 1921 since a scan of the local newspapers at the time uncovers one ad and several mentions in the "Brief Happenings" column in the *Nevada City Nugget*:

September 16, 1921 — "When you go to Schreiber's Restaurant for a meal, you are assured of the very best of food and service. A new addition to his place that is taking well is a piano-orchestrion which he has installed."

September 25, 1921 — "If you haven't heard the new piano-orchestrion at Schreiber's Restaurant and Cafe, you have missed a real treat in high-class music. He has a fine variety of choice selections for the instrument which is an added attraction to his already popular cafe."

September 30, 1921 — "Have you heard the new piano-orchestrion at Schreiber's Restaurant and Cafe? If not, you have missed a rare treat in the line of choice music. He has an excellent selection of music for this instrument, ranging from jazzy dance pieces to overtures."

Felix played almost non-stop from 1921 until 1941, an amazing 20-year service record. Ernie Schreiber located the machine such that it faced into the bar, and the back of the machine faced an opening into the restaurant. A nickel worked hard in those days — Felix entertained two sets of patrons. In fact, I've learned that wallboxes were installed at each dining table so diners did not have to go into the bar to hear Felix play. The four Schreiber daughters would often come to the restaurant in the evenings so they could drop a nickel in to hear their favorite roll.

Felix Leaves Nevada City

In 1941, Ernie Schreiber, at age 60, found the onslaught of World War II made it difficult to find anyone who could keep Felix running. He sold the old music machine to R.M. Stagg to be part of a museum of music machines and guns in Reno, Nevada.

When Felix left town, it was big news and sad news, as evidenced by this excerpt from the local *Union* newspaper in 1942:

FELIX TO PLAY FOR DOLLARS IN RENO

Early yesterday afternoon, Nevada City bid farewell to "Felix," the mechanical Orchestrion housed for nearly a quarter of a century in "Schreiber's Cafe."

It was carefully dismantled and loaded on a trailer . . . by the new owner, R.M Stagg, who will make the remarkable old player a museum piece to furnish entertainment for lovers of fine music.

"There's a thousand dollars worth of music going with it," the new owner said, adding "the masterpieces of German composers, the marches and the operas America has come to love."

Friends coming and going for two days since word of the sale got around, are concerned over the loss of a favorite source of entertainment. The new owner has his museum, the "Old Corral" at Moutainview along the Bay Shore Highway, but plans to move to Reno to open what will be known as "The Bell of Reno." Felix will no longer play for nickels, according to the plans of the museum collector, but for dollars. When properly set up, the entertainment will include lighting effects and even a dancing figure. All that the famous organs, the operas and world renowned orchestras have to fine music lovers, this German made orchestrion will be able to reproduce, according to the opinion of the experts. "This one is an especially rare example," Stagg remarked. (sic)

In the late 1940's, Stagg's entire collection was sold to a gambling and entertainment club in Reno. Along with Felix were other music machines including a Seeburg G, Seeburg J, Seeburg KT, Wurlitzer CX, Coinola CO, Mills Violano, Multiphone, Welte Cottage orchestrion and a hoard of cabinet machines. They were all stored in a corrugated-metal storage building right in the middle of Reno, and there they sat for 35 years, forgotten and unnoticed. For all practical purposes, Felix had disappeared from the face of the earth.

While in hibernation it was becoming even more of a museum piece, and an antique as well. Beginning in the 1960's, collector interest developed in automatic music machines, and by the 1980's Felix had unwittingly become one of the world's few remaining prizes in its field. But it

Original photo of the Popper Felix on location in Schreiber's Cafe, Nevada City, California. Ernest Schreiber presiding.

The Wonderful Piano-Orchestrian

NOW IN OPERATION

Come in and hear the tuneful music furnished by this marvelous instrument.

Schrieber's Restaurant and Cafe

An ad heralding the arrival of Felix, from the Nevada City-Grass Valley Gazette, September 16, 1921.

languished in its shed until a local citizen, claiming he could smell antiques in those buildings from his car as he would periodically drive by them, finally satisfied his itch by gaining permission to look inside. There he saw a hoard that was enough to open anyone's eyes. He proposed an exchange for the one machine too big for use in the club . . . the Popper Felix.

So in 1978 the machine surfaced, but knowledge of its existence was not widespread. In late 1981, I heard about its possible existence from Hayes McClaran, the well-known California restorer.

Discovery!

McClaran knew I was looking for a prime example of a large Popper with two or more pipe ranks, such as a Rex or Luna, and preferably with some animation or lighting effects. He had never seen the machine personally, and since the Felix model was undocumented in the published literature, only partial knowledge of its specifics was available.

But he knew it was there and it didn't take me long to contact Felix' owner to ascertain its availability. I then endured a six-month sequence of events familiar to most collectors. Felix was complete, but taken apart in many pieces — not a good condition for its owner to think of selling it, even if he was so inclined, which at first he was not.

The owner had other non-music collector interests and, even though Felix in its unrestored condition still seemed quite a prize, priorities prevailed. Felix' owner was a collector of military artifacts and there were items he wanted to acquire that were more important to him than the music machine. We found a formula, and so the collector's world turns. I became the proud owner of a hulking case and cartons full of parts, pipes, drums and the like.

From the telephone descriptions and Polaroid photos, I had the feeling Felix was something special due to its extensive lighting, animation, art glass and instrumentation. It was thought to have several pipe ranks which thrust it into the "large classic" category.

But it wasn't until McClaran and I showed up in a rented 22' truck with hydraulic rear lift at Felix' hiding place, opened the garage door and saw the view shown in Figure 4, that I realized how unique it was. We unpacked all the cartons and laid out the pieces on the floor. By the time we were done, we saw that Felix had six ranks of pipes (158 in all), and it was truly one of the few remaining large concert orchestrions made by Popper.

The amazing part about the find was that after all those years and all those trips, including a boat trip in 1921 across the Atlantic and through the Panama Canal, 157 of the 158 pipes were still present, and all the art glass was intact! Felix deserved nothing less than a total restoration to be returned to the status of a grand orchestrion.

I was overwhelmed at first with the idea of a machine with such credentials. The next day we settled into the task of dismantling the machine and packing it safely onto the truck for transport back to Fresno. While McClaran began planning the restoration, I researched the

The castle on the left art glass has been identified as Burg Rheinstein.

The castle on the right art glass has been identified as Schloss Stolzenfels.

207

origins of Felix. Werner Baus and Hans Schmitz came to the rescue. It was Hans who learned the castles painted on Felix' art glass were Burg Rheinstein (Castle Rhinestone) and Schloss Stolzenfels. These were two of three particular castles on the Rhine (the third one is Burg Sooneck) which were rebuilt and reconstructed from the ruins by the Prussian Prince Friedrich and Crown Prince/King Friedrich Wilhelm IV between 1820 and 1860. That was a period of national renaissance — the culture and fine arts of the period being referred to as the "Biedermeier" style.

Finally, the prize piece of literature surfaced: from Werner Baus I received a copy of a 1908 Popper catalog page, and there was Felix! The Felix from Nevada City was identical to the catalog except, instead of the woman throwing roses, the catalog machine seems to show a costumed actor with moving arms. Indeed, the catalog description spends equally as much time describing the lighting effects as the complement of instrumentation.

Popper and Co.

The only existing large Poppers known to this author are the Gladiator and the Salon Orchestra at San Sylmar, California, the Luna in the Werner Baus collection, and the Iduna in the Doyle Lane collection.[1]

Popper and Co. was a leading automatic musical instrument firm from the 1890's to the 1930's. In the year 1911, (coincidentally Schreiber's Cafe was just opening and Felix was just two years old), Popper and Co. received an award for the quality of its music machines in Turin, Italy, as evidenced by the following article in *The Music Trades Review:*

GRAND PRIX FOR POPPER & CO.
Leipzig House Honored at Turin International Exhibition
Leipzig, Germany, October 15, 1911

Popper & Co., manufacturers of automatic instruments, has been awarded the Grand Prix at the International Exhibition in Turin, Italy, on account of first class construction and artistic abilities.

Since the foundation of the house, Popper & Co. has received the following awards:

Prize of Honor from the King of Saxony
Five State medals
A number of gold medals from numerous exhibitions.

From the *Encyclopedia of Automatic Instruments* (Bowers, The Vestal Press, 1972), we learn:

"The most spectacular of all Popper instruments were the huge piano orchestrions of the 1900-1920 era . . . these large Popper orchestrions are interesting for some of their unusual effects . . . the Con Amore orchestrion displayed tiny mechanical birds which fluttered and tweeted while the music roll rewound so the patrons would not lose attention during the normally silent rewinding period.

"The arrangements on Popper & Co. orchestrion rolls are excellent, for the most part, and collectors today consider Popper instruments to be among the finest orchestrions ever produced.

Copy of a 1908 Popper catalog page.

"These huge Popper orchestrions, once made by the hundreds, are exceedingly rare today."

Popper Roll Arrangements

As with many music machines, Popper roll arrangements had differing characteristics between early rolls (#1-1999 — circa 1908-1918) and later rolls (#3000 and 8000 series, post - World War I to the early 1930's).

The earlier rolls made more elaborate use of pipes for string, wind and reed instruments to achieve variations in musical "color" similar to actual orchestral arrangements. Apparently the earlier music arrangers were educated in real orchestra-arranging strategies. The fullness of the music contained in a Popper roll can really be appreciated on the Felix, particularly the way the rolls employ the clarinets, piccolos and bells.

In real orchestras, the piccolo is the shrillest of instruments. Its brilliant tone color is almost always used for picturing frenzied merriment, infernal rivalry or other climactic passages. Popper arrangements use the piccolos sparingly and only when powerful, bright highlights for musical peaks are needed. Without the piccolos, the Felix has variety and a normal range of expression, but when piccolos speak, fire rages and the blood rushes.

The clarinets set the Felix apart as they would in any machine because they add full, mellow color. The richness of the clarinets makes Felix' music sound full without being loud. Solos on the clarinets are very effective.

Popper arrangements use the viol da gamba (soft) and violin (loud) ranks as the workhorses of the music, as in a live orchestra. Expression is achieved either by playing the gambas only (which are soft and subtle) or the violins (louder) or both.

The cellos are really a bass extension of the violin rank. They are the base line of the orchestra and are used for depth and presence, never as a featured instrument.

The flutes are versatile and clear with medium power. They are also workhorses and used for livelier portions of the music. When used in combination with the violins, they mold another component of expression.

The bells or glockenspiel are metal bars struck with metal beaters. They have a bright, lingering sound, especially effective for tuned accents, and are used sparingly.

The piano in the Felix is powerful. The bass is rich, noticeable and almost always present. The piano bass and the cellos provide the bass component of the music. The piano treble is separated from the bass and is used for piano solos, for melody accompaniment, and at times is turned off to let some pipe rank or the xylophone perform a solo.

The xylophone is a 27-note, single-stroke instrument with wood bars and wood beaters. It has a great sound and is often used with popular songs. One later jazz roll actually plays *The William Tell Overture* on the xylophone — with great results.

The above comments apply to the original Popper factory arrangements, but not to the Belgian arrangements. The latter are quite different and far less complex. They play the Felix like a small band organ, using the flutes more often than the violins and almost ignoring the clarinets and cellos. In this author's opinion, the only redeeming quality of Belgian arrangements is that some tunes are well-known American songs that strike a familiar ring in the U.S. collector's ear.

Early original Popper rolls covered a broad range of classical, dance and novelty music. The classical songs are exciting and rich as are some waltzes; whereas other waltzes and the marches are repetitive and were clearly meant more for dancing than listening.

Happily, the Popper arrangements use only the instrumentation needed at the moment, rather than having to bear down on the listener with all it has all the time. The effect can be likened to a lightweight prizefighter — dancing, bobbing and seemingly able to invoke any of his resources at will, with grace and selectivity.

Later rolls have similar sparkle, but lack the fullness in the pipe section. These later arrangements catered to the changing nature of the machines being produced — with greater emphasis on piano and percussion (xylophone and drums) and less on wind and string instruments. The arrangements are often "jazzier" and less serious, but definitely fun to hear.

Fortunately, a surprising number of American tunes can be found in both early and late rolls, including Sousa marches, show tunes and even

Restorers Hayes McClaran (left) and Brad Reinhardt performing the final tuning before installing the facade.

familiar songs such as:
Broadway Melody
Fascination Waltz
Ramona
Alexander's Ragtime Band
Yes, Sir, That's My Baby

The layout (scale) used in Popper rolls maintained surprising consistency over the 25 to 30 years that rolls were produced, and the orchestra roll was compatible with all sizes of orchestrions. The only real change was the addition of piano-stack expression (high and low vacuum) on later machines which supplemented the loud/soft hammer-rail expression. According to Werner Baus, this extra level of piano expression was added when Popper had a falling out with Welte and brought out the Popper *Welt*, an expression piano/small orchestra competitor to Welte.

Another modest difference in the later jazzier machines is the addition of a woodblock. Care must be taken when playing early rolls on later machines since the hole used for the woodblock controlled a pipe register in earlier days.

The compatibility of Popper rolls across a broad line of orchestrions

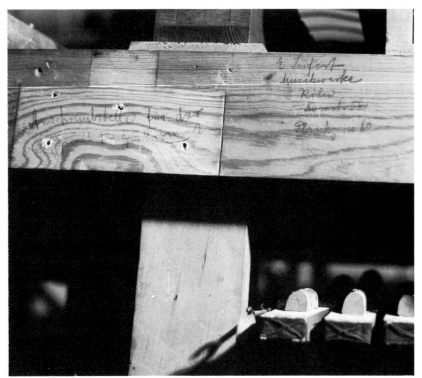

Some of the writings discovered inside the machine. Above the xylophone pneumatics: "E. Seifert Musikwerke, Koln (Cologne)?, Plangasse 60." This was probably a refurbisher who worked on Felix during the 1915-1918 period. Also found was the later (1944) inscription: "Refinished by C. Herschman and P. Schoenstein, May 1944 - 30 years after. (Our contribution to the art of organ building)."

Herschman and Schoenstein were famous San Francisco organ restorers who must have been the restorers Stagg hired.

has made it possible, through roll cutting, to preserve an extraordinarily broad range of music for the Popper orchestrion. In 1983 there were 200 different, hand-selected Popper rolls in the process of being recut on John Malone's versatile perforator. The project was sponsored by Werner Baus in Germany and Bob Gilson in Madison, Wisconsin. This author's seemingly endless chasing and auditing of roll collections provided over 550 rolls to choose from.

A Look Inside the Machine

In December of 1982 the restoration of Felix commenced in earnest. In the ensuing months, every corner of the machine was disassembled, investigated, cleaned, finished and reassembled by McClaran. At the end of a six-month effort, everything about the machine was understood.

The Europeans went about orchestrion building with some finesse because musical tastes leaned more toward the classical than in America, where music machines were made for less serious purposes. For instance, the piano in Felix is of high quality as is typical of German orchestras. Usually Feurich pianos were used, but in Felix' case, the only identifying mark on the piano plate is a Popper logo and the serial number 5022. The plate is identical to an Otero made by the Weber Company, so a good guess is that Popper did not make the piano itself.

Musically, the bass section of the piano has 29 notes, plus the lower five notes are octave coupled. This is where each of the notes in two different octaves is coupled so when a note in the coupled range is called for from the music roll, two notes actually play. This increases the bass richness and power, which is important in an orchestrion that typically depends heavily on the bass in the piano to carry the rhythm of a musical selection.

The treble section is also 29 notes. It is separate from the bass section so the treble can be turned off, thereby allowing a pipe rank or the xylophone to perform a solo in that note range, while the piano bass can continue playing the accompaniment.

Closely associated with the piano is the mandolin rail — literally a rail with leather fingers that are metal tipped and hang close to the piano strings.

The big 25″ bass drum is struck by a beater at the same time a genuine Chinese cymbal is struck. There are actually two bass drum beater pneumatics with which expression is achieved. If the roll calls for only one pneumatic, a softer sound is produced than if both contribute their forces simultaneously. Snare drum expression is achieved differently by pneumatically controlling how far the beater is from the drum surface at rest; the loudness is thereby controlled. A kettle drum sound is achieved with the addition of two tympani beaters poised over the bass drum.

Accenting is provided by a triangle, a crash cymbal and a 15-note set of tuned orchestra bells. The crash cymbal is the same Chinese cymbal but can also be hit with a felt-covered beater, making a more fully-developed and longer-lasting crash than normal. A third level of cymbal expression is achieved by both beaters hitting the cymbal which results in a noticeable crash. Additional tuned percussion is provided by a 27-note wood xylophone which is often used for solos.

The pipe section in Felix incorporates an interesting and versatile range of reed, flute and stringed instruments. The pipes in an orchestrion are identical to the pipes in an organ. Five of the six pipe ranks which Felix has are of the *flue* variety. Flue pipes are of the whistle or recorder type whereby air passes through a narrow aperture or flue. The flute is in constant service in the orchestra, taking the melody for the woodwind group just as the violin does for the strings. Often it is combined with the violin for this purpose. This is no doubt the basis for so many orchestrions with one or two pipe ranks always having either flutes or violins.

Felix' flutes are a wooden, harmonic rank surpassed in pitch only by

213

the piccolo (short for flauto piccolo or "little flute"), which is a half-sized flute used chiefly for special effects. Felix' piccolos are of the unusual *philomela* type. They are open pipes with a double mouth, resulting in a high-pitched piccolo that is even more differentiated from the flutes than usual.

Flue pipes are of three classes: diapason, flute and string. Diapason is a generic term for a family of flue pipes that only exists on an organ and has no real instrument counterpart. Felix only has pipes that are imitative of real instruments. This fact, plus the presence of a piano, are the reasons for it being called an orchestrion rather than an organ. For example, three of its flue ranks are of the string type: violins, cellos and gambas. The violins are wood pipes registered separately from the cellos. The cellos are a short rank extending down into the 4″ range of bass pipe.

On the other hand, the gambas are a longer rank of softly-voiced metal pipes. Gamba is an abbreviation for viol da gamba, (literally "leg viol") referring to the fact that all instruments of this type are held on or between the knees.

The clarinets are a completely different pipe rank operating with wind passing over a beating reed and a cylindrical or conical resonator. Clarinets are a mellow reed pipe usually appearing only in large orchestras, and unheard of on American orchestrions.

Expression (loud and soft) is provided in various ways, including a traditional piano loud/soft pedal which controls the position of the hammer-rail percussion expression (as previously described), and overall expression from the swell shutters on the top of the case. Swell shutters are louvers which open and close partially or fully, depending on the length of the control hole in the music roll. These infinitely variable swell shades are uniquely characteristic of certain German machines. A great range of expression is also implemented by careful selection of pipe ranks that are turned on at any point. The piccolos are an expression device all by themselves in that when they are on, they seem to double the volume of the entire orchestra.

European vs. American

I have already mentioned some differences between European and American machines in several passages of this article. It is fascinating that American manufacturers were consistent in their strategy to produce music machines that were truly fun for listening as opposed to the fairly prevalent European strategy of concentrating on more musical realism and intricacy. American machines would usually permit the listener to peer through clear gaps in the art glass to see the instruments play (all part of the fun), whereas European machines were closed up tight as a drum and animated art glass effects were used to entertain the listener.

The most dramatic differences between American and European machines can be found in the roll arrangements. Most American roll arrangements are centered around the piano and music that typified player pianos. Controls for other instruments are added to the basic piano arrangements. Pipes are turned on and off for variety rather than for the aesthetics of the tune. They are snappy, popular and toe-tapping. German arrangements squeeze the most out of the machinery with a balanced demand for the instrumentation when they are needed in accordance for a more faithful rendition of the original arrangement. Classical and dance music is dominant, which means it is less piano dependent.

As a comparison, take the Cremona J, a top-of-the-line American machine with a complement of instruments identical to the Popper Rex (a Felix minus all but the violins, the flute pipe ranks and the orchestra bells). The Cremona J plays the Cremona M roll that is arranged to solo on the pipes and the xylophone. Listening to the Cremona J and the Popper Rex side by side will separate collectors into two definite groups. There is no right or wrong, just two different styles of music. The American machine was designed to entertain people in saloons with a fun, piano honky-tonk sound, whereas the European machines were meant to appeal to the more refined tastes of their continental patrons.

As a collector, I would never choose one over the other. If a collection can have two principal music machines, it should have one of each. Rarely will you find good American popular music on a European machine, and you'll never listen to the American machine for original classical music.

The base by itself weighs 1250 pounds. All music collectors should have #77 as a friend.

The four Schreiber daughters visiting the Popper Felix in July 1983 and again hearing it play, 60 years after it originally arrived in Nevada City.

Ready for the final touches.

Felix Restored

In July of 1983, Popper Felix' restoration was complete. While the machine was being "shaken down" in Fresno in preparation for delivery, Ernie Schreiber's daughters: Gertrude Murray, Elsie Sharpe, Eleanor Putnam, Louise Geddes and their families were invited from Nevada City to see and hear a distant memory — after a 40-year absence! Once again Felix delighted its former owners by lighting up — as only it could — while providing its best performance since leaving the factory some 70 years earlier.

McClaran and his assistant, Brad Reinhardt, had outdone themselves. Typical of the few top-quality restorers in this field, they felt they had left a permanent piece of themselves somewhere inside Felix' wondrous innards. As McClaran said: "You can't get through a project like this without having some feeling for the machine and what it once represented. Nearly every glue joint, every valve (all 311 of them) and every piano hammer needed redoing. After years of languishing in a baking-hot shed, Felix needed to be completely disassembled and rebuilt as it was originally done at the factory."

The restoration took 23-weeks worth of effort, including deciphering the vast and curious electrical system that controlled all of the lighting and animation. Fortunately for restorers, Renner's of Germany, a piano supply house, stocks the exact and pertinent parts for all aspects of the German piano.

When it came time for Felix to leave its restoration berth in Fresno, it was McClaran himself who rented a truck and drove it to the author's home in Michigan. "The machine is restored to the best possible condition and the case has a fine furniture, hand-rubbed finish. There's no way I could bear to see someone else handle something this large and awkward with the care it should get," declared McClaran.

On a sunny July day, the Popper Felix was installed in our living room — the only room with a ceiling high enough. I asked my wife (who is not a music collector, but who is very understanding) what she thought of the 11' high decoration in our midst. She replied wryly, "Oh, it's useful to show friends that clearly I'm married to a crazy person!"

A Collector's Dream

From my perspective, the Felix has come a long way and is now properly restored to play for nickels once again. Its exquisite condition assures its permanence in the world of mechanical music.

The hunt, the discovery, the acquisition, the restoration, the hearing of the first note, the historical research, the scouring for original music, and the preservation of a genuine artifact from the California gold rush territory surely justify the story of the Popper Felix as a classic American saga. &

FILMS, FOLLIES,
AND FOTOPLAYERS*

J. Ronald Bopp

ℐN the early 20th century the halls of vaudeville, stage shows, and the Follies underwent a change that would affect the mechanical-music industry much as Prohibition was to change the coin-operated piano industry in the 20's. Something new had come! The buildings were becoming packed with patrons who were anxious to enjoy the newest form of entertainment.

What was the new revelation that was to join vaudeville and the Follies, and later to replace entirely those wonderful stage shows? The Silent Films! Silent films, through advanced technology, were able to project on the screen pre-rehearsed plays and entertainment that could be shown over and over to the ever-growing audiences.

Films and Follies

The silent films were graced with interesting characters such as Buster Keaton, who always maintained a stoic, deadpan expression, no matter what happened; the Keystone Cops, who endlessly tried to uphold justice; Harold Lloyd, the fearless comic who performed his own stunts; Fatty Arbuckle, who directed as well as acted; Mary Pickford, the first great lady of the screen, who, along with her husband Douglas Fairbanks, became good friends with Charlie Chaplin, perhaps the greatest comic of all.

Early silent films were shown in converted vaudeville houses, but soon theaters were especially built for this new form of entertainment. These early movie houses were labeled "Nickelodeons." "Nickel" was for the admission price, and "odeon" is the Greek word for theater. Erroneously, the term "nickelodeon" has been applied to coin-operated pianos, but in the history of early movie theaters we can see how this term has been used both ways.

Owners of silent-movie theaters soon realized that music added to the film made the shows more enjoyable and brought in larger crowds. Most theaters had pianos to add that special touch, and piano players were pressed into service. The period from 1900 to 1910 coincided with the development and growth of the coin-operated piano business, and it was a natural result that coin-operated pianos began to appear in the pits of nickelodeon theaters. This form of musical entertainment was certainly

---

* Presented at the 31st Annual Meeting of the Musical Box Society International.

convenient, but no control could be exercised over the type of music played, so that often a rag or waltz would be heard with a somber setting or a melancholy tune would accompany a saloon shoot-out.

Ideally, an orchestra in the pit of a theater could provide suitable music for any scene that was shown on the screen. With only a minimal charge of a nickel for admission, however, the cost of such sophisticated music was prohibitive, and other sources needed to be found. The expense of an orchestra, the lack of control of coin-operated pianos, and the unreliability of the piano player (as well as limitations in the effects he could provide) forced the industry to find another way to accompany the silent movies.

The Photoplayers

The early teens of the century found several manufacturers of coin-operated pianos experimenting with devices to place in the theater pits. Components used for coin-operated pianos and orchestrions were easily adapted, and often were identical. Because of the nature of the orchestra pit in front of the screen, these musical machines were necessarily low in profile. Several manufacturers of photoplayers emerged at this time. It is interesting how similar some were, yet others were unique. Dave Bowers, in his article "Theatre Photoplayers" (Summer 1970 *M.B.S.I. Bulletin,* Vol. XVI, No. 5, pages 202-214), lists 15 manufacturers:

> American Photo Player Company
> Berry-Wood Piano Player Company
> Ludwig Hupfeld
> Link Piano and Organ Company
> Marquette Piano Company
> Mills Novelty Company
> Nelson-Wiggen Piano Company
> North Tonawanda Musical Instrument Works
> Operators Piano Company
> Peerless Piano Player Company
> J. D. Philipps and Son
> Piano Player Manufacturing Company
> J. P. Seeburg Piano Company
> M. Welte and Sons
> Rudolph WurliTzer Company

Recently, another has been documented, the Watson Piano Company, of St. Joseph, Missouri. Their photoplayer, the Watson Photoplayer, is a single-side-chest instrument. A surviving specimen is currently in a collection in Arizona.

Probably the most active in production of photoplayers for American theaters were the Operators Piano Company, the Rudolph WurliTzer Company, the J. P. Seeburg Company, and the American Photo Player Company. The Reproduco was the Operators Piano Company's main entry into the photoplayer business. These pianos usually had no side chest. They contained a twin roll frame, along with three ranks of pipes. Rolls for the Reproduco were usually of 10-tune length and played popular music. Some 700 theaters were said to have installed this all-purpose instrument.

The Rudolph WurliTzer Company produced a wide array of instruments. WurliTzer photoplayers were referred to as "One-Man Motion Picture Orchestras," and were suitable for movie houses of modest size. Accurate records show that over 2,200 WurliTzer photoplayers were sold from 1913 to 1927, as listed below.

Year	Units Sold	Year	Units Sold
1913	317	1921	108
1914	392	1922	50
1915	357	1923	78
1916	222	1924	26
1917	118	1925	9
1918	110	1926	5
1919	194	1927	2
1920	235	Total	2,223

WurliTzer photoplayers were equipped to play three types of rolls: WurliTzer Automatic Player Piano rolls, WurliTzer Concert PianOrchestra rolls, and 88-note player-piano rolls. Automatic Player Piano rolls and Concert PianOrchestra rolls allowed the instrument to take advantage of the perforations for traps and instrument changes. The 88-note-roll option allowed the operator to add the desired musical effects for any type of scene. These machines were made to compete with the American Photo Player Company's instruments, and most were marketed on the West Coast, where that firm was located.

Like the Rudolph WurliTzer Company, the J. P. Seeburg Piano Company diversified into several areas of the automatic-music trade and had their own line of photoplayers. Several styles were offered, from single piano to piano with two side chests. These instruments used Seeburg orchestrion rolls — some used the common "G" roll, and some the "H" or "MSR" rolls. Seeburg advertisements were clever, and scattered throughout their sales brochure were slogans meant to sell their products:

"SEEBURG value quickly seen
As music changes with the screen"

"SEEBURG music full of life —
Instant change from drum to fife"

"Combination changed at will
Keeps SEEBURG hearers all a-thrill"

"Variety and sweetest tone
Makes the SEEBURG better known"

"Without the trouble to arrange
The SEEBURG makes an instant change"

These slogans would have been equally appropriate if the name of any of the manufacturers in the list given earlier were substituted for "SEEBURG."

American Photo Player Company

Our main interest in this paper is the Fotoplayer produced by the American Photo Player Company. Along with the frenzy in the early teens to produce a machine to accompany photoplays were the efforts of the Van Valkenburg brothers of Berkeley, California (see Figure 1). Their accomplishments were discovered by Harold J. Werner, a piano salesman, who formed, along with them, the American Photo Player Company in 1914. Production was at a Berkeley plant, as well as at a second factory in Van Nuys, California.

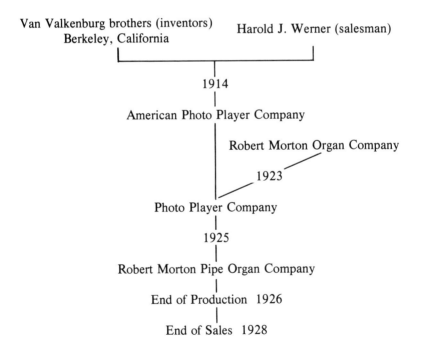

Van Valkenburg brothers (inventors)
Berkeley, California

Harold J. Werner (salesman)

1914

American Photo Player Company

Robert Morton Organ Company

1923

Photo Player Company

1925

Robert Morton Pipe Organ Company

End of Production 1926

End of Sales 1928

Figure 1. Evolution of the American Photo Player Company

222

Production went well in the teens, but in the early 20's sales dropped, and in 1923 a merger occurred with the Robert Morton Organ Company to form the Photo Player Company. In 1925 the Robert Morton Pipe Organ Company was formed, and the entire production of Fotoplayers was moved to the Van Nuys plant.

The end of production was in 1926, and the last sale was recorded in 1928. Looking at the sales record of the Rudolph WurliTzer Company (given earlier), we see a similar story. The early 20's showed a sharp decline in production, and the advent of the talking movies in the late 20's left no need for these interesting music-makers.

Several models of Fotoplayers were produced. The larger the style number, the larger and more complex was the Fotoplayer. The style 15, or Fotopiano, was made in limited numbers. It had a twin roll frame; it is not known whether any additional instruments were included.

The Style 20 Fotoplayer (Figure 2) has a single side chest. The twin roll frame allowed one type of mood music to be played while the operator was rewinding a second roll or putting the next roll in place. The anatomy of the single side chest shows three ranks of pipes—flute, violin, and violoncello—along with the percussion and sound effects.

Fotoplayer percussion and special sound effects were controlled by push tabs, pedals, telegraph keys, and leather cords with wooden handles. A diagram by Joe Rinaudo of the upper piano case details the use of the tabs,

Figure 2. Style 20 Fotoplayer with single side chest.

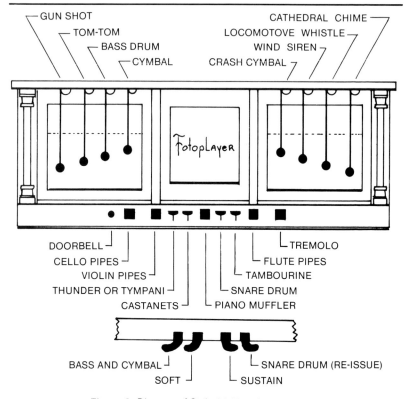

Figure 3. Diagram of Style 20 Fotoplayer controls.

pulls, and pedals of a Style 20 Fotoplayer (Figure 3). A Fotoplayer operator had to think quickly in a fast scene in order to prevent confusion.

An advertisement (Figure 4) from *The Fotoplayer—The Voice of the Screen* revealed other features of the Style 20, pointing out "its compactness and efficiency." In extrapolating from available WurliTzer data we find that their most popular style was Style G, a piano with a single side chest, so we would assume that the comparable model in the American Photo Player Line, the Style 20, would also have been quite popular.

At this point it would be interesting to compare the Style 20 Fotoplayer with similar models by other makers—the Rudolph WurliTzer Company Style G, the J. P. Seeburg Company Style W, and the Piano Player Manufacturing Company Style E.

All have single side chests. The Style 20 Fotoplayer was the most expensive (1920 prices) but had more percussion effects. Moreover, versatility was increased with the Style 20 because any 88-note roll could be played on the twin roll frame. WurliTzer's Style G also offered a twin roll frame, but its music would be limited to the orchestration on the roll.

Manufacturers	Style	Instrumentation	Percussion	Rolls	Prices
American Photo Player Co.	20	Piano, Flute, Violin, & Cello	16 effects	88-note Player Piano	$3,650
Rudolph WurliTzer Company	G	Piano, Mandolin, Flute, & Violin	8 effects	Automatic Player Piano	$2,100
J. P. Seeburg Co.	W	Piano, Mandolin, Flute, & Violin	9 effects	"G" Orchestrion	$3,500
Piano Player Mfg. Co.	E	Piano, Mandolin, Flute, Violin, & Xylophone	10 effects	?	?

The Style 25, a double-side-chest machine, was even more versatile. Sets of orchestra bells and sleigh bells were added. Also, the twin side chests are narrow enough to be pushed through a regular doorway, something that just can't be done with the Style 20 or with the larger Fotoplayers.

Styles 30, 35, 40, and 45 were increasingly larger units, each adding more pipes, reeds, and percussion effects.

The largest Fotoplayer, the Style 50, measured 21 feet in width and included 412 pipes, 195 reeds, xylophone, orchestra bells, and 26 percussion effects. With a style 50, we get not only a plain pistol shot, but pistol shots or a Gatling-gun effect; the snare drum has a jazz effect; five chimes are offered instead of one; and the horses' hoofs are improved, whatever that means.

Fortunately for collectors and historians today, literature regarding the American Photo Player Company is available in reprint form (*The Fotoplayer—The Voice of the Screen* and *Installation, Care and Operation of the Fotoplayer*). The latter includes details on the anatomy of these units. In addition, details of the case placement and wind pressures are available, and restorers of such machines can benefit from this information. In this literature it is pointed out that "The Fotoplayer is the first instrument that is manufactured for the purpose of describing motion pictures with appropriate music," and that the American Photo Player Company had a style to "fit your pit."

Music for the Photoplays

In considering silent movies and the photoplayers, we must also consider the music available for their use. Music for piano players was plentiful, and even textbooks on the subject were advertised in trade journals. Fiestyle Piano Organ Sheets were laid out on one page for easy use and had instructions as to when to add percussion effects. Other material for the piano player could be found in specially prepared music, such as "The B. F. Wood Collection of Characteristic Selections for the Motion Pictures" or

"The Sam Fox Collection of Motion Picture Music," which included such titles as "Hurry," "Dramatic Tension," and "Storm Scene."

As mentioned before, orchestrated rolls that were produced by the Rudolph WurliTzer and J. P. Seeburg companies were often used for their coin-operated pianos, and, indeed, their primary intention was for use in these instruments. Such music tends to be mechanical and, more often than

---

FOTOPLAYER STYLE 20

THE Style 20 FOTOPLAYER is a marvel of up-to-date technical construction, designed and built expressly to meet all the needs of motion picture houses of smaller seating capacity.

A special feature of the Style 20 is its compactness and efficiency.

SPECIFICATIONS FOR FOTOPLAYER—Style No. 20

Length, 10 ft.   Width, 3 ft. 1½ in.   Height, 5 ft.
Piano extends 8 inches

High Grade Player Piano—Double Tracker Device

Tremolo	Pipes for Orchestral Effects:
Piano Muffler	Violin, Cello, Flute

TRAPS AND EFFECTS AS FOLLOWS:

Bass Drum	Fire Gong
Pistol Shot	Tambourine
Cymbal	Castanets
Tom-Tom	Klaxon
Thunder or Tympani	Chinese Crash Cymbal
Snare Drum	Steamboat Whistle or
Door Bell	Locomotive Whistle
Telephone Bell	Wind Siren
	Cathedral Chime

The FOTOPLAYER is constructed of the finest hard woods throughout and the workmanship is the best.

The instrument is guaranteed both by manufacturer and dealer.

Figure 4. Specifications for Style 20 Fotoplayer.

not, did not pertain to what was on the screen when used as accompaniment.

Concurrent with the production of the American Photo Player and Rudolph WurliTzer companies' photoplayers was the development of music rolls expressly made for photoplay use. The most popular music-roll company was the Filmusic Company of Los Angeles; this firm produced

Picturolls. A reprint of a 1918 catalogue of Picturolls reveals many types. Each roll is described, and different situations are listed in which this particular music could be used. A well-prepared operator of a photoplayer would have several rolls on hand, previously selected and laid out on top of his piano. Instructions for changing tempos to suit various scenes would be noted on the rolls.

Even in the Fotoplayer literature itself, the types of music rolls were indicated, which made the choice much easier for the operator. A look at several Picturolls will show us the kinds of mood music available: Number 30, "Good Bye," was appropriate for farewell scenes; Number 49, "Sorrow Theme," was useful for sadness, grief, and depression; Number 100, "Gruesome, Mysterioso," could put patrons on the edges of their seats; and Number 5, "Mobs, Riots, and Fights," is self-explanatory.

Summary

Where were the photoplayers then, and where are they now? Photoplayers were sold primarily for use with silent movies, although other uses have been noted. It has been reported that occasionally these instruments were sold to mortuaries and to drinking establishments. An interview with Irwin Davis, a piano tuner now in his mid-seventies, revealed an original location of a tavern where he and his father serviced a large photoplayer.

Today, photoplayers are scarce—scarce as can be, when you realize that seven to eight thousand are said to have been built. It is easy to understand why the scarcity, however. The use that photoplayers underwent was tremendous—eight to twelve hours a day was common, and some reports indicate up to 24-hour usage. When something broke down it was patched up, but not necessarily correctly. When talking movies came, the photoplayers became useless. They were large and heavy, and often in disarray. It was easy to decide to haul them off, junk them, or simply use the cases for extending the stage; as a consequence, very few have survived.

Of the thousand to fifteen hundred American Photo Player Company units estimated to have been produced, only 18 to 22 are known to exist today. Bob Ayres, a historian of this company, has confirmed four Style 20's, three Style 25's, one Style 30, one Style 35, four Style 40's and one Style 50 in existence. He is aware of one Fotoplayer that was dumped into a river and one that was "cannon-balled" when a theater was demolished recently.

The Follies and vaudeville, the silent movies and the amazing rugged photoplayer are all things of the past. The Follies are gone except in memory, but fortunately some of the silent movies have been preserved for our pleasure today. Although the photoplayers are represented by only a handful scattered throughout the country, one has to marvel at the versatility and endurance of these music machines and be thankful that the few remaining still continue to provide the kind of music to set the mood. ■■

CORRECTION

$\mathcal{I}$N Ron Bopp's article on photoplayers in the last issue, there was an omission in the next to last paragraph on page 14, where the still-extant Fotoplayers are listed. The Style 45 instruments were unfortunately left out, and the sentence should read: "Bob Ayres, a historian of this company, has confirmed four Style 20's, three style 25's, one Style 30, one Style 35, four Style 40's, four Style 45's, and one Style 50 in existence." Apologies to Ron, Mr. Ayres, and the owners of the four Style 45's. ∎

Large Organs

AN INTERVIEW

Arthur Bursens and Arthur Prinsen

*M*ORE material for the history-in-our-time department of the *Bulletin*, this was sent in by Claes Friberg, who accompanied the Swedish television people to the interview, portions of which were included in the movie he showed in Saddle Brook last September. We would like to thank Mr. Friberg for having this material translated from the original Flemish by Miss Bente Howard and for making it available to us. Mr. Arthur Bursens, called the dean of Belgian dance-organ builders, was being questioned by Mr. Arthur Prinsen, a well known Belgian arranger of book-music.

Q: Mr. Bursens, at what age did you start building organs or helping to do so?
A: Well, my father was an organ builder, so I was quite naturally involved in it. When I was 14, I left school and started to work.

Q: You mean that at the age of 14 you were working with your father at the factory?
A: Oh, yes.

Q: Your father was already an organ builder at that time?
A: Yes.

Q: And was there any special reason for your starting to work there at that age – was there any particular explanation for this? Did your parents decide it (that is, were you forced), or did you like the work, or what reason did you have?
A: It used to be the rule that one started to work with one's father after leaving school.

Q: It was then . . . how shall I put it?
A: One had grown up with it.

Q: Because your father had a certain occupation, you automatically ended up with the same kind of work when you had to start working?
A: Of course.

Q: And did you already like it – making instruments like this?
A: Yes, we had to start working even before leaving school. When we came home, we had to help fix pipes, and things like that.

Q: That means you were fairly experienced before you really started?
A: Yes. I had to work for my living.

Q: Which were the so-called 'golden years' for the enterprise?
A: It has always been up and down. There have been periods when we had as much work as we could do, and then there have been bad times. Before the War in 1914, we often went to the village or parochial fairs, and then we could not relax very much. We had a cart and a horse, and went to Brussels and everywhere.

Q: As such, it was a flourishing enterprise before World War I. Those were the best years?
A: Yes, they were the best. The War broke out, and then, of course, it became . . .

Q: Before the War, before World War I, then . . .
A: Yes, then we did a good business.

Q: And is there anything from those good years that you remember especially well?
A: We needed two horses at one stage and were allowed to buy another in the middle of the summer.

Q: Just to carry the organs? Does that mean that transports took place exclusively with horses at that time?
A: Yes.

Q: Did that always turn out successfully? Did anything ever happen?
A: Well, when we had to go across water and it was low tide, we had to ask some men from a boat to help us, and the sailors pulled the cart. They put something around it and pulled it up with a rope.

Q: That means it was too heavy for the horses alone to pull up the organs? How much did such an organ weigh?
A: 2000-2200 kilos, approximately.

Q: That was a lot. And you had to load and unload this yourself?
A: Yes, but the organs were dismounted, of course.

Q: Certainly, but the case itself was in one piece.
A: A case like that weighs 700-800 kilos in itself.

Q: It must have been a very hard way to earn your living, then?
A: Yes.

Q: It has become totally different now, has it not?
A: My father had an automatic clown that could play music while it did all sorts of things if you pressed a button.

Q: A sort of robot?
A: Yes. It could walk forwards and backwards.

Q: Just by the use of registers?
A: Yes, that was what made the clown work. Once when we were in Reepermunde at a fair, we were in a room on the first floor, and at two o'clock the room was completely full.

Q: Was there so great an interest?
A: And in Vilvoorde we had to lock the clown in because people were only looking and not dancing.

Q: Then there were both advantages and disadvantages involved. Approximately how many organs have been built, let us say, from your father's time up through the time you have been building organs?
A: Approximately a thousand.

Q: A thousand organs from both of you. That is a good many. Do you have a predilection for any special kind of organ? Can you say, "I like that organ best," or, "I prefer to make this particular kind of organ," or is there anything special you can say about a certain kind of organ?
A: Not really.

Q: You like all organs equally?
A: Usually they are all good.

Q: Yes, I think that is correct.
A: But the best organs, as to tone, are Marenghis. The tone and the way of playing were best with Marenghi. They were above all others.

Q: Marenghis seem to you to be the best organs ever built?
A: Yes. They have the best tone.

Q: Now, may I ask how old you are?
A: I am 83.

Q: You are 83, approaching 84, and you are still working every day?
A: Yes, from 8 o'clock until 5:30.

Q: Every day? Then you must be very happy with your work.
A: Yes. I do it for my pleasure and because I can't sit still.

Q: You are working for your pleasure – and do you intend to build even more organs?
A: Certainly.

Q: You will keep on working as long as you can?
A: Yes. We will have to see . . .

Q: But you intend to work for a long time yet?
A: Yes.

Q: I really do admire you – to be able to make such instruments at your age. The last organ we saw – what kind of organ is that?
A: It is a . . .

Q: How many keys does it have?
A: Seventy.

Q: And is it an organ that is made to order? Or have you just made it like that?
A: No, it is in a way an order. They can come to hear it, and if they want it, that's good; but if they don't, it will not be standing here for very long.

Q: There are always prospective purchasers?
A: Yes.

Q: But the organ was originally made to order?
A: Yes, but I did not want any deposit on it.

Q: You will finish the organ, and if the customer is content, he'll take it. If he isn't, somebody else will have the possibility of getting it. To you, it is more love for your work than . . . what shall I say . . . ?
A: If you are not interested in your work it has no value.

Q: Yes. To you it is no longer a question of money; it is craftsmanship, where love for your organs is the most important thing – that is what you live for. I congratulate you, Mr. Bursens. We hope that you will long be able to build organs, for we have already heard one of your organs play; we are very pleased with it, and we hope to be able to hear many more of your works.
A: Yes, I think you will.

Q: Thank you very much.
A: *Merci.* ▪▪

Mechanical Music
at the
Circus World Museum

William O. Winston, Jr.

$\mathcal{I}$N the world of the circus, there is one element that brings all of the glamour and excitement together - and that is music. During a performance, the circus band plays music that is appropriate for each act, and as a part of some circus shows, the music of a calliope may be heard. In the circus street parades of the past, besides the brass bands and the calliopes, there were a number of other music makers, some of them mechanically operated.

The Circus World Museum in Baraboo, Wisc., is one of the most unusual attractions in the United States. It is located on the former winter quarters of the Ringling Brothers' Circus before it absorbed the Barnum and Bailey Circus to become 'The Greatest Show on Earth.' Here visitors get a presentation of real circus lore. They can see a circus parade, view a large collection of colorful circus wagons, and even attend a live circus performance under a big top.

Music plays an extremely important part at the museum. There is the rousing, screechy music of the calliopes, and the band music that accompanies the show under the big top. Besides this, there are other circus-related musical instruments, including some that are self-playing -- four band organs and a mechanically operated calliope.

The largest band organ in the collection is a Wurlitzer Model 165, which was donated to the museum by Skerbeck Shows, a Wisconsin-based traveling carnival. Organs of this type were not usually associated with circuses, but were more likely to be found with carnivals and at amusement parks. This instrument does, however, help create the atmosphere of the general world of amusement of which the circus is a part and plays daily in a large room in one of the museum's five exhibit buildings. Adjacent to the big Wurlitzer is an informative wall display that gives an explanation of automatic music and shows the band organ's part in circus history. Visitors can also step behind the large band organ and see the operation of its duplex tracker frame and its pneumatic system.

In this same room are three manually played instruments. These are an air-operated calliope, a Una-Fon, and a set of shaker chimes. The air calliope is much easier to play and has more musical range than the louder steam calliope. The Una-Fon's sounds come from a series of tuned electric bells. The shaker chimes are played by moving handles back and forth, which causes a sound something like that of a marimba. All of these instruments

WURLITZER MODEL-165, LARGEST BAND ORGAN AT THE MUSEUM.

SMALL HERSCHELL-SPILLMAN IN CENTER OF PORTABLE CAROUSEL.

added an interesting musical touch to the earlier circus parades.

Every day during the museum's operating season, a small circus parade moves around the grounds. As part of this parade, there is a glittering circus wagon pulled by a team of horses. The wagon carries a military band organ that features 13 exposed brass trumpets. It was originally built by the DeKleist firm of North Tonawanda, New York, for C. W. Parker's carousel company, and has a single tracker mechanism that uses a Wurlitzer 125 roll.

In the days when large tented circuses traveled throughout the country, the carousel was, many times, a part of the circus midway and still is a part of the carnival. These small portable merry-go-rounds, or Jennys, as they are sometimes called, lack the elaborate ornamentation of their larger counterparts. One of these Jennys, which can be ridden by visitors, is part of the action at the museum. The music for this carousel is supplied by a small but powerful Herschell-Spillman band organ, playing from a 10-tune Wurlitzer roll. Like the DeKleist organ used in the parade, this instrument sports a set of exposed brass trumpets.

ARTIZAN BAND ORGAN WITH ITS ELECTRIC LIGHTS TURNED ON.

The museum's 75 colorful circus parade-wagons, the world's largest collection of this type, are housed in a huge 400-foot long building. At one end of the building is a band organ with a heavily decorated facade, which is trimmed with lights. Donated by the late Samuel Costa of Fond du Lac, Wisc., this organ is of Artizan origin, but was equipped by its former owner

AIR-CALLIOPE WAGON, ORIGINALLY OWNED BY KEN MAYNARD WILD WEST SHOW, AT A LAKE-FRONT CELEBRATION IN MILWAUKEE.

INTERIOR OF KEN MAYNARD WAGON, SHOWING CALLIOPE. THE WORD 'CLOSE' WAS TO REMIND THE OPERATOR TO CLOSE THE COVER OVER THE KEYS TO PREVENT DUST FROM ENTERING THE INSTRUMENT DURING TRANSPORTATION.

with a duplex tracker frame using Wurlitzer 125 rolls.

Also in this building is a wagon once owned by the Ken Maynard Wild West Show. This wagon houses a National calliope that is air powered and may be played either manually or with a perforated roll.

Although its source of music had been removed before it came to Baraboo, the Orchest Melochor wagon is still interesting. Ornamented with carvings of musical instruments, paintings, and convex mirrors, it was built for P. T. Barnum in the late 1880's and once contained a large mechanical organ called 'The Golden Organ of Vienna.'

ORCHEST MELOCHORE WAGON, WITH ELABORATE DECORATION.

Adding their hooting, blasting sounds to all this other music are the museum's two steam-powered calliopes. Daily concerts are given on one of these instruments, and the music can be heard all over the museum grounds, as well as throughout a good portion of Baraboo.

What has been described above is only a part of what can be experienced by a visit to the Circus World Museum, which is open seven days a week, from mid-May to mid-September. The calliopes, band organs, and other instruments that have been preserved there provide an important element of music as part of the 'glorious, glamorous, glittering' world of the circus. ■ ■

A GAVIOLI HISTORY

Robert G. Miller

𝒥N the agricultural town of Modena in north-central Italy, Giacomo Gavioli was born in 1786. Gavioli distinguished himself for his intricate clockwork mechanisms and remarkable bell making. In 1807 his son Ludovico I was born. As the son of a renowned mechanical master, it was natural that Ludovico became learned in the trade. In time the father-son team became famous for fine musical clocks. One of their major accomplishments was the design and construction of the tower clock for the 285-foot campanile in Modena's Piazza Grande.

Ludovico I also designed and produced small barrel organs. His marriage produced two sons — Anselme, born in 1828, and Claude, born in 1831. The family business involved all three men and as their business grew, they decided to leave their pastoral environs for the excitement of Paris, known at that time as the center of art and music. Chopin, Liszt, Rossini and Verdi all had preceded the Gaviolis in moving to this fashionable capitol. The formal organization was established by Ludovico in 1843 and located at 3 Rue D'aligre, Paris.

The three Gaviolis experimented endlessly with new instrument design. They created automata of great ingenuity to meet the demand for these popular novelties. One of their automata was a figure of King David playing a real harp. Unfortunately, this valuable piece was lost while on tour with a traveling showman and was never returned to the Gaviolis.

In 1850 Ludovico II was born to Anselme and his wife. During this year the factory moved to Rue de Citeaux, Paris. The firm expanded their interests to include wind instruments. The Gaviolis created a mechanical flute for which they received a gold medal at the General Exhibition of Paris in 1855. In the 1850's Claude was given management of the firm. During this period an employee embezzled a large sum of money, causing financial hardship to them. Also during this era the Gavioli firm developed a mechanical instrument known as a Panharmonic. This provoked the interest of Rossini, who was a friend of the family.

The Gavioli firm was well established producing larger barrel-operated instruments by the year 1857. The growing market for these items necessitated a move in 1861 to a spacious building at the now famous corner 175 bis Rue de Bercy and 44 Quai de la Rappe. A limited company was formed

Figure 1. A small organ at the Gavioli shops ready for delivery.

Figure 2. A very Germanic Waldkirch Gavioli in play. *Photo courtesy M. Van Boxtel.*

241

with the expansion and Monsieur P.C.V. Iver, who invested substantial capital, became the main shareholder. The year 1863 saw the eldest son Anselme now heading the firm which was renamed Gavioli et Cie. The firm continued to win awards for their mechanical instruments.

During the Franco-Prussian war, a move to Alsace was undertaken with the loss of considerable assets resulting from war damage.

The firm returned to Paris in 1871 and soon resumed a thriving business producing barrel organs. In 1875 both Giacomo, 89, and his son Ludovico I, 68, died. Anselme, Claude and 25-year old Ludovico II carried on the business. The Gavioli organs became more ornate and the harmonic frein, a new feature, was offered in 1878. All the Gaviolis were good musicians; Claude and Ludovico II were noted for their composition and arranging. Besides organs, barrel pianos, many of them coin operated, were also being produced. The Gavioli name was very well known throughout the trade.

Into the 1880's the instruments became more elaborate, and in 1892 the most important advance in mechanical organ design was developed by Anselme — the perforated cardboard music book in place of the pinned cylinder. This concept stemmed from an 18th century principle which was used to operate the famous Jacquard lace-making loom. Anselme's application to the design of a mechanical-pneumatic key frame revolutionized the organ industry, making the pinned barrel, with its severe limitations in musical length and repetoire, obsolete. The firm produced a wide range of book organs which ranged from 35 to 89 keys.

Toward the end of the 19th century, the firm entered its golden period, which witnessed the production of some of the finest organs and facades ever made. The art-nouveau styles were truly remarkable for the high caliber of design and execution. Their 89-key instruments were now top-of-the-line. Branch offices extended to Manchester, Barcelona, Antwerp and New York. Gavioli was riding the crest of an enormous and well-deserved success and was truly world-wide in its organization with factories in Paris and a new one in Waldkirch, Germany which opened in 1900. Richard Bruder, from Gebruder Bruder, was secured as director. A young apprentice there was a fellow by the name of Karl Frei, who spent some time at their main works in France. The German Gavioli organs had a different sound from the Parisian models.

Charles Marenghi, a Gavioli-trained foreman at Paris, left the firm in 1901 following an argument with Ludovico. He took several key personnel with him and established his own business, producing beautiful organs with many Gavioli features and adding many of his own.

Demands for larger organs developed at the turn of the century as bioscope shows toured throughout Europe and especially England, bringing the new motion pictures to the masses. The use of Gavioli machines in Britain was so common that an organ operator was referred to as the "Gaviman". The design of the new 110-key organs, famous for their tonal balance and visual beauty, was fostered by the bioscope which needed full, loudly-voiced sound with elaborate appearance. These organs became the

Figure 3. A large organ-fronted bioscope show with the auditorium tent visible in the rear, about 1906. The dancing girls by the organ were usually the owner's daughters. *Photo courtesy Keith Pritchett.*

masterpiece of this old and venerable firm. Using these organs as their centerpiece, the consoles were extended as entrances forming a vast "organ-fronted show" and each showman tried to outdo his competitor in flamboyance and glitter. While Limonaire and Marenghi were popular, most of the

Figure 4. The top-of-the-line 110-key organ fully assembled at Gavioli's main works, Paris. This model was the masterpiece in the long history of the firm. *Photo courtesy Keith Pritchett.*

big shows used 110-key Gaviolis.

Not long after the loss of Marenghi, a large capital expense, necessitated by major structural repairs to the main factory building, caused severe financial drain in the ensuing years. The death of Anselme in 1902 and Claude in 1905 eroded the company's stability. Ludovico, however, maintained the policy of progressive growth and development and in 1908 introduced a radically new 112-keyless organ. These instruments have been termed the best and yet the worst. The organ musically was superb, but the new principle used a paper roll and a reciprocating compressor of wood using square chambers and parallel grooves in the pistons. The air turbulence in these pistons acted as a seal. Fragile paper rolls were damaged by poor tracking and the high wind pressure required to activate the primary valves directly. All this was no doubt an answer to the Ruth keyless ventil-system then coming into use. Many lawsuits were brought against the Gavioli firm by showmen who paid huge sums for these elaborate organs. Most 112-keyless organs were subsequently refitted with the tried and true 110-key system; each conversion rendered a financial loss to the firm. A lengthy lawsuit in turn was instituted by Gavioli against Mortier who, according to a previous agreement, was to market Gavioli organs. Instead Mortier began producing organs of their own with unauthorized use of Gavioli patents.

Around 1910 a bitter dispute between Ludovico and major shareholders regarding company policy ended with his resignation. By 1914 war clouds caused the organ market to disappear. Bioscopes ended their roamings and Gavioli et Cie, after a gesture at diversification in the form of producing bellows-operated carpet sweepers, was liquidated. Limonaire acquired the Waldkirch works and made organs scaled by Karl Frei until just after the war. The works were then taken over by Alfred Bruder and finally closed in 1930. Ludovico died in 1923 at the age of 73, and his daughter Andree died in the mid-1960's.

The Gavioli innovations were milestones in the industry and the list of people associated with and trained by them reads like a "Who's Who" of organ builders. Historically, Gavioli et Cie assumes the position of having had the most important influence in the development and manufacture of mechanical organs of the highest musical and artistic merit. ■■

THOSE FASCINATING BAND-ORGAN STATUES

Leonard Grymonprez

*S*ince the very early years of band-organ manufacture, band-organ statues have been an important part of the facade in both their stationary and animated forms. Because there is so little documentation available on this subject, this article may provide some information and ideas on the creation and manufacture of such statues.

Most art statues, beautiful as they may have been, were not used as band-organ statues. Generally, wooden statues represented well-known figures from Christianity, folk art, legendry, etc., and were usually carved from precious and hard types of wood. However, band-organ statues differed from these in that they rarely represented well-known personalities or musicians, and the type of wood used didn't play an important part.

Are we to assume that band-organ statues didn't have value? No, but they must be regarded from a purely decorative point of view, as the basic idea had an effective and amazing impression on the general public at the time.

Since some of the large French band organs had 30, 40 or more such statues, it seems that band-organ statues probably were carved on a mass-production basis. Furthermore, the construction of most statues maintained a similar pattern. Most of these statues were constructed from wooden cubes which were carefully glued together and, after being properly dried and prepared, were carved, filed, sanded and painted.

Many statues consisted of one-piece bodies, with the head, arms and legs added later. Standard models probably did not take on an important role, and so it is understandable that not all statues were carved by professional wood carvers. However, really fine artists could not be excluded, since distinctive, carved faces of male and female models, with impressive and gracious movements, exist as the proof of their artistry.

Band-organ statues were carved at various European locations and not all had that amazing, gracious look mentioned previously. Some were replicas of the better statues, but showed unskilled carving and craftsman-ship. In those instances, carvers would have made a replica of the original on a large sheet of squared drawing paper and carefully stenciled the necessary measurements on it.

Once a particular statue was carved, the decorator and painter could start their work. The statue would be prime-painted, dried, sanded, painted a second time, dried, sanded, and finally painted in detail. In any case, imaginative or not, the painter had to deliver heavy-duty work, as most band organs were made in smoky, sun-beaten, dusty workshops. Projects which required long periods of time to complete needed to be washed clean many times because of all the pollution.

Several statues had the impression of a certain period; others reflected various European periods of dress and culture. Ladies were usually represented with their hair artistically carved and painted.

Even in pre-World War I periods, band organ-statues were expensive to order. Rated at the present time (1980's) the price should average, plus or minus, five dollars per centimeter (.3937″) of height — about $300.00 for a statue with a height of 65 to 75 centimeters (25½″ - 29½″).

Today the art of manufacturing wooden statues is mostly left to advanced automatic wood-carving machines. &

Small Organs

THE SUPREME TRIUMPH OF A POPULAR SONG—ITS HAND-ORGAN APPEARANCE ON THE EAST SIDE.

BIRTH AND GROWTH OF A POPULAR SONG.

By Theodore Dreiser.

SINCE almost every one has, at some time or other, ventured the task of writing a popular song, either words or music, or both, without knowing much or anything of the difficulties which stand in the way of the ultimate success of such a composition, a slight discourse on the methods adopted at present to popularize a song cannot be far out of order. No one can truly say why such and such a song, out of the thousands that are annually written, strikes so wholly the popular fancy, netting the author thousands of dollars. The only thing that can definitely be set forth are the methods by which all songs are given publicity and an opportunity to appeal for the good favor of the public. It is all very much as a clever Broadway wit put it when he said, "I'll tell you, gentlemen, the art of song-writing is an exact thing. You can analyze it and discover the exact elements which make it up. There is just one little style or turn of strain that gives every song its popularity, and when you have found that out, learned all about it, and have it firmly fixed in your mind, why, you *can't* write the song."

Every new song success brings a fresh crop of writers. They are those who have read for the first time that of a little three-page ballad like "On the Banks of the Wabash" the daily sales are thousands of copies, that the total sales will be over half a million, and that the author is making thousands of dollars,

249

and who have proceeded forthwith to endeavor to do likewise. It looks easy, and the truth is, it really is easy for the person who has the popular-song vein in him. I know absolutely whereof I speak when I say that the words of "On the Banks of the Wabash" were written in less than an hour of an April Sunday afternoon, and that the music did not require a much longer period. The whole deed was pleasurable and easy, while the reward was proportion-

report, or, if he lives convenient to New York, he takes it about in person. Usually the publisher controlling the latest song hit is the most popular victim of aspiring writers. To him they proceed, determined of course that their song shall not fail of proper recognition of its merits, if their personality counts for anything. As a rule, however, the publisher has not time to hear a new writer play over his own piece. When he appears he is courteously informed

THE FIRST STEP IN TRANSFERRING A POPULAR SONG TO THE STREET PIANO—MARKING THE POSITION OF THE NOTES ON THE BARREL.

ately great. Yet there is not more than one good popular song turned out a year, and a great success such as "On the Banks of the Wabash" is not written once in ten years.

The history of the popularization of the average song begins with the aspiring author, who, having written what he is sure must eventually be an international song hit, sends his song to the publisher of whose business ability and general success he has heard the best

that of course a great many songs are brought in every day, and consequently each one must be left a few days for consideration. Almost invariably he will also volunteer the information that there is always a demand for good songs and that royalties are paid on all sales, usually from four to seven per cent.

This being satisfactory, the manuscript is left; or if not, and the author insists on being allowed to be present at the hearing of the piece or to play it for the publisher, he is invited to bring it in again. If he does so it is barely possible that some day he will bring in his manuscript at an opportunely dull time, and lo! the publisher will really allow him to play it over and receive judgment at once.

This, of course, is the new author, for the old one who has written one or many successes has no such trouble. For him everything is published. He

lisher, and that it is accepted. The next thing is to bind the author or authors by a contract, which reads that in consideration of, let us say, four per cent of the net price of every copy sold, he or they relinquish all claim to right, title, or interest, etc. The manuscript is then sent to a professional arranger of music, who looks it over and rearranges the accompaniment to what is, in his judgment, the best for general piano purposes, and the song is printed.

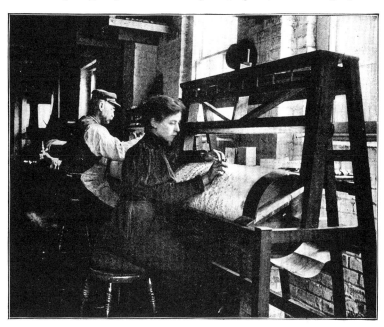

ANOTHER STEP IN THE WORK—MAKING THE HOLES FOR THE PINS.

goes to dinner with the publisher, has the freedom of the office, can even get the average songs of his friends a hearing, and is generally smiled upon and attended to, as beseems and befits the great in every field.

Granted, for the sake of forwardness, that the song is a good one and possesses that indefinable shade of sentiment in melody and words which make for popularity, and that it appeals to the very commercial judgment of the pub-

Usually the first copies of the song printed are what are called "professional copies," for which the thinnest kind of news paper is used. Probably five thousand of these are struck off, all intended for free distribution among the singing profession on the stage. The giving of professional copies and orchestra parts to all singers of some standing is considered a very effective method of pushing a new song before the public.

PLACING THE PINS IN POSITION ACCORDING TO THE MARKINGS LAID OUT BY THE FIRST WORKMAN.

TESTING THE FINISHED BARREL TO SEE THAT IT CORRECTLY GRINDS OUT THE POPULAR DITTY OF THE HOUR.

252

A BANJOIST AND SINGER TRANSFERRING THE IMMORTAL MELODY TO THE TENDER
MERCIES OF THE PHONOGRAPH.

If professional people, on hearing the song played for them in the publisher's parlors, think well of it, the publisher's hopes rise. It is then his policy to print possibly a thousand regular copies of the song, and these are sent out to "the trade," which is the mercantile term for all the small stores throughout the country which handle sheet music. A clever plan followed by some publishers is to enter into a contract with all the small dealers whereby the latter agree to take two copies of each of the publisher's new songs issued during the month, at, of course, a reduced rate. These copies being sold to the dealer at a cheaper rate than the older music, it is naturally to his advantage to sell them, since he makes a larger profit than on the copies of older songs regularly ordered. Thus the new song, being sent out at once under this contract, comes into the hands of singers and dealers throughout the country in very short order.

If, after a few months' standing, the song shows signs of the public's interest in it, if dealers occasionally order a copy, singers occasionally mention it as "going well" with their audiences, and the publisher likes the melody himself, he will endeavor to "push it" by advertising it on the backs and the inside margins of all his good selling pieces. Furthermore, if some able singer announces that he is going to "feature" the song in his tour, or if the sales of the song increase any after it has been well advertised upon the good selling pieces, a large advertisement will be placed in one of the papers which all the "professional" singers are known to take, in which the merits of the song are dilated upon and where it is announced as a coming success. Where a publisher has a reputation for good judgment and has already published a number of successes, the professional singers throughout the country are quite apt to take him at his word, or his advertisement, and write in for professional copies of the song. These are sent gratuitously, and the singers, finding it good, give it possibly an early trial before their audience. If the latter show any appreciation of its merits, it is very likely to be retained or "kept on" throughout the entire theatrical season by the keen vocalist.

In New York the work of booming the song is followed with the most careful attention, for it is well known among music publishers that if a song can be made popular around New York City it is sure to be popular throughout the country. Consequently canvassers are often sent about to the music halls where a song is being sung for the week, to distribute little hand-bills upon which the words are printed, to the end that the music-hall frequenters may become familiar with it and the sooner hum and whistle it on the streets. Boy singers are often hired to sit in the gallery and take up the chorus with the singer, thus exciting attention. Friends and hirelings are sent to applaud uproariously, and other small tricks common to every trade are employed to foster any early indication of public interest in the piece.

While the above tactics are more or less familiar to those who have essayed ballad-writing, very few know of the important part played by the hand and street organ and by the phonograph in familiarizing the masses with the merits of a song. Nearly all the piano-organs so numerously dragged about the city are controlled by an Italian padrone, who leases them to immigrant Greeks and Italians at so much a day. This business is quite an extensive one, involving as it does hundreds of organs and organ grinders, a large repair shop, and a factory where the barrels, upon which the melodies are indicated by steel pins, are prepared. The organs are quite intricate affairs, and their manufacture and control require no little knowledge and business skill, albeit they are of such humble pretensions.

With the organ-master-general the up-to-date publisher is in close communication, and between them the song is made a mutual beneficiary arrangement.

THE AUTOMATIC PIANO WITH ITS GRIST OF MELODIOUS AGONIES.

AMORETTE
WITH DANCING DOLLS

Joseph H. Schumacher

$\mathcal{S}$EVERAL YEARS AGO, I bought an Amorette organette with dancing dolls in the Mart at an East Coast Chapter meeting. At that time it played quite well, though later the sound became weak and the dolls turned sporadically. In order to return the instrument to good working order, I disassembled the organette and made the needed repairs, and during the restoration took photographs of the mechanism and made notes on its operation.

According to the books on musical boxes, the Amorette with dancing dolls was made by the Euphonika Musikwerke of Leipzig, Germany, about 1905. Although some organettes have a date stamped on the bellows board,

FIGURE 1. OVERALL VIEW SHOWING THE SHAPE OF THE CASE.

FIGURE 2. THE DRIVE-PLATE MOUNTED ON THE BACK.

FIGURE 3. ZINC DISC NO. 4176 READY TO PLAY.

there are no markings on this instrument to indicate the exact date of manufacture. Imprinted on its base is the number 1085 85, which may be a serial number or a coded date.

This small table model hand-cranked organette has the shape of a toy upright piano. The design of the case is different from that of most organettes – the back is built higher than the front (Figure 1) and the organette mechanism is housed within this back section. Two china-head dolls (three and three-fourths inches tall), dressed as a boy and a girl, are set in mirrored nooks in the front portion, creating a shadow-box effect. The polished black case, with incised and gilded ornamentation, measures approximately 13 inches high by 13 inches wide by 11 inches deep.

The instrument has 16 steel reeds and uses a key system in its operation – one key or lever for each note. It plays an 8-7/8-inch zinc disc that is fitted vertically onto a small drive-plate mounted on the back of the case (Figure 2). A metal arm, similar to those used on regular disc boxes, holds the disc in place (Figure 3).

The discs have projections that are formed by punching the metal and bending the resulting tabs at right angles to the disc – on the outer edge of the holes. The length of time a note is to be held determines the number of projections. A long note may have as many as 18 contiguous tabs (Figure 4). Long projections appear to be solid, but magnification reveals they are composed of a number of very slightly overlapping individual tabs.

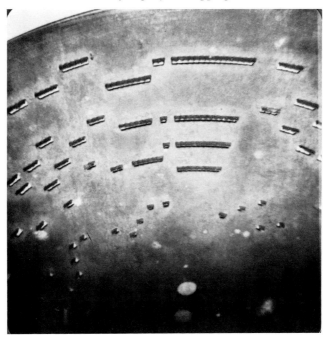

FIGURE 4. THE BACK OF A DISC, TABS BENT AT OUTER EDGE OF HOLES.

257

The organette works on a pressure system. When the crank at the left side of the case is turned, the crankshaft, by means of a worm gear, moves the center drive-plate clockwise. Simultaneously, a pulley on the shaft, connected by a belt to a central pulley, and, in turn, to a pulley at the base of the dolls, causes the dolls to rotate in opposite directions (Figure 5).

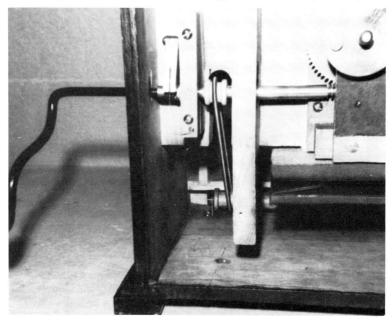

FIGURE 5. PULLEYS AND BELT FOR TURNING DOLLS.

As the disc turns and a projection appears, the corresponding metal key is moved downward (Figure 6). This movement, via a small metal rod attached to the keys and then to the spring-loaded valve flap, causes the flap to rise, allowing air to pass through the reed and thus sounding the note. The air pressure is produced by two bellows and a reservoir – the pumping bellows are operated in the customary manner by a pump rod attached to the crankshaft.

The overall condition of the organette was relatively good. One can only speculate why – perhaps it was purchased for a child and then packed away after he grew tired of it. The china-head dolls were in fine condition, except for the clothes (of white silk faille), which were tattered from the continuous turning. As this appeared to be the original clothing, I felt it best not to re-dress them, so merely washed the glazed porcelain parts and did minimal mending to the clothes.

The bellows had been re-covered with a rubberized material, and leather straps were used for stays or stiffeners. These straps were not effective; consequently, the bellows and reservoir puffed outward, losing their shape with a resulting loss of power. Rather than attempt to patch up the bellows,

258

FIGURE 6. KEYS AND FLAP VALVES.

it was decided that they should be completely re-covered. The procedure used for covering bellows is given on pages 22-31 of *Rebuilding the Player Piano,* by Larry Givens. These instructions and accompanying illustrations are excellent, and if closely followed, one can expect good results.

The bellows were re-covered with a double-weight cotton cloth with a thin layer (0.11 inches thick) of air-tight rubber between. Replacement of the valves was not necessary because this had been done by the last restorer and they were still in good condition. Re-covering bellows is somewhat more involved when an organette operates on pressure rather than suction because it is essential to apply stiffeners to the bellows and reservoir. Stiffeners are usually attached to the inside of the bellows cloth, but since the original ones had been removed when the bellows were previously done over and no pattern was available, I attached them to the outside. This course is easier, and the results are just as effective. Also, if removal or re-gluing of the stiffeners is necessary, the bellows do not have to be torn apart.

When the re-covering was finished, I creased the bellows and proceeded to make a pattern for the stiffeners. In forming the side pieces it isn't necessary to extend the cardboard to the tip of the hinge end – three-fourths to four-fifths of its length is adequate. The stiffeners were then cut from six-ply black poster board. This board was selected because it is thin and stiff and most nearly duplicates the original used in organettes.

FIGURE 7. STIFFENERS ON BELLOWS CLOTH.

FIGURE 8. REED BOARD (BASS REED 'E' HAS A CARDBOARD COVER).

After gluing the stiffeners to the outside (Figure 7), rubber strips a fourth of an inch wide are inserted between the folds before closing to hold the stiffeners in place until the glue is dry.

Because the gaskets had been glued in place, they were damaged when the unit was taken apart, so I cut new ones from chamois. Chamois was chosen because the bellows boards were slightly warped and this soft pliant leather produced a tighter seal. The facings on the valve flaps had previously been re-leathered and did not leak.

There was a small amount of rust on the tips of the keys, which was easily removed with a fine rotary wire brush without dismantling the key-frame assembly.

Elastic bands had been used for belts. Here I substituted spring-wire belts of the type used in the Celestina organette. This belting is sold in coils for use in projectors and recorders and is available from photo supply houses. It can be cut to the length needed and the ends joined with the fasteners supplied. The wooden pulley on the crankshaft was missing, so I made one patterned after those at the base of the dolls.

The reeds are mounted on a reed board within the air chamber in a rather rudimentary manner – with a tack at each end, and then sealed in place (Figure 8). Without removing them from the board, the individual reeds were carefully cleaned with isopropyl alcohol. Each reed is imprinted with a number, 1 through 16, and the scale of notes is: E F♯ B C♯ D♯ E F♯ G♯ A♯ B C♯ D♯ E F F♯ G♯.

With repairs completed and the mechanism reassembled, the organette plays well and the dolls revolve with renewed animation.

FIGURE 9. FRONT VIEW - RESTORATION COMPLETE. ■■

ORGELBAU RAFFIN

Jack Hardman

$\mathcal{J}$oseph Raffin has apparently built organs for many years, but about eight years ago, he started to build small crank organs for the growing number of devotees around the world who appreciate these marvelous instruments. Judging by his backlog of orders and the extended deliveries, he has been very successful. Perhaps most significant is Raffin's departure from the traditional "German" sound of bright trumpets. He voices his instruments with what I think of as the "Dutch" sound, primarily characterized by the addition of celested bourdon flute pipes.

Herr Raffin's home is located in the town of Uberlingen, West Germany, on the northern shore of Lake Konstanz 10 or 15 minutes west of the popular little medieval tourist resort of Meersburg. His well-equipped shop of perhaps 8,000 feet or so is located in an attractive modern building behind his residence. The Raffin family, many of whom help out with the business, are justifiably proud of their factory, and are eager to show willing visitors through the tidy facility.

His first model was a 20-keyless, 31-pipe organ which incorporated some progressive design features intended to make the organ more reliable over the long run, and musically more interesting. For example, Raffin's primary valves are built as pistons in aluminum cylinders; no leather is used. Structural plastics are employed where wood would be inferior. A lever connected to the top of the reservoir allows the organ grinder to add a degree of dynamic expression to enhance the music. Interested readers are referred to a review of this model organ (R20/31) by Hank Waelti published in *The Music Box Journal* of the Musical Box Society of Great Britain, Volume 10, No. 7, Autumn 1982. The article includes a number of pictures of Herr Raffin, his organ factory and personnel, together with some of the assembly operations.

We recently received a 31-keyless, 84-pipe organ (R31/84) and have had lots of fun playing with this lovely instrument. It is attractive to look at and beautifully constructed. But best of all, it has a marvelous sound! It arrived safely in spite of what U.S. Customs "inspection" accomplished with heavy-handed crowbars that totally destroyed what should have remained a well-constructed, reuseable wooden box built with as much care as the organ itself. It arrived via Lufthansa about six months after we placed the order.

The organ is 28" wide including the two sturdy handles, 19" deep, excluding the removable crank handle, and 30" high. The traditionally styled, optional wagon has steel-tired, dished, wooden artillery wheels. They can be easily removed when required, without tools, to make the assembly considerably more compact. The suspension for the wagon consists of four sets of opposed leaf springs. A separate wagon handle is attached with countersunk carriage bolts and large wing nuts. Mounted on its wagon, the top of the organ is about 48" off the ground.

Photo 1. Mildred, Jack and Laurie Hardman with their new Raffin 31-keyless, 84-pipe organ.

Herr Raffin's organs are played by conventional perforated rolls, although he uses a tough non-hygroscopic plastic film instead of paper for improved dimensional stability. I don't think they will ever wear out. The tracker bar is divided into two sections. In the lower section, there are five holes for the bass pipes which play simultaneously at two pitches, 8' and 4'. The next 10 holes are for the accompaniment flute pipes. The pipes are chromatic except for two whole-tone intervals. The upper section consists of 16 holes controlling the melody pipes. Our organ has four slide registers, or stops, to control the flow of wind into four corresponding ranks or sets of pipes. There is one rank of piccolo pipes, one rank of violin pipes and two ranks of bourdon flutes. Each rank consists of 16 pipes chromatically tuned except for one whole-tone interval. The bass and accompaniment flutes, which are not controlled by a stop, sound at all times to provide the underlying harmony and rhythm to the music played.

The two ranks of bourdon flutes are identical except for the way they are tuned; one rank is tuned to the correct pitches, and the other flute rank is "celested" or tuned very slightly higher in pitch. Either flute rank played alone sounds virtually the same as the other because the pipes are the same, and the difference in tuning is almost impossible to hear except in a direct A-B comparison. When the two flutes are played together, however, something exciting happens; a kind of "chorus" effect is heard along with a noticeable tremolo resulting from the "beats" or periodic constructive and destructive interference of the two sets of pipes sounding at the same time. The pitch difference amounts to only a few hertz, and the second flute rank should probably be adjusted to something around seven hertz sharp when tuning.

Photo 2. Detail of the tracker-frame assembly.

The existence of the registers (stops) has some distinct benefits. For one thing, the different kinds of pipes can be used very effectively since one sound quality, or timbre, can be contrasted with another to provide more interest and "color" to the music. Also, and significantly, there is the additional involvement on the part of the organ grinder, since on this small organ the registers are not automatically controlled from the tracker bar. If not the organ grinder, then a (hopefully) musically perceptive assistant can take part in the registration process. At any rate, the registers are fun to play with, and do add to the satisfaction derived from the exercise of developing arms like Popeye.

Registering the organ is easy. All you do is slide the registers in and out to change the timbre of the sound by turning ranks of pipes on or off. My nine-year-old daughter, Laurie, enjoys registering the organ while I crank. The only problem was that, at least in the beginning, she would move the wrong stops at the wrong time! This was a rather painful experience for my somewhat more discerning ears. But not wanting to discourage her interest and curiosity, I would grin and bear it, and try to explain later what the register stops were for, and how to decide which ones to move and when.

The piccolos have a pretty shrill sound when played alone, especially when the rear lid is hinged open, and therefore probably won't be played "solo" very often except for special effects. But they can do wonders for other voices when played in combination by changing or enhancing the overall sound heard. This again offers more variety to the basically limited number of voices available. The piccolo pipes on Herr Raffin's model R31/84 are situated along the rear of the instrument case. They are clearly visible through a nicely framed, clear plastic window which effectively allows them to be seen—Raffin's workmanship is truly superior—but helps direct their sound output toward the front of the organ. Incidentally, on a slightly different model Raffin organ, the R31/68, a set of tuned, brass saucer bells replaces the piccolo pipes. Reiterating beaters are mechanically driven through a belt drive from the main crank. On this model, it is the brass bells and their action that are revealed through the window.

The violin or string pipes are, like all the other pipes, made from wood. Their long, skinny shape and harmonic bridge encourage the generation of a harmonically rich string sound that is a delightful complement to, and contrast with, the plainer flute sounds. The violin pipes have a nice, crisp, bright sound, and depending on the musical arrangement, can sound very nice "solo." They can also be used in combination with one of the flute ranks to produce a more mellow and full-bodied sound for some of the louder parts of an arrangement.

The two flute ranks are positioned at the front of the organ, one behind the other, and in front of the violin pipes. Convenient access to

Photo 3. An example of the workmanship on the pipework.

Corrected Tuning Scale
for the Raffin 31 Keyless Organ

1. B	11. E	22. F
2. C	12. F	23. F#
3. D#	13. G	24. G
4. F	14. G#	25. G#
5. G#	15. A	26. A
6. B	16. B	27. B
7. C	17. C	28. C
8. C#	18. C#	29. C#
9. D	19. D	30. D
10. D#	20. D#	31. D#
	21. E	

Photo 4. A view of the casework, marquetry and the register stops.

the melody pipes is made easier by removable decorative panels on the organ's front and rear. Like the violins or piccolos, each flute rank has its own draw knob which is pushed in to turn off the flow of wind, and pulled out about 1/2″ to allow wind to flow to the pipes. The flute sound is basic to all organs, and is the most frequently used stop. It is sort of the starting point for most voicing arrangements.

There seems to be a good balance between the size of the main bellows and the number of pipes, but depending on the particular musical arrangement and the number of open tracker-bar holes, there can be the situation where the pipes are starved for air if both flutes and other melody ranks are all playing at once. The flutes especially consume a lot of wind. I have only one roll on which I have noticed this problem.

Incidentally, the crankshaft of the 31-keyless organ has two throws at 90 degrees driving double-acting bellows. It is supported by a sealed ball bearing on the hand-crank end, and a lubricated, split-wood pillow block situated between the two crank throws.

The sound of the two celested bourdon flutes playing together seems best reserved for smooth-flowing melodies and glissandos that are not confused by too much detail. I think they sound best when played alone, without competition from the violins or piccolos. For special effect, the piccolos can be briefly added for purposes of accent, but as a rule, I prefer the pure sound of the two flutes playing alone. In this way the celeste effect is most pronounced and therefore, most successful.

For faster-moving or more densely-packed melodies, the violin pipes might be a good choice since their brighter sound more clearly defines the melody's direction and motion. They seem to be equally effective on single-note melody lines as well as for chords or melody lines supported by additional notes in harmony.

Choosing appropriate voices for the music being played becomes fairly obvious once you are familiar with the musical arrangement. Music has a beginning and an end, and in between, it expresses a variety of emotions. Usually there are recognizable blocks of melody which are sometimes repeated at different points along the way. Music, like speech, is spoken in phrases or sentences, and for larger works, in movements. The organ grinder has all kinds of op. rtunities to "color" the music as it comes off the roll; but in general, voicing changes should be timed to coincide with the natural phrasing or sectioning of the music being played.

A little thought and common sense go a long way toward achieving the desirable changes in mood and expression that the composer is trying to convey. And a little practice helps a lot too. Incidentally, Laurie can now do a very satisfactory job of registering, and I especially like to hear *her* way of doing it, which quite properly is often different from mine. That's what we have found so exciting about this latest addition to our collection of mechanical music: it is not totally passive. It quickly involves the grinder and/or his or her assistant for the fun and enjoyment of all! &

ANOTHER WAY TO SKIN A CAT

Marion I. Levy

ONE of the early calamities of my life was to get a new Brownie Kodak, sans film, on Christmas Day. This sad situation was repeated last year -- only this time with a beautiful Cabinetto Organette with rolls too badly damaged even to try to play. Never a person to do it the simple way if a more involved procedure can be developed, I went to work at once to rectify the music shortage.

If the Cabinetto rolls had been anything but the monsters that they are, I might have just cut out the slots with a ruler and an X-Acto knife, but when you consider that just one roll is 65 or more feet long and has 25 notes, each with a slot of more than average length, the prospect of many boring hours ahead was not inspiring. Furthermore, having been a production man, it was unthinkable to make a setup of any kind for just one piece. The direction from this point on was clear -- at least to me, just as it would have been to 'Rube Goldberg' -- dig around in the scrap bin, and come up with a machine to make three at a time. Hence this saga.

The first step was the selection of paper. I decided that freezer wrapping paper had the best potential. It is tough and is coated on one side with plastic, which adds to its strength and slide-ability. It was available in 1,000-foot 18-inch-wide rolls. Since I had decided to make three music rolls at a time, plus test pieces, I needed approximately 300 feet, cut to 13-5/8-inch width. To cut the paper the desired width, I made a wooden stand, with a shaft to hold the roll of paper, and clamped this firmly to my lathe. I had previously turned up a couple of wooden plugs to secure a 1½-inch-diameter cardboard tube to a 3/4-inch steel shaft that I put between centers on the lathe. With the lathe set at slow speed, in back gear, I was ready to wind the desired length off the roll onto the cardboard tube. Next, I made a wooden framework 18 inches wide to ride on the paper as it was wound from the roll to the cardboard tube and fastened a razor blade at a distance of 13-5/8 inches from one edge. After a few adjustments and with a considerable degree of finesse, the 18-inch paper was transferred to the cardboard tube slit in two parts, the 13-5/8-inch-wide piece and a 4-3/8-inch-wide offal. The lathe and wooden stand were also used to transfer 70 feet from the 300-foot roll to each of three reels, duplicates of those used in the organette.

The next activity centered around the 'cutting board' shown below. This consisted of a bed 14 inches wide by 96 inches long made of 3/4-inch plywood, with various things added to it. Referring to the illustration, reading from right to left, there is a notched stand holding the three rolls of paper, then a wooden clamping bar secured with thumb screws. Next is a chisel for cutting out the ends of the slots and the 'cutter assembly' and 'slide,' about which more later. Another clamp and a slotted stand to hold the three finished rolls complete the cutting board.

FINISHED PAPER   CLAMP   CHISEL   CLAMP   UNCUT PAPER

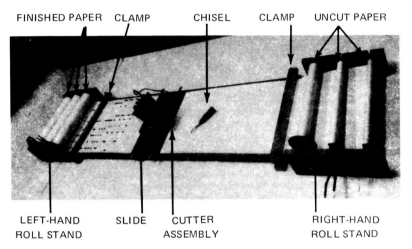

LEFT-HAND   SLIDE   CUTTER   RIGHT-HAND
ROLL STAND   ASSEMBLY   ROLL STAND

FIGURE 1.   CUTTING BOARD, SLIDE AND CUTTER ASSEMBLY.

Before any cutting could be done, however, the location and length of the slots had to be marked on one of the new rolls, using an original roll as a template. The cutting board, with the cutter assembly and slide removed, was used for this purpose. A roll of new paper and the original roll were placed in the left-hand roll stand; the two layers of paper were stretched across the board with the original paper on top. The ends were fastened to empty reels on the right-hand stand, the edges were squared up, and the clamps put on and tightened. Using a soft pencil, a line was drawn through the approximate center of each slot. When all of the slots exposed between the clamps (approximately five feet apart) had been marked, the clamps were loosened, the marked section and its corresponding original were wound onto the reels on the right-hand stand, and five feet more of the new and original rolls were stretched out, clamped, and marked. This procedure was repeated 14 times to complete the transfer of the slot markings from the original to the new roll.

To set up for cutting, three empty reels (copied from the original reels) were placed in the left-hand stand. Three 70-foot rolls of new paper (one being the marked roll) were placed in the right-hand stand, with the marked roll in the first slot. All three strips were stretched along the cutting board with the marked strip on top, and attached to the empty reels on the

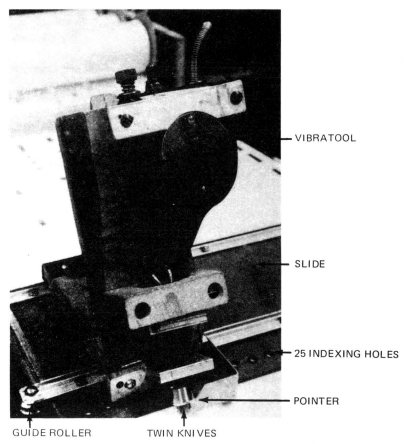

VIBRATOOL

SLIDE

25 INDEXING HOLES

POINTER

GUIDE ROLLER   TWIN KNIVES

FIGURE 2.   CUTTER ASSEMBLY AND SLIDE.

left-hand stand. Lining up the edges and tightening down the clamps completed the preparations for cutting the slots.

Please refer to Figure 2 for the cutter assembly and slide detail. A Burgess Vibratool, such as is used for cutting and embossing leather and marking metal and glass, was mounted on a simple wooden stand, at an angle, as recommended. Instead of using the regular single knife-holder, however, I made a chuck that would hold two knives 5/16-inch apart -- the width of the slot that I intended to cut. Slightly in front of the knife blades is a pointer to make it easier to follow the markings while cutting. There is also an adjustable indexing pin attached to the cutter-assembly base. This pin fits into holes in the slide, to position the cutter for the particular row of slots to be cut.

The cutter assembly rides on the slide, which is made of transparent plastic, reinforced with metal strips, and fitted at each end with guide rollers. The slide can be moved back and forth on the cutting board and will always be perpendicular to it. Twenty-five holes were drilled in the slide to

271

correspond to the 25 slots to be cut. The indexing pin on the cutter assembly fits into these holes. So that the slide and cutter assembly could be moved about freely without the knives cutting the paper, the cutter assembly is held up from the slide by a spring underneath.

One final device was needed to complete the setup, a nice sharp chisel, ground to the exact width of the slots. This was used to cut out each slot end, between the longitudinal cuts made by the knives.

With the locating pin of the cutter assembly in the top hole and starting with the slide in its far left position, the top and bottom edges of each slot in the first row were cut simultaneously, using the pointer as a guide for the beginning and end of each slot. After running the length of the first row, the pin was moved to the second hole and the second row cut, and so through 25 rows. The chisel was then used to cut each end of each slot, and the slivers lifted out. In Figure 3 you can see an example of the pencil markings, a slot partially completed with the slivers lifted near the chisel, and some completed slots.

SLIVER CUT FROM SLOT   CHISEL

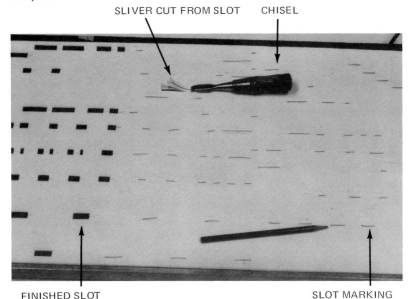

FINISHED SLOT   SLOT MARKING

FIGURE 3.   SEMI-FINISHED ROLL.

After cutting all of the slots for one setting, the paper was wound on the left-hand reels and the process continued -- setting, cutting, chiseling, until the roll was done.

A couple of hours a day for about a week finished the cutting, and finally there came the day when the last slots were cut, the ends trimmed, wire loops attached, and the tunes labeled. Now -- beautiful music! -- and two extra re-cut rolls that may relieve the frustrations of some other Cabinetto or Tournaphone owner who cannot enjoy music from his fine instrument because of what 70-odd years have done to the original rolls. ■ ■

Comparison
of
Roller-Organ Scales

Wesley B. Reed

𝓜EMBERS who collect roller organs might be interested in a comparison of scales that I have made recently. The original motive was to determine, for my own collection of 22 instruments, what similarity there might be among the various paper rolls as to hole spacing. For instance, could a multiple-hole punch made for a 25-note compass be used also to turn out 17-note and 14-note tune sheets? Another concern, of course, in arranging music for roller-organ reproduction, is how many key changes and melody accidentals are provided for. The popular songs of the period frequently jumped out into left field (the conventional term is modulating into a foreign key) and then worked back to home base (the original key) through a series of major and/or minor seventh chords.

The table shown deals only with paper-roll or cardboard tune sheets that have come to my attention. I hope other members will publish supplementary information.

COLUMN I represents several 14-note instruments, all using an approximately 20 cm.-wide tune sheet with 13.6 mm. hole spacing: Mechanical Orguinette Co., 831 Broadway, New York City -- roller feed, 18 mm. per crank revolution -- reeds above the 20 cm. card -- direct valving. Reed Pipe Clariona, Merritt Gally -- spool to spool, initial speed 16 mm./rev. -- reeds below 20.2 cm. paper -- direct valving. McTammany -- roller feed plus spools -- reeds below 19.8 cm. paper -- direct valving. Mechanical Orguinette Co. -- roller feed plus spools -- direct valving -- reeds above 19.8 cm. paper. Two with no identification -- spool to spool at 17 and 21 mm./rev. -- direct valving -- reeds below 20.1 and 19.9 cm. paper. L. H. Fairbanks, Webster, Mass. (dealer) – roller feed -- direct valving -- reeds below 19.9 cm. paper. Jubal Orchestrone reported by Art Reblitz (M.B.S.I. *Bulletin,* Spring/Summer 1975) -- except that the two lowest notes are pitched an octave lower.

COLUMN II represents two more of the 14-note instruments: Gately Automatic Organ, 32 Pearl St., Boston, Mass. -- spool to spool, at 17 to 22 mm./rev. -- mechanical relay, paper 20.2 cm. wide. The Melodia reported by Ralph Heintz (M.B.S.I. *Bulletin,* Summer 1972).

COLUMN III: Gately, a duplicate of the one listed above, but tuned a semitone up.

COLUMN IV: Columbian Orguinette reported by Art Reblitz (M.B.S.I. *Bulletin,* Spring/Summer 1975).

COLUMN V: Organina, American Automatic Organ Co., -- roller feed at 12.5 mm./rev. -- mechanical relay -- card 14.5 cm. wide with holes spaced 8.7 mm. apart.

COLUMN VI: Musette, Mechanical Orguinette Co., reported by Ron Goldstein (M.B.S.I. *Bulletin,* Autumn 1972).

COLUMN VII: Aurephone Harmonia, Tournaphone Music Co. Serial No. 9725 -- spool to spool at 18 to 23 mm./rev. -- direct valving, reeds below paper -- tune sheet 24 cm. wide with holes 13.5 mm. apart.

COLUMN VIII: Celestina, Mechanical Orguinette Co. Serial No. 578 -- spool to spool at 10 mm./rev. initial speed -- pneumatic relay -- tune sheet 14 cm. wide with holes 6.3 mm. apart.

COLUMN IX: Celestina reported by Ralph Heintz (M.B.S.I. *Bulletin,* Summer 1972). Orchestrone Pneumatic Organ, Gately Mfg. Co. -- spool to spool at 13.5 mm./rev. initial speed -- pneumatic relay -- tune sheet 9.25 cm. wide with 4.2 mm. hole spacing.

COLUMN X: Autophone, H.B. Horton, Ithaca, N. Y. -- sprocket feed -- direct valving, reeds below card -- tune sheet 13.65 cm. wide with holes 5.05 mm. apart.

COLUMN XI: Organina Thibouville, Paris, France -- roller feed at 29 mm./rev. -- mechanical relay -- card 15.45 cm. wide with 6.25 mm. hole spacing.

COLUMN XII: Tournaphone floor model -- spool to spool at 49 to 56 mm./rev. -- direct valving, reeds below paper -- tune sheet 30 cm. wide with 13.5 mm. hole spacing.

One thing that is interesting is that slightly different tunings were sometimes used for the same model of instrument, although of course the tune sheets would fit interchangeably because the pattern was the same. Less surprising is the essential interchangeability of the 14-note tune sheets. This design is the 'Model T Ford' of the roller organs.

As to musical arrangement possibilities, the 14-note scale is an example of the utmost in economy. By adding just one extra note to a diatonic scale (A, for instance), you have the choice of reproducing a melody in the key of

	I	II	III	IV	V	VI	VII	VIII	IX	X	XI	XII
									1			
A								1			1	
B												
c											2	1
d								2	2 3		3	2
e												3
f						1	1	3	4		4	4
g		1	1			2	2	4	5	1		5
a	1	2	2			3	3	5	6	2 3	5	6 7
b	2		3	1	1	4				4		8
c'		3	4	2		5	4	6	7		6	9
d'	3 4	4 5	5	3	2	6 7	5 6	7	8 9	5 6	7	10 11
e'	5		6	4	3 4	8 9	7 8	8 9	10 11	7 8	8 9	12
f'	6 7	6 7	7 8	5 6	5 6	10 11	9 10	10 11	12 13	9	10	13 14
g'	8	8 9	9	7	7 8	12	11 12	12 13	14 15	10	11 12	15 16
a'	9	10	10	8 9	9 10	13	13	14 15	14 15 16	11 12	13 14	17 18
b'	10		11	9	11	14	13	16	16	13	14	19
c''		11	12	10			14	17	17		15	20
d''	11 12	12	13	11	12	15	15	17	18	14 15 16	16	21
e''	13	13	14	12	13 14	16	16	18	19	17	17	22
f''	14	14		13	15	17	17	19	20	18	18 19	23
g''				14	16			20		19	20 21	24
a''										20	22 23	25
b''										21		
c'''											24	
										22		

A between the limits of *do* and *la* an octave above, or in the related key, D, between *sol* and *mi* an octave above. The limitations obviously are that the melody can contain no accidentals and the harmony has to be simple.

The more ambitious scales provide, first, a few extra notes to accommodate accidentals, and then perhaps two or three bass notes to give the rendition more body. Also, the scales of 16 or more notes afford the possibility of arranging a melody in one of three related keys, and using more complex harmony if the right key is chosen as the tonic. It is interesting to note that an arrangement written to fit the Celestina could be copied for the Orchestrone (see Columns VIII and IX), although the physical dimensions require two different punch guides. There are probably other such similarities.

Turning attention to the tune sheet dimensions, it is apparent that a multiple-hole punch made to fit the 25-note Tournaphone would serve equally well for making 17-hole tune sheets for the Aurephone Harmonia and 14-hole tune sheets for many smaller instruments. Another, more dubious, possibility might be using the same punch for Thibouville cards and Celestina tune sheets. ■ ■

AUTOPHONE MUSIC
"A STRIP IN TIME"

Gary G. Stevenson

𝒩OT TOO LONG AGO, while looking for hand-cranked organettes, I came upon a Symphonia on the shelf of an antique store near Springfield, Missouri. After buying this rather broken-down Symphonia organette, I asked the owner to keep his eye open for other self-playing organs, for I would be interested in them in any condition. He told me he had an odd harmonica squeeze box that did not work, brought me to a back room of his shop and showed me a cardboard box filled with parts. He told me he had owned the machine for quite a while and was not sure how it was put together.

After looking over the contents I bought the box of dusty parts. We talked a short while longer and I started out the door with the Symphonia and Autophone parts. When I turned to say goodby, the owner had returned to his shop. In a moment he appeared with another old box, this one full of original Autophone music strips. He told me these went with the box of parts, but he had forgotten where he had put them. I almost had not purchased the box of Autophone parts because of the price, but I was glad I did after seeing the music strips.

When I returned home, I contacted Carl Semon in Elk Grove, Illinois, to talk to him about my new acquisition. Carl makes recut rolls for various organettes, so I asked him to send me lists of his recut Symphonia and Autophone music. When I received them, I combined his Autophone list with the list I had compiled of my own strips. One interesting point soon became apparent — none of our strip numbers exceeded No. 313.

After receiving my combined list, Carl wrote back saying, "I would *assume* that the Autophone, being one of the earliest, if not the first organette, was quickly outdated by all the others which followed." This, we felt, was enough evidence for us to propose that only about 300 different Autophone music strips were ever punched by the company.

Our theory was tested almost immediately. In the *Silver Anniversary Collection,* (Musical Box Society International, 1974) an article on roller organs appeared on page 593. The author, Mr. Larry Givens, states that, "by 1883 the Autophone Company had issued nearly a thousand different musical selections for the 22-note Autophone . . ." There was also an article in the Spring, 1974 *Bulletin,* (Vol XX, No. 4, page 220) called *Local*

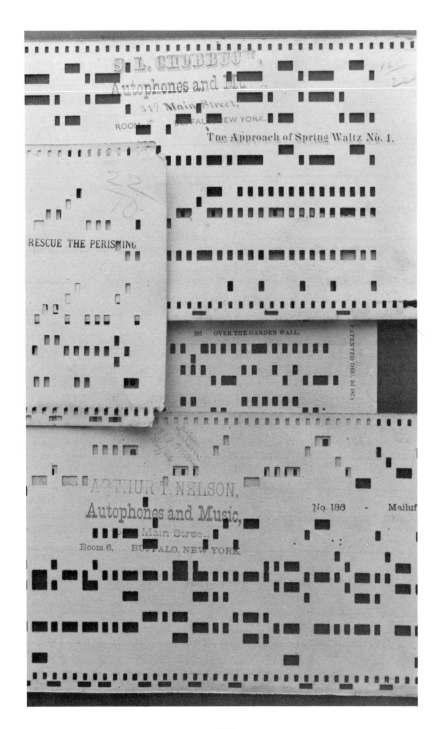

Histories as Source Material. That information was found in a book called *Ithaca and its Resources*, which did not give an original publishing date other than the nineteenth century. The information given in this book must be questioned, based on the fact that of my 179 strips and the 97 of Carl's, one would think that at least one strip would have a number higher than 313, if in fact a thousand strips had been made by 1883. (One thing to keep in mind, however, is that a boast in those years may today be misunderstood as fact.)

After the 1974 *Bulletin* article was published, another piece of the Autophone puzzle surfaced. In 1975 M.B.S.I. member Paul Wilkinson shared his Autophone music catalogue with the Society (*Bulletin*, Vol. XXI, No. 1, p. 39) and for the first time in many years an Autophone catalogue was published. The music was divided into two categories: sacred music was listed from song No. 1 to No. 86, and popular airs from No. 101 to No. 255. No songs are shown from No. 87 to No. 100 on this list,

originally compiled by The C.E. Wendell Co., of Albany, New York. At the end of the Wendell Company list is this footnote: "other songs will be added."

Mr. Howard Fitch provided me with another Autophone music-strip catalogue that shows more songs were added. This catalogue, lent to us by Mr. Glenn W. Grabinsky, adds ten more sacred strips and 87 more popular airs. This list of squeeze-box music strips again comes from a New York state company. This makes three different New York cities used as part of the Autophone Company's history. Some of my strips also came from two places in Buffalo, New York: the S.A. Chubbuck Autophone and Music Company, 19 Main Street, Room 1; and Arthur T. Nelson Autophone and Music, 317 Main Street, Room 6. Were they both there at the same time or were they one and the same company with different owners?

Some of Carl's strips came from the following places: The John H. Stredrers Book and Music Store, No. 268 W. Water St., and W.P. Parker, Agt., 41 Oneida Street, both in Milwaukee, Wisconsin; and J.H. Erb, 92 E. Randolph at 57 S. Dearborn St., Chicago, Illinois.

As you will see in the list at the end of this article, some of the strips appear to be of Scandanavian origin. They were bought by Carl and John Bernhardt from Claes Friberg in Copenhagen. These original, new, old-stock strips are marked "The C.W. Skänström, Hórrebrogade 23 Hj. af Blaagaardsgade, Kjóbenhvn, N." The music shop names are marked on strips along with other bits of information. In the accompanying photo are some of the different strips in my collection to show their markings. These marks indicate the strip title and price in American cents. The prices varied from one distributor to another. For instance, "Rescue the Pershing" shows 22/10 on my strip, No. 22 at 10 cents. The Wendell catalogue lists this song at 12 cents and the Barber Company sold it for 9 cents. Price differences could have come about because of bulk buying, differences in profit margin, or a drop in demand. The Barber catalogue appears to be the latter of the sources for this article.

Only one of my strips came with a patent date marked on it. In the accompanying photo, No. 281 "Over the Garden Wall" shows a date of December 3, 1878. This indicates the inventor, Mr. Henry Horton, made an improvement on his original patent dated October 30, 1877.

Following is a list by number of the Autophone strips known to exist and those shown in the catalogues. I invite Autophone collectors to challenge my theory by submitting the names of sacred songs between 87 and 100 or popular airs numbered higher than 342.

Perhaps some response article could give titles owned by other collectors, so that the Society will be able to compile a complete listing of all the songs produced by the Autophone Company.

The songs listed here are keyed for ownership: Carl Semon's strips are marked with a dagger (†), Howard Fitch's are marked with a double dagger (‡), and the author's strips are marked with an asterisk (*). Those without a symbol are listed in one of the catalogues referenced earlier.

AUTOPHONE MUSIC STRIPS

22-note Scale:
A, A#, B, C, D, D#, E, F, G, A, A#, B, C, D, D#, E, F, G, A, A#, C, D

SACRED MUSIC

1 Balerina*
2 I Need Thee Every Hour†
3 Antioch*
4 Nearer My Home†
5 Menoah
6 Nearer My God to Thee†
7 Rhine*
8 America
9 Loving Kindness†
10 Hold the Fort†
11 Mendon-Suwanne River*
12 Horton
13 Louvan*
14 Even Me
15 Sweet Hour of Prayer
16 Ithaca*
17 Golden Hill
18 Come to Jesus
19 St. Thomas*
20 Gather at the River†
21 Silver Street*
22 Rescue the Pershing*
23 Dennis
24 Pass Me Not‡
25 Shirland
26 I'm Coming to the Cross*
27 Italian Hymn
28 Pull for the Shore
29 Beulah Land†
30 Close to Thee*
31 There'll be Joy
32 Rest for the Weary†
33 Rock of Ages
34 Shining Shore
35 Old Hundred
36 Oak*
37 Pleyel's Hymn*
38 Spanish Hymn
39 Webb
40 Portuguese Hymn
41 What a Friend We Have in Jesus†
42 Home over There
43 Marching Along

44 Hallelujah, 'tis Done†
45 Greenland's Icy Mountain†
46 Morris*
47 Hail Virgin, Dearest Mary
48 Now I Lay Me Down to Sleep
49 I Long to be There*
50 Only an Armor Bearer
51 Rise and Shine*
52 When the Swallows Homeward Fly†
53 We Shall Meet Them*
54 Precious Name†
55 Coronation†
56 Ring the Bells
57 O, Do Not Be Discouraged*
58 Duke Street
59 He Leadeth Me*
60 Onward Christian Soldiers†
61 Will You Meet Me at the Fountain?*
62 Joyfully*
63 Eventide
64 Worthing
65 The Gate Ajar for Me*
66 I Love to Tell the Story
67 The Great Physician
68 There is Life for a Look*
69 Nuremburg*
70 Autumn (Spanish Melody)*
71 Brownell*
72 Hayden's Morning Hymn
73 Guide Me O Thou Great Jehovah
74 Over the River*
75 Psalm 89, (Hauff)
76 Psalm 119
77 Weary of Earth
78 Jesus of Nazareth Passeth By
79 What Shall the Harvest Be?
80 Just As I Am
81 Mary and Martha
82 The Lord Is My Shepherd
83 Today the Savior Calls
84 My Beautiful Dream
85 Yield Not to Temptation
86 Greenville

POPULAR AIRS

101 Auld Lang Syne‡
102 Listen to the Mocking Bird†‡
103 Baby Mine†
104 Bonnie Eloise*
105 Blue Bells of Scotland*
106 Money Musk*
107 Grandfather's Clock, and Chorus†
108 When I Was a Lad (Pinafore)*
109 Home, Sweet Home†‡
110 Farewell My Own (Pinafore)*
111 Suwanee River
112 Little Buttercup (Pinafore)
113 Sweet Bye and Bye
114 Last Rose of Summer†
115 Annie of the Vale
116 Fisher's Hornpipe
117 Autophone Polka*
118 Girl I Left Behind Me†
119 Ellen Bayne
120 Robin Adair†
121 Die Wacht am Rhein†
122 Cinderella Waltz†
123 Mutterschmerz*
124 Hours That Were, Waltz*
125 Abscheid*
126 Ah! So Pure (Martha)*
127 Der Landmann†
128 Old Kentucky Home†
129 Yankee Doodle*
130 Traumerei*
131 Bonnie Doon*
132 Swiss Waltz
133 Irish Washer Woman*
134 Speed the Plough*
135 Then You'll Remember Me
      (Bohemian Girl)
136 Nettie Moore*
137 Nancy Till*
138 John Brown†
139 Annie Laurie*
140 Tramp, Tramp*
141 Old Uncle Ned
142 Rally Round the Flag†
143 Cagliostro Waltz No.3 (Strauss)*
144 He Is an Englishman (Pinafore)*
145 Merry Maiden and the Tar (Pinafore)*
146 Farewell to Erin*
147 Scots Wha Hae*
148 O'er the Sea (Pinafore)*
149 Dem Golden Slippers†
150 Eileen Alanna*

151 Ithaca March*
152 Pretty Jane*
153 When the Corn Is Waving*
154 Wearing of the Green*
155 Marching Through Georgia†
156 Come Back to Erin
157 Morning Journal's Waltz, No. 4
158 One Thousand and One Nights Waltz,
      No. 3*
159 Manuscript Waltz, No. 4*
160 The Approach of Spring Waltz, No. 1*
161 Leap Year Waltz, No. 1*
162 Grandmother's Chair†
163 Red, White and Blue†
164 Old Black Joe†
165 Coming Through the Rye*
166 Dearest May*
167 Bonnie Blue Flag†
168 Forest Glen Waltz†
169 There's a Light in the Window*
170 Babies on our Block*
171 Dixie
172 Full Moon Union†
173 Take Back the Heart*
174 Take This Letter to My Mother†
175 Wait for the Wagon*
176 Flower from my Mother's Grave
177 Nelly Gray†
178 Cheer, Boys, Cheer†
179 Theme from Mozart's 12th Mass*
180 Rosalie the Prairie Flower*
181 Pirates Chorus*
182 Hark! the Angels Sweetly Singing
183 St. Patrick's Day†
184 Scotch Lassie Jean*
185 Secret Love*
186 Mailuttle*
187 Tyroler Kind*
188 Old Wooden Rocker
189 Slavery Days*
190 See That My Grave's Kept Green†
191 Gathering Shells from the Sea Shore†
192 Jar Furwahr, Martha*
193 Racquet Galop*
194 Vive l'Amour*
195 Secret Love, No. 2*
196 Dar am Honey on Dese Lips*
197 There's Music in the Air*
198 Jamie's on the Stormy Sea*
199 Marseillaise Hymn†
200 Twinkle Little Star, or
      Meet Me at the Bars*
201 Cradle's Empty, Baby's Gone

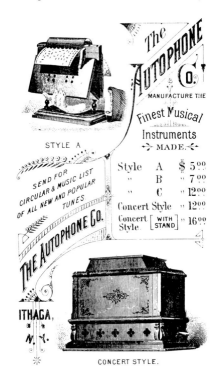

A "MANTEL" ORCHESTRONE

Robert L. Calland

𝕮HIS Orchestrone is a 26-note reed organ with two extra holes in the tracker bar that are used for automatic swell. The pneumatic pouches are a little larger than those used in the Celestina, and they give a sharp response.

Figure 1. Mr. Calland displaying the pneumatic pouches.

The three pump-bellows extend the full length of the action (26 inches), and with a 1½-inch stroke they have sufficient capacity to allow the reservoir return-springs to be adjusted to give 4½-inches maximum vacuum pressure. That provides approximately 3½-inch pressure while the organ is being played, and this gives the reeds excellent expression. Near the base of the tracker bar there are 28 lead tubes leading to the various pneumatic units.

Thanks go to Henry E. Laubach of Sarasota, Florida, for donating the

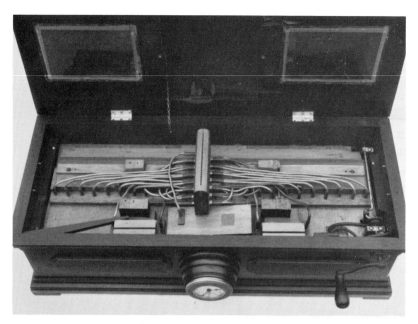

Figure 2. The new lead tubing.

Figure 3. View showing a roll in playing position.

Figure 4. The case of the Callands' Orchestrone.

necessary tubing that was used in restoring this organ to its original condition.

Mounted in the front of the cabinet is an eight-day Ansonia clock that is quite attractive.

The music rolls used on this organ are like those used on the Style 26B Orchestrone, except the music must be rolled on the spool in the opposite direction.

Along with eight newly cut rolls of music, this organ makes an interesting addition to our collection. ■■

Pianos

ROBERT HOPE-JONES
INVESTIGATES VIOLIN PIANOS

Q. David Bowers

David Junchen, the well-known theater organ scholar, recently furnished me with an interesting letter written in 1911. It revealed that Robert Hope-Jones, who had recently signed up with the Rudolph Wurlitzer Company in North Tonawanda, New York, was asked to evaluate two violin pianos and submit a report.

Robert Hope-Jones was the foremost exponent of the theater pipe organ and was the father of the so-called unified system, whereby portions of pipe organ ranks could be played from various keyboard positions which could be changed at will by the organist. After operating his own company in Elmira, New York, he joined Wurlitzer. Although Hope-Jones committed suicide in 1914 and was not able to see the true fruits of his labors, the Wurlitzer Theater Pipe Organs which he designed went on to become world famous. Eventually, over 2,000 units were built. Although Robert Morton, Kilgen, Link, and a host of others produced pipe organs to accompany silent films, the name Wurlitzer was dominant.

Hope-Jones, who possessed a keen mind and who engaged in many experiments concerning tone quality, musical mechanisms and the like, was undoubtedly America's best candidate to perform a violin piano analysis.

At the time, the category characterized as "violin pianos" was a popular part of the automatic musical instrument scene. In brief, a violin piano consisted simply of an automatic player piano to which one or more ranks of violin-toned pipes were added. Some, such as those made by Seeburg, were very simple and treated the violin pipes as an extra instrument which mechanically turned on or off according to instructions in the music roll. Others, particularly the products of certain European makers, were more sophisticated and had degrees of tonal shading, one or more violin pipe ranks arranged in a solo position on the music roll, and so on.

In 1911, at the time of Hope-Jones' report, Wurlitzer had an ongoing relationship with J.D. Philipps & Sons of Frankfurt-am-Main, Germany. From Philipps, hundreds of large orchestrions were purchased and sold in America under the names of Concert PianOrchestra and Mandolin PianOrchestra. No mention of Philipps was ever made in any Wurlitzer catalogue, and the intending purchaser would have no reason to doubt that they were American-made products by Wurlitzer's own factory.

Among the many smaller instruments handled by Wurlitzer, most were indeed made at the Wurlitzer factory in North Tonawanda. Included were several minor variations of a violin piano, a typical model of which contained a rank of pipes mounted behind the sounding board of the piano, and which used the Wurlitzer Automatic Player Piano rolls.

Apparently, in 1911 Wurlitzer contemplated building a more sophisticated model. Later, the Wurlitzer Solo Violin Piano was created following some of the ideas from the Philipps Paganini, a popular European instrument.

In 1911, Hope-Jones apparently had on the premises two violin pianos, one made by Popper & Company of Leipzig, Germany, and the other a Philipps Paganini. Exactly which Popper and Paganini models were evaluated was not stated in the report, but they were somewhat similar in size.

Although Wurlitzer had a close relationship with Philipps, from time to time they had a "wondering eye" and sought to do business elsewhere. For example, in 1909 and also on other occasions a strong attempt was made to forge a liaison with Ludwig Hupfeld, the premier maker of automatic musical instruments in Europe. Hupfeld was a gigantic organization with a broad product line containing instruments from home player pianos to immense orchestrions. Particularly attractive to Wurlitzer was the Phonolizt-Violina which utilized three real violins in combination with an expression piano. Farny Wurlitzer, who ran operations at the North Tonawanda plant, saw and heard one of these at a German trade show and was immediately captivated. In later years he told the present author that this was his favorite of all automatic musical instruments he had ever heard in his lifetime (a remarkable statement when one considers the items he produced as well as the many competitive items with which he was in a position to gain acquaintance!).

Hope-Jone's test results follow:

The Popper was described as a "piano expression divided into bass and treble," whereas the Paganini was "not divided."

For the Popper the notation "violin expression moderate" was given, while the Paganini simply rated the notation "poor."

In the next category the Paganini scored its only victory, albeit a minor one. The tremulant or vibrato device on the Popper was considered to be "moderate" in quality while the Paganini was ranked as "good."

The voicing of the violin types in the Popper was "excellent," compared to "moderate" for the Paganini.

The tone of the violins, certainly one of the most important considerations of all, was described as follows: "Popper—violin tone *living*—two pipes per note used; Paganini—violin tone dead, one pipe per note."

The Popper had "general effect a little softer," while the Paganini was described as "a little louder."

Another extremely important consideration was the subject of music rolls. Those of Popper were designed as "more artistically arranged," while those for the Paganini were written off as "inferior."

Lest there be any doubt as to which instrument Hope-Jones in his analysis considered to be the better, it was noted that for the Popper: "Violin part excellent, natural and poetic," while for the Paganini "unnatural and sometime impossible of performance, chords inartistic."

So far as the piano part of the instrument was concerned, for the Popper it was described as "artistic, although sometimes lacking in vigor," while the Paganini merited the brief note "not artistic."

Overall workmanship for the Popper was described as "excellent," in comparison to "moderate" for the Paganini.

The particular instruments evaluated were probably about the same cost and probably had the same general characteristics. The Popper measured 5'6" wide by 3' deep by 7'6" high while the Paganini measured 5'6" wide by 2'9½" deep by 7'10" high.

Robert Hope-Jones was consistently overruled on his musical and artistic suggestions. It was largely because of this that he eventually became despondent and committed suicide. Those who ran the Wurlitzer enterprise were more practical—indeed, perhaps they had to be—and the name of the game was sales and profit. It is largely because of this that very few musical innovations were ever created within the factory walls at North Tonawanda. Most of the good ideas came from the outside. I do not mean to condemn Wurlitzer for, certainly in his day, Farny Wurlitzer was nice to me and I am still indebted to the Wurlitzer Company for many kindnesses and favors for my research which led to *Put Another Nickel In* and *The Encyclopedia of Automatic Musical Instruments,* not to overlook many articles. It is just that Wurlitzer had so many opportunities to do so much, and so little advantage was taken. Unique among American firms with a wide product line in automatic pianos and orchestrions, Wurlitzer borrowed ideas elsewhere or simply had things made in other locations. The enchanting Wurlitzer Automatic Harp was a product not of the Wurlitzer factory but of the J.W. Whitlock Company of Rising Sun, Indiana. As noted, the PianOrchestras, the most elegant automatic musical instruments ever to bear the Wurlitzer name, were produced in Germany by Philipps, a firm which also inspired the Wurlitzer Automatic Roll Changer. The Mandolin Quartette and Sextette were products of Eugene DeKleist whose business was acquired by Wurlitzer in 1909.

Despite Hope-Jone's analysis, which pointed directly toward Popper as the logical instrument to copy or for which to acquire some type of a licensing arrangement, his thoughts were apparently ignored, for Paganini units were purchased from Philipps and sold under the Wurlitzer label. Later, when the Wurlitzer Solo Violin Piano was built in the North Tonawanda factory, copied ideas were from the Paganini not from the Popper.

Farny Wurlitzer possessed an extremely keen mind and could often remember virtually to the day when something transpired. I remember that during one visit to his office we were discussing the Automatic Roll Changer (which Wurlitzer always capitalized in its advertisements and reading copy). He summoned his secretary, Alice Matthies, to his office and instructed her precisely where to locate the information from over a half century earlier! Although we often talked of competitors such as Mills, Hupfeld, Link, and so on, I do not recall ever discussing Popper, although he was familiar with Popper and possessed several Popper catalogues from years earlier, catalogues which I eventually acquired.

In fairness to the memory of Farny I mention that he was a close personal friend of Hope-Jones, but was overruled on many counts by his brother Howard, who was the business manager of the Wurlitzer firm (operating from the Cincinnati, Ohio, office) and who had the final say. Howard was quick to bring suit against someone he didn't like or to fire an employee without notice. Farny, on the other hand, was warm, compassionate and understanding. Not that this makes any great deal of difference today except to observe that had Howard not been on the scene, Farny probably would have listened to Hope-Jone's ideas, Hope-Jones would have lived longer and the musical quality of Wurlitzer instruments and the rolls arranged for them would be different from what we know today.

In summation, Hope-Jones wrote:

If building violin pianos, it will be easy to make the power anything desired whichever model we follow. With the Popper model the range of expression may be increased several hundred percent at little or no added cost. If we follow the Paganini model, the range of expression can be increased, perhaps doubled, but this will involve added cost and wait. If following more closely the Popper model and using the Popper music or copies thereof, the instrument we build will be extremely beautiful and artistic. If we follow the Paganini model and use its music we cannot achieve this end, simply because of the music arrangement. It may interest you to know the Seigfried, Martini and Beach have each formed the same opinions on this subject as I have.

(Signed) Robert Hope-Jones.

THE STEINWAY COMPANY AND MECHANICAL PIANOS

Harvey N. Roehl

$\mathcal{M}$EMBERS of the East Coast Chapter of the Musical Box Society International were honored at their April 27, 1981 meeting in Binghamton and Vestal, New York, by the presence of Henry Z. Steinway and his wife, Polly. Mr. Steinway is the retired Chairman of the Board of the company bearing the family name, and he had been asked to meet with the group so they could hear him talk about his firm and the activities it was involved in back in the days of mechanically played instruments. Mr. Steinway spoke extemporaneously after the evening dinner, and unfortunately no transcript of his talk is available. He has, however, provided certain notes and documents (Exhibits A and B) in order that this article might be put together.

The general history of the Steinway Company has been well documented, and need not be repeated here. A lengthy and very good article describing the firm's history, beginning with its founding in 1853, appeared 100 years later in the October 1953 *Music Trades Magazine,* but even this interesting story fails to make any mention of the Steinway Pianolas or the Aeolian Duo-Arts and their impact on the business.

Mr. Steinway opened his remarks by suggesting that probably everyone in the room (there were 162 registered members at the Chapter meeting) would know more about mechanical instruments than he, but with that in mind he would try to bring us some "inside" information that was not generally known. The two most significant items that were brought forth were (A) the Steinway & Sons contract with the Aeolian Company and (B) the listing, by year, of the quantities of player pianos produced.

The following notes offer some interesting sidelights, and are paraphrased by the writer, based partially on memory of the Steinway talk:

". . . The post-Civil War expansion period was when the piano and the sewing machine were the principal 'home appliances' of the day, and this was the time when all the modern techniques — good and bad — of selling to consumers were developed, all of which are still used: time payments, advertising gimmicks like 'balance due' and 'only one (or four or seven) of this model left,' fire sales, bankruptcy, and so forth.

Henry Z. Steinway, at the left, and Walt Bellm during a visit to the Roehl collection on April 27, 1981. (Photograph by Jim Feller)

". . . the fight we had with WurliTzer in the early days stemmed from the fact that our contract with them for the sale of Steinway pianos in their stores stated that they were to get the lowest and best price. At some time after the contract was executed, they learned that Steinert's in Boston was actually getting an extra two per cent, and this precipitated a battle that culminated in a severing of the relationship.

". . . the piano as it is built today is, in spite of popular opinion, not of European origin, but is American. This is because the iron plate is strictly an American development, as is cross-stringing, and for many years there were the usual arguments about the merits of the latter compared to the European practice of straight stringing, but eventually the 'American method' prevailed, and today all instruments are built this way.

". . . following the end of the market for player pianos, the contract with Aeolian and Steinway was terminated 'by mutual consent' in April of 1933, and we took back from Aeolian 241 pianos specially constructed for players, which we eventually sold as regular pianos.

"... there must have been hundreds of Duo-Arts from which we removed the player mechanisms, but no records exist to tell just how many.

"... so far as I can determine, the last Steinway player was an 'L' in Walnut, Louis (no number given) style, our serial number 290,000, into which Aeolian fitted an Ampico player. It was sold to our dealer (Wells Music) in Denver, Colorado, in December of 1937.

"... pursuant to the Aeolian contract, our Hamburg factory shipped pianos to the Orchestrelle Company in England through our London branch, and to the Choralion company in Berlin, both of which were Aeolian subsidiaries. Our Hamburg factory retained its relationship with Welte. I believe they favored it over Aeolian whenever possible, because Steinway controlled the distribution — in Germany, anyway. I regret that we have no record of the number of pianos made for players in Hamburg, as our records were destroyed in the War."

EXHIBIT A — The Steinway-Aeolian contract. Note that the Aeolian Company was obliged to "downgrade" the Weber piano as one of the provisions.

Copy of Agreement between Steinway & Sons and the Aeolian Company, approved and executed as per minutes of Directors' meeting held March 9, 1909.

* * * * *

Memorandum, as per the negotiations between Chas. H. Steinway for Steinway & Sons and Edward R. Perkins for the Aeolian Company, covering the general terms of an agreement to be entered into between Steinway & Sons, of New York, a corporation organized under the laws of the State of New York, and the Aeolian Company, of New York, a corporation organized under the laws of the State of Connecticut.

The term "Aeolian Companies" shall mean the Aeolian Company and its affiliated companies.

This agreement is to be for a term of twenty-five years from date and is to cover, in its provisions, the entire World.

Steinway & Sons to agree to build pianos to allow of the incorporation of automatic actions, for the Aeolian Companies only: and the Aeolian Companies agree not to supply the Pianola action for incorporation in any piano that they do not control the wholesale and retail selling of. Steinway & Sons agree to discontinue furnishing their pianos to the Welte Artistic Player Piano Co., for the incorporation of their Welte-Mignon players for the United States of America, on and after June 1, 1910; but the present existing relations, arrangements and contracts between Steinway & Sons, Hamburg, and Steinway & Sons, London, and the Welte Company are to remain in full force and are, under no circumstances, to be questioned by the Aeolian Companies as long as the Welte Artistic Player Piano Co. does not incorporate in the Steinway Piano an action operated by foot power or hand lever control.

Steinway & Sons agree to furnish their pianos of present styles, with such changes as may be necessary for the installation of Pianola actions, to the Aeolian Companies at approximately Fifty Dollars per piano in excess of their regular wholesale prices.

The Aeolian Companies to have the exclusive sale of Steinway Pianola Pianos in those cities where both the Aeolian Companies and Steinway & Sons have their own branches. In other cities, towns and territories all over the World where the Steinway Pianos and the instruments made by the Aeolian Companies are sold by separate dealers, both the Steinway and the Aeolian dealers shall have the Steinway Pianola Pianos on exactly the same terms, prices and conditions, and represent the Steinway Pianola Piano faithfully; and it is positively understood and agreed that any Steinway or Aeolian dealer in any such city, town or territory who violates the conditions shall be deprived of the agency, or representation of the Steinway Pianola Piano.

Steinway & Sons agree to supply to the Aeolian Companies a minimum of not less than six hundred new Steinway Pianos per year, and the Aeolian Companies agree to purchase these pianos and pay cash for them — barring strikes, fires or earthquakes which might curtail the facilities of either party to supply or use this minimum number of pianos.

The Aeolian Companies agree to handle, market, advertise, push and recommend the Steinway Pianola Piano as their unqualified leader, and to obligate their branches, dealers and representatives to do likewise, as well as to use their best endeavors at all times to maintain the standing of the Steinway Piano.

The Aeolian Companies agree to officially relegate their Weber Pianola Piano to second place under the Steinway Pianola Piano; and they further agree to withdraw from the artistic concert field and that they will exploit the Weber Piano in public only through such minor pianists as Steinway & Sons may permit.

In the matter of territory, the Steinway Pianola Piano shall follow the same territorial lines as the Steinway straight piano, as regards Steinway dealers.

The Aeolian Companies are to have the exclusive marketing of the Steinway Pianola Piano, both wholesale and retail, throughout the World.

The Aeolian Companies agree to incorporate in each and every Steinway pianoforte that they may buy from Steinway & Sons under this agreement their best and most up-to-date full scale Pianola player, made of the finest material and with the best possible workmanship, and containing all of their latest improvements and devices.

Signed and sealed in
the presence of:

F. Reidmeister.

New York, March 9, 1909.

Steinway & Sons,   (Seal)
Chas. H. Steinway
President.

Signed and sealed in
the presence of:

(seal) H. M. Wilcox.

The Aeolian Company,
E. R. Perkins,
Vice-President.

EXHIBIT B — This list does not differentiate between 88-note players and Duo-Art reproducing instruments. If we may assume that all made after 1913 were actually Duo-Arts, then 6,458 Grands and 1,931 Uprights were produced for a total Duo-Art Steinway production of 8,389 instruments.

* * * * *

Player Pianos Shipped to Aeolian
1911 — 1931

Year	Grands	Uprights	Total
1911	125	327	452
1912	214	210	424
1913	254	290	544
1914	108	325	433
1915	100	324	424
1916	25	477	502
1917	223	271	494
1918	363	66	429
1919	274	55	329
1920	250	140	390
1921	444	45	489
1922	390	76	466
1923	448	56	504
1924	667	20	687
1925	762	18	780
1926	804	20	824
1927	514	16	530
1928	456	3	459
1929	319	19	338
1930	209	—	209
1931	102	—	102
Totals	7,051	2,758	9,809

■■

NOTE ACCENTING
ON PLAYER PIANOS
– A Survey –

Arthur W. J. G. Ord-Hume

𝒥N a previous issue of the M.B.S.I. *Bulletin* (Winter 1979, Vol. XXV, No. 3) in which my paper on the fidelity of the reproducing piano was published, reference was made to a British invention connected with the Aeolian Duo-Art—Isolated Instantaneous Theme. Details of this have never before been published, and I believe that members would be interested in such details.

Before moving into a description of this, however, it is advisable to consider the many ways by which inventors across the world thought to achieve the accenting of notes in a piano roll, so this paper will relate the history of note accenting.

The principle of note accentuation was the first step by means of which the basic pneumatic player piano might be elevated into acting as a reproducer. At the time note accentuation was first conceived, though, that ultimate goal was as yet undreamed of. The ability to accent a note—making it play louder than any others which might be played at the same time—would make it possible to pick out the melodic line—the theme—from counter-melody or accompaniment.

Recounting the history of theme emphasis, the *Scientific American* for May 20th, 1916, wrote:

> There is probably no element in the player that has been made the subject of so much patient investigation and clever invention as that of theme or solo expresssion, and, during the past decade, some very ingenious devices have been tried out and placed upon the market with more or less gratifying results.

The first attempt at melody emphasis, precursor of theme emphasis, came with the division of the pneumatic stack into two separate compartments, bass and treble, so that by means of hand controls the vacuum tension in the two halves could be controlled independently. This enabled one half—usually the accompaniment—to be subdued while allowing the melody (presumably in the treble) to play louder. The idea of dividing the compass of the player in this manner came from Hupfeld and was first used in their Phonola and Claviola pianos, although soon it was taken up by manufacturers world-wide. In operation, it was no different from the earlier systems employed with barrel pianos wherein a mechanical link could be pivoted about the keyboard center, notes to the left sounding progressively weaker and those to the right progressively louder and *vice versa*; but, as with the mechanical subduing control, the system was non-selective in that every note in one half of the stack played louder or softer than the notes in the other half, meaning that melody and accompaniment notes were invariably given the same degree of accent. Other systems were tried out experimentally, one being the provision of every note on the piano with two tracker openings—one for the striking signal and the other to regulate the vacuum tension. The difficulties of manufacturing the tracker bar and punching a roll accurately with perforations of varying widths rendered this impractical for production; however, such a system was the subject of a patent taken out by Robert Willard Pain, described as a manufacturer of 261 West 23rd Street in New York. Pain made use of a special tracker bar having two rows of holes that were staggered, not unlike the 116-note tracker bar of the two-manual Aeolian Orchestrelle player-organ. Pain described how, in order to adjust the vacuum tension for any note whatsoever, all that was necessary was to make that particular perforation slightly wider, or twice the width, so that both upper and lower tracker holes were uncovered. The problems of roll perforating for such a system would have been uneconomical, one feels. Still, he was granted British Patent number 19,527 in 1904 for such a system, and, significantly, this patent was acquired by Aeolian.

The system that was adopted almost universally was that whereby certain theme notes could be emphasized regardless of the overall level of the rest of the notes by means of special theming ducts at either end of the tracker bar and special precisely cut perforations at the sides of the roll to give pneumatic impetus to the required notes. Aeolian was the inventor of this system, or rather Aeolian acquired the patent for it. The inventor was James William Crooks of Boston, and it operated via a single special perforation on the left side of the roll and was intended to be used on a player action having a single, undivided stack. The British Patent for this was numbered 13,715, of 1900. The system was improved in the patent granted to Ernest Martin Skinner of Dorchester, in the county of Suffolk, Massachusetts. Here again, a single stack was controlled by one hole on the left side of the music roll. The British Patent for this was 15,518, also of 1900.

A very interesting variation was the subject of another Aeolian patent, the British coverage being 17,884, of 1910. So far, accenting had consisted of building up the vacuum tension for a note to sound above its neighbors, which had been subdued, and to achieve this, the theme note was to be cut slightly after the unthemed notes. Aeolian's experimental system worked exactly the other way about. The note to be themed was cut in advance of the notes not required to be themed and was subjected to whatever was the ruling vacuum tension; however, the other notes were subdued to a lower level by means of a sort of anti-theme perforation which subjected the stack to a tension-relieving chamber. In operation, allowing for the resultant different speeds of the action hammers, this must have brought the theme notes considerably ahead of the subdued notes and thereby permitted the possibilities of using varying hammer velocities to work against the satisfactory production of themed music.

Barely a few months later, Aeolian patented the system that was to succeed the twin-perforation theming holes. Now the use of two side-by-side very small perforations, aptly called "snakebites" by some American collectors, is very interesting and very clever, for by having the small perforations side by side, it ensures operation even if the roll is slightly off track, but, more to the point, the twin holes admit adequate control atmosphere air pressure for a very short space of time. This ensures very precise theming capabilities. This system is the subject of British Patent 20,352, of 1910, and the system was so successful that it survived from thenceforward with many other roll-making companies licensed to use the Aeolian patent. It did, furthermore, make specific allowance for use with a divided stack and thus had theming holes at both roll sides.

The successful Aeolian invention did not mean that theming devices had come to an end and that inventors would not continue to try and improve. The question of the Aeolian license was another spur to the inventive mind; however, the gradual standardization of piano rolls and the sheer size of the Aeolian empire and its massive production of both players and rolls were destined to kill off the alternative systems.

One of the last to appear was, in fact, a hark back to Robert Willard Pain's 1904 patent—the work of Paul Brown Klugh, of Chicago, who was granted British Patent number 112,632 in 1916. Klugh's tracker bar had normal openings, but above each opening, and slightly to one side, was a narrow vertical slit. The system was not only very complex, but must have been a non-starter on grounds of production costs. It operated by regulating the distance through which the hammer traveled to strike the string. The normal tracker openings worked in the usual way. Mounted above the hammers in the piano were a set of pneumatic motors, one to each pair of adjacent hammers; since piano music normally does not make use of intervals of a minor second, it was safe to assume that adjacent hammers would seldom be called upon to move together, let alone to require theming. These motors controlled an adjustable rest for the hammers, there being no conventional rest rail. The normal location was at a forward position, but when a note had to be themed, the pneumatic motor was collapsed via its own valve stack, and the hammer rest travelled back from the strings, so allowing the hammer plenty of distance in which to build up velocity. Like Pain's system, Klugh's patent required roll perforations of two sizes. Normal notes were sounded using normal-sized perforations, but themed notes had to be punched with larger openings so as to bridge both tracker-bar ducts.

There was another system that enjoyed great popularity for a while, and this had the ability to accent any note while having none of the complexity of

Pain's arrangement. This was the invention of Macarius Maximilian Kastner, the young German who created the Triumph and Autopiano players. The so-called Kastonome was an ambitious system that worked very well. It employed an individual accenting pouch for every note, the accenting pouches being connected to a common windway to which atmospheric pressure could be admitted via special additional openings in the tracker-bar sides and controlled by special music rolls featuring marginal holes for the notes to be accented.

The advantage of the Kastonome system was that it became unnecessary to modify the tension of the vacuum within the whole stack in order to accent one note, as all that was necessary was to alter the tension in a very small volume of space so as to operate the expression pouch. The disadvantage was that the system was difficult to maintain in perfect order, and although perfect when new, deterioration of the Kastonome pouches produced uneven playing, i.e. unintentionally accented notes, which was virtually impossible to mask.

The operation was very ingenious. Each of the additional perforations admitted air at atmospheric pressure to a cut-off pouch that governed the control of suction or atmosphere to a special ring-shaped pouch that formed a seat for the secondary valves. In the same way that one of Aeolian's patents covered the creation of a subdued piano with the accented notes being given 'normal' conditions, as distinct from a normal piano stack under the overall control of subduing controls through which accented notes were produced by increasing vacuum tension, the Kastonome worked on the principle of softening all the notes being played with the exception of the notes required to stand out. A correct musical interpretation required the Kastonome control to be switched on and off according to printed instructions on the music roll. Whereas the Themodist might be described as a passive system in that it did not need to be disconnected when not in use and was operational only when the Themodist perforations dictated so, the Kastonome was an active arrangement because it served to subdue the instrument overall.

Invented jointly by Kastner and C. Katz, British Patents were taken out for the system as follows: 12,761, of May 25, 1910; 8,723, of April 7, 1911. The special Kastonome music rolls, characterized by a central pair of parallel tempo-indicator width lines and a series of small green arrows between them to show speed variations, were the subject of British Patent 26,553, of November 15, 1910.

This ingenious system obviously called for special rolls suitable only for the Kastner piano, so with the pre-1914 spread of 88-note pianos with the Themodist type of accenting system, Kastner dropped the Kastonome, and the later Autopianos had what was called the "Triumphodist" control—the now universal Themodist system.

As demostrated, then, it was Aeolian's arrangement that was to survive the battle for theme expression with the Themodist, and although much later on, with the era of the reproducing piano, expression and theming came in

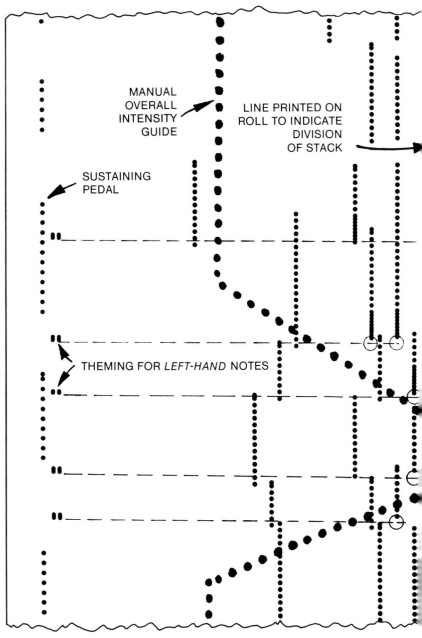

MANUAL OVERALL INTENSITY GUIDE

LINE PRINTED ON ROLL TO INDICATE DIVISION OF STACK

SUSTAINING PEDAL

THEMING FOR *LEFT-HAND* NOTES

𝕿HIS print of part of a Hupfeld roll shows how the themodizing notes (known in Hupfeld terminology as Solodant) are marked. Note that they are indicated visually (as well as audibly) by the use of a length of continuous punching to indicate the start of the note, while un-accented notes have no

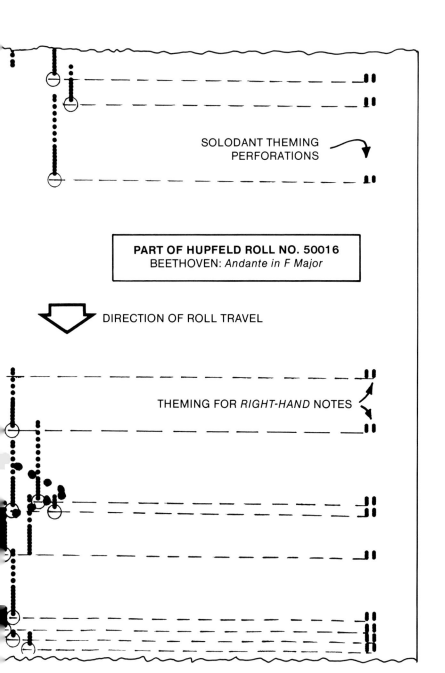

SOLODANT THEMING
PERFORATIONS

PART OF HUPFELD ROLL NO. 50016
BEETHOVEN: *Andante in F Major*

DIRECTION OF ROLL TRAVEL

THEMING FOR *RIGHT-HAND* NOTES

such indication. The narrow rule down the center of the roll shows the division of the stack between left accenting and right accenting. Hupfeld rolls were most advanced in this way and gave the player operator more guidance than most other makes of roll.

for closer scrutiny and refinement and although other systems were looked at, at the end of the reproducing piano era, whereby individual levels of theming were the goal, the snakebites were here to stay.

The principle of operation is simple and straightforward and relies on two things: first, a slight displacement of the start of the note to be themed so that it is separated from other notes that play at the same time, and second, a trigger signal to increase the operating suction to the stack at a precise moment, this suction being elevated above the level selected by any other means such as control levers. To achieve this precision, the themed note is signalled by a very short yet wide port in the tracker bar, and to ensure sufficient atmospheric air entering, two small side-by-side perforations are used.

The theme signal holes were connected to a regulator pneumatic, the overall level of vacuum tension therein being controlled by means of a knife valve. The instant a theme hole was uncovered, the regulator moved, opened the knife valve, and admitted a higher tension vacuum to the half of the stack in which the note to be themed lay. More than one note, of course, could be themed at any instant, and the response of the action was instantaneous.

In practice, the faster the traveling speed of the roll, within reason, the better the accenting effect. This is a bit of a generalization, yet it remains true that many of the earlier, slow-traveling rolls (cut at speeds of 40 and below) were intended to economize on paper, and therefore far greater accuracy was needed to position the theme holes. Usually, there was insufficient length of music slot to allow creative theming. This will be understood in a moment.

As already outlined, accenting one note calls for increasing the vacuum tension at the moment of exhausting the pneumatic motor to strike a particular note via one of the piano's hammer actions. Although this action takes place almost instantaneously, there is a minute time lag, which is only a mere fraction of a split second. With a roll cut at, say, 35 speed, this time represents virtually no distance on the paper, but if the roll is traveling at a greater speed, such as 60, then that split second becomes a noticeable fraction of an inch. It is this literally marginal distance that can now be put to use in a very subtle way.

Consider for a moment a chord of, say, four notes cut into the paper roll so that, as one might assume, all the notes start at the same instant and their starts thus represent a straight line across the paper. If we want one of these notes to stand out louder than the others, there are two ways to do it. One is to cut that note with a longer slot in the paper, leaving the other three very short. This means that the unwanted three will damp quickly, leaving the "accented" note singing out longer because the damper is held off the string.

Now that system is all very well, but it is not actually making one note physically louder and thus more predominant than the others. If we choose to punch theme holes to line up with the chord, they must affect all four notes, and we are back to where we started. The trick is to rely on the fact that the real live pianist seldom if ever will strike four notes evenly all at once. In an exaggerated case, they will sound as an *arpeggio*, and probably not in the logical order 1 2 3 4, but maybe 4 1 2 3, or whathaveyou. This pianistic shortcoming, though, is seldom discernible to the human ear and really shows only when we have a pianist cutting a roll melographically so that we can actually see his problems in the way the lines of perforations are presented.

So it does not matter all that much if, in cutting our roll, one or more notes are cut marginally late or early relative to our straight line. Remembering that the accenting of a note can take place only at the second that that particular piano action is set into motion, and that once the piano hammer is moving toward the string, nothing we can do with a paper roll can alter the hammer's velocity (short of thrusting the paper roll down inside the piano!), the trick is to select the note to be accented and cut it with a very slight delay and then theme that note.

This little trick has far greater potential than may at first appear, for it makes it possible for one note to stand out louder regardless of where the "soft-loud" controls are held—up to a position, of course, of maximum loudness. This means that it is a practical proposition to make one note stand out louder in a chord of apparently simultaneously sounding notes, regardless of whether it is the note at one end, or in the middle. Used in its developed form in the reproducing piano, this technique of theming individual notes takes precedence over the general level of vacuum in the stack as controlled by the special perforations for controlling the reproducing action.

Now we come back to my statement about roll speed and the faster speed giving greater effectiveness. It goes without saying that absolute precision is a prerequisite of positioning the theme perforations and that this precision is a factor of time rather than distance, meaning that the faster the paper travels over the tracker bar, the greater the distance in front of the note to be accented the theme holes have to be. If you visualize our fast-traveling roll and come back to our four-note chord within which we want note number three to stand out, the effect is noticeable only when the piano is being played at a level of sound below maximum loudness—this is the same whether the pianist is live or it is you with a paper roll and, if you think about it, is a very obvious statement. So, with the expression levers in use, we come to our four-note chord, and as the paper traverses the tracker bar, the perforations for notes 1, 2, and 4 uncover the ducts in the tracker bar and in the usual way set the hammers for those notes on their course to strike the strings. A split second later, our theme duct is uncovered, and note 3's perforation uncovers its tracker-bar duct. Under high tension, the pneumatic slams the piano hammer at the string at a greater speed than the other three. Depending on the degree of vacuum tension used for the first set of notes, it is now quite possible for all four hammers to strike their strings at one and the same time, since three were traveling at a slower rate than the fourth, hence we can explode the oft-repeated comment from non-*aficionados* (both concert pianists and laymen alike) that accenting one note in a chord is impossible by player piano.

In this résumé of the history of various methods of note accentuation, I have made specific references to the Kastonome and the Themodist and passing reference to the Triumphodist. These were but a very few of the names used in describing so-called accenting methods and the rolls from which such effects were produced. There is no doubt that in English-speaking countries the most common was the Themodist of Aeolian, which, on the roll and box labels, was always indicated by the word Themodist and the presence of a letter T before the roll number. This was found on the Aeolian rolls produced under the Universal name and, of course, Meloto when Universal changed its name.

Many other rolls equipped with perforations to operate the Themodist type of accenting were just marked with the word "Accented" and of course this was a characteristic of the so-called "hand-played" rolls. In Germany, the word Solodant was used for the same thing.

As distinct from physically emphasizing melody notes in the piano roll, Aeolian considered that it was worth making these notes easier to identify in the roll by punching them with a different type of perforation. British Patent number 14,325, dated September 1, 1904, was granted for a system in which, while accompaniment notes are chain-punched, the melody notes have contiguous perforations, i.e. separate holes separated by a narrow neck of paper. In fact, in the years to come the system was reversed, and the accompaniment often had contiguous perforations while the melody line had slotted openings, and in the case of longish notes, a slotted opening followed by contiguous holes. Aeolian's differentiation of types of note perforations stood it in good stead when it came to the Aeolian Pipe Organ with its double-row tracker bar wherein upper manual notes were in single perforations and the lower manual ones were in the form of slots, the arrangement being so that the operator of the instrument could see at a glance where the melody was.

All the makers of reproducing pianos made claims for their instruments that were sometimes extravagant,* while standards of advertising were often downright objectionable, particularly in America, where Ampico engaged in a public denigration of its rival, the Duo-Art. How the two companies fared when the exigencies of commercial interest and the Depression brought the two systems under one and the same roof has never been related.

One of the things that all the makers made a great thing of was the ability to perform absolutely faithfully in the manner of the original roll. Now it must be said that thanks to skillful and masterly editing by persons whose knowledge of both music and the pneumatics of their piano systems was second to none, this was a goal more often than not achieved within the overall limitations that certain types of music were difficult if not impossible to re-enact pneumatically. There were, toward the end of the era, for

---

* Although one should bear in mind the large number of testimonials, back in the days of the piano-player, from, apparently, top-quality pianists who claimed that the instrument gave them the satisfaction that only a live player could hitherto provide. Testimonials, one tends to feel, were bought at high prices.

example, some Ampico rolls that must be rated as interpretational failures not on the basis of their having been badly played originally—this cannot have been the case—but because the system could not cope with the demands made upon it.

The key to this was the ability to theme any note anywhere in, for example, a rapid *arpeggio* or counter-theme. In truth, this was just what Pain had done, somewhat arbitrarily, back in the early years of this century, while Kastner had striven a long way toward this with the Kastonome, but both these systems had the disadvantage that, as already stated, they were not passive systems, but fully interactive. In the intervening decades, player actions and music had together come along considerably. With the availability of the Aeolian-created action pattern that was by then used worldwide, whatever new system was created had to be fully compatible with normal Themodist and Duo-Art rolls.

The first company to attain this goal would obviously reap a rich reward in the market. Several other systems had been invented, perhaps the most interesting, yet impractical on the grounds of economy, was that conceived as early as 1909 by Arthur Ronald Trist of the Trist Piano Player Company. Trist had begun with a push-up player and an under-capitalized company, which went into liquidation. He re-formed into a new company and spent much time and money perfecting an isolated-theme system. It does seem, though, that he never actually produced any pianos incorporating his invention. Trist felt that the admixture of pneumatics and electricity was the key to isolated theme, and between 1909 and 1912 he patented at least five electro-pneumatic devices—and these were developed from an even earlier Trist patent of 1906. The key to his system was a three-ply music roll made of thin metal sandwiched between paper. Note theming was achieved in the accepted way by marginal perforations that passed right through the roll; however, note sensing was achieved by electric tracker brushes, and the music rolls contained "partial" perforations that exposed only the metal foil, or full perforations that operated the pneumatic chest. One major advantage of the Trist system, which no doubt would have been of a certain attraction, was that it was possible to control up to three instruments at once from one music roll and spool box, and these instruments could be organ or piano. The high cost of making a saleable player on this system more or less killed it off, and Trist went on to perfect a three-color printing process.

It is at this point that Gordon Iles came into the picture. A man of immense talent—he built the Duo-Art Robot remote-controlled *vorsetzer*— Iles spent the war years making pneumatic synthetic trainers for bomber pilots, using Duo-Art technology,* and today runs the Artona Music Roll Company at Ramsgate. Iles succeeded where others had failed, only to be beaten by the financial collapse of Aeolian in London.

Born in 1908, Iles studied music at Cambridge under Dr. Cyril Bradley Rootham (born 1865, died 1938) where he had charge of the University's

---

* See article: "How the Duo-Art Won the War" in *The Music Box,* Volume 7, p. 131.

Duo-Art, a Weber Model 12 pedal-electric grand. Dr. Rootham, a composer in his own right, used the instrument more as an ordinary piano than as a reproducer, and although he had contributed to the Aeolian "World's Music" series, he did not have an especially good opinion of it and was never slow to point out the occasional lack of what came to be termed *isolated simultaneous theme* or IST for short. He conceded that IST was extremely good in the case of certain recordings, but not all. Gordon Iles was a pianist of above average ability, and he was also aware of this shortcoming. Fortunately, he had the time to study the problem in some depth.

It should be pointed out that his father, John Henry Iles, had at one time been a journalist and became president of the London Press Club. His prowess as a one-time County cricketer who had played with the legendary W. G. Grace for Gloucestershire brought him to the notice of the managing director of Aeolian in London, G. F. Reed, and they became firm friends. Iles Senior became public relations and advertising adviser to Reed. Through this, the Iles home had every model of the Pianola from the 65-note push-up to the most sophisticated electric Duo-Art, and all of these instruments Gordon Iles stripped down to the smallest part until he had become thoroughly acquainted with the art and practice of pneumatic action.

Ultimately, Gordon Iles succeeded in producing a prototype Duo-Art action of his own, which was accredited as being "remarkably fine." Both Iles Senior and Reed were much impressed, and the suggestion was made by his father that Gordon Iles should tackle the problem of IST. Acceptance of the challenge was met with the immediate shipment of a special Weber Duo-Art to Gordon's workshop at his home, and here research and experiments in IST began in real earnest. This was around 1925. Aeolian's chief technical superintendent at Hayes, in Middlesex, was Harry W. Palmer, and he made all the special components designed by Gordon Iles and sent them to Iles's home at Broadstairs, in Kent.

Finally, Gordon Iles completed his IST Duo-Art in his workshop. At this time Aeolian was spending vast sums of money on special-purpose equipment to manufacture educational music rolls under the label "The World's Music." The company had also redesigned the basic piano-playing stack and taken out a patent (number 323,005, dated September 17th, 1928) in the names of C. F. Cook and H. W. Palmer for an action featuring hingeless, square striking pneumatics as distinct from the usual wedge-shaped ones.* Unfortunately, the financial collapse of the company was nigh, and IST was abandoned.

The entire program of work on IST had been conducted in secrecy, for company policy demanded that the public should be told that Duo-Art with its Themodist constituted the ultimate in perfection and left nothing further to desire. Nevertheless, those who heard the IST in operation immediately

---

* The use of parallel striking pneumatics had been included in British Patent number 4,804, dated February 26th, 1909, in the name of C. Katz and M. M. Kastner.

became aware of the very definite improvement in reproduction that it gave.

The operation of the Aeolian-Iles IST system hinged on the use of a special twin valve chest* employed in conjunction with a tracker bar having a double row of holes, the two rows being very close together. The top row included Themodist ports but were fixed with a minimum (extremely soft) level of accompaniment. The lower row of ducts were accompanimental only and were under the influence of the usual variable Duo-Art level as set by the music roll accompaniment perforations.† This bottom row was not provided with Themodist ducts.

The tracker bar was made in an interesting way. Some of the early pre-Duo-Art tracker bars had comparatively narrow slots, so two of these were cut lengthwise and the portions with the slots joined together to form a single bar in which the two rows of holes were very little wider than the single row in a standard bar.

In operation, if a themed note was provided with a theme perforation, as normally found in a roll, and set back by a fraction of an inch corresponding to the space between the two rows of holes in the double tracker bar, then the themed note or notes arrived at the first row at the same time as the forward-cut accompanimental notes. These, having no Themodist perforations, will either not have sounded at all when they passed the first row, or at most would barely have played due to the low level setting of that valve stack. The result of this was that themed notes could be played simultaneously with the accompanimental notes. In this way it was only necessary to arrange rolls to play at a tempo setting of no more than 100, and sometimes even less, in order to provide full IST without losing maximum repetition. An added advantage was that the rolls would also play satisfactorily when used on standard Duo-Art instruments although without, of course, the IST effect.

Conversely, ordinary Duo-Art rolls would also play in the normal way on a special IST instrument. The "stop" slot position between the treble Themodist and soft pedal slots in the tracker bar was used, in the case of an IST piano, to bring the mechanism into operation, otherwise only the lower row of holes functioned. One or two patents were taken out, but were allowed to lapse when the Aeolian Company folded up.

This perfection of IST was actually built into a piano on a commercial venture. Iles Senior built the Dreamland Super Cinema at Margate about 1936, and Gordon Iles cooperated with the John Compton Organ Company in designing the organ. Part of the installation was an IST Duo-Art on the stage that could also be played with expressive touch from the organ

---

* Aeolian had used the twin chest as the basis of a rudimentary, non-automatic theming system as early as 1916, when, on November 28th of that year, it was granted British Patent number 111,349 for variable-tension striking pneumatics under the control of a tune-sheet or from special buttons provided for the purpose in the key-slip.

† In truth, the double-row tracker bar used in conjunction with two valve chests, one at a high vacuum tension and the other at low, combined with accenting ducts, had been the subject of British Patent number 7,698, dated March 26th, 1914, in the name of D. Kennedy.

console. This unique piano and installation was destroyed by enemy action during the war.

Aeolian had also experimented with another method of achieving IST, which used a standard tracker bar but had the disadvantage that it required the use of special rolls that could not be used on standard instruments. In this system, each slot in the tracker bar had three functions, which, as before, were brought into action through a perforation aligning with the "stop" position. These three functions for each note-playing hole were: (1) to play a note; (2) to cancel the playing power of the adjacent tracker note-playing hole; (3) to theme exclusively the note corresponding to the slot on the left. Spelled out, then, this system used the normal tracker hole next to the one being played for theming by first signalling a cancel to its normal playing function, and then causing it to react to the opening of the note channel to its left. This assumed that in normal music intervals of a minor second are seldom encountered, for in such instances the theming of one of the notes would be impossible by this method, although imaginative Themodist cutting could no doubt be used to some advantage. In use, if a note to be themed had a single pip perforation next to it on the left, it would be themed without the production of what might appear to result in a discord. Naturally, the operation of this IST system was achieved in conjunction with a special twin valve chest of similar design to that employed in the twin tracker-bar system described above, and a rather complex bank of cancel membranes was also required.

Although this system proved completely reliable, it had obvious limitations and was restricted to using for its full effect special rolls that could not be used on any other playing mechanism.

So ended the quest for themed notes. Like many other inventions, it reached perfection at a time when nobody wanted it. Significantly, the demand is there again today. Perhaps some latter-day engineer may resurrect the work of Gordon Iles.

It is to be regretted that no pictures ever existed of that very special Duo-Art in the Margate cinema and, in the artificial surroundings that affect values during times of war, nobody bothered to try to salvage any of the remains after the bombing. ■■

THE PIANO MAN —
CONLON NANCARROW

James Spriggs

CONLON Nancarrow has one advantage over most living composers. When he produces a new piece of music, he is sure that he will be able to hear it performed. He can also be sure that the performance will be perfect.

That's because Nancarrow gave up writing for human performers and began writing for a machine nearly 40 years ago. Nancarrow's music is written on piano rolls for the player piano.

"The recording can be a very different experience," Nancarrow stated in a recent interview. "In the right conditions it can be as good as the original performance. At the New Music America Festival in San Francisco, with a good tape and good acoustics and equipment, I thought the recording sounded better than the original."

Since World War II, there have been essentially two kinds of composers: those who are like Nancarrow and those who are like John Cage or Roger Sessions, who was one of Nancarrow's teachers. Nancarrow went on: "Sessions once said that if he heard the most perfect recording in the world of his favorite piece of music, after hearing it once he would want to throw it away, he couldn't bear to hear it again, because it would be always the same thing. I don't understand it. People read 'War and Peace' and it's the same every time, or Shakespeare's sonnets or view a Rembrandt painting, and it's always the same. But a piece of music has to be a different thing each performance. I just don't understand that. You would think a composer would go after the most perfect performance he could get and just keep it there."

A composer like Cage believes in spontaneity, indeterminacy, pure chance in its extreme form, this attitude includes the feeling that whatever happens during a concert is music. Nancarrow (who is a friend of Cage despite philosophical differences) believes in ideal forms that can have a perfect embodiment. "That's my approach," he said. "The other approach is perfectly valid, but it's not mine."

Essentially, Nancarrow said, he is "self-educated" as a composer. "With Sessions," he said, "I studied counterpoint. I would write little pieces and take them to him, and he would say, 'That's interesting; where's your counterpoint exercise?' "

Born in Texarkana in 1912, Nancarrow fought against Franco in the Abraham Lincoln Brigade during the Spanish Civil War. Because of his

Conlon Nancarrow (1912-   ), American-born composer in exile in Mexico City, April 1977.

service in Spain, he was denied an American passport in 1940. "I guess you could call that harassment," he said. "Anyway, that's all it was. I wasn't planning to go anywhere, I just wanted to have a passport, just on general principles, and the idea that I couldn't have one bothered me."

He moved to Mexico and became a Mexican citizen, and in the past few years, he has started traveling again. Since the late '70's, when his music began to be known largely through recordings, he has averaged about one concert trip per year. Before then, he used to stay at home working on his Studies for Player Piano on a specially-built machine.

He had two primary reasons for choosing this outlet: One was the technical limitations of human performers, the other was that he couldn't get them to play his music. "I remember once I was asked to write a trio for clarinet, bassoon and piano. I wrote and went to a rehearsal. They read through it very badly. Then afterward, the pianist told me that the clarinetist and bassoonist refused to play it because the public would think they were playing the wrong notes.

"I have written a few things for piano live, but it's much more work than writing for player piano. For one thing, I have to think of the limitation of 10 fingers. Another is that I'm interested in hearing my music. Before I started on the player piano, I had written quite a few things for other instruments and none of them were ever played. Last year in California, they played for the first time a piece for string quartet that I composed 40 years ago."

How did he live in Mexico when his music was totally unknown? He laughed at the question and said, "Odds and ends — for some time, mainly on my wife's earnings. A while back, I had a little inheritance, so there was a little income, but that got to be less and less until it was finally nothing." In 1982, he received a $300,000 grant from the MacArthur Foundation, which should help a little.

There are only two composers he admires completely: Bach and Stravinsky — particularly Stravinsky. "He is one composer who always chose the right note at the right time. And probably more important, he knew what to throw away. Most artists feel, 'This is my child, and I can't part with it.' I've thrown away quite alot." ♎

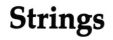

Strings

An Insight into
Mills Novelty Company,
The Industry Maker

Donald D. Barr

℃HE following is a résumé of interviews with Bert Mills, a mechanical innovator with Mills Novelty Co., Chicago, Illinois. To the collector of musical antiques, the name, Mills Novelty Co., is synonymous with Violano-Virtuosos, slot machines, and jukeboxes. Mr. Mills credits himself with having developed or contributed to every successful product manufactured by the Company during his employment, which dated from his early teens. He refers to himself as a high school dropout because of his lack of formal education. His lack of education did not hinder his inventive mind nor preclude his financial success, and his ability to recall distant facts would be enjoyed by anyone one-quarter of his 82 years. We thank him for answering the numerous questions propounded to him, to which he responded without hesitation. The following contains many of the questions and answers relating primarily to the musical items made by Mills Novelty Co., its history, and the personalities involved. All bracketed material has been inserted by the author in the interest of clarification.

Q: Mr. Mills, to present-day collectors, the Violano-Virtuoso is probably the most familiar of the Mills Novelty Co. products. During the long period of its manufacture, numerous modifications were obviously made. Can you describe the machine as it existed in its early period of development?
A: Yes. About 1904, Henry K. Sandell [hereafter, Sandell] brought into the factory his patented mechanical violin. It was not encased and was mounted in what we call a 'breadboard design.' The fingerhead was high above the strings. The most important feature it had was the revolving discs which played the strings in place of a violin bow. The bow motor ran at a constant speed, and so, naturally, there was no expression. Tuning was done by screws similar to a guitar. Naturally, it would get out of tune whenever there was a change in temperature or a draft.

My brother, Herbert S. Mills [hereafter referred to as HSM] who owned the Company, liked violin music and thought that the machine could be improved, and if so, would have commercial possibilities. Sandell worked on it for about the next six years. The machine was improved somewhat, and a few were put out on the market about 1906 or 1907. It was called the 'Virtuosa' and was an automatic violin only. These instruments sounded poorly, but the people played them anyway because they were so unusual.

They were definitely not played for the enjoyment of the music. The piano with the symmetrical harp was added about 1911 or 1912, all of which did not really make the machine any more practical but did make it more interesting. The name of the instrument was then changed to the 'Violano-Virtuoso.' About 1915 or 1916, the Violano-Virtuoso was more or less turned over to me for commercial development. I developed many patents for the machine that made it more practical for commercial use. Many of my early patents were put in my brother's [HSM] name or in Sandell's name, but I was given credit for almost all of my later ones. I have roughly fifteen or sixteen Violano patents in my name and was paid a patent royalty on every Violano sold.

Q: How many of the Virtuosas which contained no piano were produced?
A: Probably about fifty of them. The Virtuosa which had no piano was the instrument that won a prize in the Alaska-Yukon Exposition. Most of the Virtuosas were later taken or traded back to the factory. On the curved-case model, which housed the Virtuosa, we built a cabinet addition to the rear in which we put the piano. [This is today sometimes referred to as the 'bow front' model.] This was also done on some other case designs as well.

Q: Is it a fact that Kaiser Wilhelm bought one of the Virtuosas [without the piano]?
A: Yes, that's true. He got his machine about 1912 or 1913.

Q: How did the Company promote the early Virtuosas?
A: Well, they weren't promoted very much or well. Of course, being such a novelty, we sold a few of them, but as I said, they were so impractical we took most of them back. Few of the buyers kept them.

Q: Did you send them out to dealers for distribution?
A: No, they were all sold by us directly to the user. We didn't have any dealers in the early days as we did later on.

Q: Did the early machines generally go into homes?
A: No, the early ones actually went to taverns and that sort of thing. They were coin-operated right from the beginning. We made a few for home use without coin operation, like for Mr. Charles G. Dawes, who was later Vice-President under Coolidge. Mr. Dawes asked me to come out to his home in Evanston to dinner. He said that he wanted to talk to me and see if we could take the Violano he had in his house and fix it up so that he could sit back and put in the expression as he wanted, rather than have it use the expression which was cut into the rolls. I said that it would be very simple to do. I went to the factory the next day and made a little device whereby he could sit down and give the expression to the violin by remote control. I just cut out the brushes so that they would get no current from the perforated rolls and wired in the remote-control buttons. That one, however, was the only one of that type that was ever made.

318

Q: Early advertising pictures of the Violano show a piano harp or plate that wasn't the familiar symmetrical design that was patented in 1912. It was the more conventional type, being from low to high. Was this design manufactured in quantity?
A: No, we never manufactured them, and I don't recall even seeing any in the experimental room.

Q: Looking at the early Home Model Violano [see the cover], we find that it was made pretty much like the June 4, 1912 patent drawings. To your best recollection, how many of that model were made?
A: I would estimate that not over twenty of those Violano-Virtuosos that have the fingers over the strings were made.

Q: That machine also plucks the strings?
A: Yes. I developed that pizzicato. It wore out the strings, especially the D and G, which were gut, but wound with aluminum and silver. They would be scored by the pluckers and then break, so the idea was dropped.

Q: This Home machine seems to have far more expression devices than the later ones. For example, it will put on more bow pressure and can reverse the bows, and do other things that the later Violanos do not do. Why were these seemingly good ideas dropped?
A: Well, this machine was quite complicated. There was an adjustment to the bows at the top of the bow solenoids which were over the bows. People handling the machine would adjust these bows so that they would scrape, and just wouldn't or couldn't adjust them properly. I changed that method by setting the bow solenoids to the rear and employed a lever device to actuate the bows. The height of the bows would be regulated by turning an adjusting screw on the lever. Later, I put little springs underneath the bow lever to cushion the bows and did away with the adjusting screw. That made the machines on location more practical. The adjustments on the early Home model, if properly made, would give you better expression, but if they were out of adjustment, they would be just terrible. I didn't know what the musical term for moving the bow back and forth was, but I saw musicians do it rapidly and I thought it would be interesting to see if we couldn't do that with a roll. The sound effect did not justify the involved mechanism, and that idea was dropped.

Q: Why was the violin string fingering changed from the top to the side?
A: The overhead fingers made a lot of noise. I suggested to Sandell that we put them underneath the strings and just bring them up. He said, "No, you don't finger a violin below the strings." I said, "That's because you can't." All you have to do is mute the string at a given point. He said, "Well, go ahead, try it and see if it works out." I made one up with a couple of finger magnets, and I called Sandell in. I put the bow down on the string, and I said, "Well, how does that sound?" He said, "I don't see any difference." I said, "The only difference is that there is no noise to that finger when it

comes up." I did not like the big magnet box above the strings, and so my arrangement was better for that reason, too. It opened up the violin and was more interesting to the public because they could see the fingering.

Q: The early violins were tuned by turning a worm gear and later by moving weights hung on a lever. Who came up with the idea of tuning by weights?
A: I did. One day when I was working on devising a better method of tuning, I went in to see my brother, Herbert, and I told him that for a string to stay in tune, it must have a certain amount of tension, whatever it be, say ten pounds, and that if a system could be devised with a weight, it should keep the tension constant and the string in tune. He listened intently, picked up the phone and asked to have Sandell sent in. He came in and listened to my idea and [Sandell] said, "That will work, and I will have one made up right away." This he did with the weights hanging down into the lower part of the machine. Because I was so young at the time, I believe that the patent on tuning may have been put in Sandell's name. After that incident, my brother gave me a pretty free hand in further development work. We argued quite often about my ideas, and very frequently the argument would be settled when I got fired. Customarily, in a day or so, my brother would visit our parents' home where I lived and after an apology one way or the other, would re-hire me at a slightly increased salary.

Q: Early Home model machines had a feeder which is quite different from the later ones. It didn't rewind automatically. The end of the roll is cut out on the left side just before the end. A roller rides the left side of the roll, and when the roll comes to the end, it contacts the metal core of the spool where the paper is cut away, thus energizing a solenoid which pulls a switch that shuts off the machine. Then, the operator shifts gears to reverse, starts it up again, and the machine rewinds, shutting itself off when the roll is rewound.
A: That's the way that some of the first Home models were originally made. Later, and for the coin-operator, the feeder had an automatic rewind which in effect and with about 20 more parts than the ultimate design, would reverse the feeder motor as distinguished from reversing by shifting gears. Basically, the rewind was dependent upon the diameter of the paper remaining on the spool. The roll would play and would get to a point when the diameter of the paper on the feed spool would be small, then with a riding wheel and other parts would throw a switch that energized a reversing switch. It was quite similar to the wheel and mechanism which rides the take-up spool and causes the machine to stop rewinding at the proper point.

One incident that I remember is when I went to Calgary, Canada, where there was a machine purchased by Northwest Novelty Company. I went up there to set it up. It was back about 1919 or 1918, and it was 15 or 20 below zero outside. When I got into Calgary that morning it was 43 below zero. That afternoon it warmed up, and we opened up the packing box. The machine was white with frost and condensation on the top. The music rolls were like putty; you couldn't adjust the machine to rewind properly; it was just simply impossible. We had brushes on the machine that we weren't using, and I remembered that one of them was the 19th brush. I thought to myself, "Well, why not wire the 19th brush to the solenoid for the reversing switch and cut a hole in the music roll at the end where the 19th brush is so that when it plays and comes to the end of the roll where the hole is cut, it can throw the switch." I asked Mr. Fenwick, who was in charge, to let me unroll the rolls on the floor so that I could modify them. I made up a little template and took a pen knife and cut the slot in the proper place but just a little wider to make sure that the brush would go through. It even played a violin note because I made the hole so wide. I fixed all his rolls up and took all the other junk off the feeder. I wired back to Chicago, and I said, "Don't send any more music rolls to Canada until I get back." I didn't want to send up any more without the rewind slots cut in them. When I got back, my brother [HSM] said, "Now, what did you do in Canada?" And I said, "Well, I took all this junk off the feeder and made the rolls rewind with a brush," and he replied, "I don't want you monkeying with these machines on the outside — you're fired." And I said, "Fine, I quit." On the eighth floor of the factory, we had an experimental room. I went up there without him knowing it and got one of the men aside, and I said "Now, I can't be around this machine because my brother [HSM] may come up and raise the devil," so I said, "Now, here's what I want you to do. Tie that rewind arm [roller] down so that it can't operate, and take one of these rolls and cut a hole where the 19th brush is." At first, he was hesitant and said, "I'm going to get fired, too." I assured him that he wouldn't. He did it, and I went down to my brother's office and said, "Herbert, I want you to see something." Well, after a little argument with him, I got him to come up. I said to him, "You see how that junk is tied down; we don't use it anymore." He watched the roll get down to the end and rewind, and he said, "How did you do it?" I said, "Find out for yourself," and I turned around and walked out. Of course, he could tell from the men how it worked. I used to play pinochle with my brothers and my father every Sunday, and Herbert came over the following Sunday and he said, "Bert, where have you been for the last three or four days?" I said, "I've been fired, don't you remember?" He said, "I didn't fire you. You get down to work," and I replied, "I will like the devil — I quit!" "Well, he said, "I'll give you a ten dollar raise," and I said, "Okay, I'll be back."

Q: Some of the very early rolls that are still around have written in pencil, "No automatic rewind." What, if any, is the reason for that?
A: That is because the 19th brush, which is the automatic rewind, was not cut in by the factory. The factory probably did not put the writing on the rolls. Someone probably cut in the hole at the 19th brush but never crossed out the marking.

Q: The violin expression tracks on the early rolls seem to be very short in length, but on the later rolls, they were longer. What is the reason for this?

A: Well, there was just more expression in the later rolls to be used with an improved motor. That was all.

Q: The later rolls were described as 'hand played.' If the earlier ones were different, how were they made?
A: Originally, when the musical department made up a roll, the musicians, of whom we had fourteen, would each sit at a long table with uncut master-roll paper, going from one end to the other, that was lined vertically and horizontally. The horizontal lines were to determine the length of the notes. They would sit down with their music in front of them, and they'd pencil-mark out all the notes. It would take one man probably a week or two to make just one selection. Then we had girls who would chop out the

GRAND MODEL VIOLANO

322

marked-up master roll, all by hand. I did not like the musical arrangements of the early rolls. Once I said to Professor Fredrickson, the head musician at Mills, "Why don't you put some jazz on that piano so there is more than just the ump thump thump that you have there?" He got mad at me, and went to my brother and said, "You keep your brother out of here, or I quit." My brother called in his secretary or the timekeeper and said, "Professor Fredrickson just resigned." He then called me at my office and he said, "Well, you're going to make the music rolls now." All the other musicians quit in sympathy after my brother refused to rehire Professor Fredrickson. I was in a heck of a pickle! I did not know anything about music, but my wife knows music, so I took a roll of the master-roll paper home with me one night, and I said to her, "Now look, I'm going to make a roll, but I've got to make it mechanically. You read music. Tell me what those notes are, and I'll mark them on the master-roll by hand. Then, I'm going down and make a machine that will do it automatically." Actually, the first machine I designed to hand play the music was the keyboard for the violin. There was an upper keyboard and a lower keyboard for the violin, which took care of the overlapping notes. I had on the side a little deal whereby you moved your knee to put in the tremolo. The pedals were for the expression. I didn't know how to play the keyboard machine so I had a musician come out, and I said, "Now, you put your fingers on these keys. Tell me what they are, eighth notes, quarter notes, or whatever they are, while I move this roll of paper by hand." I had a cable going up to the marking machine which was designed so that it would put little lines or marks on a master roll as the keys were played. After practice, within a couple of hours, two musicians [violin and piano] and I could make up a marked roll. We then had the girls chop out the markings. This became the 'hand played' music. That method worked pretty well until I thought up a better way. I wondered why I couldn't cut out the master roll as the musicians played by connecting the cutting machine to perforate while the musicians were playing. Furthermore, why couldn't I hook up a violin and let the musician hear the violin as he played and do the same for the piano? These modifications were made up. I knew a couple of musicians at the Tip Top Inn in Chicago whom I got to come over [one was Walter Blaufus]. So then I said, "Now sit down and try this for a while, and one of you play the violin and the other play the piano." They got intrigued with the setup and liked the violin because it played like an organ. I connected the violin and piano keyboards to one of our cutting machines that made regular rolls. They sat down and played, and when they got all through, I took that roll off, which was then a master roll, and put it on a machine to play. Expression and everything were in there. It worked just fine. So, instead of using fourteen men, each of whom would take two or three weeks to make one selection, in three minutes we had a whole song. In an afternoon they [the musicians] could come over and make two or three rolls.

Q: Labels on the music rolls indicate that a lot of your music was arranged by a fellow named J.F. Stelzel.

DE LUXE MODEL VIOLANO

A: Yes, Stelzel was one of the first musicians that we had, and he played the keyboard-operated violin.

Q: How did the roll-cutting machinery work, and how was it set up?
A: Well, two sets of copies were run off from each master. Each set consisted of ten sheets. Each set was run through a separate perforating head and would be cut in about an hour and a half. The master roll and reader was in the center between the two perforators. The reading was done electrically, and the punches were actuated by solenoids but driven mechanically.

Q: Was the master roll just as long in length as the production roll?
A: Yes, it was identical. You could take the master and play it on a machine, or you could take a production copy and use it as a master for

making other copies. In fact, the later master rolls looked identical to the ones you would play on a machine.

Q: Your cutting machines were evidently high-speed units. Is that true?
A: Yes, they were. The one on which I made the master rolls was run at very high speed, but in the production of copies, it would take about four times as long to cut the copy. When we made a master, we cut two copies at a time and, of course, the perforator could run much faster. The perforated slots of all rolls are slightly scalloped because the punches were round. Because in making the master roll it went faster and the punching head did likewise, the master rolls were no more scalloped than a production copy.

Q: Well, your perforators were evidently much more high-speed than the pneumatic-actuated perforators used by the makers of piano and other rolls.
A: Oh, yes, definitely yes.

Q: Did you have any problems developing a suitable paper with which to make rolls?
A: Yes, we had some problems, but the paper mill helped develop a paper for us that wouldn't expand and contract too much. They came out with one that was pretty good and could stand quite a little change in the temperature and humidity. We still had problems if the temperature and humidity went extremely low.

Q: Who developed the Melody Violins?
A: The violin arrangement used in roll cutting gave me the idea of making the 'quad' [Melody Violins]. We made up a unit for a symphony orchestra, where one man played sixteen violins, that is, both the first and second violins from a double [organ type] keyboard. The one man took over the whole string section. That was quite a concert, and so unusual to have one man play the whole violin section. Of course, the musicians kicked at the whole thing.

Q: When using the multiple violins, did you use relays to handle the switching, thus minimizing the arcing?
A: I didn't on the quad [Melody Violins] but I did on the sixteen. We made up one group of violins for The Fair Store in Chicago. It was an anniversary event – 40th or 50th anniversary, something like that. The owner of the store was a very close friend of my brother [HSM]. My brother offered to install violins in the store for the event and asked me, "How many can you put in?" I replied, "Well, how many do you want?" He said, "Well, they figured that they'd need about fifty in there," and I said, "Okay, we'll put in fifty." Well, then I had to have relays, of course, because the keyboard's contacts would have burned up. We made that up, and it was terrific. That was the only installation ever made like that. I don't know how many thousands of dollars it cost, but it was done just for the week-long celebration.

Q: How many of the quad or Melody Violin units were built?
A: They were never produced in quantity, and we probably made about a dozen.

MILLS MELODY VIOLINS

Q: Mills Novelty Co. made a unit called the 'Four Feeder.' It consisted of four Violano feeders. What was the primary purpose and use of that unit?
A: Well, the reason for its use was because there were only five selections of music on a roll, or say, five popular songs on a roll. These feeders would work on relays so that you could either select different rolls with perhaps different types of music, or you could let them run continuously so that you could get twenty different tunes instead of five before repeating any of them. They were not too popular, and we did not build over a dozen of them.

Q: How did musicians regard the Violano?
A: Some of them commented favorably. I remember the time when Mischa Elman, who was one of the top violinists of the day, came over to the factory and we played 'I palpiti'* by N. Paganini. He listened to it, danced around, and was quite favorably amazed with the quality of the fingering.

*Niccolò Paganini's Introduction and Variations on "Di tanti palpiti" from Rossini's *Tancredi.* – Ed.

MILLS PIANO ORCHESTRA

Q: The Mills Piano Orchestra was pictured in some of your advertising of the late 1920's. No known collector of today has one. A former customer of Mills recalls that he saw one at a convention in Chicago. What is the story about them?

A: They came out rather late as an effort to compete with amplified music, which was just coming into being. They were not competitive musically and were never put into production. Not more than about six were produced.

Q: The 'Orchestra Attachment' for the Violano was a percussion unit that was in a separate cabinet and wired to the Violano. A few have survived. Do you know how many were made?

A: We probably made about thirty to forty.

Q: You made another unit called the 'Expression Piano,' and with the addition of a race track, called it the 'Race Horse Piano.'
A: Yes. Both of the pianos were the same, but the Race Horse Piano had a half-dozen moving horses. This was not a gambling device per se. I mean, it was intended as a gambling device, because you and I could gamble on it. That was the idea. We'd put our nickels in, and then you'd take the book and let me bet on the horses, or you take three and I take three, or any other combination. All types of bets could be made, and that was the idea.

Q: Your advertising gave the message that it was very good for use among friendly people.
A: That's right. That was the idea. It was intended as a gambling machine, but it wasn't gambling as such because it didn't pay out — it didn't take your money, except for the music.

Q: What year was the Race Horse Piano introduced?
A: I would say probably 1924 or 1925, or thereabouts.

COMPLETE ORCHESTRA FOR DANCING

328

Q: Were many of them made?
A: Oh, probably fifty to a hundred — not over that.

Q: Well, some of the surviving Race Horse Pianos in this country came back from England.
A: Yes, Samson Novelty Company bought most of them from us.

Q: Did the Expression and Race Horse Pianos use the same roll?
A: Yes. It was narrower, and, of course, different from a Violano roll. They, like all of our instruments, used electrical contacts. We never made anything pneumatic.

MILLS RACE HORSE PIANO

MAGNETIC EXPRESSION PIANO

Q: Now, did you have different roll-making machinery to make the Expression Piano rolls?
A: No, we just had a different feeder, but they all ran through the same cutting machine.

Q: Did you use the same piano-type keyboard for making up the piano rolls?
A: Yes.

Q: What kind of roll did the Piano Orchestra take?
A: We used the same size roll as for the Expression Piano, but the tracker scale was quite different.

Q: On the original Violina that had no piano, were the brushes for the notes on the violin arranged the same as on the later Violano?
A: Yes. We just added an additional group of tracks for the piano. For the Violina, the feeder and the roll weren't as wide as those for the Violano.

Q: Violanos which had the orchestra units attached to them had some rearranging of the expression tracks. I think they disconnected a couple of expression tracks on the bow motor and used them for other purposes, and so on.
A: That's right.

Q: Now, on the orchestra attachment, your catalog says that you could attach that to any machine that had a serial number on the piano harp higher than 1200.
A: Yeah, that's true.

Q: What was the big difference at 1200?
A: We always started numbering our products with 101 — we never started with No. 1, so 1200 was actually 1100. There was probably a change made at that point, but I can't recall what it was.

Q: What method did you use for making the rolls with the orchestra attachment? Were they hand played by the musicians?
A: The master rolls for this were made the usual way, and the other tracks for the orchestra attachment were edited and cut in by hand. We didn't use a keyboard to play in the percussion because we never got that far with it. We could have done that, but we never made enough of them to make it worth while.

Q: Was the number of a machine the one that was on the piano harp, or was it somewhere else on the machine?
A: When we made the piano and the violin as one unit, the number of the machine was then on the piano.

Q: Gano Senter, who was a distributor for Violanos in the Rocky Mountain states, said that the Company was always very sticky about selling just the violin and that you had to have a good reason before the factory would sell one.
A: Well, not really. We used to sell the violins to a lot of musicians and would get $500 to $600 for them. They were very well built and very fine instruments. The front and back of each violin were matched tonally. Of course, those sold to musicians were fitted with tuning pegs and a fingerboard. The wood was seasoned. The Company was always seeking out sources of seasoned wood from which violins could be made. On one occasion, Herbert [HSM], while touring Europe, procured a large quantity of suitable spruce lumber taken from old buildings being demolished. It was carefully stacked and shipped to the Plant in Chicago where it lay in a pile for a few weeks. The Plant Manager, thinking it was waste, had it hauled to the dump. Luckily, his job survived the episode.

Q: Was the factory aware of the German machine that played the violin and the piano, which was called the Hupfeld Phonoliszt–Violina?

A: Yes. I remember that they were actually out with their machine before we were out with ours. They played pretty well, but I think they were quite complicated. They could play several notes, the same as we could. They were not as rugged as our machines, and the public could not play them. If any machines were fitted for coin-operation, they would really get the gaff of the public, that didn't really know how to play them and that can break all but the best-made machines. I doubt that those German machines would have stood the test of coin operation. They had a better full-scale expression piano, though.

Q: Was the Mills Violina which was exhibited at the Alaska-Yukon Pacific Exposition given to the Smithsonian Institution?
A: No. The Smithsonian was given a later model with a piano. The one in the Exposition that won the prize had no piano.

Q: Did Mills Novelty Co. have any kind of commercial relationships with Seeburg or Wurlitzer, or did Mills distribute for them or vice versa?
A: No. J.P. Seeburg Co. at that time made automatic pianos, and we knew them very well but had no relationship with them. Later, many years later, I sold my coffee-machine business to the Seeburg Company, which by that time had been taken over by others. We had no arrangement with competition, just direct distributors.

Q: Did the Mills Novelty Co. ever think in terms of building bigger orchestrion units, like Wurlitzer used to market?
A: Not really. The closest we came to it was the drum unit and so forth.

Q: Did you ever accept other manufacturers' machines as trade-ins?
A: I don't believe we ever did, but we took our own in trade.

Q: Not long before Farny Wurlitzer passed on, he said that the Mills Novelty people were real scrappers, that they were constantly in litigation, and had many lawsuits with the Wurlitzer Company.
A: Well, we had some lawsuits with Wurlitzer. Nevertheless, Farny would come to the factory and have lunch with my brother [HSM], and so forth. They were friendly enemies. The litigation was over patent infringements, and we beat them all the time. They never sued us for anything.

Q: Some early literature would indicate that there was a separate division or company called the Violano-Virtuoso Company. Was that just publicity, or was there a separate company with that name?
A: I don't recall it ever being a separate company, but it could have been a sales company organized for that purpose.

Q: Were the fancy curved-case Violanos [bow front], which had the piano added, made before or after World War I?
A: The cases were made before World War I, but the pianos could have

been added after the War.

Q: Do you recall what year it was that you switched over from the cast-iron feeders to the cast-aluminum feeders?
A: I don't remember exactly when we switched over. The Violano feeder was revamped a great deal from the original cast-iron model. I designed the last model, but I don't remember exactly what year it was.

Q: In England, there are at least a couple of old Violanos which have cases not seen in this country. They have leaded art glass on the front window, etc.
A: Yes, some of the early ones were made with art glass. They were not our very first models but were made before the ultimate design.

Q: Did you ever put the Violanos in custom cases on special order?
A: Not that I can recall.

Q: Were special installations made, like in churches or dance halls and so forth?
A: Yes, we had various keyboard-operated violins. We put them in some churches, where they were attached to organs so that they could be played right from the organ keyboard by putting in the stops. We made a special installation for the Fishers, who were the people who built the car bodies for General Motors. For a Fisher brother, I set one up in his home and attached it to a big organ which had pipes that went up through two floors.

Q: A collector in San Francisco has a double, or twin, Violano that is fitted with a keyboard that slides out so that the violins can be played manually. Are you familiar with that?
A: Yes, we made just a few of those units. Some people ordered those with the keyboard so that they could play the violin as the roll played, thus adding to the music on the roll; or they would let only the piano play, and they would play the violins from the keyboard.

Q: On the cover for the finger magnets there are numerous patents listed as being issued by various foreign countries. What was the purpose of getting the patents issued in the different countries?
A: Well, so that no one manufactured them in the other countries.

Q: In many of the listed countries it would seem as though there would not have been much of a market.
A: That is true, but we figured that if they manufactured them in those countries, they could sell them elsewhere. On most of our stuff, we took out patents in England, France, Germany, and in other countries where a particular item could receive competition.

Q: Did you sell many Violanos in countries other than the United States

and England?
A: No.

Q: *Regarding the Violano patents, many appear to be secured by Bertie E. Mills. Who is that?*
A: I'm Bertie. My family is of English descent on both sides. That goes back many generations, of course. All of my brothers had English names; Cecil, Franklin, Guy, then Oliver, and Steven Herbert. He liked Herbert better so he switched his name around — it was never registered or legally changed; he just adopted the use of Herbert S. instead of Steven Herbert. When they got to me, they ran out of names, so I was christened Bertie. When I was in grammar school, the kids used to kid me about my name. I later cut off the 'ie.' All my first patents read 'Bertie.' Our patent attorneys were Darenforth, Darenforth Lee, Crittenden and Wiles, in Chicago at that time. Mr. Darenforth was an old friend of the family, and he always called me Bertie, and he always put 'Bertie' on my patents, regardless of what I wanted.

Q: *You patented a mute device for the Violano. How successful was that?*
A: Well, it was added to all the machines right after that time. They were later disconnected, because if this device wasn't adjusted properly, it would sometimes make a fuzzy sound. It had to be adjusted about once a month, and didn't work out too well.

Q: *A patent for rosin compound was issued to your brother [HSM]. What was unusual about that formula?*
A: We used to make our own rosin into little squares. We needed something that wasn't too hard or too soft. The rosin that a violinist uses is pretty soft, and when we used it on the Violano, it would just powder all over and cover the violin. My brother had a chemist make it up but had the patent put in his own name.

Q: *You secured a patent on Motor Controlling Means. This idea was used on the bow motor of late-model machines, and it is essentially a governor-controlled limit switch. What gave you the idea for that?*
A: The bow motor was made with four field magnets. Some of the magnets had more than one winding. They were wired together in shunt and in series so that the bow motor would work fast or slow, depending upon which magnets were energized. As a matter of fact, the idea of the governor was to ease the speed changes and eliminate the jerking. The limiting switches on fast and slow were to avoid stalling or too high a speed.

Q: *The patent for the continuous tremolo is yours.*
A: Yes, the tremolo on the violin is comprised of a weight that hangs on a rod. The weight would be pulled to a solenoid and would, as it got close, break the electrical contact, thus falling back and giving a tremolo effect through the movement of the rod that was attached to and would shake the

violin tailpiece. You could have one long tremolo track cut in the roll which would not affect the operation of the tremolo because it would break the contact and move back and forth. Sandell came out with still another tremolo device, which we never used. He always got very jealous when I would come up with a better idea. He would invariably say to my brother [HSM], "Your brother doesn't know what he's talking about. His idea is contrary to all electrical ideas and theories." I would reply, "If we always worked by theory, we'd never invent anything. We have to go contrary to what the books say once in a while."

Q: The after-tone damper patent is also yours and was quite an improvement. Before that, was there any damping device?
A: No. The after-tone resulted when the bows would come up after playing. Before the damper was put on, you had to be satisfied with hearing the after-tone.

Q: You have another patent for tremolo effects. What was the need for it?
A: Yes, that was devised for the following reason. There was a Canadian ocean liner that had a Violano placed in one of its lounges. A ship always lists, and those tuning weights would go wrong, so the violin couldn't be played as there was no way to tune it. They came back and said that they couldn't use the violin on ocean voyages. In quiet waters, it was all right, but when they started to move on the ocean, it wouldn't work. Peterson, one of our machinists in the experimental room, and I did the mechanical work necessary to eliminate the weights after I had invented the method. Basically, it employed springs instead of weights to put tension on the strings. Adjusting screws would increase the tension on the springs. It worked almost as well as the weights. I had a patent for a tremolo device used in conjunction with the spring-tension tuning system. It had little pistons underneath each spring-controlled tuning arm that were in turn connected to the tuning arms and vibrated the arms when the pistons were actuated by another larger piston. We actually never used it very much, but as I say, it was all right for the ships. The tremolo effect would be obtained because the piston bobs up and down, thus changing the string tension. It would naturally not vibrate the tailpiece, as the other tremolos would do, but as I said, the weights for tuning or tremolo could not be used on ships.

Q: Who made the pianos for the Violano?
A: We made our own.

Q: The early ones had 'Strauch' on them.
A: That was the company that made the actions. We didn't make the actions. We made the sounding boards. We didn't cast the plates ourselves. We had our own plate patterns, and Superior Foundry cast them for us.

Q: Did Strauch always supply the actions?
A: They did in the early days. Later on we got them from somebody else,

335

but I can't recall who it was.

Q: *Where did you get the percussion items for the orchestra units?*
A: I'm not sure. We could have gotten them from Wurlitzer.

Q: *Was there any profit made on the Violanos?*
A: Well, in the last few years, yes, but if you take it over a period of time, all in all, no. They used to say my brother was a nut because he spent about a million dollars trying to promote the machine before it was really ready. He was just crazy about it. He never kept track of what it lost, cost, or made, because he didn't want to know.

Q: *Was it true that your brother [HSM] was a 'scrapper?'*
A: Oh, well, he liked to box, but I mean, not in anger. The minute you walked in the place he wanted to box with you. He used to box with me. He'd say, "Now I'll tell you something – just put your hands down – I want to show you something," and then he'd swat you and then say, "You see, you can never trust anybody."

Q: *Is it true that he liked his whiskey?*
A: Yes.

Q: *Was that also true of the son, Fred, who later ran the Company after his father's death?*
A: Yes. Fred liked Scotch whisky. He was told by the doctors that he had to stop drinking, so Fred went to sherry wine. He would drink a bottle of that in the morning, and he would brag that he was off the hard stuff.

Q: *Did the Company pursue an aggressive export business?*
A: Oh, yes. As a matter of fact, in Johannesburg, South Africa, we used to do about two or three hundred thousand dollars a year. We did a lot of business in France and England.

Q: *Are you familiar with the early Mills jukebox of the old carousel design?*
A: Yes. I invented it. I should recall it. That was in 1925, and we were in production in 1926. We were out first, about a year ahead of Seeburg. Capehart was the second one on the market.

Q: *Was it the jukebox that killed the Violano sales?*
A: Yes, to a degree. Amplified music took over and eliminated all other mechanical music machines. My brother [HSM] used to spend six weeks in Florida every year, and before he left for Florida in 1925, I said to him, "Herb, there is going to be amplified music now. There are going to be coin-operated phonographs made with amplified music. While you're away, I'll make one." He said, "Don't you dare touch or make anything. We're making the Violano, and that's it. We don't want any more music." As soon

as he left, I started in the experimental room on making one. I had to work like the devil and have it done before he came back, because I knew he would stop us. When he came back, I had the first one playing. It wasn't ready for production, but it was playing, and it sounded pretty darn good. It took me several days before I got my brother to go in there to hear it. In the meantime, I got fired because I made it against his wishes, but I would still come down to the factory every day just the same. When he seemed ready to go home, I'd ride with him. I wanted to talk to him and try to show him this thing. I finally got him in there about six o'clock one night. We didn't leave till one o'clock in the morning. We played all the records we had in the place about four times over, and he just sat back and listened to them. The next morning when I got down to the factory about 9:30, he was already there and was down in the tool room where we had the model jukebox. He told them to tool up for it. I went in and said, "Herbert, it's not ready for tooling, and it's not ready for the market. Let me work on it another couple of months, and it will be ready." He said, "Get out of here. I'm doing what I want." He tooled up for it. Thereafter, I had to make a lot of changes, and we had to scrap a lot of the tools. The first jukebox was not selective. It just played the twelve records as they came. Afterwards, I made it selective. The recordings in those days were not uniform. Some played real loud, and some were soft. When you'd put them in a jukebox, some would blast out if you had the volume set loud enough to hear soft ones. So I had a little gadget on the front hub of the machine so that when you put the discs on the machine, you could set the volume for each record so that they would all play at the same volume.

Q: Did the Company ever experience problems with the pot-metal or die-cast parts they used?
A: Yes, we had trouble. There was pot metal in the Violano weight-arm tuning devices that gave the most trouble. They had a steel fulcrum insert that would break out when the pot metal swelled. In those days, the pot metal wasn't so good.

Q: Well, seemingly, some of the pot metal on the very earliest Violanos has held up very well, and some of the ones on the intermediate models fell apart.
A: We didn't cast the parts ourselves, we had it done on the outside.

Q: Did't Sandell have some patents on pot-metal formulas?
A: Yeah, and those were the ones we had trouble with.

Q: There is a tale about Sandell knowing the whereabouts of the body of a person who got washed overboard from a Mills boat. If you know the story, would you tell it?
A: Yes. Well, Sandell was a spiritualist of sorts. He claimed that all of his ideas came from the spirits in the spirit world. I always used to kid the devil out of him. We had a factory manager by the name of King. My brother had

MILLS AUTOMATIC PHONOGRAPH

a sailing yacht on Lake Michigan, and King and his two sons asked to take the yacht out one time so that they could go up in Wisconsin. My brother let them take it. They were in quite a heavy storm on their way back, and King was washed overboard about 20 or 30 miles out of Chicago. His sons stayed around on the lake for a couple of hours but couldn't find him, and they finally had to give up. There were boats and everything else out looking, but they couldn't find the body. One morning, Sandell came down to the factory, and we were in the experimental room, and he said to me, "You know where King is?" I said, "No," and he said, "He's at the Randolph Street Bridge in the piling," and I said, "Oh, is he? Was that in the paper this morning?" He said, "No, no. It just came to me — that's where he is." Two hours later they found King's body at the Randolph Street Bridge, washed into the pilings. So whether the spirits told him or what, he was right, but that was the only spirit thing he was ever right about.

Q: Mr. Mills, the November 1932 issue of Fortune Magazine contains an article about the Company entitled, "Plums, Cherries, and Murder." Do you remember that article?

A: Yes, I remember it. The reporter who wrote the article came to me to ask about all the percentages on the reel machines. I made up all of the percentages from the very beginning. They had a phony story on the reels and asked me to help them correct it. I helped them out, but they didn't publish it the way I told it to them. It was erroneous.

Q: Rumor has it that someone who knew your nephew, Fred [son of HSM], very well said that Fred, who was at that time President of the Company, believed that the Company was going to get a million dollars' worth of good publicity out of the article. Is that true?

A: That whole article backfired, and he [Fred] said and swore up and down that he would never let another reporter in that Company. You see, they twisted the story. They took stuff out of context and said that we said it. Like most reporters, they wanted to build up the story, and so they changed it to suit themselves.

Q: In the article, it is said that you sold these machines to the biggest gangsters in the country. Was that true?

A: As a matter of fact, before Prohibition went out, the gangsters never bought any machines. They were peddling booze. They didn't have to operate machines during Prohibition. After Prohibition went out, they had to find something to do, and they would come in and buy slot machines. These slot machines purchased by gangsters were never located in the right places. Most of the legitimate operators didn't put them in where there were school kids to play them, and they didn't put them in saloons and so forth, where there were poor people and where the machines would get their salaries. When the mobs took over the slots, they didn't care whether they put them in grocery stores or any place else. Women would come in to buy groceries and spend their money in the slot machine. It turned out to be pretty lousy, but it was beyond our control. As a matter of fact, one of these same mobsters came to me to buy coffee machines. He had been in the jukebox business. He said, "I want to get some coffee machines to put around Chicago," and I said, "What do you want them for?" I said, "There's no money in it. I sell them, but the people who buy them are suckers. There's no money in these things. It would take you about two years to get your money back. I wouldn't buy it if I were you." I had to lie a little bit because some of the machines had paid for themselves in thirty days. Well, I talked him out of it, and they never got into the coffee-vending business. What they would do is go into your plant and ask you to take a certain machine or else. You know, the first coffee machines I put out helped a lot of operators who were really on the rocks. In the wintertime, their business in cold-drink machines dropped down very far, and coffee built up their winter business. They used to tip their hats as they went past my factory. We had machines regularly selling a thousand cups a day.

Q: Did you think that Mills products were the leader in the industry?
A: Yes. We had a reputation for making quality products. That is one thing my brother struck for - no junk. Some of our stuff held up too long. People copied our products. Tom Watling copied our slot machines, which by law couldn't be patented. Watling was in the scale business and made coin-operated scales. Caille Brothers in Detroit did the same thing, and so did Jennings, who once worked for us. Pace also worked for us. Jennings, who became the second largest manufacturer to us, was our Philadelphia manager, and he'd go down to these towns that had been operating slot machines, after they were closed down. People would have twenty-five or thirty slot machines down in their basements, that he would buy. He would put them in new cabinets and then call them Jennings machines. The mechanisms were ours, and the cases were his.

Q: What kind of quality did the Caille Brothers products have?
A: Well, Caille was the first other good manufacturer that made things well. As a matter of fact, Caille would come into our experimental room, and we would let him see what we were working on. They never actually stole anything from us. Caille Brothers were in the motorboat business in Detroit. They made outboard motors, about the first ever put on the market. They later went into making slots.

Q: Can you tell me briefly something about your family and the organization of Mills Novelty Co.?
A: Yes. Herbert [HSM], who really was the Mills Novelty Co., was my third oldest brother and was born in Iowa in 1870. The family moved to Chicago about 1874 or 1875, a few years after the big Chicago fire [1871]. I was the youngest in the family and was 22 years younger than Herbert.

Q: Is it true that your brother Herbert was curly haired and started out as a newsboy?
A: That's possible. Of course, everybody that was a success is always said to have sold newspapers.

Q: Was your brother Herbert's first major invention the cigar vendor, or was that your father's invention?
A: My father was quite an inventor, and that was his invention.

Q: What was Herbert's first major invention?
A: I don't think he invented much of anything. He used to take some of my Dad's inventions and call them his own, but he didn't invent much of anything.

Q: Your brothers, Cecil and Herbert, together, are said to have invented the 'Owl' [an upright slot machine]?
A: No, my father invented the 'Owl.' My brother Cecil, being like my brother Herbert, was one of those who, if you told him to take a

screwdriver and tighten up a screw, he wouldn't know which way to turn it. They were not, aside from my Dad, myself, and one other brother, very mechanical or inventive.

Q: How did the Mills Novelty Co. come into being, and who developed its early products?
A: My father, M. B. Mills, founded the Mills Railroad Gate Company during the 1880's. They manufactured my father's invention, pneumatic gates. After selling out in 1893 or 1894, my father started the M. B. Mills Manufacturing Company, which produced some of the very first vending machines, including his patented cigar vendors. M. B. Mills [who passed on in 1938] was an active inventor, with over 140 patents. He was quite proud of me when I had acquired more patents than he. I was the youngest of the family, and my brother, Herbert S. Mills, was President of Mills Novelty Co. during its tremendous growth period. My brother Herbert took over the Company at the turn of the century and changed the name to Mills Novelty Co. The Company, when owned by my father, built several slot machines, the first of which was called the 'Klondike.' The first big floor-model machine made in 1898 was called the 'Owl,' and the owl, which was pictured on the machine later, became the Company's trademark.

Q: Why was the Mills Novelty Co.'s gambling machine named the 'Dewey'?
A: Well, this is because it was introduced right after the Spanish-American War, and after the fight at Manila, everything was at that time 'Dewey.' Admiral Dewey was the hero of the day.

Q: Was it just a sales idea, or did Admiral Dewey have an interest in it?
A: It was just a sales gimmick.

Q: Did Mills Novelty Co. invest in Company-owned arcades?
A: Yes, I think we were the builders of practically all the arcade machines, and back in the early days toward the turn of the century—in 1905, 1906, and 1907, along in that era—our biggest business was arcade machines, much bigger than the slot-machine end of the business. We owned arcades and sold arcade machines to the people who operated them, which included a couple of the movie magnates, such as the Warners.

Q: Were the arcades owned in partnership with others?
A: No. We never went into partnership.

Q: It has been said that Charlie Fay invented the slot machine in '95, and thereafter he manufactured them and put them out on location. One of his machines on location was stolen and turned up at the Mills Novelty Co. factory where it was copied and then manufactured in quantity.
A: That is entirely untrue. Charlie Fay invented the one-arm bandit in 1905. He was at that time a customer of ours and bought machines from us and operated them on the West Coast in the San Francisco area. I was there

in the factory on the day that Charlie Fay brought his machine in. It was in an iron case, and he called it the 'Liberty Bell.' It had the cracked Liberty Bell cast on the front of the machine. It was a very crude machine, but it operated all right. It was very easy to cheat. I mean, the players could cheat the machine. Charlie Fay did have a good idea but could not do anything with it because he was not in the manufacturing business. When he brought it in to my brother, he said, "Herb, if you'll give me the first fifty machines you make, you can have it." He said, "I know you can copy it and steal it if you want to, but I know you won't." And so we built the machine, and my brother gave him the first fifty machines we built. This was after I had revamped the machine and made it practical. Nearly 75 per cent of the parts in the redesigned machine were to keep the public from cheating it.

Q: Is it true that the Liberty Bell Machine would take the money much quicker than the Dewey, thus making it more desirable?
A: The operation cycle of the machine that was called the Liberty Bell took about six seconds to complete, and the people could drop their money in faster because they didn't have to stop and select colors, etc., as you did with the Dewey. Players would do a lot of things to try to win, and they'd take a little longer time before getting the money into a Dewey, but with the Liberty Bell machines, it only took six seconds to get the money. Often, people have the idea that the machine was 40 or 50 per cent against the player, but the worst machine, the strongest machine we ever made, was 20 per cent against the player, and those didn't get much play and, therefore, never made any money for the operator. The most liberal machines would make the money because the player put it all back in the machine. We jokingly called it working on the cupidity of the public.

Q: Is it true that your brother, Herbert, got into some trouble selling pictures through the mail and was given a jail sentence of some sort?
A: Yes and no. If what he did had been done today, he could have gone on selling those pictures without problems. We had a machine that was called the Stereoscope, which was made for use in the arcades. My brother was away on a trip. His father-in-law was managing the business and got hold of some pictures that were considered very lewd in those days. They weren't as bad or revealing as a bikini today, but they were considered very lewd, so the Federal Government arrested him because he was the president of the company, and he was the one to take the gaff. He protected his father-in-law and took the rap. They gave him the sentence of a year and then suspended the sentence.

Q: Did he ever serve any time?
A: No. He was not sentenced to a Federal prison. He was sentenced to jail in Chicago. I mean, he could report once in a while, but that was all.

Q: With the good connections that your brother had, how is it that the case got that far?

A: Well, that's probably one of the reasons why he never was sentenced to jail. I remember it all very well. I was a young fellow when it happened back in 1904. The Judge was a good friend whom we all knew very well.

Q: There were several boats that were Company or family owned, one of which was called the 'Minoco.' It was kept off the Florida Coast, was it not?
A: Herbert bought a boat in Florida, back in, or some time in, the 'Teens. It was a small boat, about fifty feet. It was not called the 'Minoco.' After my brother [HSM] died, his four sons inherited the business, and they bought a boat which belonged to Dr. Baruch, a brother of Bernard Baruch. It was a 98-foot yacht, and when they were wondering what to call it, I said, "Why don't you call it the 'Minoco'?" That is made up of the first two letters of each word in the Company name. They liked the idea, and so named it. Then, after they had that boat for about a year, they had a new boat made at the Mathis Yards around Philadelphia. It was a larger boat - 110 feet. We carried an eleven-man crew. We kept it off the Florida Coast in the winter, and would run it to Chicago up through the canals and down to Chicago during the summertime.

Q: Did both boats have Violanos on them?
A: No, neither one had a Violano. The boat Herbert bought in Florida had a Violano on it for a short time. I remember it well because it almost sunk the boat. He was crazy about the Violano.

Q: Gano Senter, of whom we spoke earlier and who was a friend of your brother Herbert, said that Herbert used to listen to the Violano a great deal of the time.
A: Yes. My brother would sit down and listen to the Violano all day long.

Q: Was your brother referred to as the 'Commodore'?
A: Well, he was Commodore of the Yacht Club - the Chicago Yacht Club, or the Columbia Yacht Club in Chicago. He was no real Commodore, and I don't think he ever wanted to be referred to as such, but they did refer to him as Commodore.

Q: A gentleman in Chicago who wrote for one of the trade papers said that your brother did things in a big way. Once he wanted to entertain on the boat, which was then on Lake Michigan, and in order to get a good show, he had to buy all the tickets to a New York show for every performance during an entire week.
A: Yes, that was on a powered houseboat. It was about 150 feet long and had a beam of about thirty feet. You could put a lot of people on it. It had two decks, so he used to buy all the tickets and have the show come over to the yacht club, etc., and put on a big party. He was always full of the devil.

One time we had about twenty Judges out to dinner. He had me wire the table up so that underneath the tablecloth I ran a wire to a piece of tin that was under each plate and on the sides underneath the forks and knives.

343

When I was given a signal, I would press a button, and when they'd go to pick up their knives and forks, they'd get a shock and throw their knives and forks up in the air. Herbert didn't care who it was, he liked to play practical jokes.

Q: Could you describe the facilities for eating and so on that were located on the top of the factory at 4100 Fullerton in Chicago?
A: Yes, we called that area the 'Bungalow.' It was a suite. The dining room would accommodate about thirty. We had another area where we had handball courts and steam baths and that sort of thing. We could go up and play handball, take a steam bath, and come in to eat. We had an excellent Japanese chef, whom my brother called Tu and who had been over in this country for twenty-odd years. The funny part of it was that at that time, he had already been over here about twenty-four years, and he had sons over there twenty years old of whom he was very proud. He had never seen his wife in twenty-four years. I used to say to him, "Tu, how, under the circumstances, did you have sons over there?" He would reply that he had good neighbors.

Q: A rumor has circulated to the effect that on one occasion Herbert was wearing a very expensive diamond ring, which was stolen from him. After a few well-placed phone calls, he got it back the following day. Do you recall that incident?
A: Yes. It was not a ring. It was a watch charm that hung on a chain. It was in the form of an owl, which was our trademark. It was about one and a half inches high and a little less in width. It had several hundred small diamonds, and two ruby eyes. He had this made up, or somebody gave it to him, I'm not sure which. He wore this owl, and clipped it on his watch chain. After it was stolen, a few telephone calls were made, and they finally discovered where it was and returned it.

Q: The owl as a trademark was filed on in 1906?
A: Yes, it was a red owl.

Q: What was the origin of the use of the owl?
A: Well, the Owl slot machine was invented by my Dad in 1898. My Dad was building the Owl in our basement because the factory at Jefferson and Washington burned down. That factory was only about 1000 to 1500 square feet or so. At the time it burned down, my Dad had been working on the Owl. When the fire started, the first thing one of my brothers did was save the Owl, which was in the process of invention. My Dad finished it in our basement, and so the owl became the trademark. They didn't protect it as a trademark until around 1906, but it was actually first used as a trademark around the turn of the century.

Q: The trademark was originally claimed by the Mills Novelty Co. but was renewed in 1946 by Mills Industries. What caused the name change?

A: Our name was a misnomer. We didn't manufacture novelties. We manufactured coin-operated machines and all kinds of vending machines, arcade machines, and slot machines. During the War, the English Government came over to seek out different manufacturers to make things for them, ammunitions and so forth, and they wanted some bomb releases manufactured, and we were recommended. Well, the people from England thought that it was ridiculous to go to a novelty company to build bomb releases. They flew to Chicago, and we met them at the factory on a Sunday. They saw the plant and the type of equipment we had and knew that there was no question about our ability to make what they wanted. We changed the name of the Company just after that to Mills Industries. When the United States got into the War [World War II], we went into making war materials for the government and stopped making vending machines.

I retired in 1944 just before the War ended. It got too tough to be retired. I was too young. I had belonged to two different golf clubs at the time, and I grew bored with them because I had nobody to play with. It's not like out here in Arizona. In Chicago, people that I played golf with were working except for the week-ends. During the week, I'd go down to the Club and have to play with the pro or a caddy. So, in 1945, I started working on my own. I worked on the coffee machine. My first patents were issued in 1945. In 1947, I went back into manufacturing on my own, and in February of 1947 I shipped my first coffee machine. I started with 20 men, and when I sold out to Seeburg in 1959, I had just under 500 employees.

Q: We know that the Mills Novelty Co. no longer exists. When did it go out of business?
A: During World War II. Nothing was manufactured except war material. When the War was over, there were no new products to come out with. The slot-machine business was down to nothing because of laws that prohibited the shipment of machines or parts across state lines. There was never a Company bankruptcy or anything of that kind. The Company was sold. The people that bought it and the patents, which had practically run out, got it all for around $100,000. A separate purchaser bought the factory and all of the tools, which were absolutely top quality. The equipment in that factory was worth about $5,000,000, and I think that the new people bought it for $2,000,000. That ended the Company. One of my nephews thereafter manufactured slot machines in Reno, Nevada.

Q. What was done with all of the spare parts, etc.?
A: They were all junked out periodically after the items became obsolete.

১৩৬১৩

Mr. Mills, on behalf of myself and fellow collectors, we thank you for your time and patience. ■ ■

The ORPHEUS
Mechanical Zither

Joseph H. Schumacher

$\mathcal{R}$ECENTLY I had the opportunity to buy an Orpheus Mechanical Zither. The Orpheus is a sister to the Ariston organette in that both were made by Ehrlich of Leipzig, Germany, and they play the same 24-note disc.

THE SAME DISCS MAY BE PLAYED ON EITHER THE ORPHEUS OR THE ARISTON, WITH DIFFERENT SOUND QUALITY.

According to its original owner, this mechanical zither (or piano, as it is sometimes called) was purchased around 1900 from Thomas O'Hare, 62 Water Street, Pittsburgh, Pa. O'Hare's stamp on the yellow cardboard discs reads (complete with misspelling): "Mechanical Musical Instruments Of All Discription, And Their Music." The instrument had been used for about 10 years and then put in a storage shed. It was complete except for the legs, which were discarded years ago, and the staff that supports the lid in the open position.

Quite an unusual and interesting instrument, the Orpheus has the outward appearance of a miniature grand piano and is 34 inches long by 17 inches wide by six inches deep. The unit has 24 strings (ranging in length from 23 to 27 inches) and uses a perforated cardboard disc 13 inches in diameter. The disc extends beyond the end of the case, and the lid may be open or closed when playing; there is a cut-out section to allow operation when the lid is down. The sound of the Orpheus is different from that of any other instrument I've ever heard -- it has a light reverberating sound character, due to repeated hammer action.

The discs are center-driven. As the crank handle is turned, a spirally cut worm gear on the crankshaft drives a horizontal toothed wheel two and a half inches in diameter. Fastened to the top of this brass wheel is the center drive plate. The plate has four positioning pins and a large center spindle to

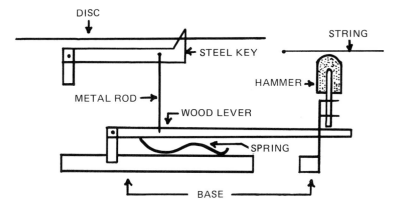

HAMMER STRIKING MECHANISM

drive the disc, which rides over steel key-shaped levers. Attached to these keys are metal rods that are inserted toward one end of spring-loaded wooden levers positioned under the hammer assembly. When a disc is placed on the machine, the wooden levers move downward against the springs. When a note is called for by a perforation in the disc, a key pops through the appropriate hole in the disc and this action cuases the wooden lever to thrust the hammer upward against the string (see illustration). The 12 lower notes have tiny felt dampers to mute the strings after they have sounded.

When I purchased the instrument, it was covered with black coal dirt and was not operative. I realized that this zither was definitely 'in the rough' and, to work properly, had to be fully restored. The restoration was rather basic and straightforward: remove the components from the case; clean each component, and repair if necessary; then reassemble.

First, I removed, in turn, the center drive plate, the disc-holding bracket, the brass frame that separates the keys, and the board to which the latter two are fastened. Next, I examined the strings, one of which was broken and the rest quite rusted, so I decided to have it restrung. After the strings were removed, I took out the cast-metal plate, held in place by five large screws. The next step was to remove the hammer striking mechanism, which I examined carefully before proceeding, to be sure that I would be able to put it back in its original position and not disturb any adjustments. I then removed the unit.

Now that the major components were disassembled, the cleaning process could begin. The hammer striking mechanism was in three parts: the steel keys, a row of wooden levers, and a row of hammers. Fortunately, the

SHOWING THE CLEANED STEEL KEYS, THE TUNING CHART, AND THE ATTRACTIVE CARTOUCHE.

steel keys were in excellent condition, and I had only to polish the ends of the keys that come in contact with the disc. Several of the wooden levers had splits at the ends and had to be glued. The hammer-head felts were cleaned with K2r aerosol spot remover, which dries as a powder and may be brushed away with a soft brush. Two applications were sufficient to remove

THE HAMMER STRIKING MECHANISM REASSEMBLED.

the dirt. I then used a dry lubricant on all the metal parts that come in contact with wood.

The large center drive plate was cleaned with fine steel wool and then sprayed with Krylon gold enamel. The brass frame that separates the steel keys from each other needed only cleaning and polishing. I washed the cast-metal plate and disc-holding bracket and sprayed them also with gold enamel. With the tuning pins still in the pin block, minor rust was removed with a small rotary wire brush and the pins were then polished with very fine steel wool. Several applications of Gun Blue gave a rich blue-black finish to the pins. The case had become unglued in several corners, so these corners were reglued. I then cleaned the case with Van Sciver's wood cleaner and polish. This is a hardwood cleaner and polish that removes film and grime and preserves the finish. I was surprised at how much of the original finish was concealed under the dirt. My experience with old wood cases has been that the nearer a piece can be kept to its original condition, the better, so no other work was done on the wood pieces except coating the decorative area inside the case with acrylic spray.

The components were now ready for reassembly. First, I installed the hammer striking mechanism, which was glued in place and then fastened with screws. Before proceeding, I tested its operation. My reason for doing it at this point was that it would be difficult to make adjustments after the metal plate and strings were installed. In order to make the test, I had to put back on temporarily the disc-holding bracket, the brass frame and its supporting board, and the center drive plate. I placed a disc on the machine and turned the crank handle. The disc went around smoothly, and the hammer action was snappy, indicating that it was working properly. The temporarily installed parts could then be removed, and I could continue with the reassembly. The cast-metal plate was inserted and went into place easily; it was then fastened with its five holding screws. I next replaced the velvet trim around the inside edge of the case. Then came the installation of the new strings, the restringing done by a fellow MBS member. After the strings were installed, they were tuned to the scale printed on a chart under the strings. (The notes, in ascending order, are: A B D E A B C♯ D E F♯ G♯ A B C♯ D D♯ E F♯ G G♯ A B C♯ D.) Next, the board that holds the disc-holding bracket and brass frame and then the center drive plate were fitted in place and fastened securely, the final step.

THE RESTORED ORPHEUS IN ALL ITS GLORY.

With the unit fully assembled, I put a disc in place and checked the hammers again for proper operation. The felt dampers were adjusted so that they touch a string just after it has sounded, and the Orpheus was ready to play again after a silence of some 65 years.

Custom prints by David R. Young. ▪▪

Toys, Self-Playing

The Wolverine
ZILOTONE

Martin A. Roenigk

€VER SINCE 'discovering' the Wolverine Zilotone several years ago, I have been fascinated by this ingenious musical toy of the Depression years. The toy combines the mechanical attributes of the early piano-playing automatons with the convenience and variety of music provided by disc musical boxes. While not entirely successful, and neither the complexity of mechanical action nor the quality of music comes anywhere near that of its far more illustrious forebears, it is nevertheless a delightful toy.

The Zilotone was invented by Howard N. Barnum of Cleveland, Ohio. On Oct. 7, 1930, he received U. S. Patent No. 1,777,712 for his 'Musical Toy.' The design itself is quite simple. The clown plays the xylophone with two basic movements: 1) an up-and-down stroke of his arms to strike the various bars, and 2) a sideways motion of his entire body to select the proper note. The patent illustration shows the various mechanical parts and their assembly. In essence, rod 19 rides up a spiral track 18, shown in detail in Figure 4 of the drawing, and then drops off, causing the arm of the figure to rise and then drop, thus striking a note with each turn of the shaft 17, driven through a train of gears from the spring arbor. Interchangeably attached to the spring arbor is a cam plate (29 in Figures 1, 2, and 5 of the patent drawing) that operates via a cam follower 32 and a rack-and-pinion arrangement to turn the figure back and forth and thus position the hammer over the desired note in the tune sequence.

The production model was considerably simplified and improved, principally by riveting a second, serrated disc to the cam plate, as shown in the photo of the two sides of the tune disc, each serration acting through simple levers on a spring-loaded rod that runs through the body of the figure and moves the arms, and thus the striker, up and down. This eliminates items 12 through 22 shown in the patent drawing and has the great advantage of permitting phrasing in the music, since wherever a tooth is not cut on the serrated disc, a pause or rest will occur, and these are, of course, synchronized with the notes selected by the contours of the cam disc to which the serrated disc is riveted. The xylophone has 12 notes (C-G, A-G) on the production model versus seven on the patent drawing. The motive power is a large spring motor that is hand wound and that drives the disc, which in turn drives the clown. The production model is entirely of metal,

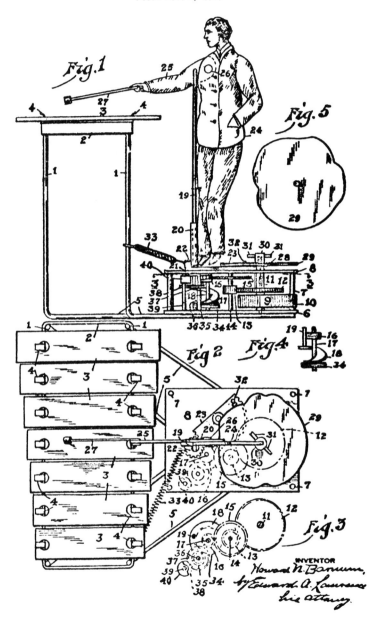

INVENTOR

Howard N. Barnum,

by Edward A. Lawrence

his attorney.

FRONT VIEW, SHOWING THE NAME OF THE TOY.

brightly lithographed (in a variety of color schemes over the years), and weighs a hefty two pounds.

The No. 48 Zilotone was produced by the Wolverine Supply and Manufacturing Company (now a subsidiary of Spang Industries) in their Pittsburgh, Pennsylvania, factory complex. Although production records were destroyed in their 1970 move to Boonville, Arkansas, Mr. James L. Lehren, current President of Wolverine, has been most helpful in providing background information. Wolverine was founded in 1903 by Mr. B. F. Bain of Wolverine, Michigan. Mr. Lehren's father joined the company as Sales Manager in 1906, and Mr. Lehren joined the company in 1938. During the period of the 1920's through the 1940's, the company produced a number of tin mechanical toys that have delighted toy collectors ever since. Noted for their complex mechanical actions and sturdy metal construction, these included sand- and marble-activated toys, tin wind-up toys, and a number of musical toys, such as the No. 27 Drum Major, No. 49 Educational Chimes, and No. 50 Semi-Chromatic Chimes. Today, at their 600,000-square-foot plant in Arkansas, the company remains an important manufacturer of children's toys and games.

The Zilotone was introduced in 1929 (Mr. Barnum filed for his patent in November of 1929) and was last catalogued in 1935. When first sold, the Zilotone was priced at $2.50, including a set of six tune discs. Although the price changed little over the following six years, the number of free discs that were included declined from six to three. Optional sets of discs were available at three for 50c. For reasons unknown, perhaps lack of interest, the number of available tunes apparently reached only nine during the life of the toy. Following is a listing of all known titles:

200	Wearing of the Green
201	My Bonnie Lies over the Ocean
202	Good Night, Ladies
203	Listen to the Mocking Bird
204	Silent Night
205	Yankee Doodle
206	Sidewalks of New York
207	My Old Kentucky Home
208	Farmer in the Dell

In 1930 discs 203-208 were included, and 200-202 was the only optional set, while in 1935 discs 206-208 were included, with 200-202 and 203-205 offered separately.

FRONT AND REAR VIEWS OF THE TWO-PART TUNE DISCS.

A colorful piece of sales literature used during the early years takes considerable liberties in describing "The Outstanding Musical Novelty of the Season." Anyone who has heard even a properly working Zilotone would have to take exception to the statements that "The tone is clear and harmonious. Each note is full-bodied, rich and true to the melody rendered." The tunes are clearly recognizable, however, and the music is a delight to listen to when one accepts the toy as the mass-produced item that it was. I have even been told how to tune the notes, but I won't bore you with the details. (If anyone has a Zilotone that is badly in need of tuning, I will be glad to send this information upon request.)

356

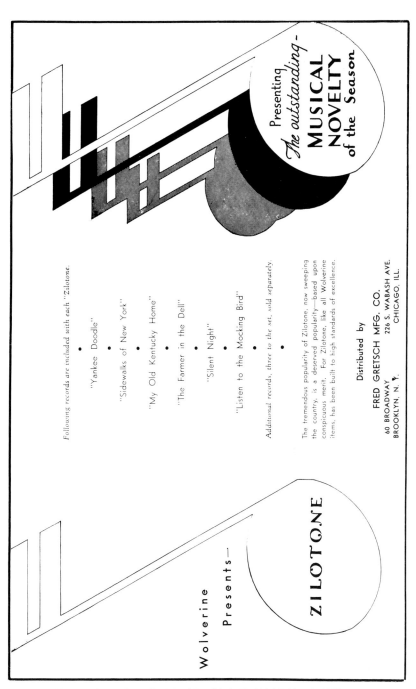

ORIGINAL BROCHURE, REPRODUCED COURTESY OF MR. JAMES L. LEHREN.

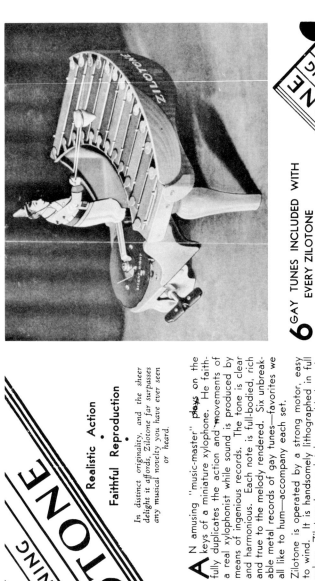

ZILOTONE

NEW
DIFFERENT
COLORFUL
ENTERTAINING

Realistic Action

Faithful Reproduction

In distinct originality, and the sheer delight it affords, Zilotone far surpasses any musical novelty you have ever seen or heard.

AN amusing "music-master" plays on the keys of a miniature xylophone. He faithfully duplicates the action and movements of a real xylophonist while sound is produced by means of ingenious records. The tone is clear and harmonious. Each note is full-bodied, rich and true to the melody rendered. Six unbreakable metal records of gay tunes—favorites we all like to hum—accompany each set.

Zilotone is operated by a strong motor, easy to wind. It is handsomely lithographed in full colors. Zilotone is completely assembled, ready to be played. Packed in attractive box.

WOLVERINE SUPPLY & MFG. CO.

Factory: New York Office: 200 Fifth Avenue
Pittsburgh, Pa.   Tel. Gramercy 3453—Room 406

ZILOTONE

EVER-INTERESTING
MERITORIOUS
FASCINATING

6 GAY TUNES INCLUDED WITH EVERY ZILOTONE

Entire set to retail at . . . **$2.50**

See Back Page for List of Records

Additional records are available retailing at 3 for $.50

AN ANGLE SHOT, SHOWING THE TUNE DISC IN PLACE.

TWO LATTER-DAY XYLOPHONISTS, MADE IN JAPAN.

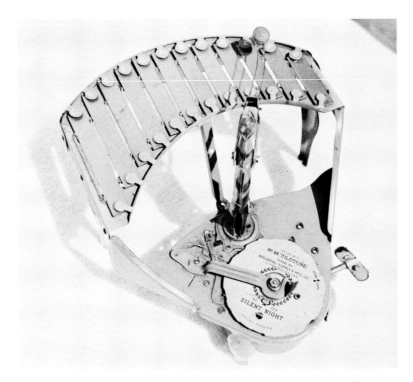

THE TUNE DISC IS DIRECTLY OVER THE SPRING HOUSING.

It is not known how many Zilotones were actually sold, but they are rather difficult to find today. This suggests that production was not great, perhaps reflecting the dual obstacles of a high price ($2.50 versus the average of $1.50 for musical toys in the Wolverine line) and the depression economy at the time of their production.

The concept of a toy automaton playing a xylophone remained popular, and a number of toys of this genre were imported from Japan in the 1950's and 1960's. These toys were battery-operated and limited in repertoire to a single tune. Illustrative of this more recent type of automatic xylophone are the two examples shown; mechanically 'Dennis the Menace' and the 'Musical Clown' are identical, with both playing "London Bridge" on six-note xylophones. Interestingly enough, these battery-operated toys use exactly the same basic principle as the Wolverine Zilotone. Riveted together are two discs – one (with a template-like edge) directing the back-and-forth motion of the body while the other (with a serrated edge) directs the up-and-down motions of the arm/striker. The major difference is that the discs are driven electrically rather than by a spring-wound motor. One can only wonder if the Japanese designer, when working out his automatic xylophone, had a Wolverine No. 48 Zilotone sitting on his desk.
■■

Other
Art—History—Reference

COUNTRIES KNOWN TO HAVE BEEN ASSOCIATED WITH MECHANICAL MUSIC

Arthur W.J.G. Ord-Hume

Alphabetical List

ARABIA
ARGENTINA
AUSTRALIA
AUSTRIA
BELGIUM
BOHEMIA
BOLIVIA
BULGARIA
CANADA
CHINA
CZECHOSLOVAKIA*
DENMARK
ESTONIA
EUROPEAN RUSSIA AND
   THE GRAND DUCHY
   OF FINLAND
FINLAND
   (see under European Russia)
FRANCE
GERMANY
GREAT BRITAIN
HOLLAND

HUNGARY
ITALY
INDIA
JAPAN
JAVA
LATVIA
LITHUANIA
MEXICO
MOROCCO
NORWAY
POLAND
PORTUGAL
RUSSIA
   (see under European Russia)
SPAIN
SWEDEN
SWITZERLAND
SYRIA
TURKEY
UNITED STATES
   OF AMERICA
YUGOSLAVIA

*The territory known today as Czechoslovakia is unlikely to have produced any mechanical musical instruments since, following the establishment of the state in 1917, there are no records of any indigenous industry. The countries which were divided up into Czechish or Czechian state were nevertheless steeped in such activities and references to this work are listed under their respective names. Similarly, what is today called the Soviet Union or, more correctly, the Union of Soviet Socialist Republics, has no recorded history of mechanical music since incorporation. In prerevolution Russia, the story was very different.

363

Annotated Alphabetical Listing

ARABIA
Early center of advanced mechanical engineering with development of sophisticated automated machinery and automata by 6th century A.D.

ARGENTINA
Production of cylinder musical boxes in Buenos Aires between 1889 and 1910 by Charles Francois Lecoultre.

AUSTRALIA
Manufacture of player piano rolls, assembly of player pianos under license, manufacture of bells and the production of a very limited number of carillons, mainly created as a result of English expertise and with English guidance.

AUSTRIA
The manufacture of a wide range of mechanical organs extending from organ-playing musical clocks through street organs to orchestrion organs. Musical boxes, mechanical and pneumatic pianos and piano orchestrions.

BELGIUM
As part of the Low Countries territory with Holland, a very wide tradition of mechanical instruments. Bells and, in particular, carillons flourished in the period 15th-18th century and the creation of musical clocks and clocks with automata was well established by the end of the 18th century. Later excelled in the manufacture of street organs, dance organs and the particular Belgian breed of cafe organs, clockwork pianos and entertainment orchestrions.

BOHEMIA
Mechanical pianos, piano-orchestrions, musical boxes, musical clocks, largely in the Viennese tradition, barrel organs and street organs, bells and carillons, pipe orchestrions.

BOLIVIA
Piano roll manufacture.

BULGARIA
Piano roll manufacture, street organ and piano manufacture.

CANADA
Player pianos and piano actions, piano roll manufacture.

CHINA

Musical clocks and watches with automata. Industry inspired by British exports during the 18th century. Many items made using parts imported from Britain. Automata. Much of achievements of the Far East formed a commonality between concepts, aspirations and ideals which rapidly spread to the Middle East.

DENMARK

Musical clocks and watches, street organs, player pianos, piano rolls.

ESTONIA

Street organs, musical clocks.

EUROPEAN RUSSIA AND THE GRAND DUCHY OF FINLAND

Musical clocks and watches, automaton work, bells and a limited number of carillons. Musical box manufacture, most probably using imported components, piano-orchestrions, pipe orchestrions, mechanical pianos, mechanical harmoniums.

FRANCE

Musical clocks and watches, automaton work, musical boxes, mechanical organs of all types, mechanical pianos and piano-orchestrions, complex automata and production automata, much of it with music. Mechanical harmoniums and reed organs in general.

GERMANY

A very early centre for mechanical music with musical clocks and automata going back to the 16th century. Clockwork spinets, automaton work of a very high order, mechanical musical instruments of all types including organs, orchestrions, disc and cylinder musical boxes, show organs, dance organs and cafe organs, street organs and pianos, reproducing pianos, advanced electric and pneumatic playing systems.

GREAT BRITAIN

Musical clocks and watches, complex automata, bells and carillons. small quantity of musical box manufacture, street organs, street piano and clockwork organ and piano manufacture, dance organs and fairground organs, automata. Church and chamber barrel organs.

HOLLAND

As part of the Low Countries, founding nation of the carillon and also the Dutch-style musical clock. Most of the many styles of domestic clock were built with musicwork at one time or another. Also devised the Dutch-style street organ. Piano roll manufacture. A significant influence on European mechanical music as well as music itself.

HUNGARY

Musical clocks and watches, musical boxes, street organs and orchestrions.

INDIA

Automata and elementary figures.

ITALY

Street pianos and organs, clockwork pianos, cafe pianos, musical clocks and watches, automata.

JAPAN

Automata, player pianos.

JAVA

Primitive automata and moving elementary figures. Dancing automaton dolls and wind-powered figures, self-moving devices to scare evil spirits.

LATVIA

Musical clocks and automaton work.

LITHUANIA

Player piano assembly, piano roll manufacture.

MEXICO

Piano roll manufacture, simple automaton work.

MOROCCO

Mechanical automata well established by the 14th century. Water-powered clocks, automatic flutes.

POLAND (strictly speaking part of European Russia and Duchy of Finland)

Musical clocks and automata, piano roll manufacture.

PORTUGAL

Musical clocks, automaton clocks, automata, piano roll manufacture.

RUSSIA (see under European Russia)

SPAIN

Street pianos and organs, automaton work, musical clocks and watches with automata, piano roll manufacture, assembly of player pianos.

SWEDEN
Musical clocks, mechanical pianos.

SWITZERLAND
Automaton work, musical clocks and watches, mechanical organs, orchestrions and show organs, disc and cylinder musical boxes.

SYRIA
Rich source of very early mechanical contrivances which, together with Arabia, represent the earliest documentary evidence of automata and mechanical musical instruments.

TURKEY
Automaton work, musical clocks (many made in Britain or assembled from parts imported).

UNITED STATES OF AMERICA
Musical clocks, initially in the European style but later in a well-defined American style, invariably with carillons. Street pianos and organs, mechanical pianos and organs, pneumatic pianos, reproducing pianos, piano-orchestrions, electro-pneumatic ditto and pure electric models. Disc and cylinder musical boxes, initially assembled from imported components. Wide range of automated musical instruments from banjo through to harp. Piano and organ roll manufacture. 𝄞

A RESEARCHER'S GUIDE TO MECHANICAL MUSIC

Frederick Fried

𝒯HE FOLLOWING INFORMATION was presented by me to the East Coast Chapter, MBSI, at its meeting in Westbury, Long Island, on May 1, 1982.

The resources are intended to be a starting point as more extensive research must include census reports, city directories, insurance and death records, and accounts of fairs, expositions, etc. This information is not intended to be a definitive listing.

ORGANIZATION JOURNALS

Bulletin, Musical Box Society International.

The Key Frame, Fair Organ Preservation Society, Staly Bridge, Cheshire, 1965–78.

The Music Box, Musical Box Society of Great Britain.

Merry-Go-Roundup, National Carousel Association.

Het Pierement, Netherlands Mechanical Organ Society.

AMUSEMENT PARK PUBLICATIONS

Amusement Business, Billboard Publications, Inc., Cincinnati.

The Billboard, The Billboard Publishing Company, Cincinnati, 1897–1969.

Amusement Park Management, Sylvan Hoffman, Washington, NJ, 1926–33.

The World's Fair, Oldham, England.

PERIODICALS

"Harper's Monthly".

"Harper's Weekly".

"Frank Leslie's Weekly".

"New York Clipper".

"Scientific American".

FAIRS, CENTENNIALS, EXHIBITIONS

American Institute of the City of New York, "Catalogue of Exhibits and Awards".

"The Centennial Exhibition", J. S. Ingram, Philadelphia, 1876.

"Official Catalogue of the International Exhibition of 1876", James D. McCabe, Philadelphia, National Publishing Co., 1876.

"Dictionnaire du Théâtre", Paris, Libraire de Firmin, Didot et Cie, 1885.

RESEARCH CENTERS AND LIBRARIES

Harvard Business School (Library), Cambridge, Massachusetts.
Dunn Business Records of 19th century manufacturers of music machines.

Library of Congress, Washington, D.C.
Music catalogues, not in the Union File, bundled and stacked in the folio section, (stack pass required). U.S. Patent Office — Records, Reports & Gazettes.

New York Public Library, Library of Performing Arts, Lincoln Center, New York — Music Division.
Scrap books, photos, miscellaneous collections.

GENERAL REFERENCE

Bonhote, D., & Baud, F., *Au Temps des Boîtes á* Musique, Editions Mondo, Lausanne, 1975. (Available in French, German or Italian; no English).

Bowers, Q. David, *Encyclopedia of Automatic Musical Instruments,* Vestal Press, 1972.

Bowers, Q. David, *Guidebook of Automatic Musical Instruments,* Vestal Press, 1967, 68.

Buchner, Dr. Alexander, *Mechanical Musical Instruments,* Batchworth Press, London, 1954.

Crowley, T. E., *Discovering Mechanical Music,* Shire Publications, Buckingham, Buckinghamshire, 1975.

Haspels, Dr. J.-J. L., *Muziek op Rolletjes,* Utrecht, 1975.

Hoover, Cynthia A., *Music Machines – American Style,* Smithsonian Institution Press, 1971.

Marini, Marino, *Museo de Strumenti Musicali Meccanici,* published by the author, Ravenna, Italy, 1973.

Reblitz, Arthur A., & Bowers, Q. David, *Treasures of Mechanical Music,* Vestal Press, 1981.

Simmen, Rene, *Men and Machines,* Van Lindonk, Amsterdam, 1968.

The *Silver Anniversary Collection,* M.B.S.I. 1974.

Weiss, Eugene H., *Phonographes et Musique Méchanique,* Librairie Hachette, Paris, 1930.

Weiss-Stauffacher, H., & Bruhin, R., *Mechanische Musikinstrumente un Musikautomaton,* published by the author, Seewen (Switzerland), 1973. English translation by James Underwood, Distributor: U. S. Kodansha International/U.S.A. Ltd. through Harper & Rowe Publishers, Inc., New York, N.Y. 1976.

THE PIANO

American Steel & Wire Company, *Piano Tone Building,* Vols. 1 and 2. "Proceedings of the Piano Technicians' Conference", New York, 1919, Volumes 1 and 2.

Autopiano, *Selling the Autopiano,* Autopiano Company, 1925.

Billings, F. C., *Helpful Suggestions,* "How to Keep Your Piano Better Tuned and the Action Better Regulated", Milwaukee, 1918.

Bowers, Q. David, *Put Another Nickel In,* Vestal Press, New York, 1976.

Cooke, James F., *Every Man His Own Tuner,* Oxford, England, 1906.

Dolge, Alfred, *Pianos and Their Makers,* Covina Publishing Co., Covina, California, 1911. (Appendix lists makers of all nations, lists firms manufacturing pianos [1911] and supplies).

Faust, Oliver C., *Tuner's Pocket Companion,* Boston, Massachusetts, 1902, 1949.

Fischer, J. Cree, *Piano Tuning, Regulating, and Repairing,* Theodore Presser Co., Philadelphia, 1907.

Givens, Larry, *Rebuilding the Player Piano,* Vestal Press, New York, 1963.

Givens, Larry, *Re-Enacting the Artist,* Vestal Press, New York, 1970.

Hammacher, Schlemmer & Co., *Piano Material,* Catalogue No. 275, 5th Edition, New York, n.d.

Howe, Alfred H., *Scientific Piano Tuning and Servicing,* J. J. Little & Ives Co., New York, 1941.

Maitland, George L., *How to Change Pitch of Pianos,* Philadelphia, 1915.

McTammany, John, *The History of The Player,* New York, 1913.

McTammany, John, *The Technical History of the Player,* The Musical Courier Co., 1915. (Reprint available from Vestal Press).

Meahl, P. J., *How and Why,* R. E. Fox Co., 1914

Norton, Edw. Quincy, *Construction, Tuning and Care of the Piano Forte,* Boston, 1887.

Ord-Hume, A. W. J. G., *Player Piano,* Allen & Unwin, London, 1970.

Reblitz, Arthur A., *Piano Servicing, Tuning and Rebuilding,* Vestal Press, New York, 1976.

Roehl, Harvey, *Player Piano Treasury,* Vestal Press, New York, 1961.

Schultz, M. Co., *Tuner's and Repairman's Manual for Schultz Player Pianos,* 1922.

Spillane, Daniel, *The Piano,* (Technical and Practical Instructions Relating to Tuning, Regulating and Toning), E. L. Bill Publ., New York, 1913.

Talbot, H., *National Self Tuner,* 1903.

Van Atta, Harrison Louis, *The Piano and Player Piano,* Dayton, 1914.

White, Wm. Braid, *The Player Piano Up-To-Date,* Edw. Lyman Bill, New York, 1914.

White, Wm. Braid, *Regulation and Repair of Piano and Player Mechanism,* together with *Tuning as Science and Art,* Edw. Lyman Bill, New York, 1909.

Wing & Son, *The Book of Complete Information About Pianos,* New York, 1897.

TRADE PUBLICATIONS

The International Directory of Music Industries
Edited and compiled by F. D. Abbot and C. A. Daniell, editors of "The Presto", the weekly journal of the Music Trades and Industries, Presto Publishing Company, Chicago, 1911. (Lists makers of pianos, organs, player pianos, orchestrions, and small instruments. Also repairers of music boxes, phonographs, talking machines, records and supplies. Has index to advertisers. Also, street pianos, carousels and merry-go-round organs, supplies, and importers of all musical instruments of all countries.)

The Piano & Organ Purchaser's Guide
Compiled by John C. Freund, Editor of the *Music Trades* and *Musical America* published by the Music Trades Co., 1918. (Lists all makes of pianos and organs, pipe, reed, etc., also parts and makers.)

Presto Buyer's Guide
Pianos and Player Pianos, 1910. (Lists all makers, logos on grained wood, history, care, popular and medium grade, trademark pianos, stencil or special names, manufacturers.)

"The Presto"
American Music Trade Weekly, Vol. 1, No. 1, 1882–1921. (News of the trade — excellent source for photos, engravings, etc.)

Swiss Trade Directory
Musical instruments of all types, 1902. (Good source for orchestrions, disc and roller players, organs and all instruments.)

Weltadressbuch der Musikindustrie
Paul de Wit, compiler, editor, publisher, Leipzig, 1893–1927. (Perhaps the best source for locating makers of instruments made between 1893 and 1927. Excellent illustrations of mechanical musical instruments.)

ORGANS

Audsley, George Ashdown, *The Art of Organ Building,* Dodd, Mead & Co., New York, 1905.

Barnes, William Harrison, *The Contemporary American Organ, Its Revolution, Design, and Construction,* J. Fischer & Bro., New York, 1937.

Beaumont, Anthony, *Fair Organs,* Model Aeronautical Press, Watsford, 1968.

Bedwell, G. G., *The Evolution of the Organ,* William Rider & Son, London, 1907.

Bowers, Q. David, *Encyclopedia of Automatic Musical Instruments,* Vestal Press, New York, 1972.

Boyer, Jacques, *The Manufacture of Mechanical Organs,* Scientific American, New York, April, 1908.

Chapuis, Alfred, *Automates, Machines Automatiques et Mécanismes,* 1928, *Histoire de la Boîte à Musique,* Edition Scriptar, Lausanne, 1955.

Church, John, *Organ Voicing and Tuning,* John Church Co., Cincinnati, 1881.

Clarke, William H., *Clarke's Outline of the Construction of the Pipe Organ,* Indianapolis, 1877.

Cockayne, Eric V., *The Fair Organ and How It Works,* Fair Organ Preservation Society, Northampton, 1967; *The Fairground Organ,* Newton Abbott, David & Charles, 1970.

Dickson, William Edward, *Practical Organ Building,* Crosby, Lockwood & Co., London, 1882.

Edwards, C. A., *Organs & Organ Building,* Bazaar, London, 1881.

Faust, Oliver C., *Organs, Construction and Tuning,* 1935. (Includes reed organs, Orchestrelle, and the player piano.)

Fried, Frederick, *A Pictorial History of the Carousel,* A. S. Barnes, New York, 1964.

Greville, Father P. R., *Memories of the Fairground,* L. Brown Stocton-on-Tees, 1965.

Grove, Sir George, *Dictionary of Music & Musicians,* McMillan, New York, 1879.

Hinton, J. W., *Organ Construction,* Weekes and Co., London, Third Edition, 1910.

Langwill, Lyndesay G. and Boston, Canon Noel, *Church & Chamber Barrel Organs,* Langwill & Boston, Edinburgh, 1967.

Leichtentritt, Hugo, "Mechanical Music in Olden Times", Music Quarterly, Vol. XX, New York, January, 1930.

Mathews, John, *Handbook of the Organ,* Augener, London, n.d.

Miller, John, *Recent Revolution in Organ Building,* Charles Francis Press, New York, 1902. Reprinted in 1913.

Ord-Hume, A. W. J. G., *Barrel Organ,* Allen & Unwin, London, 1978.

Page, Arthur, "Hints to Young Organists", *On Organ Playing,* Vincent Music Company, London, 1899.

Protz, Albert, *Mechanische Musikinstrumente,* Bahrenreiter, Kassel, 1939.

Rimbault, Edward F., *An Historical Account of the Organ,* London, 1855.

Schifferli, Peter, *Kleiner Drehorgelgruss,* Sanssouci, Zurich, 1968.

Sumner, William Leslie, *The Organ, Its Evolution, Construction & Use,* MacDonald, London, 1952.

Tootell, George, *How to Play the Cinema Organ,* Paxoon, London, n.d.

Waard, Rompke de, *Van Speeldoos tot Pierement,* Amsterdam, 1965; Het Draaiorgel, Alkmaar, Uitgeverij De Alk, 1972 (Translated into English by Wade Jenkins, "From Musical Boxes to Street Organs"), Vestal Press, New York.

Wedgewood, James Ingall, *Dictionary of Organ Stops,* G. Schirmer, New York, 1907.

Wicks, Mark, "Organ of the Month", — 19 copies, April 1942 to October 1943, (small pamphlets).

Wieffering, F., *Glorieuze Orgeldagen,* Utrecht, 1965.

MUSICAL BOXES

Buchner, Dr. Alexander, *Mechanical Musical Instruments,* Batchworth Press, London, c. 1954.

British Patent Office, *Musical Instruments 1694–1908, Abridgements Class 88,* London.

Chapuis, Alfred, *A History of the Music Box and Mechanical Music,* 1955, (Translated from the French.) — no index; has references and notes by chapters.

Clark, John E. T., *Music Boxes, A History and An Appreciation,* Fountain Press, London, 1948. Has appendix, makers of musical boxes, mechanical song birds, and automata.

Hoke, John and Helen, *Music Boxes, Their Lore and Lure,* Hawthorne Books, Inc., New York 1957.

Jacot, J. H., *The Jacot Repair Manual,* New York, 1890.

Mosoriak, Roy, *The Curious History of Music Boxes,* Lightner Publ., Chicago, 1943. Names of boxes classed by types and arrangements of music produced. Chronological listing of all U.S. patents granted for musical boxes and improvements in musical boxes from 1869 to 1904. Bibliography, index, list of makers.

Ord-Hume, A. W. J. G., *Collecting Musical Boxes and How to Repair Them,* Allen & Unwin, London, 1967.

Ord-Hume, A. W. J. G., *Clockwork Music, An Illustrated History of Mechanical Musical Instruments,* Allen & Unwin, London, 1973.

Ord-Hume, A. W. J. G., *Musical Box — A History and Collector's Guide,* Allen & Unwin, London, 1979.

Ord-Hume, A. W. J. G., *Restoring Musical Boxes,* Allen & Unwin, London, 1979.

Tallis, D., *Music Boxes,* Muller, London, 1971.

Templeton, Alec, *Music Boxes,* Wilfred Funk, New York, 1958.

U. S. Patent Office, Washington, D. C.

Webb, G., *The Cylinder Musical Box Handbook,* Faber & Faber, London, 1968.

Webb, G., The Disc Musical Box Handbook, Faber & Faber, London, 1971.

Young, David R., *How Old Is My Music Box?,* published by the author, Rochester, NY, 1980 (pamphlet). A chronology of the mechanical development of cylinder and disc music boxes.

SNUFF BOXES

Curtis, Mattoon, M., *Story of Snuff & Snuff Boxes,* Liveright, New York 1935.

Norton, Richard & Martin, *A History of Gold Snuff Boxes,* S. J. Phillips, London, 1935.

AUTOMATA

Carroll, Charles M., *The Great Chess Automata,* 1975.

Chapuis, A. and Droz, E., *Automata,* translated Reid, Editions du Griffon, Neuchatel, 1958.

Chapuis, A. and Gelis, E., *Le Monde des Automates,* Société Anonyme des Impressions Blondel la Rougery, Paris, 1928 (two volumes).

Devaux, P., *Automates et Automatisme,* Presses Universitaires, Paris, 1941.

Hiller, Mary, *Automata and Mechanical Toys, 1976.*

Maingot, E., *Les Automates,* Librairie Hachette, Paris, 1959.

Conservatoire Nationale des Arts et Matiéres, *Automates et Méchanismes,* Paris, 1960.

Conservatoire Nationale des Artes et Matiéres, *Les Boîtes à Musique de Prague,* (catalogue), Paris, 1966.

Ryder, Steven, "Animated Androids", 1978.

MUSICAL CLOCKS

Bassermann-Jordan, *Uhren,* Klinkhardt & Biermann, Braunschweig, Germany, 1976.

Bender, Gerd, *Die Uhremacher des hohen Schwarzwaldes und ihre Werke,* Muller, Villingen, Germany, 1975.

Holzhey, Gunther, *Flotenuhren aus dem Schwarzald,* Berliner Union, Stuttgart, c. 1971.

Juttemann, Herbert, *Die Schwarzwalduhr,* Klinkhardt & Biermann, Braunschweig, Germany, 1972.

Ord-Hume, A. W. J. G., *Musical Clocks & Watches,* published by the author, London, 1973.

CARILLONS

Lehr, Andre, *Leerboek der Campanologie,* Nationaal Beiaardmuseum, Asten, Netherlands, 1976.

Lehr, Andre, *Van Paardebel tot Speelklok,* Europese Bibliotheek, Zaltbommel, Netherlands, 1971.

Price, Frank Percival, *The Carillon,* Oxford University Press, London, 1933.

Verheyden, Prosper, *Beiaarden in Frankrijk,* Beiaardschool te Mechelen, Antwerp, Belgium, 1926.

THEORY OF MECHANICAL MUSIC

Engramelle, Marie Dominique, Joseph, *La Tonotechnie ou l'Art de Noter les Cylindres,* Paris, 1775 (facsimile reprint, Minkoff, Geneva, 1971).

Ord-Hume, A. W. J. G., *The Mechanics of Mechanical Music,* published by the author, London, 1973.

Schmitz, H. P., *Die Tontechnik des Pere Engramelle,* Barenreiter, Kassel, 1953.

RESEARCHER'S GUIDE TO MECHANICAL MUSIC ADDENDUM

Peter Schuhknecht

To the article "A Researcher's Guide to Mechanical Music" written by Frederick Fried (Vol. XXVIII, No. 1) I would like to add the following books authored by me: "Mechanische Singvogel" and "Die Drehorgel in der Graphik." Both books are available under my address in Hannover, Germany.

[Ed. note: Members are encouraged to submit names of other publications which were not included in the original article, as it was not intended to be a complete listing of all books in all languages.] 𝄞

New Information About Mozart's Clockwork Pieces

Hans Haselböck

During his lifetime, Wolfgang Amadeus Mozart demonstrated a special interest in the organ: his father, Leopold Mozart, had himself been a first-rate organist, and both of them missed no opportunity to see all the noteworthy organs which lay along the routes of their concert tours. Church music duties constituted another factor which enforced a constant interaction with the organ.

That Wolfgang Amadeus Mozart nevertheless wrote no organ works is explained by the musical practices of Catholic liturgy: the essential liturgical chants, the ordinary and propers of the feast days of the time, were performed by the choir. There was no real place within the Mass for the organ to be prominent and independent. The organist merely had to provide intonations for the individual chants and then to play organ continuo in the orchestra. The interludes, normally short, had to be strictly matched to the timing of the liturgical acts, and were therefore usually improvised.

Nevertheless, we have three compositions for automatic organs, all from the last period of Mozart's life. The interest of organists has always been drawn to them, and they are the subject of the present study.

THE COMMISSION

The three clockwork pieces, K.594, 608, and 616, were commissioned by the owner of an art gallery, as background music for his exhibits — namely by Joseph Deym-Müller (1750-1804), one of the most interesting personalities of Vienna's cultural life in the closing years of the eighteenth century.

Count Josef Deym von Stritetz — his more complete name — came from an old and noble family in Bohemia. During his military service he was involved in a dual in which his opponent was killed. Deym then took flight all the way across Europe to Holland, where he adopted the name Müller

BROUGHT to our attention by both Bill Edgerton and Jim Feller, this article is reprinted through the gracious permission of Arthur Lawrence, Editor of THE DIAPASON, in which it first appeared in November 1977. Mr. Lawrence kindly sent a supplementary illustration (of the beginning of K. 608) that appeared in February 1978. The following is quoted from THE DIAPASON: "Dr. Hans Haselböck is professor of organ and improvisation at the Hochschule tür Musik in Vienna .. His article was translated by Bruce Gustafson, assistant professor of music at Saint Mary's College."

and managed to support himself by building wax figures. Several years later he went to Naples, Rome and Florence, where he gained entree to the most important collections of antiquities, and produced plaster copies of significant ancient Greek art objects. About 1780, he brought his collection to Vienna, rented a store front quite near St. Stephen's Cathedral on Stock-im-Eisen Place, and charged admission to see about one hundred copies of famous ancient statues (including the Medicean Venus, the Venus of Knidos, the Farnesi Hercules, the Apollo of the Belvedere, the Laocoön group and various others). Deym's collection contained yet other showpieces: life-size colored wax figures of important and recently deceased personalities (Kaiser Leopold II, Franz II, and the princes Lobkowitz and Esterházy), paintings and sketches, and artistically ornamented vases, along with musical clocks, mechanical figures, and other curiosities. The entire show, which became a noted attraction of the old Kaiser city under the name "Müllersches Kunstcabinet," must have had the character of a wax works whose artistic worth — according to a contemporary[1] — was of middling quality.

On July 14, 1790, the important Austrian field marshal, Laudon, the winner of the battles of Kunersdorf (1759) and Belgrade (1789), died. Deym, who had made a life-size wax likeness of the field marshal the year before his death,[2] rented new quarters in Vienna's Himmelpfort Street, across from the winter palace of Prince Eugen, not far from Mozart's last residence, and set up a memorial exhibit in Laudon's honor. It was in this connection, then, that Deym ordered a funereal piece from Mozart in August or September, 1790.

Mozart travelled to Frankfurt on September 23, 1790, to take part in the coronation of Leopold II. Clearly, he left with the intention that while on the trip, which lasted until the tenth of November, he would write the composition for Count Deym's automatic instrument. This is mentioned in his famous letter of October 3, 1790:

. . . So I have definite plans to write the Adagio for the clock maker at once in order to put a few ducats in my beloved little wife's hands; and I have done so — but as it is a hated chore for me, unfortunately can't finish it — I write every day on it — must put it aside because it bores me and indeed if there were not such an important basic reason for it, I would surely put it aside totally — so I hope to wring it out little by little — yes, if it were a large clock and the thing sounded like an organ, I'd be happy; but as it is, the mechanism is made out of nothing but little pipes which sound too high and, to me, too childish . . .

Earlier Mozart scholarship relates this letter to K.594.[3] There is much evidence, however, that Mozart's writing of October 3, 1790, concerns K.593a, or another lost work. All of Mozart's efforts to the contrary, the work did not come to fruition. It appears that Deym had

Beginning of K.594 (copy in private Viennese collection)

planned on too small an instrument, which, to the composer, did not seem to be suitable for funereal music, and which sounded "too childish" — that is, one of the well-known rococo flute clocks (for which Mozart later wrote K.616). In spite of Mozart's labors, the work was not finished, and not until December, 1790, when he was once again back in Vienna, did he write an entirely different piece, K.594. There is some basis for the assumption that Deym was able in the meantime to get a larger automatic instrument which Mozart thought more suitable to the purpose.

During the period through March, 1791, the piece was set on barrels (i.e., the pins which allow the pipes to speak were positioned and driven into the barrels — *trans.*) , and on March 26, 1791, a notice appeared in the *Wiener Zeitung* that the Laudon-Mausoleum had opened three days previously and that "with the striking of each hour there is funereal music, and it will be different each week. This week the composition is by Herr Kapellmeister Mozart."[4]

Count Deym kept his Laudon-Mausoleum, as he called it, open until about the end of July, 1791. In August, he moved, together with these show pieces, to Stock-im-Eisen Place and displayed the Laudon memorial show together with his other art objects. The automatic instrument was also moved, and the *Wiener Zeitung* wrote the following on August 17, 1791:

The Müller art collection on Stock-im-Eisen Place . . . is presently set up almost completely new, and is considerably enlarged . . . One hears at the end various musical clocks, one of which imitates a pianoforte to the point of deception, another the transverse flute, a third the canary bird . . . When one has looked through the first two rooms, he will find the splendor of the mausoleum of the great Baron von Laudon . . . There one is surprised during the inspection of it all by select funereal music composed by the famous Herr Capellmeister Mozart, which is very suitable to the subject.[5]

The surprise which the reporter spoke of is obviously Mozart's second barrel organ piece, K.608, which must have alternated with K.594 in the new arrangement of the exhibit. Deym must

have commissioned K.608 immediately upon the completion of K.594. Mozart gave March 3, 1791, as the completion date. The months of March through August would have been used again for the barrel pinner's work. We have some justification to assume that both pieces were to be performed on one and the same clock work.

Before this work (K.608) could have been performed by an automatic instrument, however, Mozart wrote a third similar work, the Andante K.616, which is from May 4, 1791. The commissioner was again Count Deym, who put the piece in another scene of his show, in the so-called "Bedroom of the Graces."

The later fortunes of Müller's exhibit will only be briefly described here. In 1795, four years after Mozart's death, Deym moved his exhibit to another location on the Kohlmarkt in Vienna's inner city. The automatic instruments which played the three Mozart pieces were transferred at the same time. The Laudon-**Mausoleum** was not re-erected. Laudon did not lie as before in a glass casket, but stood upright and was portrayed together with the likeness of Kaiser Josef II (who died February 20, 1790) , in the center of the "Elysium."

There is an exact description of the new exhibit by a contemporary reporter,[6] explicitly mentioning Mozart's music:

One hears every hour specially written suitable funereal music by the unforgettable Mozart, which lasts eight minutes and surpasses in precision and purity everything which has been tried with this kind of artistic endeavor.

The two Mozart pieces, K.594 and 608, seem to have been set to alternate. K.616, on the other hand, sounded on another smaller instrument in the "Bedroom of the Graces:"

In the famous bedroom of the graces stands a resilient bed which is dimly lit in the evenings by alabaster lamps, with a beautiful sleeping figure, and behind these the most enchanting music which was composed especially for the place and presentation. In an eighteen-foot niche stands the beautiful Kallipygos Venus admirably colored, and with the aid of the artfully placed mirror, the three graces from which the bedroom takes its name.[7]

Two years later, in 1791, Deym — who had been rehabilitated in the meantime — moved for the last time with his collection: he had his own palace-like building constructed at great expense near the Rotenturmtor, by the Donaukanal, and there he showed his "Royal Privileged Kaiser's Art Gallery."

In 1799, Deym married a visitor to the gallery, Countess Josephine Brunsvik, the daughter of a Hungarian countess. At the same time, Deym also met with Beethoven about the joint production of a flute clock piece. (Beethoven produced three pieces and made a copy of K.608 for himself as preparation.)

Deym died after a rather joyless marriage, before the birth of his fourth child, on January 27, 1804, and left his wife in great financial difficulties. Josephine Deym-Brunsvik left Beethoven's great attraction for her unrequited (she enters his biography as the "undyingly beloved"), married Baron Christoph Stackelberg from Riga in 1810, and died on March 31, 1821. After her death, the lawyer who was appointed trustee by the children sold the works from the collection to settle the claims of the creditors. The Müller building was subsequently put to use as a dance hall and for musical performances, and was completely torn down in 1889.

THE INSTRUMENTS

While we know at least three flute clocks associated with Haydn and which come from the composer's time, there is no trace after 1821 of a single one on which Mozart's works once sounded.

The only one of the Mozart organ barrel pieces which can be heard on a flute clock is the Andante, K.616, which plays on Music Cabinet 2052, dating from about 1810, in the Leipzig music instrument museum. It is important to keep in mind that this music cabinet is *not* the same as the instrument in the Deym collection. The barrel, in any case, comes from a later time: since the old barrels had become unusable, the former owner of the music cabinet, Paul de Wit, had three new barrels completed towards the end of the nineteenth century. Mozart's Andante was set on one of them. In the autograph of this piece, which has a compass of f-f³, there is also a suggestion by Mozart for shortening the length of it, reducing it from 144 measures to 111, if the barrel should have too little room. The Leipzig music cabinet in its present state does not use Mozart's suggestd cut, but has only measures 1-53 and 125-144, a total of 73 measures.

Mozart had been familiar with the sound of automatic instruments from his earliest youth. In Salzburg and in the immediate vicinity of the city, there were three famous music mechanisms in the eighteenth century:

—the "Dutch carillon" from 1704, in the tower of the "reconstruction" of the archbishop's residence; it played daily, morning, noon and evening.
—The water organ at Hellbrunn, finished in 1752 by the Salzburg organ builder, Rochus Egedacher.
—The trumpet mechanism in the fortress Hohensalzburg, whose barrel organ had been rebuilt in 1753; the instrument's twelve pieces were published by Leopold Mozart in a version for keyboard.

In his later concert tours as well, Mozart must have continually encountered mechanical musical instruments because it was just at this time that decorative clocks and flute mechanisms were greatly favored in aristocratic circles.

Next to Berlin and Dresden, Vienna was the foremost production center of automatic instruments. A great number of flute clock makers is known to us: Franz Egidius Arzt and Joseph Arzt Johann Bauer, Joseph Gurk, Christian Heinrich, Franz and Johann Adolf Hoyer, Johann Nepomuk and Leonhard Mälzel, Joseph Niemecz, Anton and Rudolf Reinlein, as well as Johann Georg Strasser and son. Among the surviving flute clocks, three can be cited with original works by Joseph Haydn (1772, 1792, and 1793), which contain between 17 and 29 pipes. As a rule, the musical mechanisms did not contain all the chromatic pitches, so that one was restricted in the choice of keys.

The question of the identity of the builder of the flute clocks on which Mozart's pieces were played can be answered here for the first time. In the archives of the *Gesellschaft der Musikfreunde* in Vienna, there is a letter which has not been previously discussed in Mozart scholarship; it was written by Ignaz von Seyfried (1776-1841) to an unnamed music publisher as he planned to arrange and publish Mozart's F Minor Fantasy, K.608, for orchestra under the title, "Fantasia fugata." The missive, dated January 18, 1813, gives unique details about the builder and sound of the Mozart flute clock:

Mozart's Fantasy in F Minor, composed here in Vienna for the organ

380

machine of the late *Frater Primitiv*, is, to my knowledge, little known; yet it occupies, it seems to me, one of the first places among the masterworks of the immortal [composer]. I still remember from my youth the strong impression made by the repeated — often repeated — hearing of this genial product, which cannot be erased from my memory . . . [A detailed description of K.608 follows.]

Here we discover, therefore, who built the automatic instrument on which Mozart's pieces had been played: "Brother (Frater) Primitiv" was the monastic name of Joseph Niemecz, who was born in Bohemia on February 9, 1750; he entered the monastery of the Brothers of Mercy as a novice in 1768; in 1776 was ordained as a priest in Königgrätz, and in 1780 took the position of librarian for Prince Esterházy at the Esterháza palace. Niemecz had great literary gifts, but also played a number of instruments and was one of Haydn's composition students. His special talent lay, however, in the area of building automatic instruments and there were supposedly a number of such instruments — some very odd — in the palaces of Eisenstadt and Esterháza.

When Brother Primitiv died on January 9, 1806, his complete estate, "large and small musical playing clocks and machines . . . were sold for the cheapest prices."[8] The three small flute clocks with original pieces by Haydn are still known, but there is no trace of the other automatic instruments.

How, then, were the instruments on which Mozart's pieces were played procured? It is fairly certain that the three pieces by Mozart were intended for two different flute clocks: K.594 and 608 for a large instrument, built by Primitiv Niemecz; K.616, however, for a small rococo flute clock, apparently from the same builder. In this connection it is important that Mozart himself stipulated that his K.616 was "for a barrel in a *small* organ," whereas a copy of K.594 now in private possession in Vienna, carries the title, "Machine Composition v[on] H[errn] Capellm[eister] Mozart." (See illustration on page 160.)

Prof. Hans Haselböck has sent this illustration as a supplement to his article on Mozart's Clockwork pieces (November 1977). It is the beginning of the Fantasy, K.608, from a manuscript copy in the Gesellschaft der Musikfreunde, Vienna (reproduced through the courtesy of that institution).

The constructional details of small flute clocks is sufficiently known: instruments of this type usually have a set of narrow-scaled gedeckt pipes producing a delightful chamber music effect. It is more difficult to imagine the sound of the larger automatic instruments. We should remember that the composition which "has such an important basic reason for it" (the imminent opening of the exhibit? — Mozart's pressing debts?) must be completed, and yet it was not being finished because the instrument was of too small pipes; that is, the sound had too little gravity. After the return trip "in December," came K.594, which in no way gives the impression of a "hated chore." Obviously, the exhibitor, Count Deym, had been able to put another instrument to use. Its difference from the small rococo clocks lay not in a larger compass, as is sometimes assumed,[9] but in different disposition and scaling.

These assumptions are supported in other passages in Seyfried's letter, cited above, which gives information about the sound of Niemecz's clock with the Mozart pieces. According to his account, the device "consisted of flutes and bassoon!" It follows from this account that this automatic instrument contained one or more labial voices and a reed register. There is further proof that both of the large Mozart pieces (K.594 and 608) were played on this instrument:

both pieces are in the same key,
they were approximately of the same duration.
they are titled similarly in copies,
they have the same notation (four staves).

The sound of this automatic instrument undoubtedly was about half way between that of the small rococo flute clocks and the later Orchestrion, more-or-less as Mälzel built them.

There is still further information about K.608: in the *Allgemeine Musikalische Zeitung* of July 28, 1801, a doctor named Doppelmair gave a report from Petersburg (Leningrad today) and wrote that a large automatic instrument was being exhibited by a clock maker named Johann Georg Strasser, who had emigrated from Vienna. His "mechanical orchestra" had seven registers on two separate chests, including two 12' voices and a reed stop! Among the fifteen barrels, each of which had a performance time of about ten minutes, was Mozart's "Fantasie à 4 mains" — K. 608 was circulated under this name.

Here are the most important passages of the letter:

For several pleasurable months art-lovers in St. Petersburg have had the joy of seeing the completed mechanical orchestra which is uniquely and notedly splendid for this type of art work, the invention and workmanship of the famous clock maker, Mr. Johann Georg Strasser, from Baden near Vienna, and his son . . . This work is divided into two orchestras [and] the one has the following voices:
1) Viola di Gamba 12 foot.
2) Flöte 12 foot.
3) Flöte 8 foot.
4) Flöte 4 foot.
The second consists of:
5) Vox humana 8 foot.
6) Fugara 8 foot.
7) Flöte 8 foot.
The pipes are in part from wood, in part from metal, built by the famous organ and instrument maker, Mr. Gabrahan in St. Petersburg . . . . Only those who understand musical expression so well, such as Messrs Strasser, father and son, could furnish such barrels and build the organ of the art work in such a way that one would think that he were hearing virtuosos who, through the gliding, articulating, swelling, and dying of the tones and of whole sections . . . . knew how to give the pieces their own special life. . . .[10]

Mozart, to be sure, could not have heard this automatic instrument, but he could have known the clock maker Strasser, since his wife's vacations led him frequently to Baden near Vienna. It is therefore possible that Mozart became acquainted with other automatic organs by Strasser, or at least that he was informed of the plans for them. Mozart's wish in his letter of October 3, 1790, "yes, if it were a large clock and the thing sounded like an organ," was fulfilled here in Strasser's work.

An even larger sound was finally produced by Johann Nepomuk Mälzel's musical machines, which he built in Vienna around 1813 and which he supplied with the name "Panmelodikon" or "Panharmonikon."[11] It is known that Beethoven had written his composition, *Wellington's Victory*, for this automatic instrument (Wellington, with an English army, had been victorious over the French army on June 21, 1813). The piece never sounded on an automatic instrument, but was orchestrated a little later by Beethoven and was performed

W. A. MOZART IN 1789.

with great success in Vienna on December 12, 1813.

Admittedly we have strayed considerably from Mozart's time with these automatic instruments. This brief overview should clearly show that from a developmental point of view, and aided by hindsight, Mozart's organ barrel compositions (with the exception of the Andante K.616) were written for a type of automatic instrument which stands half way in size between the rococo Haydn instruments and their successors, such as Mälzel's Panharmonikon, which included percussion instruments for the first time and led to the Orchestrion.

THOUGHTS ON ORGAN
INTERPRETATION

The tradition of playing Mozart's organ barrel pieces on an organ with manuals and pedals does not have to be defended: of all of the arrangements (piano four hands, string quartet, brass quintet, orchestra, etc.), surely the sound of an organ comes closest to the sound that Mozart had in mind.

The least of the interpretation problems are soluble in the Andante, K.616. The appropriate sound for this piece would undoubtedly be to play it straight through with a single registration (Holzgedact 8' on a secondary division). The alternation of Gedackt 8' and Flöte 8' would also be conceivable, using the model which the flute clock from 1819 in the barrel organ museum in Utrecht gives us.[12] If the voices were not sufficiently clear, one could opt for the Gedackt 8' and Kleingedackt 4' (the

South German "Klein-Copi"). A disposition in octaves is known, by the way, in exceptional old flute clocks: in the music instrument museum of what is today the Karl Marx University in Leipzig there are at least two instruments (one from Johann Nepomuk Mälzel's shop, with a 4' and a 2' register in an empire clock; a second by Franz Egidius Arzt from Vienna, rebuilt in a display case with clock, also with 4' and 2') which also have the choice of registers programmed on the barrel. An alternation of registration in K.616 from 8' to 8' with 4' is therefore not to be ruled out, but it is not required.

The situation with the pieces K.594 and 608 is more difficult. For the former composition, the original has still not been published, and the arrangements for organ which are available are based on a reworking. The uncertainty is, however, the same as for K.608: namely, if one takes the copy which was intended for the flute clock as the basis of a text of an organ version, then the composition can be played almost completely as written, note for note, if one couples the pedals to the manual in order to help the hands, leaving the independent (16') pedal stops off.[13] On the other hand, one might return to the thought that Mozart himself complained, "yes, if the thing sounded like an organ." The sound of a larger organ is, therefore, at least not contradictory of the composer's intentions, and it is appropriate, if not necessary, to the musical dictates of both pieces, especially K.608. That the choice of the adequate sounds is a basic presupposition if a piece is to have its proper effect needs no detailed defense here. The attempt at a performance which has the "authentic" sound must therefore not merely adhere to the score, but must take into account the fact that Niemecz's and Strasser's organ machines surely had no mixtures, but possibly were similar to the sound of the later orchestrion (on the organ this sonority corresponds to a *grand jeu* registration,[14] which in any case was not possible on a south German or Austrian organ of Mozart's time).

A registration of corresponding intensity and weight can be found in the *plenum* of the Hauptwerk of historic Austrian organs: it was of flue pipes throughout and was always — and this is of considerable consequence for the interpretation of Mozart's barrel organ pieces — played with a 16' pedal, just as every ensemble from a certain size on used a 16' foundation in the bass, according to conventional practice. Therefore, an interpretation of K.594 and 608 with 16' pedal is possible, and it is even useful for the desired musical effect, but we have to take a few octave transpositions into the bargain as well. For the use of pedals in K.608, one can also refer to the piano 4-hand arrangement which appeared just after Mozart's death.[15] In the interpretation of these pieces on the organ, a decision must be made between a rather literal performance which shuns a 16' pedal line (quite imaginable for small organs having a chamber-music character) and a rendition with "full" organ and 16' pedal — which Mozart's earlier intentions do suggest and which is more suited to the sound of a large organ, at the price of a few insignificant octave transpositions, to be sure.

We know from Mozart's improvisation in the monastery of Strahov / Prague in the fall of 1787 how he himself registered pieces with similar movements. According to the report of the monastery organist, Father Norbert Lehmann, he played the organ first with a coupled "pleno choro," and created "meisterhafte Accorde" ("masterful chords" — a registrational suggestion for the dotted sections of K.608?). Then Mozart took the manual couplers off and also reduced the pedal: "All four reeds were too loud for him. In addition to the normal pedal without mixture, he chose the eight-foot Posaunbass." With this registration he played polyphony, involving ornamentation at the same time, however (are the fugal sections of K.608 and the allegro part of K.594 parallel to this?): "Then he began a four-voiced fugue theme, which was even more difficult to execute because it and its answer were constructed from a series of mordents. . . ."[16]

In contrast, a quieter flute color, 8' or 8' and 4', should be chosen for the beginning and ending of K.594, as well as for the middle section of K.608. In general, in places where the dynamic contrast between the plenum registration and the flutes would be too great (such as at the transition to measure 159 in K.608), an increase to 8' and principal 4' (8', 4', 2', at the most) is called for. Too many changes in registration should be avoided in the A-flat major section of K.608.

"... yes, if the thing sounded like an organ": in spite of all of the arrangements of Mozart's organ barrel pieces, it is only the organist who has the means to make the composer's imagined sound a reality. There are a number of technical difficulties to master in the process, but the reward for all the trouble is certainly considerable: under skilled hands and on sympathetic instruments, Mozart's three organ barrel pieces show themselves to be masterful music of the Viennese Classic — organ compositions which have no counterparts in that style.

FOOTNOTES

[1] Theodor Frimmel, "Ein altes Wachsfigurenkabinett," *Alt Wiener Kalender* (1922), p.131 ff.

[2] Cf. Otto Erich Deutsch, *Mozart—Die Dokumente seines Lebens* (Cassel, 1961), p.341.

[3] Nottebohm, Nohl, Jahn, Albert, Köchel.

[4] Deutsch, p.349.

[5] Ibid., p.351.

[6] C.M.A., "Beschreibung der kaiserl. königl. privilegierten, durch den Herrn Hofstatuarius Müller errichteten Kunstgalerie in Wien, 1799."

[7] 1814 edition, no. 37, p.76.

1796 edition. Quoted in Frimmel, *Wachsfigurenkabinett*, p.130.

[8] *Wiener Zeitung*, May 28, 1806.

[9] Ernst Simon, *Mechanische Musikinstrumente früherer Zeiten und ihre Musik* (Wiesbaden, 1960), p.75. Simon suggests a compass of F-d³, but a compass of c⁰-d³ is fairly certain.

[10] *Allgemeine musikalische Zeitung* 3:44 (July 29, 1801): 376 ff.

[11] Detailed description in Hanns H. Josten, *Württembergisches Landesmuseum, Die Sammlung der Musikinstrumente* (Stuttgart, 1928), p.97 ff (cf. *The Diapason* 68:5 (April, 1977), p.6—*trans*.).

[12] Built by Diderick Nicolaas Winkel. The flute clock plays a composition which is supposed to be by Mozart (written on the barrel); however, there is no proof of the authenticity of this work.

[13] A version on this basis appeared in the edition of the Mozart organ barrel pieces by Doblinger (Vienna, Diletto musicale, 587).

[14] That is, a sound dominated by reeds and cornets (—*trans*.).

[15] Pianos at this time had a range down to contra F at the most, which corresponds approximately to the compass of a contrabass in an orchestra.

[16] Deutsch, p.444.

CHRONOLOGY OF MOZART'S CLOCKWORK PIECES

c. 1780	—Count Josef Deym, who took bourgeois name Müller, opened the "Müller Art Gallery" on Stock-im-Eisen Square, Vienna.
1780	—Brother Primitivus Niemecz became librarian at Prince Esterházy's palace in Eisenstadt. He later became known as a maker of automatic instruments.
July 14, 1790	—Death of Austrian field marshal Baron von Laudon (victor over Frederick the Great at Kunersdorf, 1759, and over Eroberer at Belgrade, 1789). Deym, who had made life-size wax bust of Laudon, conceived of erecting a memorial show.
Aug-Sept, 1790	—Deym commissioned Mozart to write a funereal piece for a flute clock.
Oct. 3, 1790	—Date of Mozart's letter to his wife, written in Frankfurt. Contents: he was not progressing with the piece because the instrument stipulated did not suit his plan.
	—Deym procured a large automatic instrument, perhaps at Konstanza's urging; it was in contrast to the little rococo flute clock's "flutes and bassoon." Builder: Father Primitivus Niemecz.
Dec., 1790	—Mozart composed the Adagio and Allegro, K.594, in Vienna.
Mar. 3, 1791	—Mozart finished the F-Minor Fantasy, K.608. The piece was intended for the same automatic instrument in the Laudon-Mausoleum as K.594.
Mar. 23, 1791	—Deym opened the Laudon-Mausoleum on Vienna's Himmelpfort Street. Mozart's funereal piece, K.594, sounded hourly.
May 4, 1791	—Mozart wrote the Andante, K.616, intended for Deym, and apparently composed for the flute clock for which Deym had originally intended the funereal piece. It later played in the "Bedroom of the Graces."
August, 1791	—Deym moved the Laudon Mausoleum to his gallery on Stock-im-Eisen Place. As an added attraction, K.608 was played there for the first time.
Dec. 5, 1791	—Mozart's death.
1795	—Deym set up his collection at the Kohlmarkt.
1797	—Deym displayed his collection in the new "Müller Building" near the Rotenturmtor. The flute clocks with Mozart's pieces also made these moves.
1799	—Deym married Josephine Brunsvik.
July 29, 1801	—Report in the Allgemeine musikalische Zeitung: In Petersburg one can hear Mozart's F-Minor Fantasy, K.608, on a large automatic instrument ("Mechanical Theater") by Johann Georg Strasser, which has seven registers. Strasser came from Baden near Vienna, where Mozart had repeatedly played.
Jan. 27, 1804	—Joseph Deym's death. Beethoven's dedication to Deym's widow ("undyingly beloved") was not reciprocated by her, perhaps because of her standing.
Jan. 18, 1813	—Seyfried's report about the "organ Machine" by Father Primitiv, on which he heard K.608.
Mar. 31, 1821	—Death of Josephine Deym-Brunsvik. Dispersal of Deym's collection to pay the claims of creditors. From this time, all trace of the flute clocks with Mozart's pieces is lost.

THE COMPOSITIONS

In 1784, Mozart began to sketch an index of his works, which he continued until his death. In this index, the exact dates are given for the genesis of the three flute clock works:

Overview from Mozart's index	Listings from Koechel's catalog
— — —	*K.593a; Adagio for keyboard or organ barrel.* Composed about the end of 1790 in Vienna; fragment of 9 measures, written on 3 staves (2 in 𝄞, 1 in 𝄢). Autograph in the Mozarteum, Salzburg. Range: d°-d³.
No. 121, "in December," (1790)	*K.594; Adagio and Allegro for organ barrel.* Autograph unknown. Copy from beginning of 19th century from Beethoven's estate, in New York Public Library. [Another copy in private Viennese collection (3 staves in 𝄞, 1 in 𝄢).] Range: c°-d³.
No. 130, "the 3rd of March," (1791) An organ piece for a clock	*K.608; Fantasy for organ barrel.* Autograph unknown. Copies in Preussische Staatsbibliothek, West Berlin, and Gesellschaft der Musikfreunde, Vienna (3 staves in 𝄞, 1 in 𝄢). Beethoven made hand written copy. Range: c°-d♭³.
— — —	*K.615a; Andante for barrel in small organ.* (Preliminary sketch for K.616.) About April, 1791; 4-measure fragment on 4 staves (3 in 𝄞, 1 in 𝄢). Autograph in University Library, Uppsala (attached to sketches for *Die Zauberfloete*). Range: f°-d¹.
No. 136, "the 4th of May," (1791) An Andante for a barrel in a little organ	*K.616; Andante for barrel in small organ.* Autograph in the Mozarteum, Salzburg; written in 3 staves, 𝄞. Range: f°-f³.

SUMMARY

1. Mozart composed three pieces for automatically activated organs, between December 1790 and May 1791. He had possibly written earlier for automatic instruments.

2. These pieces were commissioned by Count Joseph Deym-Müller, who ordered them for his art gallery.

3. Of the three pieces, only K.616 survives in an autograph.

4. K.594 and 608 were played by a large automatic organ (Seyfried: "organ machine") in Deym's Laudon-Mausoleum. The instrument had labial pipes and a reed register; the builder was Father Primitivus Niemecz, librarian for Prince Esterházy. The Andante, K.616, was meant for a normal small flute clock (builder: also Niemecz?) and was played in Deym's "Bedroom of the Graces."

5. The F-Minor Fantasy, K.608, was later heard in Petersburg on a large automatic organ, Johann Georg Strasser's "Mechanical Theater." This instrument had two divided chests with a total to seven registers, including a reed and two 16' stops from F. It had the capability of playing solo voices (as on a two-manual organ), letting the lower parts sound at 16' pitch. Strasser had worked in Baden, near Vienna, until 1795; it is probable that Mozart knew the "clock maker" Strasser and his musical machines.

6. Mozart's organ barrel pieces were written for two different types of automatic instruments: K.616 for the type like those which have survived with Haydn's original pieces (only 4' gedeckt stops, having an intimate sound); K.594 and 608 for an instrument with an intense sound, which also had a reed voice (and could, in the case of Strasser's automatic organ, even have the effect of 2 manuals and a 16' pedal).

7. None of the original automatic organs which sounded Mozart's compositions have survived. An excerpt of K.616 can be heard on a barrel in the Leipzig music instrument museum, but this cannot be considered a primary source, because the piece was initially pinned on the barrel toward the end of the 19th century. ∎ ●

MECHANICAL MUSIC
IN DUTCH ILLUSTRATIONS

Hendrik H. Strengers

𝒎ANY Dutch painters, etchers, and illustrators enjoy international fame, although theirs is one of the smallest countries of the world. Perhaps there is a reason for this remarkable fact. We have an old saying in Holland: "God has created the world with the exception of the Netherlands. That we have done ourselves." Believe me or not, but it is true. We have made land out of the sea, and created our own polders and landscapes, from Roman times to this day. Does this explain our love for extensive plains and for tiny details? I do not know, but our painters are famous for their landscapes and our illustrators for their gift of noticing details.

This patriotic introduction has been written to call your attention to a rather neglected aspect of our common hobby: the history of depicting mechanical music in the art of painting and in related arts. The M.B.S.I. has reproduced many magnificent old photographs, advertisements, paintings, lithographs, and engravings concerning automatic musical instruments in the *Bulletin* during the past years, but nobody has tried to write a thorough study on this subject. How interesting it should be to trace the development of the popularity of mechanical music in different countries by looking for pictures in children's books, newspapers, periodicals concerning music, et cetera--to say nothing of the nursery rhymes and poems that match these pictures!

As for the Netherlands, I'll try to make a start now. The first three illustrations were made by well-known artists, and the rest come from children's books. The translations of the nursery rhymes are not literal, of course, but are faithful to the sense of the originals.

In this article, it is my intention only to give an introduction to a little-known aspect of our hobby, and I hope that members of our Society living in other countries all over the world will follow this example and publish the part of the story relating to their own countries. Who is next?

FIGURE 1.

Title: *Jalousie de métier,* or Professional jealousy. Published by Van Holkema & Warendorf en K. Groesbeek, at Amsterdam. A fine pencil drawing by Johan Coenraad BRAAKENSIEK, born May 24, 1858, at Amsterdam, died February 27, 1940, at Amsterdam. He was a very

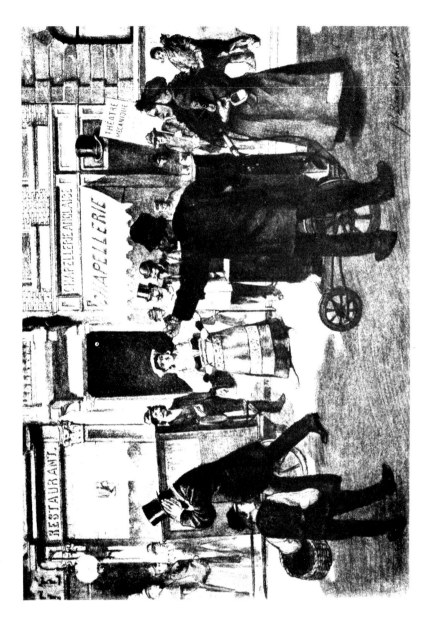

FIGURE 1. PROFESSIONAL JEALOUSY, PENCIL DRAWING BY BRAAKENSIEK.

⊰⊱

THE photographs of Figures 1 through 5B are courtesy of Mr. Theo Strengers of The Hague.

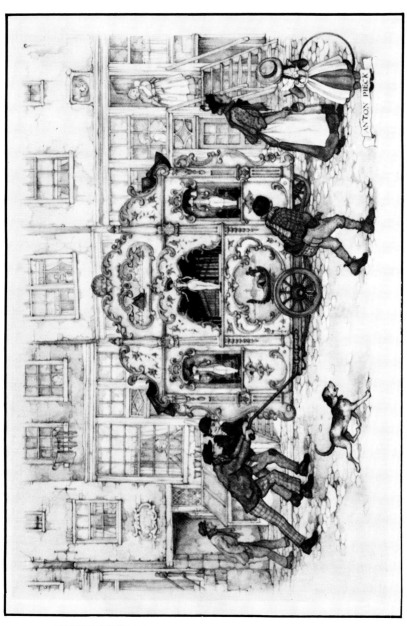

FIGURE 2. THE STREET-ORGAN, WATER COLOR BY PIECK.

THIS illustration is reproduced by the kind permission of Mr. Anton Pieck, given on January 3, 1978, to the author, Mr. Strengers.

well-known artist, and became famous for his mocking political prints, published in important Dutch and foreign newspapers and weekly papers. There were exhibitions of his work at Amsterdam in 1899, The Hague in 1896, and Rotterdam in 1902.

This drawing (original, 9-¾ by 7 inches) dates from the *last decade of the 19th century*, and depicts the professional jealousy of two men with barrel pianos. Some details are rather comic: 1) left, the man with the top hat covers his ears with his hands to escape the cacophony of two pianos playing at the same time; 2) right, the woman with the collecting box (*mansbak* in Dutch) looks furiously at the musical intruder standing near the entrance of a restaurant, but victory radiates from her eyes; 3) right, a sandwich man carries a board with the words *'Théâtre Mécanique'* (Mechanical Spectacle); and 4) *'Chapellerie Anglaise'* means 'English Hatter's Shop,' but the man with the old-fashioned English bowler stands before the shop, while the top hat above the entrance is not necessarily English. What did I say earlier about details?

FIGURE 2.

Title: The street-organ. A water color by Anton Franciscus PIECK, born April 19, 1895, at Den Helder, and working to this day with indomitable energy. Mr. Pieck is one of our most famous living artists in the field of book illustration. He is also the designer of an extensive fairy-tale park call *"De Efteling"* at Kaatsheuvel in the Netherlands.

This water color (original, ca. 16 by 11½ inches) dates from the *pre-World War II period,* and was colored in pastel tints, such as pink, brown, and blue in very soft shades. Some children look out of the windows; the tired organ-grinders push their organ forward; the woman with the collecting box shambles in front; and the little dog trots along in between. Even the little girl stops trundling her hoop and looks at the scene, as does the small boy with the basket, who has been shopping. Can the organ be a Gavioli? Note the gondola in the belly, the ships in the paintings and the carved shell ornament at the top.

FIGURE 3.

Title: Music. One of many illustrations from *The Picture-Book of Ot and Sien* (*Het Prentenboek van Ot en Sien*), probably the most famous children's book of the Netherlands. Written by Jan Ligthart and H. Scheepstra in *1905*; published by J. Wolters at Groningen; illustrated by Cornelis JETSES, born June 23, 1873, at Groningen, died June 9, 1955, at Wassenaar. Nearly every Dutchman older than 30 years has grown up with this book. The typical Dutch sphere of his work, combined with an almost perfect feeling for accenting only important details, is the basis of his immense success.

In this water color, the scene in the foreground was sketched first in dark lines, so it forms a contrast to the background. Quite simple, but very effective! The organ is clearly a Harmonipan-type from the last decade of

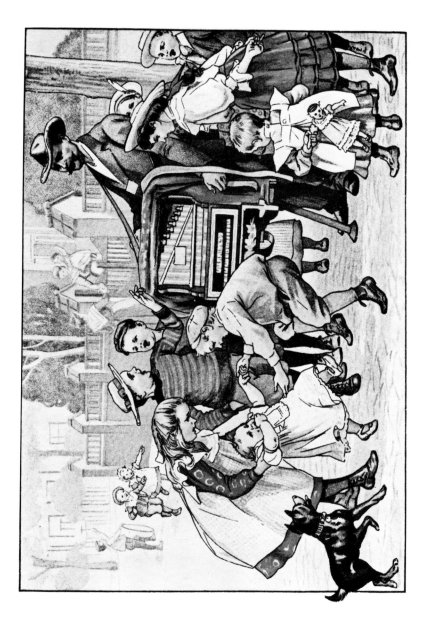

FIGURE 3. MUSIC, WATER COLOR BY JETSES.

the 19th century, as built by Cocchi, Bacigalupo and Graffigna (Berlin). Note the fine panpipes in the front. The accompanying poem follows, in both Dutch and English.

MUZIEK

Muziek! roept Sien. Muziek! roept Ot.
Hij rukt het hekje haast kapot,
Muziek! daar moet hij heen.
De kindren dansen op de maat,
En zoo maar midden in de straat,
De dansvloer is van steen.

Een kleintje springt zoo leuk in 't rond,
En bij haar blaft een jonge hond,
Of danst die ook wat mee?
O neen, hij zingt een huilpartij,
Die hoort er voor de mooiheid bij,
O wee, o wee, o wee!

MUSIC

"Music!" Sien shouts. "Music!" Ot cries;
He nearly smashes the garden door.
"Music!" Out he runs, and there he flies.
As if it were a dancing floor,
Right in the middle of the street
The children dance on nimble feet.

A chubby baby jumps for joy.
A puppy barks at a happy boy --
Or is it dancing, in its way?
Oh, no! It howls now, out of time --
Accents the music as a chime.
O, dear! Please chase the pup away!

FIGURE 4.

Title: The organ-grinder and his monkey (above), and The present-day street-organ (below). Published by The Koster Brothers at Amsterdam in *1901*; text by F.H. van Leent; illustrations by Jan Frederik RINKE, born March 27, 1863, at Schildwolde, died May 20, 1922, at The Hague. He was a draughtsman, painter, engraver, and lithographer, and made many trips through England, the United States, Germany and Belgium. The title of the book is: *In former and present days -- from 1801 to 1901* (*Toen en nu -- van 1801 tot 1901*). The technique of Rinke is a little like that of Jetses, but it is not as refined. Nevertheless, his illustrations are very interesting. A translation of the upper and lower poems follows.

De orgelman en zijn aapje.

Hier ziet ge nu een orgelman
Die blijde wijsjes spelen kan,
En op diens orgel danst een aapje,
Zoo fraai gekleed als menig knaapje;
Zoo'n orgelman bracht aan de jeugd,
Voorheen de ware kermisvreugd.

Het hedendaagsche straatorgel.

Nu hoort men daag'lijks, vroeg en laat,
De orgeltonen ruischen langs de straat;
De fraaiste aria's van menig opera
Speelt zulk een orgel keurig na.

FIGURE 4. THE ORGAN-GRINDER AND HIS MONKEY, AND
THE PRESENT-DAY STREET-ORGAN, DRAWINGS BY RINKE.

THE ORGAN–GRINDER AND HIS MONKEY

The organ-grinder you see here
Can play his tunes so well with cheer
That on the organ, like a youth,
His monkey twirls, in coat and hat;
The boy and girl are pleased, in truth,
To hear the organ play like that.

THE PRESENT–DAY STREET ORGAN

From dawn to dusk you can enjoy
The organ, well-played by the boy,
Performing many lovely airs
In the streets and at the fairs.

FIGURES 5A and 5B.

Title: The organ-cat (*De orgelkat*), from the book *Admiral Kwek-Kwek,* by Beata (Mrs. B. Zegers Veeckens), published by Lentz & De Haan at Utrecht. The date of this nursery-book is unknown (*probably around 1910*), just as the name of the illustrator is not known. The style of these illustrations is undoubtedly from an English source (compare Kate Greenaway's *Under the Window* and others). Illustration 'A' is an extremely fine watercolor, and 'B' shows sketches in black ink. Although a translation of this children's Dutch is nearly impossible, I'll try to give you some idea of the rhyme.

THE ORGAN–CAT

TSCHING, tschang! TSCHING, tschang!
Little kittens, such a BING, bang!
Dance, dance! What a pleasure!
As you dance, I beat the measure!

Kling, klang! Turelay!
Kittens! Well, what do you say?
Please put money in my tray
When you hear the poor cat play.

All the kittens in the town
Dance in rhythm, up and down,
As a quartet in a row,
Tails upright, and quick, quick, slow!

De Orgelkat.

TSCHING, tschang!
  TSCHING, tschang!
Kleine katjes, weest niet bang!
Dansen, dansen! Wat plezier!
'k Speel mijn mooiste
    deuntjes hier!

Kling, klang!
  Turelu!
Katjes! Wel,
  wat zegt
    ge nu?

Geef nu elk in 't zakje wat
Voor de arme Orgelkat.

FIGURE 5A. THE ORGAN-CAT, WATER COLOR BY UNKNOWN ARTIST.

In the kitchens of the street,
Mice dance on their tiny feet!
Hurrah! The cats are out! Let's feast
At last, and undisturbed, at least!

Cheese and bacon, bread and cake,
They drag off all that they can take

En al de katten uit de straat
   Ze dansen samen op de maat,
Soms met hun vieren op een rij
   De staarten in de lucht er bij!

    Maar in de keukens van de huizen,
    Daar dansen op de maat de muizen!
    „Hoera! De katten uit! Nu zullen
    We ongestoord toch ook eens smullen!"

En kaas en spek, en brood en koek,
Ze sleepen alles in een hoek
En eten zich 't buikje rond,
En maken het haast al te bont.

Maar stil! Het
orgel speelt niet meer,
En al de katten
   komen weer.
Gauw weggekropen,
   muisjes! Snel!
Of ze eet u op, die
   stoute Nel!

FIGURE 5B. SECOND PAGE OF THE ORGAN-CAT, DRAWING IN BLACK INK.

And eat their bellies fat and round,
Then lie replete upon the ground.

But quiet, please! The play ends now,
And Organ-Cat must take his bow.
Quickly! Mouselings, run! Here all the kittens come --
As you know, they're very, very troublesome.

FIGURES 5C and 5D.

The front and back of a sand toy that uses the organ-cat as its illustration, with an additional mouse performing flips. This toy was made in Japan, and even has a Japanese patent number -- No. 704322. The Dutch illustration used on a Japanese toy is very interesting because of the fact that for centuries the only contact that Japan maintained with European civilization was at the Dutch center of trade on the island of Desjima, connected by a bridge with Nagasaki. This long-term contact explains the very close relations between Japanese and Dutch artists. The painter Vincent van Gogh owned a magnificent collection of Japanese woodcuts (presently in the van Gogh Museum at Amsterdam), and Japanese artists and members of the upper crust owned Dutch paintings and read Dutch children's books; yes, believe it or not, they even spoke Dutch. This illustration is a fine example of the influence of Dutch art all over the world.

FIGURES 5C AND 5D. SAND TOY WITH ORGAN-CAT ILLUSTRATION.

FIGURE 6.

Title: The canary-bird, from the book *Prenten-Magazijn voor de Jeugd* (*Picture-book for children*), *Deel: Natuurlijke Geschiedenis* (Part: "Natural History"), *Sectie: Vogelen* (Section: "Birds"), page 142. Published by J. Schuitemaker at Purmerend, *1851*. (There is only one complete example of this book known.) Woodcut by Mozes Henriques PIMENTEL, born March

De Kanarievogel.

Men leert met veel gemak en weinig oefeningen,
Deez' vogel menig liedje of deuntje fluitend zingen.
En volgt hij andren na, toch zingt die vogel schoon:
Zijn stem is liefelijk, en helder is zijn toon.

FIGURE 6. THE CANARY-BIRD, WOODCUT BY PIMENTEL.

2, 1828, at The Hague; died June 27, 1902, at The Hague. He was a pupil at
the School for Wood-Engraving at The Hague (1840-1844) and at the
still-existing and very famous Academy for Plastic Arts in the same city
(1841-1846). He was a wood-engraver, draughtsman, and mathematician.
The woodcuts were printed by Prenten-Fabriek van D. Noothoven van
Goor, at Leiden. The name of the poet who wrote the verse under the
illustration is unknown, but the style recalls that of Willem Bilderdijk, one
of our first great romanticists, born Sept. 7, 1756, at Amsterdam; died Dec.
18, 1831, at Haarlem. Here is a translation of the quatrain.

THE CANARY

With a short spell of practice -- he's easily taught --
He sings very well, and he also has caught
The song-style of all other birds he can hear:
His voice is sweet, and his tone is clear. ■■

THE NOT-SO-SILENT FILMS AND SOME SOUND EFFECTS

The Dramagraph, Drumona, Kinemataphone and The Automatic Snare Drum.

Frederick Fried

Some effects for the silent movies have been well covered in past issues of the M.B.S. Bulletins, and by David Bowers in his *Encyclopedia of Automatic Musical Instruments.* These and other piano-style instruments were activated by "picture" and piano rolls; however, the Dramagraph, the Drumona Orchestral Cabinet, the Kinematophone, and the Automatic Snare Drum were controlled by the hands and feet of the piano player, and have not been recorded in the above publications.

On August 5th, 1911, Samuel Lapin of Philadelphia, Pennsylvannia filed for a patent for his invention, the "Stage Noise Cabinet," which he later renamed the "Dramagraph," and on December 10th, 1912, received his patent No. 1,047,090. Mr. Lapin's letterhead listed his address as 1740 N. Gratz Street, and also noted that he was ". . .the inventor of the Dramagraph sound machine, that created a sensation at the Grand Central Palace Exposition, New York, week of July 17th, 1913." To attest to the performance of his invention, he listed as references fifteen theatre, amusement and film companies in America, and one in England.

Most of the elements in the Dramagraph were incorporated into his second patent for which he applied on October 12, 1912, and on June 23rd, 1914, he was granted patent No. 1,100,833 for a "Sound Effect Machine." The patent was assigned by Mr. Lapin to the Excelsior Drum Works, a New Jersey Corporation that manufactured the machine under the name "DRUMONA."

The "Drumona" Model-D was exhibited in Booth 43 at the Second International Exposition of Motion Picture Art, in Grand Central Palace, New York City, New York the week of June 8th, 1914. As the invention was exhibited before the date of patent, his attorney, Victor J. Evans of Washington, D.C., issued to him a "Certificate of Patentability" which warned that he "will prosecute all infringement."

SAY, MR. EXHIBITOR

SUPPOSE an expert trap-drummer offered his services indefinitely without pay or any consideration, other than that you purchase his outfit, "WOULD YOU REFUSE"?

This is precisely what it means when you install

HOW IT
LOOKS
WITHOUT
PIANO

MODEL-D
PRICE $350.00
F. O. B. FACTORY

The new Orchestral cabinet, which can be combined with any make piano, talking machine or other musical instruments and made to serve the duties of an expert trap-drummer and effect man, eliminating the weekly expense of several musicians.

For motion picture theatres "DRUMONA" is positively the latest and best invention yet introduced, and figuring the salary paid the trap-drummer, "DRUMONA" will pay for itself in a very short time. The only operator required is the pianist, who can without the least exertion instantly produce simultaneously with the playing of the piano the much desired tone of the Bass and Snare Drums. the familiar crash of the cymbal, the grotesque sound of the tamborine and spanish castanets the weird tones of the tom-toms, for indian and oriental scenes, the fascinating ring of the triangle, the jingle of sleighbells and the soulful, sacred music of the church organ and chimes.

**AS IT LOOKS
WHEN COMBINED
WITH PIANO**

Certificate of Patentability issued to the inventor by Victor J. Evans & Co., Washington, DC who will prosecute all infrigements.

"DRUMONA" is not connected with your piano by the use of tubes, belts, pulleys, nails, screws, etc, the instrument is merely placed in position as shown in cut and is immediately ready for use.

Independent of the musical effects, other pedals are provided to produce the sound effects of Locomotive, Fire, Patrol, Ambulance, Door, Phone and other Bells, Horse-trot, Clog-dance, Crash of Burning building and roar of Flames, Cannon, Thunder, Bear-growl, Lion-roar, Automobile-horn, Fog-horn, Sawmill, Starting of Automobile. Steam Exhaust, Telegraph, Typewriter, Wireless Telegraphy, Waterfall, Ocean and other water effects.

The below halftone shows the new foot-board of *"DRUMONA"* on which are attached large numbers opposite each pedal, corresponding with numbers shown on our instruction sheet placed on the piano in the maner as sheet music and enables the pianist to quickly grasp the the wonderful possibilites of *"DRUMONA"* in a short time.

Taps and roll on Snare Drum, also Indian Tom-tom and other effects produced with No. 1 pedal.

"DRUMONA"
will adjust itself in any small space, as its dimensions are only
36 inches high,
32 inches deep,
36 inches wide.

Weight of "DRUMONA" boxed ready for shipment 275 pounds.

"DRUMONA"
Is the result of five years laborous effort by
MR. SAMUEL LAPIN
the well known inventor of dramatic sound effects.

Number 2 and 3 pedals produce almost as many effects, and eliminates the shifting of foot from one pedal to another.

COMPLETE INSTRUCTIONS FURNISHED WITH EACH "DRUMONA"

Loud and soft tones are governed by degree of foot pressure on pedals and even the expensive orchestrions now on the market cannot compare with *"DRUMONA"* for real drum and picture effects, as it entirely eliminates the mechanical sound so prominent in so called picture players. and one of the many important features is the fact that you are under no continual expense for upkeep, no motors or intricate machinery to get out of order and the only regret you will have installing *"DRUMONA"* will be, that you did not know about it sooner.

On this page you get an inside view of "DRUMONA" Bass and Snare Drums, and all other musical instruments used therein, are of the highest quality and such as used by the professional man, in fact few trap-drummers can boast of as conpact and complete an outfit as contained in "DRUMONA".

"DRUMONA" created a sensation at recent expositions of Motion Picture Art, held at Grand Central Palace, New York, and Memorial Hall, Dayton, Ohio.

A few of the many exhibitors who consider "DRUMONA" the most effective, practical, and necessary musical instrument ever devised for the photoplay industry:—

E. L. LENHART,	Best Theatre, Birmingham, Ala.
CHARLES FISCHER,	Forepaugh's Theatre, Phila., Pa.
CHARLES BRODIE,	Elite Theatre, Bridgeport, Conn.
M. E. HALL,	Dixie Theatre, Fellsmere, Fla.
EUGENE COOK,	Aurora Theatre, Baltimore, Md.
GRAND PICTURE OPERATING Co.	Central Theatre, N. Y.
E. F. MOYER,	Electric Theatre, White Haven, Pa.
P. F. KEEFER,	Alpha Theatre, Kingston, Pa.
HURTIG & SEAMON,	Lyric Theatre, Dayton, Ohio
A. E. THORP,	Rex Theatre, Richmond, Va.
L. T. LESTER,	Lester Theatre, Spartanburg, S. C.

DON'T let your competitors spring all the new surprises. Introduce a new drawing attraction on your own hook, install LAPIN'S "DRUMONA".

For sale and demonstrated by

The "Drumona" was advertised as a "one-man orchestra" although the advertisement showed a woman at the piano. The retail price was $350, F.O.B. Philadelphia. A small illustrated promotion piece notes: "Suppose we could show you how by using the Drumona you could reduce the necessary expense. Suppose we could show you by combining the Drumona with your present piano, you could have the most salient musical features of a $1000 to $5000 orchestrian, yet eliminate the objectionable mechanical sound.

"Suppose we could show how your pianist can operate the Drumona simultaneously with the playing of the piano. Suppose we could show you how Drumona could eliminate the expense of a trap-drummer! Give you the much desired tone of brass and snare drums, the familiar crash of the cymbal; the grotesque sound of the tambourine and Spanish castanets; the weird tones of the tom-tom for Indian and Oriental scenes, the soulful sacred music of church organ and chimes and the jingle of sleigh bells and triangle.

"Suppose we could show you how, independent of the musical features, you could produce the sound effects of the train, ambulance, patrol and fire bells, phone and door bells, horse trot, the roar of the cannon, automobile horn, telegraph, typewriter, wireless telegraphy, bear growl, lion roar, thunder, automobile and other engine effects, steam exhaust, waterfall and ocean, locomotive.

"The Drumona is not a monotonous, mechanically operated instrument, has no intricate parts to get out of order, no electric motors, can be used with any make pianos; all effects musical and otherwise, are produced by a series of extension foot pedals protruding from the lower frame of the cabinet. Its operation is simplicity itself. . . ."

From a file of correspondence it seems that Mr. Lapin was not doing a land office business. In July of 1914, Mr. Lapin replied to an inquiry by offering the Drumona for $350.00. On August 8th, 1914, he offered an agent's discount of 25%, and ten days later, not having word from the inquirer, he wrote, "I will go the limit with you as collections are bad and am up against it for ready cash I will allow you a discount of 40% if you will take advantage of it at once."

The following was pencilled on the reverse side of the letter by George Messig, an organ and orchestrion repairman, who had worked closely with the B.A.B. Organ Company in Brooklyn, New York.

"Gliding pedal changes drum from snare to tom-toms. Also fire bell to chimes by sliding a piece of felt in front of plate. Locomotive - quick movement of sand box, causing sand to drop up and down. Horse trot - clog dancing thump, sawmill - automotive horn bell if down continuous. Starting auto same as locomotive. Thunder and lightning vibrating hammer with soft end vibrating on top of brass chime cymbal. Soft tones were governed by the degree of foot pressure on pedals."

The Drumona was 37 inches high, 32 inches deep and 36 inches wide. It weighed 275 lbs boxed.

THE KINEMATOPHONE

A one-page annoucement reproduced from an undated advertisement in *Variety,* a theatre publication, notes:

"To Moving Picture Managers - Just what you have been waiting for - Gaston Anchini's Remarkable invention THE KINEMATOPHONE which will positively give life to any moving picture." For each key above the 42-key board is an illustration depicting the sound of the instrument, fowl, animal, etc. By the combination of keys, the effect of the starting of a railroad train, the escape of steam, the ringing of the engine bell, the rumble of cars could all be produced. A patent search covering a span of twenty years in the Records, Reports and Gazettes, including trademarks, design patents, and patents, yeilded no "Kinematophone" and no inventor with the name Gaston Anchini in the U.S. Patent records.

The Kinematophone Co. (Inc.) was located in the Geo. M. Cohan Theatre Bldg., 1482 Broadway. The firm was listed as Counihan and Shannon. W. J. Counihan is listed as President and General Manager. The instrument was 43 inches high, 47 inches long and 25 inches wide.

THE AUTOMATIC SNARE DRUM

This instrument sold for $15.00 by Carl Fischer, Cooper Square, New York, was an automatic snare drum with electric attachment which was operated by the piano player as an accompaniment to the piano and for dramatic effects.

The electro magnet attached inside the drum to the drumstick was controlled by the footboard placed near the pedals of the piano, and by wires attached to the battery. The manufacturer was the Excelsior Drum Works of New Jersey. The instrument sold for $25.00 but was marked down as a "Great Bargain For a short time only for $15.00."

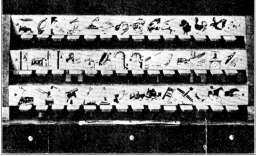

PHILADELPHIA Aug, 8, 1914

George Messig

755 Gravesend Ave

Brooklyn, N.Y.

Dear Sir:-

On July 24th, last I answered your inquiry relative to "Drumona" but up to date have failed to hear from you.

Upon reading your letter again it occurd to me that you desire to act as agent in making the sale for "Drumona" and accordingly will give you agents discount of 25% If you make the effort you will find that you can make a good many sales in your city and I earnestly advise you to get busy, as now is the time when the exhibitors are making preparations for the fall business.

You can see and hear a "Drumona" at 771 Ninth Ave Central Theatre New York

Take your prospect there and ask the folks connected with the Theatre what they think of it and I feel confident I will have your order, Yours truly

S. Lapin

THE GREAT
SNUFF-BOX MYSTERY

Ralph Heintz

*E*veryone has heard, at one time or another, that delightful little piano sketch by Anatol Konstantinovich Liadov entitled "A Musical Snuff-Box". The dainty melody, played entirely on the upper half of the keyboard, has no trouble in conjuring up visions of a beautiful little tortoise-shell case with a jewel-like movement inside. The work was composed around 1880, and has been considered a fitting tribute — perhaps the only one — to the snuff-box-maker's art. It is still played by budding young pianists, frequently as an encore (because it is short) or to provide lighthearted relief to an otherwise heavy program.

Recently evidence has come to light indicating that Liadov was not the only composer to be enchanted by snuff-box music. Several sheet-music covers have been found showing that at least three other nineteenth-century composers felt inspired to honor the snuff-box musically. Unfortunately, only the covers have been found; the scores themselves are still missing. Nevertheless, the covers provide a tantalizing glimpse at the popularity of the snuff-box in the last half of the nineteenth century. None are dated, but from the publishers' addresses given it should be possible to check the early occupancy records and come up with an approximate publication date.

The first cover, shown in Figure 1, lists "Three Snuff-Box Waltzes for the Piano Forte" by Charles Chaulieu. The fact that there are three is emphasized by pictures of three identical sectional-comb boxes at the top of the page, designated "No. 1 in C," "No. 2 in G" and "No. 3 in A". The publishers, R. Cocks & Co. of Princes Street, London, also proudly attest that they publish the works of Czerny, Herz, Hummel, Hünten, Mayseder, Pleyel, Pixis, Weber & c. as well as those of Chaulieu. It is interesting to note that, of the composers listed, only Chaulieu is *not* listed in *Grove's Dictionary of Music and Musicians*. At least he is in good company.

In the absence of further evidence, it seems reasonable to assume that Chaulieu was a contemporary of the others on the list, and since they *all* fall within the time frame 1790-1880, we can, perhaps, arbitrarily assume Chaulieu lived in the 1800-1875 time period. If this is true, then there is also a good likelihood that the three waltzes were written in the 1860's or even earlier, giving them considerable seniority over the Liadov composition.

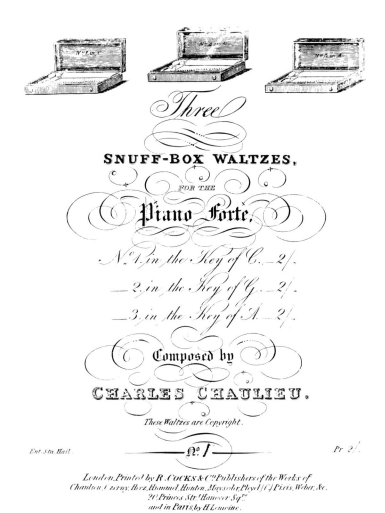

Figure 1. Three identical sectional-comb snuff-boxes.

A second cover, shown in Figure 2, appears rather stark in comparison with the highly embellished cover of the Chaulieu Waltzes. It shows a single, sectional-comb box in some detail, although the governor fan does not appear to have a worm, and the geneva on top of the spring barrel could not possibly work. With a little imagination, however, one can see approximately 60 teeth in the comb, arranged two-per-section, with all screws properly slotted. Even the stopwork arm can be seen reaching to the great gear on the cylinder. The pinning density

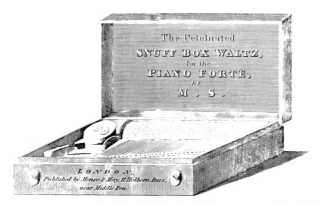

Figure 2. An interesting mechanism; it's hard to find a governor without the fan. Note the two-teeth-per-section comb.

on the cylinder is a collector's dream, and, since the buttons at the front of the case indicate that this is supposed to portray a two-air movement of conventional design, an actual cylinder this highly orchestrated should provide good competition for the Vienna Philharmonic.

The title of the opus, printed inside the open lid of the box, proclaims it to be *The Celebrated* "Snuff Box Waltz for the Piano Forte," by M. S. Either the composer felt that he, himself, was so celebrated that no identification beyond his initials was necessary, or he was so ashamed of the composition that he refused to have his name associated with it. In any event, a search of *Grove's Dictionary* failed to turn up any nineteenth-century composer who fit the initials, so we are faced with still another relatively unknown composer.

The publishers, Monro & May, of 11, Holborn Bars, near Middle Row, London, did not bother to tell us who else was in their stable of composers; nor were they about to waste ink on information other than the price of two shillings. Although, again, no date is shown, the quality of the paper and the style of printing suggest that the work was published at about the same time as the Chaulieu Waltzes.

The third cover, shown in Figure 3, provides an exercise in self-cancelling phrases. The title is "The Snuff Box *Extravaganza*" (italics are the author's) and the snuff-box illustation bears a remarkable similarity to that used on the preceding cover. There are, however, some interesting differences. Although the cylinder pinning is equally dense in both cases, the comb on the "Extravaganza" appears to have only about 28 teeth in a one-per-section configuration (possibly just the work of a

THE SNUFF BOX
EXTRAVAGANZA

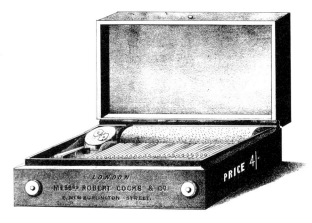

FOR THE
PIANO FORTE
BY
IMMANUEL LIEBICH.

BY THE SAME COMPOSER,
"THE MUSICAL BOX", PERFOMED BY HIM AT THE HANOVER SQUARE ROOMS,
& HONORED WITH A TREBLE ENCORE.

STANNARD & DIXON, IMP.T

Figure 3. This appears to be identical to the snuff-box depicted in Figure 2. However, note the fewer number of teeth and the apparently useless Geneva stop. It does have the equally interesting fan-less governor.

lazy engraver). The governor appears equally wormless, and the geneva even more useless. Evidently, the engraver in both cases could not understand the function of either the governor or the geneva, and felt free to improvise.

In all of the pictures the artist's concepts and attention to detail are manifested in strange ways. There are so many similarities that all could have been drawn by the same person. The absence of a protective inner cover and the height of the movement within the case suggest that the artist was inspired by the tin boxes used as transit cases for delivering movements to the case makers; yet, the wall thicknesses and beveled corners are typical of tortoise shell or gutta-percha cases. The lid hinges, in particular, are given special attention. In the "Extravaganza" picture, the hinge is of the integral style commonly used in the later gutta-percha boxes, while in the box of Figure 2, the hinge is of the metal "piano-hinge" style riveted in place and typical of those used on tortoise shell cases. All of this may amount to nit-picking, but in the absence of concrete information, it provides at least a basis for speculation.

It would appear that the artist for "Extravaganza" had used a somewhat later box as his model while still retaining the idea of a sectional comb. The quailty of the paper and the style of printing on "Extravaganza" suggest that it was printed several decades after the Chaulieu and "M. S." works, and a date of around 1895 does not seem unreasonable. The publishers, as for the Chaulieu waltzes, were Robert Cocks & Co., who at this point were doing business at 6, New Burlington Street, London. A look into nineteenth century, London business records should provide, at least, a rough time frame for the publishers, but that research will have to wait for a later visit to the United Kingdom. The other clue, a price tag of four shillings, shows that the ravages of inflation were present even then, and helps to confirm the theory that "Extravaganza" was published considerably later than the other works.

The "Snuff Box Extravaganza" (note the absence of the hyphen in Snuff-Box in this and in Figure 2) was composed by Immanuel Liebich, whose name joins the others in being totally ignored by *Grove's Dictionary*. The publishers may have been aware of this possibility because they have attempted to impress his name on the public with the following note: "By the same composer, 'THE MUSICAL BOX,' performed by him at the HANOVER SQUARE ROOMS, & honored with a *treble* encore." Now we're getting somewhere. Several editions of *this* work are around, although they are all relatively late. The one pictured in Figure 4 shows an ethereal young lady gazing intently into what can only be an early keywind. The quizzical look on her face probably results from the fact that the movement has obviously been mounted in the case backwards: with the comb to the rear of the cylinder.

Figure 4. The quizzical look on the young lady's face is probably due to the fact that the movement is placed in the case backwards!

Figure 5. This depiction of a music box almost defies description. The artist obviously had a sense of humor.

Although there is no copyright date anywhere on the score, a previous owner was kind enough to write the date (presumably when she acquired — or mastered — it) November 4, 1904, in the upper right corner. This edition was published in New York, and the art work appears consistent with the early twentieth century. A slightly later edition, shown in Figure 5, shows a proud papa, looking like a stage magician, demonstrating his music box to the entire family on a Sunday afternoon. Many of them look bored to tears, and the box, according to the artist, seems to be a cross between early typewriter and a dictaphone with four wildly carefree, dancing dolls. Not only has the art work deteriorated, but there seems to have been a few other changes as well: Liebich's first name is now spelled Emanuel, rather than Immanuel; the title on the earlier edition is "Musical Box - Caprice," while on the later version it has degenerated to merely "Music Box;" inside, the music *and* the titles are identical for both editions, both are called "The Music Box - Caprice" and are shown as Opus 19 of Emanual Liebich. Unfortunately, a copy of the first edition has not yet come to light, so we are unable to say at this point how it originally looked or whether it even had a picture of a music box on the cover.

At any rate, this information does help to support the assumption that Liebich's "Snuff Box Extravaganza" was probably written in the mid-1890's. Assuming that the "Musical Box - Caprice" was written at about the same time, and allowing a few years for it to achieve *treble encore* prominence, plus another few years to cross the Atlantic and warrant publication by two separate music houses, the various dates all seem to tally.

A large number (estimates run well in excess of one hundred) of musical compositions either refer directly to some item of mechanical music or depict a mechanical instrument on the cover. If we disregard the forty-odd compositions written by Irving Berlin for his Music Box Revues (each of which showed a large disc box on the cover), the remainder is very heavily biased in favor of barrel organs and street pianos. The reason is obvious: monkey organs and the misnamed hurdy gurdies were louder, flashier and more intrusive into the peace and quiet of the older residential neighborhoods; hence, their place in the time-softened realm of nostalgia is assured. It is pleasing to note that the lowly snuff-box achieved somewhat the same degree of recognition in the musical compositions of a hundred years ago. ♩

HURDY GURDY TO THE RESCUE

Robert Penna

*H*ow often have you watched a movie or television program and enjoyed the sounds of an antique musical instrument in the background? Often it is the sound of a street piano or a fairground organ. You rarely catch a glimpse of the piece, and its use is usually consigned to set a mood or lend originality to the scene. But once Hollywood actually cast an automatic musical instrument to play a pivotal role in a drama -- that's when it became *The Hurdy Gurdy to the Rescue.*

In 1935, Maxwell Anderson wrote a play entitled *Winterset.* By 1936 Hollywood had adapted this intriguing drama into a film starring Burgess Meredith, Margo, and a nameless, but hardly voiceless, hurdy gurdy.

The film was produced by Pandro S. Berman and directed by Alfred Santell. John Carradine, Eduard Ciannelli and Mischa Auer were among the notable co-stars. As with many movie epics, the story was developed from an actual occurrence. The Sacco and Vanzetti trial of the 1920's was the basis for this story.

As you may recall, Nicola Sacco and Bartolomeo Vanzetti were two anarchists who were convicted of the murder of a payroll master and guard on the basis of circumstantial evidence and anti-radical sentiment. Even today, researchers feel that mob hysteria, coupled with questionable law-enforcement procedures, resulted in their conviction and execution.

The movie copies much of what actually took place. The opening scenes of the movie show a gang of mobsters stealing an automobile, cold-bloodedly killing a paymaster of a large factory, and robbing the payroll. As in reality, an eyewitness takes the license number of the car and the police find the abandoned automobile. Italian anarchists were implicated in the crime and, in the movie, an Italian radical, as the owner of the stolen car, is accused of the deed.

Reality and fiction parallel each other further. No eyewitness could positively identify the accused. One of the anarchists had a young son and, in the movie, this child appears bearing the same first name as one of the anarchists, thereby strengthening the parallelism. Sherwood Anderson, the author of *Winterset,* did not want anyone to miss the fact that his characters were based on the individuals in the Sacco and Vanzetti affair. He even managed to leave the feeling of uncertain and hostile police procedures in his work.

The movie begins in a small town in New York State in 1920. (The actual crime took place in South Braintree, Massachusetts on April 15, 1920.) Three members of a gang steal a black touring car of a known Italian named Bartolomeo Romagna and ambush the payroll master outside his plant. Through his stolen car, Romagna is implicated, tried and sentenced to die in the electric chair. His wife and child are hounded out of town and head west.

Years later, a law professor gives his students a final exam in which they must judge the guilt or innocence of Bartolomeo Romagna. Each decides that Romagna was innocent. The results are published and this hastens the return of Romagna's son.

Named Mio, after his father, the boy (played by Burgess Meredith) seeks to exonerate his father's reputation. Following a lead, Mio tracks down Garth Esdras, a member of the gang who had been named as a possible witness. At about the same time, the actual murderer, Trock Estrella, kills the third member of the original gang, Shadow. Another coincidence finds Judge Gaunt wandering the area where all will meet. Judge Gaunt was the magistrate who presided at the Romagna trial and had become demented with uncertainty.

Photo 1. A young man begins to dance to the sound of "Siboney" before the others join him.

416

To further complicate events, and because of the dramatist's flair, Mio falls in love with Garth's sister, Miriamne (played by Margo). At this point, Lucia, the "street piano man," is introduced. He and his hurdy gurdy are in a back court behind several old and run-down tenements. Lucia complains that the police were chasing him off the streets. This was probably a complaint that many a hurdy gurdy man echoed throughout the years. Lucia exclaims, "You got the big dough, you get the pull, fine. No big dough, no pull. . . She's a good little machine, this baby. Cost plenty -- and two new records I only played twice. See this one." As he trundles the crank to his instrument, a young boy begins to dance to the 1929 tune, "Siboney." Lucia remarks, "Good boy -- see, it's a lulu --it itches the feet!"

Couples begin to dance and Lucia states, "Maybe we can't play in front, maybe we can play behind!" Warming to his task which he evidently enjoys doing, Lucia begins to bemoan the loss of his instrument and his livelihood. He cries, "Maybe you don't know folks! Tonight we play goodbye to the piano. Goodbye forever! No more piano on the streets! No more music! No more money for the music man! Tomorrow will be sad as hell, tonight dance! Tomorrow no more Verdi, no more rumba, no more good time!"

Photo 2. Lucia and a group of youngsters move the street piano into the court after being chased there by the police.

Photo 3. During a rainstorm, Lucia (in the background), covers up Mio's hurdy gurdy as the crowd disperses.

A policeman enters and begins to heavy-handedly disband the merrymakers when a young radical objects. During his tirade, the radical explains the reason why so many people loved the automatic musical instrument. He states, "We don't go to the theatres! Why not? We can't afford it! We don't go to night clubs, where women dance naked and the music drips from saxophones and leaks out of Rudy Vallee -- we can't afford that either! But we might at least dance on the river bank to the strains of a barrel organ!"

A downpour disperses the group, which had reached near-riotous proportions when the policeman threatens the crowd of music lovers. Lucia receives a final warning never to play the street piano again.

During the storm, Trock Estrella and his henchmen turn up to silence Garth, the judge, and Mio in order to stop any further investigation into the old crime. In Anderson's Broadway version of the play, Mio and Miriamne are riddled to death while trying to reach the police for assistance. The Hollywood version, true to the "lived-happily-ever-after" syndrome, introduces a new epic here: the hurdy gurdy.

Just when matters are worst, Mio dashes to the hurdy gurdy and cranks out the tune "Siboney" once again. The song melodiously echoes through the alleys behind the tenements and brings the policeman back just in time to avert the murders.

Photo 4. In the driving rain, Mio dashes to the hurdy gurdy which is covered with a canvas sheet.

Photo 5. Miriamne comforts Mio as he turns the crank to the covered up hurdy gurdy.

Not only are Mio and Miramne saved, but Garth tells the true story of Trock's murder of the payroll master, and Bartolomeo Romagna's name is cleared. Trock Estrella, who had arranged for Mio's murder, falls into his own trap and is shot by his henchmen.

However, the hurdy gurdy had saved the day. But what actually happened to the street pianos that were once so familiar on the streets of New York? Art Sanders, owner of the Musical Museum in Deansboro, New York was quoted in a *New York Times* article as saying, "Many of them disappeared in the late 1930's when Mayor LaGuardia banned them as causing traffic jams. The tragedy is that many of the operators were illiterate and thought that merely possessing the grind organs was illegal, so they burned them." A rather ignominious end for so many valuable instruments that brought such joy to so many people. 𝄞

Phonographs

DIARY DISCLOSURES OF
JOHN GABEL:
A PIONEER IN
AUTOMATIC MUSIC

Rick Crandall

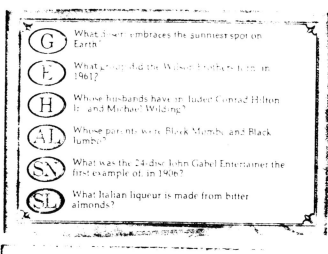

G What desert embraces the sunniest spot on Earth?

E What group did the Wilson Brothers form in 1961?

H Whose husbands have included Conrad Hilton Jr. and Michael Wilding?

AL Whose parents were Black Mumbo and Black Jumbo?

SN What was the 24-disc John Gabel Entertainer the first example of, in 1906?

SL What Italian liqueur is made from bitter almonds?

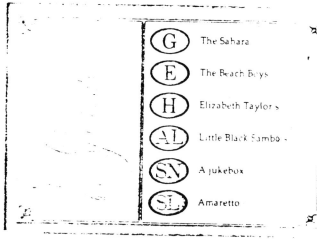

G The Sahara

E The Beach Boys

H Elizabeth Taylor's

AL Little Black Sambo's

SN A jukebox

SL Amaretto

Shown here is a legitimate card form the popular game of Trivial Pursuit. So how did the designers of the game know about John Gabel? Surely not more than a handful of music collectors could successfully answer the question. For a while I thought, somehow, that the card was written for me!

John Gabel (Photo 1) was an early inventor associated with the phonograph, but he has been lurking in the shadows of insufficient information. It is known that the first coin-operated, cylinder phonograph appeared in 1889, and that the first coin-operated, disc phonograph was introduced in 1898. But for those in search of the selective, coin-operated, multi-disc player, some collectors have more than suspected that Gabel's contributions, particularly in the area of automatic phonographs, were early, important and too-little appreciated.

Indeed, a study of the U.S. patent files turned up #1,134,603 granted on April 16, 1915, for an automatic, acoustic, disc phonograph with an ingenious device that even changes the steel needle after each record is played! True, 1915 is more than ten years earlier than the first real jukeboxes (AMI, Mills, Seeburg, etc., from 1927-29 era), but look again! The patent was actually *filed* in February of 1906. Now, that is early!

One look at the patent drawings depicts a beautiful machine that would catch anyone's eye (Figure 2): a fancy wood case with inset, bevelled-oak panels, ornate castings rivalling the art cases of the early gambling machines, bevelled-glass windows on all sides and a large brass horn on top. That would certainly satisfy the beauty criteria for most collectors, but the machine's appeal doesn't stop there.

A further look into drawings of the mechanism and a read through the dry language of the patent show great mechanical ingenuity: two stacks of twelve individual selectable 10″ disc records, a coin mechanism with an early magnetic slug detector, an advanced tone-arm design, weight and size compensators to adjust for the lack of record standards, and more. Everything, including the record changer, needle changer, tune indicator, play counter and turntable was powered automatically by one full turn of a gambling-machine-like crane.

Some of us have known existing examples of a later version of the Gabel machine, called the Gabel Automatic Entertainer. It is in a somewhat plainer case but still quite attractive, with tone quality that is indeed superb. And best of all, the mechanism is nearly identical to the patent drawings. These machines usually carry a patent plate with dates like 1909 and 1916, and so collectors have not known where to classify them. It was too early for the jukebox era, but too late to be an important development in the phonograph era. This latter design incorporated an enclosed horn. It is sought after, and known extant examples number less than two dozen as of this writing, making it a rare and desirable machine.

Photo 1. John Gabel.

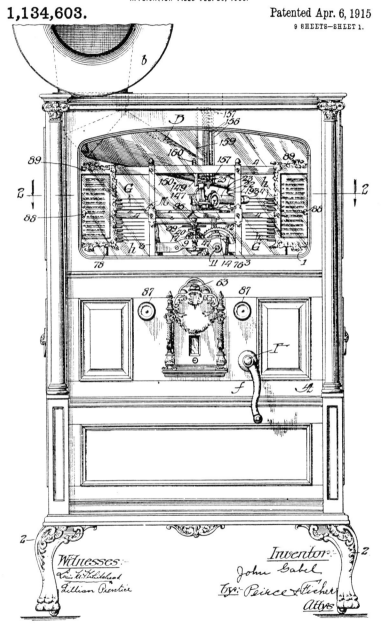

J. GABEL.

AUTOMATIC TALKING MACHINE.

APPLICATION FILED FEB. 26, 1906.

1,134,603.

Patented Apr. 6, 1915

9 SHEETS—SHEET 1.

Photo 2. An automatic acoustic disc phonograph, ca. 1906.

But who was John Gabel and what about the machine pictured in the patent filed in 1906? There is a brief but provocative mention of the Gabel in *From Tin Foil to Stereo* (Howard W. Sams & Co., 1977):

"The Automatic Machine and Tool Company of Chicago (Illinois) manufactured the first truly selective disc mechanism. Although spring-motor operated, it was automatic, permitting a choice of 24 selections stored in racks at either side of the turntable. . .As in the earlier cylinder mechanisms, Gabel's device had a screw-feed mechanism to carry the sound box across the record; it was also equipped with a magnetic-slug detector. The entire operation by the patron was confined to one handle at the front of the cabinet that changed the record, the needle, and wound the motor all in one turn. In the industry, the John Gabel Automatic Entertainer is recognized as the true progenitor of the modern juke box, yet this one only 1906!"

The progenitor. So why has there not been more coverage of John Gabel and his wonderous machine? A thorough check around the collector community yielded a possible answer. No examples of the 1906 machine were known to exist and no advertising or other literature had yet surfaced to describe the man, the machine or the company.

So who was John Gabel and would we ever see his early machine? Was it ever commercially manufactured?

In 1981 the first breakthrough occurred. A gambling machine dealer in Chicago was given a lead to check out a "horn phonograph in a slot machine case" located in a factory building south of Chicago. In rapid succession, the machine (serial #711) flew through the hands of a picker, a slot dealer and a collector, with breathtaking price appreciation along the way. Finally, there it stood, in all its unrestored, non-working but complete glory, in my own spare bedroom.

Piece by piece the machine was nervously dismantled. Each sub-assembly and then each screw, gear and spring was photographed. The dismantling procedure was carefully recorded. This machine was a one-of-a-kind for the moment, and I was not going to be the one to have taken it apart beyond reassembly. A year and several stripped-gear restorations, cleanings, buffings, platings, etc., later, it was ready for final regulation. Chuck Pheiffer, who had much experience restoring phono-graphs and who had restored the Gabel reproducer, came for the weekend to assist.

The result is as pictured in Photo 3. A magnificent appearance, flawless repetitive operation (as of this writing the Entertainer has played more than 400 records without a single jam) and in Chuck's words: "The best tone I've heard from a phonograph of comparable age." Anyone who takes more than a casual glance inside a Gabel machine will concur that he must have been a mechanical genius.

Photo 3. Author's horn model Gabel Automatic Entertainer serial #711 produced ca. 1907-08. The mirrored back is removed for best photo contrast.

IDENTITY A MYSTERY

But who *was* John Gabel? Some information trickled in from slot-machine collectors. There are some floor-model gambling machines that date back to the 1898-1903 period built by the Automatic Machine and Tool Company with John Gabel's name on them. Also, a serial number study of the later versions of the Automatic Entertainer indicates an astounding estimate of over 7,000 machines having originally been produced — during a time when no other automatic, disc phonograph had been able to establish itself, and when a life cycle run of 2,000 to 3,000 units was considered successful.

The author's horn model received some publicity in 1983 when an article he produced was printed in Russ Ofria's *Nickel A Tune* magazine in a several-part series. It was then that a second example of the horn model surfaced with serial #702. Without close inspection, the only thing that can be said is that the two extant examples appear nearly identical except that #702 has a cast, front sign with *The Automatic Entertainer* and the author's #711 has a similar sign but cast in it is "Gabel's Automatic Entertainer."

Then a third horn model surfaced with an even earlier serial number: 646. Its marquee also omits the Gabel name and uses the lower capacity needle changer shown in the patent drawing in Figure 2. Otherwise #646 appears identical to #711.

DIARY DISCOVERED

The second real break in the mystery finally came. My friend and noted author on collectables, Richard Bueschel of Mt. Prospect, Illinois, hinted to me one day that there existed a major and historically-important document on John Gabel. He put me in contact with the owner and subsequently, one Saturday morning I received a copy of a several-hundred page, typewritten diary of John Gabel's entire life. Most important were the dozens of pages covering his trials, tribulations and thoughts while inventing the Automatic Entertainer. Also included were his perspectives on his competitors and documentation of a colossal, extended legal and competitive battle with the Victor Talking Machine Company, which didn't even have a competitive product at the time.

For the first time anywhere, the full story of John Gabel and his Automatic Entertainer appeared in Allen Koenigsberg's *Antique Phonograph Monthly,* (Vol. VII, No. 8) in the summer of 1984.

Since that time, additional information has gradually surfaced which I've included here, along with the aspects of the APM story that are of interest to MBSI readers.

John Gabel, born in Hungary in 1872, and prevented by early illness from having more than two years of public school education, became an immigrant to the United States. That was in 1886 when John was 14 years of age and before he could speak a word of English. His father was a nailsmith which, in the fashion of the day, set John on a course of metalworking. He continued at odd jobs which were to help him produce some income during his stay with his brother in Philadelphia. Two years later, when John was 16, he was encouraged by a friend of the family to try his fortune in the city of opportunity — Chicago.

In Chicago he found great demand for machinists. Slowly he learned English. It was the age of the gear, the cog, the cam and the lever. Everybody was trying to do everything and anything with mechanics. He wound up with a good job at Felt & Terrants assembling the intricate mechanisms of adding machines, known as Comptometers.

Gabel's skills skyrocketed, in part from the experience, and in part due to his conviction that he was a "born machinist." During the ensuing eight years, he worked for several companies, including many early efforts at producing coin-operated, gambling machine mechanisms.

Finally, in 1898, the "inevitable" occurred. John Gabel, with his energetic spirit, inventive mind, metalworking skills, and no money, became co-founder and president of his own fledgling company. A Chicago cabinet maker put up the funds and the cabinets for Gabel's own improved version of a floor-model slot machine.

Photo 4. The Comptometer, Gabel's early training ground. It was claimed to "perform every mathematical calculation essential in business."

THE GABEL "SLOTS" INTRODUCED

By Christmas of 1898, his Automatic Machine and Tool Company, with three employees, had its first all-mechanical, floor-model, gambling machines ready for market. Acceptance was immediate, even though Gabel had no training in selling techniques. By 1900, the Automatic Machine and Tool Company already employed 50 men. Perhaps only in America could a 26-year old, uneducated immigrant, self-taught in English, and whose only skill was mechanical inventiveness, start his own company and grow to prosperity in two years!

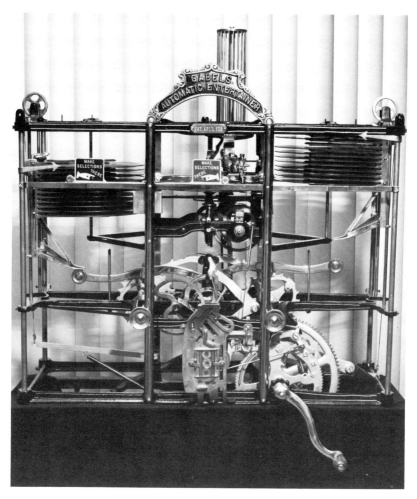

Photo 5a. Horn model #701 restored mechanism, front view. Note record stacks holding 12 records on each side; vertical cage on top is the needle magazine which appears to be of higher capacity than the patent drawing.

J. GABEL.

AUTOMATIC TALKING MACHINE.

APPLICATION FILED AUG. 18, 1909.

1,182,551.

Patented May 9, 1916.

7 SHEETS—SHEET 1.

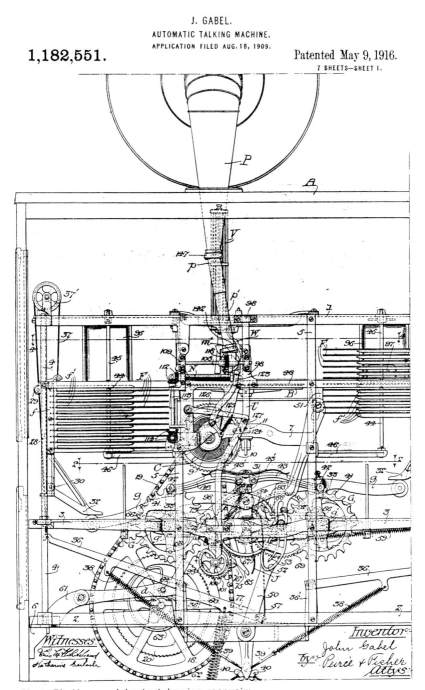

Photo 5b. Horn model patent drawing, rear veiw.

But the story does not end there. We haven't gotten to the music yet. In 1903, he followed the lead of some other slot-machine producers who sought to establish the legitimacy of the gambling machines through the installation of Swiss music boxes that played whenever a nickel was deposited for a chance at a pay out.

During Christmas of 1903, Gabel went to see Mr. Vosey from the Lyon & Healy Department Store, who was in charge of the brass instruments and Swiss music boxes. After concluding the sale of music boxes, Vosey drew Gabel's attention to the talking machines. Gabel was biased against their "noisiness" and lack of musical quality — undoubtedly a correct judgment of the Victor with front-mounted horns and the early type of rigid tone arms. But sometime in the Victor IV or V time frame (ca. 1903), a newer, tapered, tone arm was designed which made dramatic improvements in sound quality.

GABEL STUDIES PHONOGRAPH

He took the Victor home, along with Vosey's selection of ten records, and surprised himself by liking them so much that he played all ten every night for some time. Gabel recalls:

While I listened to the music, I thought of the possibilities of this new talking machine for public use. At that time there was only one automatic nickel-in-the-slot instrument on the market that made money. It was very crude and the music was awful. It had a wooden roll with iron pegs driven into it.

While the roll was rotating, the pegs would contact the keys and operate the piano keys to produce music. The entire system was copied from the Swiss music box, but it was really the best on the market.

We know that the machine he was referring to was the Wurlitzer Tonophone, indeed a crude affair, but it was the first on the market and Wurlitzer did well with it.

INSPIRATION STRIKES

It occurred to me that an automatic talking machine would give better music to the public as well as a variety of selections both instrumental and vocal. I made sketches of an instrument of this kind and could not dismiss it from my mind.

This recollection is a rare opportunity in the research of automatic, music-machine history. Here, 80 years later, we can read the thoughts of an important, early inventory, in the first person, at the very moment of conception of the world's first automatic, multiple-disc phonograph.

Gabel envisioned many advantages of this new machine, not the least of which was that, contrary to the gambling machines, it would be obviously legal to operate in all states. He couldn't give up his normal responsibilities of selling on the road, so development of a prototype went slowly.

In the spring of 1905, the first model of my automatic talking machine was ready. It was very crude but worked well enough to demonstrate. I needed money. . .I had to make a model to be used for patterns and another to send to the patent attorney.

Mr. Mikkelson, who had been making the beautiful wooden cases for Gabel's machines all along, reappeared as an investor with $2,000 for a small piece of the company. Another $2,000 came from Mr. Sherwin, the head of Chicago Hardware Foundry Company. The foundry was the supplier of castings to the Automatic Machine and Tool Company, and to others in the slot-machine business in Chicago. This accounts for the similarity in appearance of the fancy leg castings on the first Entertainers and the earlier gambling machines produced in Chicago.

THE FIRST MODEL. . .AND AN OMEN

In the middle of August, 1905, Gabel took a machine to patent attorneys Pierce, Fisher and Clapp, who were, fatefully, also the patent attorneys for the Victor Talking Machine Company. By the end of October the patterns were ready and Gabel had three music machines made.

On Christmas Day, 1905 we held a party at the company's office. We played the three machines, one after the other. . .and we all began to dance.

A few days later one of the machinists named the device *The Automatic Entertainer*. One was given to Joe Hallner, a Wisconsin operator and dealer in slots. There was no trouble with the mechanical part, but after three days the sound deteriorated. Hallner went through the machine in detail and Gabel concluded the only thing wrong was record wear. "The original grooves were actually cut out." All three machines developed the same problem.

NEEDLE CHANGER CONCEIVED

Gabel recalls: *To improve the sound was not in my line. I was a mechanic, not a musician. It was necessary for me to think fast. The first thing I did was to look for the cause of the record wear. That was easy. The needles had been made with a fine black diamond point, believing that the point would be permanent. I was mistaken in this as the continuous grind of the record wore down the fine point of the needle and the dull point wore out the records.*

Photo 6a. Close up of #711 tone arm with chute (arrow) down which a new needle would drop from the cage-like magazine above and then "fingered" into position. Note ejected needle still in tray next to the record stack, poised to roll down into the catcher bucket.

J. GABEL.
AUTOMATIC TALKING MACHINE.
APPLICATION FILED AUG. 18, 1909.

1,182,551.

Patented May 9, 1916.
7 SHEETS—SHEET 7.

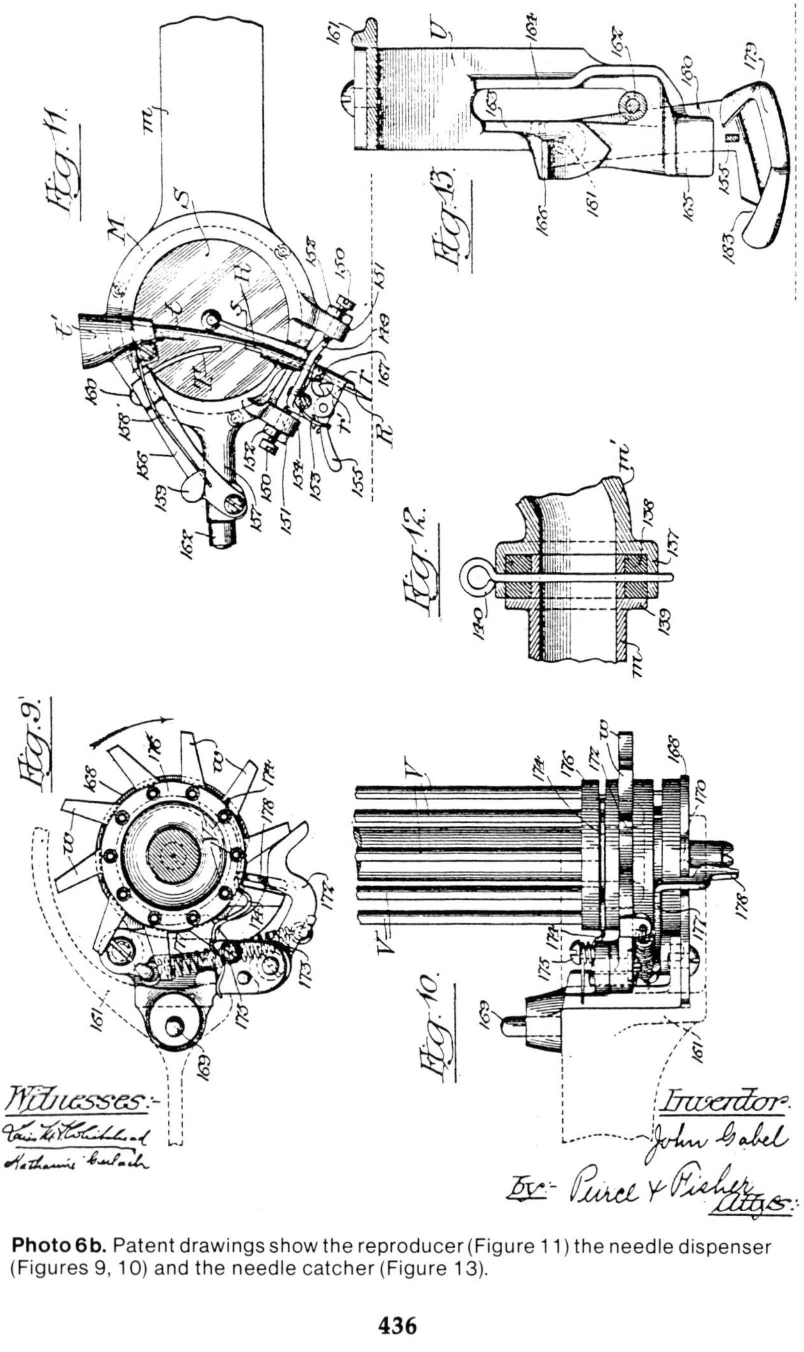

Fig. 11.

Fig. 13.

Fig. 12.

Fig. 9.

Fig. 10.

Witnesses:-

Inventor.
John Gabel
By- Pierce & Fisher
Attys.

Photo 6b. Patent drawings show the reproducer (Figure 11) the needle dispenser (Figures 9, 10) and the needle catcher (Figure 13).

436

I wondered what could be used to substitute the diamond point so that the operator would not have to change the needle too often. First I experimented on an adjustable needle, using a steel wire which I fed through a brass needle and fastened it to the end of it. This gave a lot of grief. If I used a wire fine enough to reach the bottom of the record groove, it would cause vibration and the sound would not be clear enough. If the wire was stiff enough to prevent vibration, it would scratch and spoil the records. This convinced me that the record grooves were V-shaped and that it would be necessary to use a needle with a point to fit the V-shaped groove for the record. That is the reason why the Victor Talking Machine gave the best results when played with the Victor needle.

So I decided to make an automatic changing device. Within a week I had solved the problem and made a needle magazine as well as a movement in the machine to operate the magazine so that a fresh needle could be dropped into the sound box for every record.

This was done in time to incorporate the needle changer in the diagram for the first patient application.

The needle-changing mechanism completed my experimental work on the (mechanical part of the) Entertainer. The needle-changing mechanism was used on the Entertainer until 1929 — a period of 23 years.

When the experimental work on the mechanism was completed, I set my mind on improving the sound. That was my greatest problem. I worked day and night including Sundays. . .until I was satisfied that I had the best sounding machine on the market. This included the Victor Talking Machine which was considered the best talking machine in existence.

In 1915 at the Panama Pacific International Exposition in San Francisco, the Judges decided that my machine was the best sounding machine and it was awarded the first price (Gold Medal) in competition with all other talking machines including the Victor.

But even back in 1906 when the Entertainer was put on the market, trouble brewed immediately with the Victor Talking Machine Company.

PATENT DISPUTES. . .AND MORE

The patent law firm was concerned about the conflict because they were in the middle, and Victor was an enormous client. They arranged a meeting at the Victor factory in Camden, New Jersey, where Gabel had had a machine crated and sent.

The meeting was with Mr. Geisler, the manager, possibly of the legal department. Geisler's reaction to the Entertainer:

"This is a disgrace to our machine. We have a fine, rich looking machine and we are selling to the finest class of people in the best homes. This thing must be operated in the cheapest type of saloon and will play our records. It will cheapen our machine."

The president of the Victor Company, Eldridge Johnson, was in Europe, and Geisler may have been interpreting Johnson's envisioning of the Victor machines as a genuine musical instrument intended for the best homes.

Upon Gabel's return to Chicago, Pierce, of the law firm, told him that Victor had a special fund of one million dollars on reserve for interference law suits. "If they do not like a person, they find a way to bring suit. Last year (in 1905) we put a firm in Michigan out of business."

Then ensued an interesting debate between Clapp and Pierce, both of the same law firm. The worry was the Berliner groove-driven reproducer patent. Victor was so confident of its patent strength that it felt compelled to boast in ads in the *Talking Machine World*. The ads stressed the importance of its Berliner patent #534,543:

"That the Victor Company controls the disc reproducing machine and disc record, where the reproducer is vibrated and *propelled* by the record. . .(emphasis added). . .the Victor Company hesitates at anything like bragging, but the Victor Company is on top."

SMALL PATENT DETOUR PLANNED

Clapp said: "I mean that we can get around it, John. Is it possible to bring the sound box across the records by means of a screw instead of that free-swing motion?" Clapp felt this would get away from the Berliner patent and Gabel implemented it in one day.

The first patent, #1,134,603, filed on February 26, 1906, shows the machine that must have been prototyped and then triplicated in late 1905. It reflects the addition of an early version of the needle changer in that it does not yet show the finger on the reproducer that positively pushes the new needle into place before playing a new record. The patent also does not show the change to the feed-screw propellant for the tone arm.

The machine shown in the patent drawing is, therefore, a pre-production model. Once the feed screw was added, the horn was moved to the center of the case and a spring-loaded, telescopic connection made from the horn to the tone arm.

The Gabel machine is loaded with features, many of which are there to insure the reliability of operation under adverse conditions. For example, the Entertainer automatically adjusts for the small differences in actual record size (owing to a lack of standards in 1905). The mechanism also permits listener's selection of the next disc to be played while the current disc is still playing via an ingenious double-clutch arrangement.

Best of all is the unified, automatic operation that powers all functions from one simple turn of the crank. The Gabel Entertainer eliminates the bothersome problems that undoubtedly were the undoing of the contemporaneous cylinder record changer called the Multiphone.

Photo 7. Close up of the front window. The tune card holders hang on each side, the coin counter is visible below the "Make Selection There" sign and the needle magazine is shown upright in the center. The tag above says "Pat. Apld. For".

The horn has a movable baffle: a metal tab that slides in and out of the base of the horn and controls the volume. In the closed position, the listener can comfortably hear the record while standing in front of the horn. With the baffle pulled out, the listener can be across a 30-foot room and catch every word easily.

The coin slot displayed the last three coins played so that the proprietor could tell if patrons were trying to slug the machine with fake nickels. Putting the last three coins on display was a preventive measure that had already been used in gambling machines.

Another feature was the visible coin counter which allowed the proprietor to see that employees weren't stealing from the coin box. The only other early automatic-music machine that sported a coin counter was the Encore Automatic Banjo, invented in 1893 and commercialized in 1896. Since the Banjo was still on the market in 1905, it is possible that John Gabel got the idea from seeing one. The second patent (#1,182,551), filed August 18, 1909, contained all of the improvements mentioned, but no additional features. The second patent depicted a mechanism that is identical to the horn model in the author's collection, indicating that once the mechanism design stablized, no improvements were needed over long periods of time.

After the patent application was filed in February, 1906, Gabel brought the machine to market. It was a beauty in its quartered-oak case, richly figured and decorated with bevelled panels and opulent nickel-plated castings, and best of all, the large, polished brass horn gleamed on top. This 1905 version of the Automatic Entertainer was an immediate success. During 1906, Gabel, as salesman, made many sales to music houses and to dealers of the Victor Talking Machine Company. The success of the machine did not go unnoticed by Victor.

VICTOR THREATENS SUIT

In January of 1907, Pierce told Gabel that Victor wanted to file suit. In a rare burst of ethics for that period, he said he decided to defend Gabel:

"John, money is not the only thing in the world. They would buy me as they have bought others. No, John, I value my pride and honor more than the almighty dollar they are slinging at me. If the Victor Company brings suit against you, they will find me fighting on your side."

Soon afterward, the suit was indeed filed and Pierce did defend. However, Gabel's business was immediately influenced. The dealers of the Victor Company backed off immediately, and some even returned machines that were as yet unsold. Gabel went on the road to protect his business. This is the kind of situation where the phrase "loneliness at the top of the corporate ladder" gets its meaning. To New Orleans, Texas, Arizona, California, Nevada, Utah, Colorado, Nebraska, Iowa and Illinois he travelled. He could not talk Victor dealers into continuing with the Entertainer due to the hold Victor had, so he concentrated on the independents. On the road he found other problems, all endemic to getting acceptance for a new product:

In Monroe, (Louisiana?) I found the Entertainer was in the hands of a piano dealer who operated electronic pianos. His help did not know a thing about automatic mechanisms, nor did they care to learn.

I asked the proprietor to show the machine to me. When I removed the door I pointed to a small spring that had been unhooked from the screw feed nut. Someone had deliberately unhooked the spring.

Early in March, 1907, a short time after the earthquake, I arrived in San Francisco. Two of the music houses there had my machine, Bacigalupi and Eilers.

Both Bacigalupi and Eilers were the most important distributors of all kinds of automatic music machines on the West Coast. Eilers was the Eilers Piano House, headquartered in Portland, Oregon, with outlets all over the West Coast. Neither of these houses was controlled by the Victor Company, but Bacigalupi was the father-in-law of Leon Douglass, the retired Vice-President of the Victor Company. Bacigalupi offered to take Gabel out to see Douglass, who had retired to an estate near San Francisco, California.

A SLIP OF THE TONGUE?

On the visit Gabel met Douglass and his wife Victoria on a leisurely Sunday afternoon. After lunch, Gabel managed to chill the afternoon by putting his foot in his mouth with an innocent statement that was taken to have a double meaning.

. . .in the afternoon we walked through the orange and lemon grove. It was the first time in my life that I ever picked a lemon from a tree and I remarked that it was the first lemon that I had picked since my marriage.

I don't know why I made that remark. I had no reason for it as my married life had been very happy. I suppose the remark was made to be funny.

Mr. Bacigalupi was standing beside me and kicked me in the shin. Mrs. Douglass turned and walked away. Then Bacigalupi told me that my remark was very much out of place. He told me his daughter and Douglass were not very happy together. I regretted the remark, not only for the sake of the Douglasses, but for Bacigalupi, who had been so kind to me. We soon left, but the parting was somewhat cold.

Photo 8. The coin mechanism in front of the changer mechanism.

Upon returning to the hotel, Gabel learned that Bacigalupi had paid $15,000 for one of the large Wurlitzer "organs." It was a coin-operated machine in the hotel dining room (probably a large Pianorchestra that Wurlitzer imported from Phillips in Germany) and it was out of order. He said a mechanic had been working on it for two days and was beginning to take some verbal abuse from the two Bacigalupi sons. When the service man was alone, Gabel walked over and offered to help:

Bacigalupi had wired Wurlitzer to send a mechanic to San Francisco to fix that organ and this Italian was the mechanic. I had never seen the inside of one of those instruments. However I studied the mechanism and he tried to explain how it should work.

I asked him to give me a couple of slugs and he left me alone. I placed a slug in the slot, watched the mechanism and called the man. Pointing to a pawl, I told him to take it out. I examined it and showed him where and how to file off the end. After replacing it, he put a slug in the slot and the instrument started to produce music.

The Italian was so happy that he shook hands with me and thanked me while the tears ran down his face. The two sons came rushing in and wanted to know how he fixed it. They were so pleased that they invited me to lunch with them. From that time they were my friends and promised to keep my machine as well as buy more.

Somehow that story sounds a bit too simplistic. Any problem with the coin-trip mechanism seems improbable to have been that major, but it's interesting hearing the recollection.

Gabel was ready to leave San Francisco, but had run out of money. The city was in ruins from the earthquake (Gabel was still feeling the earth tremors during the visit) and the only transportation was the horse and wagon. All classes of working men were on strike so it was expensive for him to move around.

Photo 9. Close up of fancy casting "Drop Coin Here".

With his typical, simple resourcefulness Gabel recalls:

I dared not tell Bacigalupi that I was broke. Fortunately, I met Tom Watling (of gambling machine fame) and borrowed five dollars until I could get some money from Chicago. I still had some stops to make, so I stopped in the saloons of every town that I visited and repaired slot machines to pay my expenses.

In Salt Lake City I sold ten Entertainers to Carstensen and Anson. I had to stay there two days longer to land that order. Although I was broke, I could not tell Carstensen and Anson that the President of The Automatic Machine & Tool Company was unable to pay his hotel bill. That evening I scouted around in search of a broken slot machine that needed repairing. I found one and it was tough. It took two hours to repair the machine and when I charged five dollars for the work, he (the proprietor) threatened to throw me out. When he called me a robber, I told him that the machine would take in five dollars that night. He said: 'All right, I will pay you the five dollars when the machine earns it!'

I was very tired and it was after ten o'clock, but I had to wait until after two o'clock for my pay and my train was leaving for Chicago at eight o'clock. Thanks to the old slot machine, it took in five dollars in four hours.

EVERY PART NECESSARY

In order to show how important it was to have a good man on the road in the amusement-machine business, Gabel recalls a few more stories from that whirlwind trip:

At a music store in Sacramento there were two Entertainers. I was informed that the machines were continuously out of order. I looked at the machine and asked what had become of the needle magazine. The mechanic said: 'That is what gives us so much trouble.' He brought the needle magazines to me and, as soon as I touched them I asked how the oil got on them. He told me the needles were stuck in the tubes and so he oiled them. I assured him that the needles would not stick in the tubes if the tubes were filled properly. I showed him that the needle was too light to slide through the tube with oil in it.

I gave the magazines a gasoline bath and during reassembly I asked for the needle gauge. He did not know what I wanted. I showed him where the round steel plate with a small hole in it should be placed at the top of the needle magazine to keep the dust out of the tubes and to prevent the needles from falling out.

The man said: 'I do not use that thing.' I told him he would not have trouble if he had filled the needle magazine through that needle gauge. I picked up a needle on which there was a burr. I tried to put it through the gauge and it would not go through. Then I removed the plate and put the needle into one of the tubes. It stuck in the middle of the tube. In this way I showed him the importance of the gauge to prevent the clogging of the mechanism.

I explained that our factory would not put a part on the machine unless it was needed and that this needle gauge was necessary.

That is a lesson that many a modern-day restorer could well learn about all kinds of automatic-music machines with mysterious and seemingly unimportant features. These machines should be put back to *original* condition — it generally proves out the designers knew what they were doing.

RECESSION OF 1907

The year 1907 was notable for its national, economic crisis which added to the stiff competitive methods of the Victor Talking Machine Company. Lyon & Healy bought an Entertainer and actually shipped it to Victor to ask permission to sell it. Victor responded with an emphatic "NO," and the sample machine was returned to Gabel with the message: "The Victor Company will not permit us to handle it." Such was the power of Victor.

J.P. Seeburg himself had purchased an Entertainer which was promptly delivered to his Chicago loop office for display in his main showroom. However, Seeburg judged it as a competitive threat (how prophetic!) to the automatic-piano business which was just getting up a head of steam, so nothing was done with it.

Gabel recalls: *While the Victor caused a lot of grief, the piano manufacturers, dealers and operators were also a menace. The electric piano was on the market before my Entertainer and the country was flooded with them. It was natural for those who had invested heavily in pianos to be interested in keeping the Entertainer out of the way.*

Then it seemed the big break came in August of 1907, when Howard Wurlitzer himself came to see John Gabel. Wurlitzer was, without question, the marketing powerhouse in the country and Wurlitzer was very favorably impressed with the Automatic Entertainer. He made Gabel a proposition that would make Wurlitzer the exclusive distributor of the machine. Given business conditions, the offer was like "an angel from heaven." However, John Gabel was becoming a bit more of a realist and he asked Wurlitzer how he would obtain permission from the

Victor Company to handle the Entertainer. He recalled Wurlitzer saying that the Victor Company had nothing to do with Wurlitzer and that Wurlitzer made and sold anything they wished. In his typical brash style, Howard Wurlitzer said:

". . .if the Victor Co. does not like it, let them come to us and I will talk to them as I would to my Dutch Uncle."

To prove his good intentions, even before a deal was consummated, Wurlitzer ordered 100 Entertainers that same day. During the ensuing 30 days, Gabel made all the machines he could, a total of 26. These were still the early horn models which were all shipped to Cincinnati, Ohio.

VICTOR PRESSURES WURLITZER

Soon after, Wurlitzer returned to Chicago saying that he had been called to Camden, New Jersey, and Geisler put the arm on him. Wurlitzer had a jobber's contract with the Victor Company for the cities of Cincinnati and Chicago and if Victor cancelled their contract, Wurlitzer would be stuck with $700,000 in goods that apparently could not be resold through normal distribution without a contract.

So it was back to the hard, selling life compounded by a forced move of the factory from 43 South Canal. The Northwestern Depot was scheduled to be built where the Automatic Machine and Tool Company was located, so the factory was moved to 210 Ann Street. While all this was going on, the Victor lawsuit day of reckoning was approaching and Gabel was spending an increasing amount of time being drilled by his attorneys in preparation. So far 1907 was not a great year for him.

GABEL VS. VICTOR

This case meant a lot to me. A decision in my favor would mean new life to me and the business and it would mean bankruptcy should the decision be against me. On the last day, Mr. Clapp instructed to send one of my machines to the court room and to set it up so that I would be sure it worked. I followed instructions.

The Victor Company's man set up one of their machines in the court room so that the stage was all set for the hearing in the afternoon. Judge Kohlsaat presided. The attorney for Victor, Mr. Pettit, addressed the court and explained the broad claims of the Berliner patent. Then he demonstrated on his exhibit the claims that were involved in the infringement suit. The judge had a paper before him. No doubt it was a copy of the Berlinger patent.

Mr. Clapp addressed the Court. In his calm slow manner, he started to talk. Finally, Judge Kohlsaat told him that it was not necessary to pace back and forth nor to talk further about the Berliner patent as he knew it by heart.

Mr. Clapp begged the Court to permit him to demonstrate the movement on his opponent's machine. He said: 'Your Honor, the broad claim of the Berliner patent is a swinging arm with a reproducer on the end. The stylus of the reproducer sets into the groove of the record and the grooves of the record then carry the reproducer and arm across the records. The Gabel machine has no swinging arm. Neither does the groove of the record feed the reproducer across it. I will demonstrate this fact by playing the Gabel machine.'

He said: 'Your Honor, the reproducer and arm on this machine are carried across the record by a screw feed. I will now disconnect the screw feed. Please watch the results. As soon as he disconnected the screw feed, the reproducer continued to repeat the same sound.'

He said: 'Now, Your Honor, you can see that we are not infringing on the Berliner patent.'

Judge Kohlsaat gave his decision then and there by saying that he could see no similarity in the two machines, so there could be no infringement and the case was dismissed. The Victor Company had lost the case and it gave me new life. With a free mind I was able to think of improving the business and to increase production although the Victor Company continued to spread trouble for me all over the country with their antagonistic attitude and false statements.

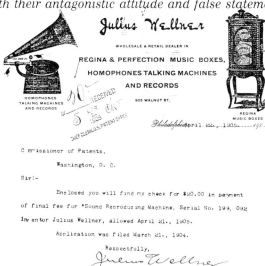

Photo 10a. Julius Wellner letterhead in 1905 showing his early emphasis on phonographs and Regina music boxes.

447

VICTORY IS SWEET

The year 1908 began on a better note. Sales were increasing and Gabel began assembling a network of state agents. Joe Hallner from Wisconsin began buying machines for resale and by 1909, Mr. C.L. Fox bought several machines for St. Louis, Missouri, and the surrounding areas.

In 1909, Gabel made some changes to the Entertainer. While the mechanism stayed the same (it had proven to be very reliable), he added an electric motor to replace the crank. He also replaced the external horn with an enclosed horn covered by grillwork in a taller case to accommodate the horn. The fancy castings were eliminated and the overall appearance was directed more toward a less showy, more refined device.

Collectors today prize the horn models of most phonograph types, but back in the 1910 era the horn was considered a necessary evil, and awkward as well. The Entertainer with an enclosed horn was considered an improvement in appearance then. The front, bevelled-glass window was retained so that the mechanical intricacies of the machine were still in view. The 1909 version achieved great success with the Victor lawsuit settled and an improving network of dealers was gradually established.

A brief cloud came on the horizon in 1910 when a well-known and successful distributor of music machines in Philadelphia, Pennsylvania, Julius Wellner, informed Gabel that he was interfering with Wellner's invention.

Photo 10b. Stock certificate from 1945 issued to a Gabel family member.

ANOTHER PATENT INTERFERENCE

That was news to me as I had never heard about it before. I asked Mr. Wellner to accompany me to our attorney's office, which he did. Wellner was truthful enough. He told us that his machine would not work, and that the purpose of his visit to Chicago was to make arrangements to be a distributor for my machine, and that a $10.00 commission on each machine should be applied as royalty.

The attorneys talked Gabel into the idea that the royalty was low enough to be a better proposition than an expensive legal fight. So the deal was accepted and Wellner bought "a substantial number of machines and we parted on a friendly terms."

As it turned out, the run-in with Wellner was fortuitous since Gabel was in need of top-notch retailers and Wellner was in the thick of the action on the East Coast. As far back as 1897, when Wellner lived in Jersey City, New Jersey, where the Regina and Criterion music boxes were made, he patented (#585,246) a novel damping arrangement for music-box teeth whereby a felt pad sandwiched in the center of the star wheel took the place of wire or spring dampers. This device never got to market.

From a Hathaway & Bowers catalog description of a Regina Sublima piano, which was originally sold to Julius Wellner on December 12, 1908, we learn that he was ". . .a music merchant of Philadelphia —a gentleman who was to become, a few years later, one of the most live-wire dealers for Seeburg pianos."

Gabel's first patent had been filed in February, 1906, and was still not issued in 1910. As to why the patent application took so long Gabel recalled:

I had confidence in my attorneys, they had proven themselves honorable when they fought my case with the Victor Co. when I did not have the money to pay them. Mr. Clapp purposely held up the patent papers. His purpose was to get all of the interferences out of the way so that a clear patent with all 106 claims would be granted.

Resolving the Wellner situation certainly was part of the plan. In 1911 Fox moved his headquarters from St. Louis to Kansas City, Missouri and he was doing good business there. Wellner was doing well in the East; Gabel continued selling machines personally through Indiana and Wisconsin, as well as in his home state of Illinois.

In 1912 the Victor Company brought another suit against Gabel. Gabel was on the stand for 17 days and answered 851 questions. His laudable stamina in overcoming obstacle after obstacle was once again rewarded. In early 1913, he learned that he had won the case and, accordingly, 23 more claims were allowed in the patent — for a total of

Photos 11 a,b. Horn model #646. This machine is presently owned by the son of a San Francisco music merchant. The son recalls: "he (his father) handled electric pianos, Wurlitzer Harps, Encore Automatic Banjoes, orchestrions and talking machines. What those were I do not know. All of these instruments were in saloons and restaurants. He changed the roll music once a week.

During the earthquake and fire a large number of these instruments were lost. In 1926 he sold out his business but he did keep one player piano, one Regina bar top music box and the (Gabels) record player. I have these with me today."

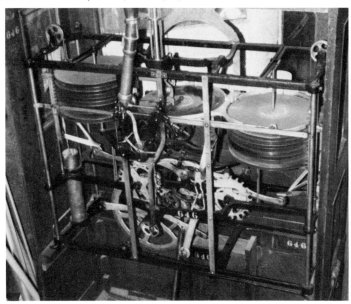

450

129 claims. Shortly thereafter, the Victory Company appealed their case all they way to the Supreme Court. After a costly preparation process, Gabel and his attorneys showed up in Washington, District of Columbia, on the appointed day in the summer of 1913 only to find that Victor abandoned the lawsuit that morning. They were playing an interference and cost-escalation game, but their bluff had finally been called. That marked the end of Victor's legal attacks.

In 1913, Mr. E.S. Garrett, who managed the Columbia Phonograph Store in St. Louis, Missouri, became so impressed with the Entertainer that he set up an agency in California and it became successful as the Golden Gate Music Company of San Francisco. Hundreds of machines were sold there.

STRUGGLES TO IMPROVE TONE

For years we had been buying sheet mica here in the U.S. We would then peel it down to size and select the clear sheets to punch out our diaphrams. If the mica was not clear the sound was cracked. If it was too thin it squeaked and if it was too thick the sound was dull.

When I began using German mica, the sound was greatly improved. But during the summer of 1914 Germany declared war on France and England and the mica diaphrams were no longer available. I decided to experiment with metal. Steel was too stiff, brass and copper would not do. Then I tried aluminum and developed a good sounding diaphram that was far superior to mica.

In July of 1915 Gabel received a surprise telegram from Garrett in which he related the excellent news that the Entertainer had received first prize for phonograph exhibits at the Panama-Pacific Exposition in San Francisco. Before the end of the same day, a representative of *Talking Machine World* magazine called and said: "Mr. Gabel, have you heard the news in San Francisco?" Gabel thought he was referring to the good news and showed the telegram. The reporter said "Oh, that is wrong. I have received a telegram from San Francisco stating that Marshall Field & Company was awarded first prize. I have a story here from Marshall Field & Company for *Talking Machine World.*"

GOLD MEDAL CONFUSION

It would appear that Gabel didn't quite have the full story about Marshall Field. An all-day perusal of the *Talking Machine World* of 1915 by Allen Koenigsberg produced a mention in the April 15, 1915, issue that the Cheney booth was *designed* by Marshall Field & Co., and other hints about a forthcoming, unusual machine which apparently never did appear.

451

Gabel perhaps did not know that Field's was only a distributor for Cheney. He goes on to recall that the Field story had to be retracted and that the Exposition Commissioners closed the Field (Cheney?) exhibit for making false statements. Allen Koenigsberg could find no such printed retraction, although he did find a September 15, 1915, *Talking Machine World* mention of the Gabel win:

". . .the Entertainer was awarded the gold medal for automatic talking machines by the exposition authorities. This includes an award ribbon and large banner. Substantial shipments of Gabel's Entertainer have been made recently to Hawaii, the Philippine Islands and Australia."

The Gabel exhibit was in the Palace of Liberal Arts. Upon entering the Palace, he found Garrett in his booth in the midst of emptiness. All the other major phonograph companies (Victor, Columbia and possibly Cheney) had cleared out. Garrett said: "Oh, Mr. Gabel, you should have been here to see the fuss that those fellows made and how angry they were."

The Victor Company appealed to the Commissioners and accused them of unfairness. Gabel recalls:

They had placed over a dozen machines throughout the grounds, free of charge, as an ad. Their action (the appeal) did not appeal to the public favor. The people were talking about them and said that they were selfish and conceited and sore because they did not get the first prize.

Mr. Charles Moore, President of the Panama-Pacific International Exposition congratulated me on my fine exhibit and wonderful invention. Then he presented me with the Gold Medal which was the highest award for any product in the Exposition. There was always a crowd at our booth. The people were fascinated by the nickel-plated mechanism which was constantly in motion, changing records and needles automatically. There was an extra needle magazine which was kept filled — ready to use when the other was empty.

Gabel had learned some principles of marketing. He tells us that he had one additional special version at the Exposition which was the one referred to above that drew all the crowds:

Before the fair, I had one mechanism nickel-plated and when it was assembled we enclosed it in a glass case. It was in operation continuously at the booth.

Can you imagine a Gabel mechanism all nickel-plated and in a glass dome? For anyone who has seen the mechanism, it would not appear difficult to imagine the captivating power it would have.

Photo 12a. Earlier version of the enclosed horn machine with the unusual option of a crank instead of motorized operation.

Photo 12b. Later version of the enclosed horn model with electric turntable drive.

OFFICIAL EXPOSITION RECOGNITION

Moore had indicated that Gabel would get a full page in the *Official History* and he kept his word. Here are some excerpts:

"The International Jury of Awards gave Gabel's Automatic Entertainer a Gold Medal, and the award was made because of superiority of tone reproducing qualities of this machine as well as its many other excellent points.

"The Jury took into account that the Automatic Entertainer possessed many novel and useful features. It was thoroughly appreciated that in the field of mechanical entertaining, Gabel's machine occupied a position which would commend itself to those who desired to use it as a coin operating machine, and also to those who wished to have a practical as well as ornamental sound reproducing device. . .it would give to the owner no trouble, as its construction was such as to make it 'fool proof'. It obviated the necessity of having an expert mechanic to attend to its needs.

"There were two styles shown at the Panama-Pacific Exposition, one being the instrument used for commercial purposes. This instrument was so constructed as to play from one to twenty nickels at a time, while the other was the home machine, which was operated by the mere pressing of a button.

"Both of the machines held twenty-four standard records, which were so arranged as to permit the playing of any selection preferred, or if the music lover desired, the Entertainer would play continuously, the machine changing records and needles automatically thus giving a lengthy concert.

"The motor, which used either a direct or alternating current, was used to wind the machine, and for places where current was not available, a handle was provided so that the machine could be prepared for its work with one turn of the crank.

"The trouble with the majority of sound reproducing devices has been the constant care and attention which must be given to them, and this has been done away with in the Gabel machine.

"Another point in its favor is its handsome exterior, possessing a rich and dignified appearance, and from an ornamental standpoint, the machine was so constructed as to grace drawing room or salon.

"The fact that numerous machines were ordered by Commissioners and visitors from foreign lands where high class music is appreciated, is another evidence of the worth of the Gabel Automatic Entertainer.

"Mechanical experts were very much interested in the machine and were loud in their praise of its construction from a mechanical viewpoint. They were unanimous in declaring that Mr. Gabel has given to the world a device mechanically correct in every detail."

Orders started pouring in from all over California and the world. John Gabel had finally made an indelible impression for the fine mechanic and inventor he was. While this was 1915, ten long years after he built his first three Entertainers, it still would be ten more years before anyone else would catch up with an automatic selector disc mechanism.

AN AVALANCHE OF ORDERS

The year 1915 was pivotal and 1916 opened with a bang. Orders were coming in so fast that it was impossible to fill them promptly. Gabel still employed 50 men, but his distributors informed him that they needed quantities such as 500 for Minneapolis/St. Paul, Minnesota, 500 for southern California, and so on.

The cases were still made by outside vendors and the mechanism was nearly identical to the first 1905 machine except for the enclosed horn, the motor and double-capacity needle changer. We learned from the Wurlitzer contract of 1907 that capacity was perhaps 30-35 per month, or 350 to 400 per year with 50 employees. Still, it is remarkable how few survive. Perhaps the policy of the jukebox industry to destroy older models contributed to this situation.

Capacity was apparently eventually expanded and the agent network grew. In 1918 Gabel changed the name of the company from the Automatic Machine and Tool Company to the John Gabel Manufacturing Company because he wanted credit for all the lean years and after the protracted fight with Victor.

Gabel went on producing the acoustic Entertainer until 1928, an incredible 23-year life span. In 1928-29 a number of competitors came on the market with electrically-amplified machines that used more permanent needles. These devices avoided the need for a needle changer and were free to compete.

The first Capehart phonograph was still acoustic and ran awry of the Gabel patents. The Capehart Automatic Phonograph Company filed suit against Gabel in September of 1929, attacking the validity of the patents. In January of 1930, Charles Bartholomew of Chicago also filed suit to do battle over the patents. These suits dragged on until 1935 when the Gabel patents expired their 17-year legal life. All suits were dropped in October of 1935 and the field reopened for reasons of both patent expiration and technological advance.

John Gabel went on to design and produce his own electrically-amplified jukeboxes in oak cabinets. He continued doing so until 1936 when he retired at age 65. The John Gabel Manufacturing Company continued in the jukebox business, joining the plastics revolution, until 1949 when it dissolved and reportedly sold some assets and patents to the Rockola Company.

John Gabel died in December, 1955, at the age of 83. His obituaries in the local papers in Chicago made some reference to his major accomplishments:

"John Gabel, 83, of 253 Linden, Glencoe, who manufactured the world's first disc-record coin operated jukebox, died Friday. . .

Mr. Gabel in 1898 founded the Automatic Machine and Tool Co. which later became the John Gabel Manufacturing Co., at Racine and Lake."

COLLECTOR NOTES

A study of serial numbers and patent labels on extant Gabel machines has been actively underway by Russ Ofria (publisher of *Nickel A Tune* magazine), Fred Roth (collector, restorer and Gabel enthusiast) and me. Here's what we have so far:

1905 - 1909 EXPOSED HORN "PATENT" MODEL

We know that extant serial numbers are in the 600's and 700's, and there is an enclosed horn machine with serial #815. It is reasonable to guess that 300 horn models were made from serial #500 to serial #800. Earlier versions have "Gabel's" omitted from the name cast into the marquee. The early needle changer was of lesser capacity, comparable to the patent drawings.

1909 - 1920 ENCLOSED HORN "1909" MODEL

As mentioned previously, the earliest of these enclosed-horn models is #815, and serial numbers extend well into the 3,000's, perhaps even the 4,000's, before a 1922 patent date begins to appear on the patent tag. A good guess is that 3,000 machines of this type were originally made. The cabinet is 68 inches high to accommodate the interior horn (behind the grillwork), the coin entry is a slot in a round, knob-like casting affixed between and level with the selector knobs, and it usually had a motor that literally took the place of the human arm in winding the mechanism. The benefit of this simplistic method of motorization was that an optional hand crank could still be offered for areas of non-standard or non-existent power. Otherwise, the mechanism is nearly identical to the horn model.

1920 - 1928 THE ENCLOSED HORN
"ELECTRIC DRIVE" MODEL

Around 1920, Gabel departed from a spring-powered machine and installed a motor-driven belt that powered both the changer and the turntable directly. This model was in a slightly smaller case with a smaller front window, and it sported a light behind the marquee to illuminate the mechanism. The coin-entry casting was changed to a wing shape and was mounted higher than the selector knobs. Otherwise, they were still mechanically similar to the original Gabel machines.

FROM 1928 TO THE EARLY 1940's

In 1928 or so, the jukebox industry was getting a start and competitors flooded in. Case style varied greatly and electric amplification replaced acoustic as the new technology. Gabel followed suit with several "modern" case styles and electrical amplification. Still, the basic mechanism was recognizable even on machines whose serial numbers break the 11,000 mark and extend at least to the late 1930's.

Russ Ofria claims that over half the earlier acoustic machines found have been converted to later mechanisms, in many instances also resulting in the case being cropped down in size because the two-foot long, main-drive spring was no longer needed.

The recycling of older mechanisms would help to explain why the acoustic Gabels are relatively rare.

SUMMARY OF ACOUSTIC GABEL MACHINES

Model	Years of Production	Est. Original Production Qty.	Approx. No. Known Today
Horn "Patent	1905 - 1909	300	3
Enclosed Horn "1909"	1909 - 1920	3,000	10 - 20
Enclosed Horn Electric	1920 - 1928	4,000	10 - 20
		7,300	23 - 43

If the "1% survival rule" for early machines is applied, there are some more 1909 enclosed-horn models yet to be found (perhaps another 10 to 20), although I have a feeling that additional publicity will turn up a few more horn models as well.

by 1935, John Gabel was no longer spending much time with the business and other competitors stole the lead with newer technologies. By 1940, Gabel machines were being regularly traded out by Wurlitzer and others.

Photo 13. A display of early coin-op machines all from approximately the same period. Left to right: Encore Automatic Banjo (1897-1912); Gabel's Automatic Entertainer (1905-1909 model); Wurlitzer Automatic Harp (1905-1910). Rick Crandall collection.

The lack of advertising and other promotional material from his early sales efforts has contributed to John Gabel's near obscurity. The discovery of his early machine and his diary (with his secretary's comments), and the subsequent disclosure of this new information in articles such as this should serve to complement the record of early endeavors in the field of automatic music.

John Gabel's contributions will now be a legitimate and remembered part of the history of automatic-music machines.

WHERE ARE THEY NOW?
The Edison Phonograph Dolls

Patty Marchal

*A*ccording to the *Scientific American* of April 26, 1890, the Edison Laboratory at Orange, New Jersey, had the capacity for making 500 talking dolls a day. With that kind of production, within 24 days, each of our present MBSI members would have one of these beauties. How I do wish!

Figure 1. The completed doll.

Figure 2. Winding the mechanism.

Figure 3. The phono mechanism.

The finished doll (Figures 1 and 2) has the same appearance as other dolls, but its body is made of tin, and the interior is filled with a mechanism much like that of a commercial phonograph of 1890, but is much simpler and inexpensive.

Much of the mechanism of the doll was made in the regular phonograph works of the Edison plant, but the adjustments, the manufacture of the record cylinders which determined the story the doll would tell, the packing and shipping were all conducted in a near-by, extensive building devoted to the manufacture of this interesting toy.

The cylinder of the phonograph of the talking doll is mounted on a sleeve which slides on the shaft, the sleeve being screw-threaded so as to cause the cylinder to move lengthwise on the shaft. A key is provided by which the cylinder may be thrown out of engagement with the segmental nut, and a spiral spring is provided for returning the cylinder to the point of starting. The cylinder carries a ring of wax-like material, upon which is recorded the speech or song to be repeated by the doll.

Above the record cylinder is arranged a diaphragm carrying a reproducing stylus. The funnel at the top of the phonographic apparatus opens underneath the breast of the doll, which is perforated to permit the sound to escape (Figure 3).

Figure 4. Making the voice recording.

Figure 5. The production room.

By the simple operation of turning the crank any child can make the doll say "Mary had a little lamb," "Jack and Jill," or whatever it was, so to speak, taught to say by girls who prepared the wax-like records. The jangle of a large number of these girls, each having a stall to herself, simultaneously repeating "Little Bo Peep," united with the sounds of the phonographs themselves when reproducing the stories, would surely have made a veritable pandemonium (Figure 4).

At the Edison Laboratory everything was done by the 'piece' system. The construction of new tools by skilled mechanics in every branch and the machinery used were the finest procurable. Every piece, without regard to its size or importance, was carefully inspected by aid of standard gauges, so that when the parts were brought together, no additional work was required to cause them to act properly.

After the little phonographs were assembled they were brought to the assembly room, placed in the bodies of the dolls, packed and carefully stored away in boxes having on their labels the name of the story the doll was able to repeat (Figure 5).

Where are they now?

GLOSSARY

Aerophone. An instrument in which sound is produced by the vibration of air, as in an organ pipe.

Agraffe. A device which clasps a piano string to prevent it from vibrating.

Air. One tune or melody in the musical program.

Airbrake. The fan fly on the endless screw of the governor.

Air motor. A series or cluster of small bellows which converts the movement of air in to or out of it into mechanical motion.

Anvil. The piece of steel protruding from the bottom of a cylinder musical box comb tooth which holds the damper pin and damper in place.

Arbor. The central shaft in the cylinder of a musical box.

Artist's Roll. The hand-played rolls made by prominent pianists and designed to play on expression and reproducing pianos.

Automatic Musical Instrument. A mechanism which automatically plays a musical program and without the need for musical knowledge or skill on the part of its operator. The term "mechanical" is often used as a synonym for "automatic" whereas, strictly speaking, automatic refers to those instruments which may be operated by a self-contained power source such as an electric motor, a clockwork spring motor, a descending weight or a wind-water mechanism. A hand-turned musical mechanism, such as a barrel organ or organette, is the true mechanical musical instrument.

Automaton (plural: automata). A mechanically-operated doll or other figure usually representing a human or an animal. A mechanically-operated model, e.g., sailing ship or landscape. Automata are frequently but not invariably, equipped with musical movements.

Band Organ (American term). An automatic organ, usually loudly voiced and designed for outdoor use. It is also called a carousel or sideshow organ. Its European counterpart is a fair or fairground organ (England); Jahrmarkt, Kermisorgel or Draaiorgel (Germany) or Pierement (Dutch).

Barrel. A pinned cylinder, usually made of wood, which holds the programmed music for use in barrel-operated instruments.

Barrel Organ. An organ, usually hand-cranked, with the musical program pinned on a wooden cylinder. The term "chamber organ" often refers to a softly voiced organ made for indoor use while "monkey organ" refers to the loudly voiced outdoor instrument.

Bedplate or Baseplate. The foundation, usually made of iron (with the early ones made of brass), which supports the components of the musical movement.

Bellows. Two or more boards covered with leather or airtight cloth, often hinged together at one end. Pumping a bellows creates air pressure or suction when the boards are pushed together or pulled apart by a lever or crank; other bellows cause a mechanism to operate when air pressure or suction is connected to them causing them to open or close (see also: Pneumatic).

Bird Cage. Usually with one to four birds, the beaks and tails move and the heads turn when the movement, located in the base of the cage, is in operation.

Bird Organ. A small hand-cranked organ with a small number of pewter or wooden pipes. It was developed in the 18th century to teach canaries to sing. The music is pinned on a wooden barrel. Synonyms: canary organ, serinette or perroquette.

Bird, Singing. Usually a tiny bird automaton in a decorated metal, tortoiseshell or composition box. The bird pops up from under a spring-loaded lid, moves its wings and, on the higher quality, early models, the head. A bird song is produced from a bellows-operated flute or whistle within the box.

Bleed. A small orifice permitting vacuum or air pressure to be equalized below a pouch after an open tracker bar hole is closed, allowing the action initiated by the hole in the music roll or book to be reversed.

Book Music. A zigzag-folded, cardboard strip with the music program punched lengthwise, used instead of a paper music roll in many European street and fair organs. Derived from the Jacquard weaving loom-control card system.

Brevete'. French for patented. Often found with the initials "SGDG " which means patented without guarantee by the government (sans garantie du gouvernement).

Bridge. A metal support which holds the arbor in place on the bedplate, as in a cylinder musical box. Synonym: pillow block.

Calliope, Air. A musical instrument consisting of a set of tuned brass whistles sounded by lightly compressed air and operated by means of a keyboard or roll-playing system. Utilized by American outdoor showmen from 1906 to the present.

Calliope, Steam. An extremely loud and uniquely American musical instrument powered by steam. It consists of a series of tuned brass whistles operated by a keyboard, although a few early models were played by means of a barrel. The signature of the circus, it was also used by packet and excursion steamboats, floating theaters and other attractions to announce their presence.

Carousel Organ. See Band Organ.

Cartel Box. A large-sized (over 13") cylinder musical box usually associated with Geneva, Switzerland, where it was first made.

Celeste. See Voice Celeste.

Cement. The thick resinous material which is used in the cylinder of a musical box to hold the pins in place and to afford a deeper, more resonant sound.

Center Spindle. The device in a disc musical box which holds the disc in its proper position for playing and has the height wheel attached to it for proper alignment of the disc.

Chamber Organ. A barrel organ in a styled cabinet which was softly voiced and meant for play in parlors and related areas.

Change/Repeat. In cylinder boxes, the finger that engages in and turns the snail, allowing the musical program to change or repeat the same song, depending on the position of the change/repeat lever.

Chordophon. The generic term for stringed automatic musical instruments which are played by hammers, bowed, strummed, etc.

Chordophone. A disc-operated instrument in which sound is produced by strings which are plucked.

Chromatic. A scale composed entirely of half tones, typically either 12 or 13 in succession.

Click Spring. The small metal spring which holds pressure against the pawl.

Cob (American term). The pinned, wooden barrel used in the Gem, Concert, Chautauqua and other similar organs.

Cock Bracket. A stand-off bracket used to support one end of a driven shaft. In a clockwork mechanism, the bracket which holds the tip of the endless screw in the governor.

Coin Piano. An automatic piano, usually played by a multi-tune paper roll, which plays one song upon the insertion of a coin, shuts off at the end of each song and automatically rewinds after the last song on the roll. Usually contains some form of automatic expression, a mandolin attachment and sometimes an instrument such as a xylophone or a small rank of organ pipes.

Comb. A group of tuned, steel teeth arranged in a musical scale and used in cylinder and disc musical boxes.

Comb Base. The base upon which a musical box comb rests. Synonyms: trestle, brass pedestal, plinth.

Courbette. The tool used by the justifier to bend and perfectly align cylinder pins so that they catch the tip of the tooth that they are to play. Synonym: pin straightener.

Croisage. The overlapping of pin and comb tooth tips in a cylinder musical box. Specifically, the tips of the treble teeth must be just a shade higher than those of the bass teeth.

Cuff. The sleeve-shaped metal cone which holds the musical program for the Capital Cuff Musical Box.

Cylinder. In a musical box, the barrel made of thin (about 0.5mm) brass. The pins of the musical program are driven through the cylinder and held in place with sealing cement.

Also, the wooden barrel of a barrel piano or organ which is studded with steel pins which holds the musical program.

Cylinder Musical Box. The genus of the term musical box. Usually containing one or more tuned, steel musical combs with the music programmed on a pinned, brass cylinder.

Cylinder Separators. The discs, made of zinc or brass, located inside of a musical box cylinder to keep the cylinder in round.

Damper. A small hair spring or bird feather (quill) in a cylinder musical box or metal finger in a disc musical box located under or beside the tip of each tooth of the comb. Just before a pin plucks a tooth it momentarily presses the damper against the tooth, preventing a buzz from occurring just prior to the tone being produced. In disc movements the dampers are allowed to rest on the edge of the tooth by rotation of the star wheel. The only time a damper does *anything* is when a tooth is already vibrating from previous action.

Damper Pin. The tapered, brass or steel brad which holds the damper in place in the anvil under the tooth of a cylinder musical box.

Dance Organ. An automatic player pipe organ, often with percussion, one or more accordions or other instruments displayed on the facade, used in dance halls, cafes and other similar locations, especially in Belgium and Holland. The musical output is softer than that of the outdoor fair and band organs owing to the use of different ranks of pipes and sometimes a solid wood facade which blocks much of the sound.

Detent. A device for holding a moveable member fixed in one of two or more desired positions; allowing for manual selection of the position. Example: allowing a mechanism to start or stop.

Disc. The circular plate, usually metal or cardboard, which contains holes or projections which represent the musical program. Typically the disc rotates against a set of star wheels or a key frame to recover the stored music. Used in the disc-playing musical box and disc-playing reed organ.

Disc Musical Box. A musical box which produces music by means of metal disc turning star wheels which, in turn, pluck the tuned steel, musical comb.

Disc-Shifting Musical Box. A musical box designed to play two tunes in two revolutions of the disc by means of laterally shifting the disc between tunes. The New Century and Sirion boxes are the best known of this type.

Double Combs. A disc musical box which has two combs mounted on the bedplate in which each star wheel plucks two teeth for each note programmed on the disc. With "interleaved" combs, every other star wheel plucks one comb, and the alternate wheels pluck the other comb. The Symphonion Sublime Harmonie system uses two combs placed on opposite sides of the center spindle. Synonym: duplex combs.

Drehorgal (German). Any hand-cranked organ. Also, Leierkasten.

Drive Gear Pinion. The gear which is driven by the spring barrel and delivers the spring tension to the cylinder arbor.

Duplex Comb Movement. A disc musical box having two combs in which each star wheel plucks two teeth tuned to the same note for each note programmed on the disc.

Duplex Musical Box. A cylinder musical box which contains two separate cylinders and two sets of music combs which play synchronously usually with one cylinder in front of the other.

Edge Drive. The type of drive used to power musical box discs. In the gear type the toothed edge of the metal disc meshes with a toothed drive gear. In the sprocket type a toothed or knobbed sprocket wheel mounted under the disc near its outer rim engages with corresponding slots or holes in the outer edge of the disc.

Endcaps. The brass plates which seal the cement in the brass cylinder of a musical box adding rigidity to the cylinder and providing the precise bearing surfaces which support the cylinder on the arbor and allow it to slide as the tunes are changed.

Endless Roll. A type of roll made by gluing the front and end of a roll together to form a continuous loop. Used in coin pianos, some organettes and in the Encore Banjo.

Endless Screw. Part of the governor assembly in a clockwork mechanism. It is the worm or helicoidally (spirally)-cut shaft to which the airbrake is attached. The airbrake fan at the top regulates the speed of the mechanism.

Endless Screw Assembly. See Governor.

Endshake. The tolerance allowed in the endless screw of the governor which allows for a properly operating airbrake. Can be applied to any shaft that employs pivots held between plates.

Endstone. The jewel, usually a ruby or garnet, upon which the pivot of the worm or endless screw bears. It is held atop the cock bracket by the endstone cap.

Endstone Cap. The removeable brass piece atop the governor cock bracket which holds the endstone in place.

Equalizer. A reservoir bellows for a vacuum or wind supply. Usually equipped with a pallet valve, the equalizer spills vacuum or wind when the bellows moves beyond a set limit, thus keeping the vacuum or wind supply regulated at a set level. Synonym: bellows without valves used to stabilize vacuum or wind.

Escape Gear. See Second Wheel.

Escapement. A mechanism utilizing a gear train which regulates the energy stored in an enclosed spring. Synonyms: governor, endless screw assembly.

Escutcheon. A decorative metal piece, usually adorning a keyhole or handle.

Expression. The capacity, in an instrument such as an automatic piano, of varying the volume or intensity of the musical output by varying the vacuum level and other means. A musical roll or musical book may have expression cut into it to operate controls which automatically vary the expression.

Facade. The decorative wood or plastic front of a band, dance or street organ. Synonym: (English) proscenium.

Fair or Fairground Organ. See Band Organ.

Fan Fly. The mechanism used to govern the speed of the musical mechanism by means of a rotating fan or air brake using air resistance upon the fan blades. Synonym: airbrake.

Feeder Bellows: The main bellows of a pump which supplies the vacuum or wind pressure to an equalizer or reservoir.

First Wheel. The wheel in the governor assembly which meshes, via its pinion, with the great wheel of the cylinder.

Flap Valve. A strip of leather (sometimes backed with stiff metal, wood or faced with blotter paper or rubber cloth) attached to a bellows or reservoir which permits air to pass in only one direction.

Flotenuhr (German). Flute or organ-playing clockwork not necessarily associated with a timepiece, but often provided with a timepiece in order to set off the music at a specified hour.

Forte-Piano. An arrangement of musical combs generally found in cylinder musical boxes where there are two combs, the louder (forte) comb toned (not tuned) to play more loudly than the softer (piano) comb.

Frein (French). See Harmonic Brake.

Freres (French). Brothers.

Friction Wheel Drive. A system used in some electric pianos and orchestrions whereby power is transferred from a flywheel to a drive shaft by means of a rubber-tired wheel affixed to the drive shaft and which rides on the lateral surface of the flywheel. Speed is regulated by moving the wheel closer or further from the center of the flywheel.

Fusee Drive. A conically-shaped drum used in both the winding and power train of a clockwork spring motor and connected to the mainspring barrel by a finely wrought chain or by a gut line to maintain the force of the spring at a constant level.

Gantry. A slotted or laminated frame designed to hold the star wheels in a disc box in the proper position for striking the comb teeth while allowing them to rotate freely.

Gebruder (German). Brothers; usually abbreviated Gebr.

Geneva Gear. See Stopwork.

Governor, Musical Box. A mechanism which controls speed by means of a fan fly endless screw with gear train, friction, pneumatic or electrical device. The basic components include: governor block, cock bracket, endstone plate, stopwork, potence, regulating screw, endless screw, airbrake, endstone, sprag, second wheel and drive pinion. Synonyms: gear train, escapement or endless screw assembly.

Great Wheel. The large gear at the end of the musical box cylinder which meshes with the governor assembly.

Gully. The grooved recess on the great wheel which controls the start/stop pin-lever assembly.

Harmonic Brake. A metal blade, usually of brass, placed at the mouth of a violin or cello pipe to stabilize the tone and to enable it to speak more quickly on high pressure without overblowing. This Gavioli invention is among the most popular methods used to create the voicing desired for a particular pipe.

Height Wheel. In a disc musical box, the small, flat disc affixed to the center spindle which gives the correct height to the musical box disc allowing it to pluck the star wheels properly.

Helicoidal. A form of cylinder or barrel in which the pins are arranged in a helix (or spiral) around the surface of the cylinder. The cylinder gradually moves sideways as it turns providing one long continuous piece of music without the usual pause for the sideways shift between revolutions. Some cylinder musical boxes and barrel organs, as well as all Gem organ rollers, were helicoidally pinned.

Hold Down Arm. The bar which holds the disc against the star wheels in a disc musical box. The bar holds the roller or idler wheels which apply direct pressure to the disc. Synonyms: pressure bar, idler arm.

In a piano, it holds the strings in position between the tuning pins and the agraffes on the upper plate bridge.

Hooked Teeth. Found in early musical cylinder box combs to allow for rapid plucking of the teeth. They improved the action of the dampers by allowing the damper to curl in and under the tooth.

Hurdy Gurdy (French: *Vielle a roue*). Historically defined, a stringed instrument with a crank which turns a rosin-covered wheel against violin strings eliminating the need for a bow. Some of the strings are "fingered" by a series of keys while others always remain open to provide drone accompaniment, as in bagpipes. Popular, but incorrect, usage: barrel organ, street piano or other hand-cranked instrument used by a street musician.

Idiophone. An instrument in which sound is produced by means of resonant metal, wood or glass. This can be a musical comb, free reeds or chimes.

Inlay. See Veneer.

Instant Stop. On early musical movements, ca. 1820-60. A lever which acts upon the governor and permits the repairman to stop the mechanism at once to allow for critical adjustments.

Interchangeable Cylinder Box. A type of cylinder box which incorporates toggles or latches that permit cylinders to be removed and replaced with relative ease.

Jewel Cap. See Endstone Cap.

Justifying. The alignment of each pin on the cylinder of a music box so that it plucks the tooth tip in the precise manner required for a particular song. Synonym: verifying.

Key Frame. As applied to barrel-operated instruments such as street pianos and barrel/band organs. The key frame is parallel with the axis of the barrel and has a number of keys or levers, one for each note in the scale of the instrument. Each key is operated by contact with a pin on the surface of the barrel. This, in turn, allows air to pass into an organ pipe or pluck a string.

In pneumatically operated band organs, the key frame is comprised of a set of small, spring-loaded levers that are activated by a book of perforated music. The perforations in the musical program cause the small levers to move changing the position of a small valve in a pneumatic control box. This, in turn, operates the appropriate musical note in the organ.

Keyless Frame. An alternative to the key frame applied to band organs which is closely allied to the tracker bar of a player piano in that it is a fully-pneumatic, music-reading system. There are no mechanical levers as in the key frame. The passage of the perforated music acts as a "traveling valve" to open and close small airways thereby allowing the proper pipe to sound.

Key-Wind Box. A cylinder musical box from the early or mid-19th century which uses a detachable key, similar to a clock-winding key, to wind the mainspring.

Laminated Comb. In a cylinder musical box, a comb arranged vertically and comprised of individual teeth stacked upon each other and played by a vertically-mounted cylinder. Usually found in early watches, musical waxing seals, etc. Incorrect usage: describing a sectional comb.

Lever Wind. A mechanism which achieves its winding action from the ratchetted lever. It was designed as an improvement to the earlier key-wind system.

Lock and Cancel. A valve which operates a particular section of an instrument, e.g., xylophone or rank of pipes. The valve is toggled on and off by perforations in the roll or book of music.

Longue Marche. A cylinder musical box equipped with multiple large springs to provide an extended playing time.

Mainspring. The power source, made of tempered steel, for clockwork mechanisms.

Mandoline Box. A cylinder musical box with four or more teeth tuned to each note in the melody and embellishment sections (not in the bass section) or to the tones used in the tunes played so that by plucking each tooth in rapid succession the sound of a mandolin is effected. The cylinder is readily identified by the obvious angled lines of pins which create the "trill" effect. Some later-period boxes were made with as few as three notes per tune, referred to as pseudo-mandoline.

Manivelle (French) Crank. Usually refers to small musical boxes which do not have spring motors but are operated by turning a small crank, hence the name. Generally applies to novelty musical boxes but also to small, disc-playing musical boxes.

Marquetry. See Veneer.

Master Diapason. A master comb used in tuning musical movements.

Mechanical Musical Instruments. Generic term used to describe all self-playing musical instruments. Instruments which are powered by a spring, descending weights, clockwork or are hand-cranked. These instruments are not powered by electricity. Most instruments which were originally designed to be powered by electricity are classified as automatic rather than mechanical.

Military Band Organ. A band organ with exposed brass pipes and drums which is intended to replicate the sound of a military band.

Monkey Organ (American term). A portable, hand-cranked barrel organ. More properly known as a hand or barrel organ, these instruments were used by street musicians who used live monkeys to collect coins offered by patrons.

Movement. The mechanism of an automatic musical instrument, especially a spring wound musical box.

Music Roll. A strip of paper on which music and control functions are arranged by a series of perforations. By passing over a tracker bar the perforations cause a roll-operated instrument to perform. Player pianos are the best known instruments of this type.

Musical Box or Music Box. Generic term for a cylinder or disc type automatic instrument which plucks one or more tuned steel combs and is typically housed in a wooden cabinet. Incorrectly interpreted to mean any type of automatic musical instrument.

Musical Comb. A series of steel teeth tuned to a scale and soldered (or in the case of a sectional comb, screwed) to a brass or cast iron trestle which is fastened to the bedplate and holds the teeth at the proper angle to the cylinder.

Necessaire. A small case, sometimes in the shape of a piano or other elegant form, with such "necessary" items as scissors, thread, needles, etc. Many also have a miniature musical movement.

Nickelodeon (American term). Originally the name of early movie theaters (pre-1920). Today, a term used to describe a coin-operated piano, orchestrion or similar instrument.

Orchestral Box. A cylinder musical box with accompaniment, usually bells, drum, wood block, organ accompaniment, etc. Popular ca. 1880-1910.

Orchestrion. A mechanical musical instrument designed to imitate an orchestra. A "piano orchestrion" (as made by Seeburg, Wurlitzer, Philipps, Hupfeld, Weber, etc.) includes a piano with or without a keyboard with extra instruments such as xylophone, ranks of pipes, orchestra bells, drums and other percussion. An "organ orchestrion" (as made by Welte, Mortier, etc.) has many ranks of pipes plus other instruments, but no piano.

Organette. A small, hand-cranked, self-playing reed organ. Usually operated by paper roll, cardboard disc, metal disc or wooden cylinder. Also, a small pipe organ.

Overture Box. A cylinder musical box with cylinders 3" or larger in diameter. Very finely made and pre-1880, containing overtures of operatic selections. In some boxes one air was pinned to play in two revolutions of the cylinder. Most played only two, three or four airs.

Pallet Valve. A small piece of leather-faced wood or metal hinged to an opening in a pipe chest, or other pneumatic mechanism, which allows air in or out when opened.

Parachute Check. See Safety Check.

Pawl. A metal finger with a pointed end which engages with a ratchet gear and holds the power in check.

Perforations. The holes in a music roll, music book, disc, etc. which are arranged in a manner to produce a musical performance when used on an automatic or mechanical instrument.

Perforator. The machine which produces perforations, especially in a musical roll.

Photoplayer. A musical instrument consisting of a piano and one or two side chests which contain pipes, percussion and novelty side effects. Often equipped with a roll-operated player mechanism. They were used to provide music and sound effects to accompany silent films in movie theaters.

Piano Player. A cabinet-style, roll-operated device which is pushed up to a piano allowing the fingers on the player to play the piano keyboard. Synonyms: push-up piano player; vorsetzer.

Piece a oiseau (French). A large cylinder musical box with one or more mechanical birds fitted into the box. The birds are made to move and to "sing" in harmony with the pinned cylinder.

Pierement (Dutch). A large, hand-cranked street organ moved about Dutch streets on a three-wheeled cart or other carriage.

Pin. The metal protrusion from a barrel or cylinder which actuates a key, lever or tooth causing the music to sound.

Pinion. The small gear which drives a larger brass gear or other device which will be the receptor of the power transmitted through the pinion.

Pitman. A push rod, made of thin metal wire or wood, used to connect a key with a pallet in a pneumatic instrument.

Platform Movement. A small musical movement used in some 18th and 19th century watches and other small items. The pins are arranged in sequence on the surface of a disc or platform. Separate steel teeth are arranged around the periphery and are plucked by the projections on the disc. Synonym: Sur plateau.

Player Piano. A pneumatically played, foot-pumped, paper roll-operated piano with manual levers or buttons for expression.

Plectrum. A device used to pluck a string, e.g., the wooden "finger" in the Wurlitzer Automatic Harp. Synonym: star wheel.

Plerodienique Box. A cylinder musical movement with the cylinder made in two parts each of which shifts inward toward the center (until the end of the program, that is, at which time they take the big leap outward and start the program over again). This occurs at different times so that one cylinder is playing while the other is shifting. This allows for uninterrupted music.

Pneumatic. Usually refers to a small bellows or air motor. Two pieces of wood hinged at one end, covered with rubberized cloth or leather which, when evacuated or pressurized, performs a mechanical function.

Polytype Box. A cylinder musical box with multiple arrangements pinned onto the cylinder. One type was a revolver movement that had a separate comb and bedplate for each cylinder and was like several complete music boxes in a single case. The other was a more conventional box with the airs arranged in different styles, e.g., sublime harmony, tremolo zither, etc.

Portative. The classical term used to describe a portable, hand-cranked barrel organ or similar instruments.

Poseur. A person who sets the comb to the cylinder. Also known as a setter.

Potence. The lower adjustable bearing for the endless screw in the governor. The potence holds the lower pivot of the endless screw and, by means of the regulating screw, allows the proper depthing of the endless screw to the second wheel.

Pouch. A pneumatic which, when acted upon by wind or vacuum, causes a valve or key to operate. Synonym: puff.

Pressure Bar. See Hold Down Arm.

Pricking. The scoring of the cylinder for a musical box which preceeds the drilling of the cylinder for the pinning of the musical program. Synonym: piquage.

Projection. The tab which projects downward from a metal disc and, in turn, operates a star wheel which then plucks the tooth of a disc musical box.

Proscenium. See Facade.

Ratchet. A stepping mechanism consisting of a gear and a spring-loaded lever (pawl) which allows movement in one direction only. A necessary part of a spring-wound mechanism.

Rebate. The scoring of pins too closely together which keeps the damper from operating properly when the cylinder pins strike the dampers in succession.

Reed. A vibrating metal tongue which produces sound in an organ. Usually made of brass and tuned to a musical tone. Synonym: free reed.

Registration. The process by which a cylinder, such as in a musical box, is aligned so that the cylinder pins are in perfect calibration with the tooth tips.

Registration Stud Pin. The threaded pin that protrudes from the end cap of a musical box cylinder and rests against the snail cam. Turning the pin allows for fine adjustment of the cylinder position in order to align the registration marks with the tips of the comb teeth.

Regulating Screw. The screw, located in the rear of the governor block, which allows for the depthing adjustment of the endless screw with the second wheel by sliding the potence in and out.

Repeat/Change Lever. The lever, located in the rear of the cylinder musical box baseplate, which allows the musical box program to either be repeated or changed.

Reproducing Piano. A self-playing piano which closely imitates a pianist's artistry by means of expression mechanisms controlled by special music rolls. Reproducing piano rolls were "recorded" by many of the greatest classical and popular artists of the era (approximately 1905-1935) on special recording devices which, with the help of human roll editors, captured the dynamics, tempo changes and other nuances of the performer.

Reservoir. A form of spring-loaded bellows which stores air at a relatively constant pressure so that a pneumatically-powered instrument may receive a steady supply of air at a pressure either above or below that of the surrounding atmosphere.

Resonator. The wooden or brass body of an organ pipe. Misnomer for tuning weights in musical boxes.

Revolver Box. A cylinder musical box with three or more multiple-tune cylinders in which each cylinder can be brought into playing position by the revolving of the cylinder-holding mechanism.

Rigid Notation. The horizontal, engraved lines found on some early musical box cylinders. The lines were said to be used to aid in timing the music in the absence of a rotary dividing engine. Mostly used by Francois Nicole.

Roll Frame. The mechanism which pulls a music roll over the tracker bar and rewinds it. Synonyms: spool box, spool frame.

Roller. See Cob.

Roller Organ. Tabletop organette using a small pinned wooden cylinder. Also called a cob or "Gem" roller organ.

Run. The occurrence when the spring power in a musical box is discharged very rapidly, as when the governor fails. In cylinder boxes this causes the cylinder to spin at great speed and can result in damage to pins, gears, teeth and tips. In disc boxes it can fracture the spring barrel and strip the gears and destroy the teeth. The British call this "The most expensive sound on earth."

Safety Check. In cylinder boxes, a mechanism designed to prevent a destructive "run" should the power of the mainspring be improperly released. Synonym: parachute check.

Schutz Marke (German). Patent mark.

Second Wheel. The gear in a governor which is engaged with the endless screw and is mounted on a shaft which has a pinion that engages the first wheel, which in turn is mounted on a shaft that has a pinion the engages the great wheel. This is the wheel that transfers speed regulation from the endless to the cylinder. Synonym: escape gear or worm wheel.

Sectional Comb. A comb in a cylinder musical box which is made from separate sections of teeth, typically from one to five rather than as one piece of steel. Late 18th, early 19th century.

Semi-helicoidal. A cylinder musical box in which the cylinder rotates in a normal fashion and is laterally shifted at one position during its rotation. To enable longer-than-normal pieces of music to be played, arrangements are made for the musical pinning to be continued during the time when the cylinder is making its lateral shift in what is known as the "dead space." There is also a secondary mechanism which prevents the mechanism from stopping in the normal way after one cylinder revolution.

Serinette (French). See Bird Organ.

Serpentine. A musical box case which typically has a double curved plan form (double "S").

Set Pins. The metal pins found under the musical comb to allow for proper alignment of the comb to the cylinder pins.

Shoulder Screw. A machine screw with an unthreaded portion under the head, slightly larger than the threaded portion but smaller than the head. Used for connecting two moving parts without the need for a lock nut. When the shoulder is tightened against the stationary part, the moving part may rotate freely around the shoulder without causing the screw to loosen.

Snail (cam). The helical gear which laterally shifts the cylinder (from tune to tune) in a musical box or other cylinder or barrel-operated instruments.

Snuff Box. A small, pocket-sized box typical of one used to carry snuff, often fitted with a musical movement, ca. 19th century. The musical movements were often placed in simple metal transit cases for shipment from the maker to the sales agent. The agent then placed the movement in a more elaborate case.

Speed Regulator. Found on some musical movements to allow for the governing of the speed of the movement.

Spool Box. See Key Frame.

Sprag. See Stop Tail.

Spring Barrel. The drum-shaped metal housing which contains the mainspring in a clockwork-powered mechanism. In cylinder musical boxes it is usually of brass, while in disc-playing musical boxes it is frequently of stamped steel or cast iron.

Spring Barrel Hook. The device, inside the spring barrel, which holds the outer end of the mainspring in place. The inner end is attached to the arbor hook, the outer to the barrel hook.

Spring Barrel Lid. The brass plate which is pressed into the open end of the barrel and which is the outer bearing for the barrel.

Stack. The mechanism which comprises the series of pouches, valves, bellows and related parts and which operates instruments such as player pianos. Synonym: pneumatic stack.

Star Wheel. In a disc-playing musical box, the toothed wheel which engages with the projections (or openings) in the musical disc and is turned so that one of its star-shaped projections plucks a particular tooth in the musical comb.

Stop Tail. The small metal finger below the airbrake which stops the movement when it connects with the stop lever.

Stopwork. The male and female gears on the cylinder side (the winder side in double mainspring assemblies) of the spring barrel which prevents overwinding and prevents the spring from unwinding so far that the spring disengages from the spring barrel hook. On a double spring barrel drive system there are two Geneva-type stopworks: one on the first barrel on the lever side, and the other on the cylinder side of the second wheel. It is also the mechanism attached to the governor block that causes the mechanism to stop at the end of a tune. Synonym: Geneva works.

Street Organ. An American/English term used to describe the Dutch pierement. An organ played on city streets for the financial gain of the operator and/or owner/lessor.

Striker. A pivoted rod terminating in a knob that is used to strike a bell, drum or castenet. The knobs are occasionally embellished with butterflies, bees or flowers.

Sublime Harmony. A musical box configuration in which two or more nearly similar combs, each with treble and bass teeth, in a cylinder musical box are tuned so that a rich "celeste" effect is achieved. In the Symphonion disc musical box it is two combs set at opposing angles.

Sur Plateau (French: *upon plate*). See Platform Movement.

Tabatier (French). Tobacco holder or snuff box.

Telescoping/Telescopic Box. The incorrect term for a plerodienique box.

Temper. The heat-treating process used to produce hardness and springiness in steel. Used in comb teeth and springs.
Also, the adjustment of the pitch of a note, instrument, etc. by temperament; tune.

Timbre. The difference in tone which causes the same note to sound differently when produced by two different instruments or voices. Synonym: tone color.

Tongue. A vibrating reed or, less common, a tooth in a tuned comb.

Tooth. A tuned tine, usually made of tempered steel, used to sound a note in a musical comb.

Touche (French). Key.

Tracker Bar. A narrow bar, usually made of brass or hard wood, with a row of small holes precisely spaced down its length over which the paper music roll (or cardboard book, in a keyless organ) passes to play the music. Typically found in instruments such as player pianos, orchestrions, etc.

Tune Card. The paper or metal card which lists the tunes for a musical box or other automatic or mechanical instrument. Attached to the underside of a musical box lid.

Tune Indicator. The device in some cylinder movements which uses a pointer to note the number of the tune being played.

Tuning Weights. The lead weights attached to the underside of the teeth on a musical box comb, especially in the bass section, causing them to vibrate more slowly and thus sound a lower note. Also, the adjustable weights in the Mills Violano which are affixed to leverage arms to keep the strings in tune.

Valve. A device which controls the flow of air and is usually activated by a pouch.

Valve Chest. The wooden housing which holds the valves and/or pneumatic action of a wind- or vacuum-operated instrument.

Veneer. A thin sheet of wood glued to various cabinet parts. The stronger, but plainer-looking, core wood is invariably first covered with "cross banding" glued at right angles to its grain, and then the cross banding is covered with fancy veneer with the grain running parallel to the core. This sandwich greatly strengthens a cabinet against cracking and warping. Marquetry consists of small pieces of veneer of various grain patterns and colors inlaid flush into the surface of the surrounding veneer to create various designs, borders, etc.

Verifying. See Registration.

Voice Celeste, (French: Voix Celeste). The tuning of two comb teeth, reeds or pipes with beats in the music which produces a pleasant sound. Sometimes known as the type of cylinder musical box which has organ accompaniment. Sometimes referred to as "Continental Tuning."

Wallbox. A small box which receives coins and is connected to a coin piano or orchestrion and operates the instrument upon command. The box may or may not be attached to the instrument.

Worm. See Endless Screw.

Worm Wheel. See Second Wheel.

Zither. A device added to many late cylinder and disc musical boxes consisting of a sleeve or rolled stiff paper which, when pressed against the musical comb, creates a banjo effect.

References: *The Encyclopedia of Automatic Musical Instruments*, Q. David Bowers, 1972, The Vestal Press. Used with permission.

Restoring Musical Boxes, Arthur W.J.G. Ord-Hume, George Allen & Unwin, 1980, *Musical Box*, ibid and *Player Piano*, 1974.

As noted in the Foreword, this Glossary is not meant to be definitive as presented. It is the first step toward what will be a glossary endorsed by the MBSI. Readers are encouraged to provide input to the editor regarding this glossary.

KEY TO VOLUME AND ISSUES

The Society began publishing the *Technical Bulletin* in a 5½" x 8½" typeset format in 1966. Prior to that there was a typewritten, informal newsletter.

From 1966 to 1974 the Society published just one magazine, the *Technical Bulletin*, six times per year: Autumn, Christmas, Winter, Spring, Summer and Reminder.

VOLUME	ISSUES	YEAR
XIII	3-6	1967
XIV	1-6	1967-68
XV	1-6	1968-69
XVI	1-6	1969-70
XVII	1-6	1970-71
XVIII	1-6	1971-72
XIX	1-6	1972-73
XX	1-6	1973-74

In 1975 the Society began publishing the *News Bulletin* to relate Society affairs and topical information. It would be published bi-monthly. The *Technical Bulletin* would then be devoted to the historical, technical and artistic aspects of mechanical music. The *Technical Bulletin* would be published three times per year: Winter—No. 1, Autumn—No. 2 and Spring—No. 3. In 1979 the sequence was changed to Spring/Summer—No. 1, Autumn—No. 2 and Winter—No. 3.

XXI	1-3	1975
XXII	1-3	1976
XXIII	1-3	1977
XXIV	1-3	1978
XXV	1-3	*1979
XXVI	1-3	1980
XXVII	1-2	**1981
XXVIII	1-2	**1982
XXIX	1-3	1983
XXX	1-3	1984
XXXI	1-3	1985

* The sequence was changed from Winter, Spring and Autumn to Spring/Summer, Autumn and Winter.

** Only two issues were published in these years so that a three-year lapse in publishing could be made up.

PUBLICATIONS OF THE MUSICAL BOX SOCIETY INTERNATIONAL

The Silver Anniversary Collection, Edgerton, 1974.
A compilation of articles from the first 25 years of the MBSI *Technical Bulletin.* Nearly out of print.

The History of The Musical Box, Chapuis. Reprinted in English and translated by Joseph Roesch in 1980.
Originally printed in French in 1926, considered one of the necessary references in the field.

SOME RELATED BOOKS

The Encyclopedia of Automatic Musical Instruments, Q. David Bowers, 1972, The Vestal Press.

The Mechanical Music Cabinet, Siegfried Wendel, 1984, The Vestal Press.

The Marvelous World of Music Machines, Heinrich Weiss-Stauffacher, 1976, Kodansha International.

Guidebook of Automatic Musical Instruments, Q. David Bowers, 1967, The Vestal Press, (Vols. 1 & 2).

San Sylmar, Connie O'Kelley, 1978, Merle Norman Cosmetics.

Au Temps des Boites a Musique, Daniel Bonhote, (undated), Editions Monda SA. (Available in English translation.)

Musical Boxes, John E.T. Clark, 1948, Cornish Bros., Ltd. (Third Edition 1961, George Allen & Unwin).

The Disc Musical Box Handbook, Graham Webb, 1971, Faber & Faber.

The Musical Box Handbook, Second Edition, Volume 1, Cylinder Boxes, Graham Webb, 1984, The Vestal Press.

The Musical Box Handbook, 2nd Edition, Volume 2, Disc Boxes, Graham Webb, 1984, The Vestal Press.

Musical Boxes, David Tallis, 1971, Muller.

Music Boxes, Their Lore and Lure, Helen & John Hoke, 1957, Hawthorn.

Alec Templeton's Music Boxes, Rachael Bail Baumel, 1958, Wilfred Funk.

Mechanical Musical Instruments. Alexander Buchner, c 1948, Batchwork Press.

The Curious History of Music Boxes, Roy Mosoriak, 1943, Lightner Publishing Company (Reprinted c 1970).

Musical Box, A History and Collector's Guide, Arthur W.J.G. Ord-Hume, 1980, George Allen & Unwin.

Restoring Musical Boxes, Arthur W.J.G. Ord-Hume, 1980, George Allen & Unwin.

The Mechanics of Mechanical Music—The Arrangement of Music for Automatic Instruments, Arthur W.J.G. Ord-Hume, 1973, Ord-Hume.

The Fairground Organ, Eric V. Cockayne, 1970, David & Charles.

Treasures of Mechanical Music, Q. David Bowers and Arthur Reblitz, 1981, The Vestal Press.

From Music Boxes to Street Organs, R. de Waard, 1967, The Vestal Press.

Barrel Organ, Arthur W.J.G. Ord-Hume, 1978, Barnes.

Church and Chamber Barrel Organs, Cannon Noel Boston and Lyndesay G. Langwill, 1967, Lorimer & Chalmers, Ltd.

Drehorgein, Helmut Zeraschi, 1979, Hallweg AG.

Joseph Hayden and the Mechanical Organ, W.J.G. Ord-Hume, 1980, George Allen & Unwin.

Player Piano, Arthur W.J.G. Ord-Hume, 1970, George Allen & Unwin.

Player Pianos and Music Boxes, Harvey Roehl, The Vestal Press.

Player Piano Treasury, 2nd Edition, Harvey Roehl, The Vestal Press.

Player Piano Servicing and Rebuilding, Arthur Reblitz, The Vestal Press.

Rebuilding the Ampico Model B Reproducing Piano, Saul, The Vestal Press.

Pianola, Arthur W.J.G. Ord-Hume, 1984, Allen & Unwin.

Restoring Pianolas, Arthur W.J.G. Ord-Hume, Allen & Unwin.

The Mechanical Dolls of Monte Carlo, Antoine Battani and Annette Bordeau, 1985, Rizzoli.

Animated Androids, Steve Ryder and Jere Ryder, 1978, The Musical Box Society of Great Britain.

Le Monde des Automates, Societe anonyme des Impressions Blondel la Rougery, Paris, 1928 (two Vols).

The Guiness Collection, 1984, Guiness.

The Mills Violano Virtuoso, Michael Kitner & Arthur Reblitz, The Vestal Press.